GOVERNING URBAN AMERICA

GOVERNING URBAN AMERICA

FIFTH EDITION

CHARLES R. ADRIAN
Professor of Political Science
University of California, Riverside

CHARLES PRESS
Professor of Political Science
Michigan State University

McGRAW-HILL BOOK COMPANY

New York St. Louis San Francisco Auckland Bogotá Düsseldorf Johannesburg London Madrid Mexico Montreal New Delhi Panama Paris São Paulo Singapore Sydney Tokyo Toronto

This book was set in Times Roman by National ShareGraphics, Inc.
The editors were Lyle Linder and Barry Benjamin;
the cover was designed by Scott Chelius;
the production supervisor was Angela Kardovich.
Kingsport Press, Inc., was printer and binder.

GOVERNING URBAN AMERICA

234567890 FGRFGR 78321098

Library of Congress Cataloging in Publication Data

Adrian, Charles R
Governing urban America.

Bibliography: p.
Includes index.
1. Municipal government—United States.
I. Press, Charles, joint author. II. Title.
JS331.A4 1977 352'.008'0973 76-26082
ISBN 0-07-000446-3

Contents

PART 2 THE POLITICS OF URBAN FUNCTIONS AND SERVICES

Preface

Shortly after the first edition of this book appeared, Lawrence J. R. Herson wrote an article for the *American Political Science Review* called "The Lost World of Municipal Government." The senior author of this book, who wrote the first two editions of *Governing Urban America* alone, was gratified to find that Professor Herson had made a partial exception of this work in his general condemnation of political scientists in the urban government field for ignoring developments in theory and empirical research taking place elsewhere in political science. Indeed, it has been precisely the intent of transcending these shortcomings in other textbooks that inspired the publication of the first edition in 1955.

What were the aims of the first edition, published when the parents of the current generation of college students were undergraduates? It was based on three assumptions: first, that structure, the policy process, functions (today we would say "policy"), and administrative operations must all be considered; second, that urban government must be viewed as part of the whole culture; and third, that local government is primarily a *political* process. Earlier writers, strongly influenced by the efficiency-and-economy movement, had treated politics as a necessary evil, not as the heart of the subject. Some of these assumptions were quite cautiously applied in that first edition, but they have remained the basis for each succeeding edition, and they provoked flattering imitation.

While we have always paid due attention to topics of current interest (the first edition reflected the contemporary interest in organized crime and local government created by Senator Estes Kefauver's televised hearings by devoting a chapter to the subject), the enduring value of the text is, we believe, the fact that we have concentrated on the topics of central and crucial importance. These topics change more slowly than persons unacquainted with history might expect. Thus in 1955 it was noted that: "Many problems remain to be solved [today, we would not claim that solutions are possible for most problems and we would only look to their effective "management"]—problems of securing adequate legal authority from the state, of making municipal government more fully representative of the interests and desires of the community, of developing high standards of municipal service and administration, and of providing the municipal government with financial means to meet the increasing demands for services." All of these are still issues and problems as the fifth edition goes to press. Other issues and problems have joined them and we have noted these with each revision.

The second edition (1961) paid special attention to the competition among interest groups, to the politics of suburbia, and to the effects of metropolitan decentralization. As in the first edition, there was more hope for the effectiveness of the interaction of pressure groups than is the case today. With the third edition (1968), Charles Press joined in making the revisions. That version placed considerable emphasis upon the politics of education, which political scientists had long ignored, and on civil rights and liberties, which had previously been considered appropriate only for courses involving the national government. In 1972, the fourth edition was especially concerned with the politics of poverty and of the ghetto, along with the effects upon suburbia of the aging process.

In this current edition, we pay particular attention to the issues of "neighborhood" government and other attempts to make urban politics more representative and with broader participation, to the changing functions of the city manager and other urban executives, to the increasingly serious fiscal problems of cities and to the effects of "revenue sharing," to the expanding involvement in urban government and politics of women and persons from minority groups, and to the changing legal concepts of home rule and urban land-use controls. With regret, we decided to eliminate the chapter on local-government ideology.

The chapters on public policy and programs have been completely rewritten and updated. The book has been shortened somewhat both in order to try to cut down on production costs and because many instructors like to add a brief second book to a term's assignments in order to develop some special topic but without unduly raising costs for the student.

We wish to thank the loyal users of *Governing Urban America,* for they have made this fifth edition—and each of the earlier revisions—possible. We also thank persons who have adopted the book and our students, past and present, for many valuable criticisms and suggestions. As always, we welcome further comments, favorable or otherwise. Finally, we wish to express our recognition of the fact that a textbook is essentially a particular way of organizing the research that has been done over the years. In revising this book, we are forcefully reminded of the vast amount of research and writing that has made our task more interesting with each new edition.

Charles R. Adrian
Charles Press

GOVERNING URBAN AMERICA

Part One

The Urban Political Process

At all levels of government in a democracy, the decision process is one of negotiation, accommodation, compromise, and the achievement of proximate rather than ultimate goals. The end result of the process is a public policy that seldom completely satisfies anyone, but leaves relatively few of the politically aware completely dissatisfied. And this is true whether one perceives government as "pluralistic" (in which there are so many ideas and interests involved in the process that no single set can dominate) or "elitist" (in which a dominant class rules in its own interests). Even a ruling elite must compromise its internal conflicts. The first part of this book, then, deals with the process by which ideas and interests are converted into urban public policy.

A

The Setting

Chapter 1

The Sprawling Metropolis

College students of today are by all odds likely to spend their lifetimes in urban communities. This textbook is designed to help gain a better understanding of the operation of city government. Particular stress is laid throughout the text upon the issues in city politics that are political in nature, that is, issues that are controversial and possess alternatives in the public policy process. As such, these issues may require the ordinary citizen to make a choice and take a stand, either at the polls, as a member of an interest group, or even as a part-time council member or member of one of the citizen advisory boards or commissions that are associated with urban government.

The possible approaches to the study of political institutions are many. In this book, the emphasis is placed upon a study of the political process with the objective of supplying to readers a method that will provide them with a tool for the analysis of political events that affect them and society. No attempt is made to supply details concerning the thousands of urban communities in the United States. Such information is available in the nearest library and in the material in the footnotes, which list ample citations.

AMERICAN VIEWS OF URBAN GOVERNMENT

American city government has changed rapidly in the present century. Unlike most state and county governments, cities have undergone extensive alteration of their structure, and they are attempting to furnish the services demanded by contemporary society. Most city political machines and bosses have disappeared. The remaining ones are adopting policies more appropriate for the environment they now find themselves in. Blatant corruption and spoilsmanship have given way before the need for governmental services performed by technical specialists.

As we will shortly note, not all has been "progress" and improvement in America's urbanized areas. Some of the most serious problems of our society have their geographic location in cities. What the student must understand is that many of these most serious problems are especially concentrated in only a part of the metropolis, and that part, the core city and often its older industrialized suburbs, is usually governmentally separate from the rest of the metropolis.

These realities of government in the contemporary American city are not well understood by the typical citizen. The folkways and folk tales of Americana saddle city government and city politicians with a stereotype that has little basis in fact. The stereotype does, however, have a *historical* basis.

The Public Attitude toward City Governments

Nearly everyone has at one time heard of the famous comment by the British political scientist James Bryce, who called "the government of cities the one conspicuous failure of the United States." That statement was made more than eighty-five years ago. Yet many Americans think of it as being appropriate today. Partly for this reason, citizens have developed a cynicism regarding municipal governments, especially the governments of the larger municipalities that make up the core cities of metropolitan areas. It is worthwhile, therefore, to inquire into the cause of such attitudes, since they are frequently an additional handicap that those who govern cities must live with.

1. Rapid Growth of Cities In the first place, difficulties in achieving confidence in city government are partly a product of the rapidity with which the American city grew after the Civil War. This nation was predominantly an agricultural one until (roughly) the last half of the nineteenth century, and its democratic traditions were oriented toward the frontier and the farm, not toward the city. The same traditions do not necessarily fit each of them equally well. Effective *democratic* government is built largely upon a sound foundation of customs and traditions that require time to build. When blossoming cities of the nineteenth century had added to their populations shiploads of immigrants, ignorant of the customs, laws, beliefs, and even language of an adopted country, the problems of government became vastly more complex. In recent times, most core cities have declined in population but have continued to add large numbers of new residents unused to urban ways, particularly blacks and whites from economically marginal areas of the rural South, as well as Spanish-speaking citizens from Puerto Rico and the rural Southwest.

2. Corruption A second consideration has been the persistency with which American cities have been plagued with varying degrees of corruption. It was long a veritable tradition in our larger municipalities when the boss system flourished and has affected a great many of our cities of any size at one time or another. Corruption may enter city government as a result of the commonplace lack of interest in the operations of the city which permits lax administration. Dishonesty and irregularities breed a greater lack of interest and a cynicism which allows for more of the same. Another cause stems from circumstances which demand that city officials enforce formally enacted laws that do not accord with the prevailing public mores of their citizens. Examples of this may be found in the case of liquor prohibition during the 1920s and of gambling and perhaps marijuana use today. Such anomalies place city officials in positions of great temptation, yet the same citizens who drink illegal liquor or insist upon gambling will be among those who will censure public officials who do not enforce the law. Individual Americans expect tougher moral fiber in their public officials than they themselves possess.

3. Decay Confidence in municipal government has waned as increasing numbers of citizens have come to view core cities as areas of decay. The flight to the suburbs cannot, of course, be attributed to the crime-in-the-streets issue alone, but threats to personal safety have become a part of the widely held image of cities as areas that provide unpleasant and unattractive living surroundings. City government, despite its relative weakness as an agency for social control, has been viewed by many citizens as somehow responsible for the aspects of urban life they disapprove of, while the services it has provided have been taken for granted, with little curiosity as to how they are made possible.

4. City as Creature of the State Cities are not mentioned in the United States Constitution and therefore exist legally as creations of state governments, though many antedate these governments. With minor exceptions, to be discussed in Chapter 8, the relationship of a city to the state in which it is located is the relationship between a child and its parent. A city can perform only those functions authorized it by state law or constitution.

American courts historically have given a very narrow interpretation to the powers of cities. This approach has been based on the theory that, if in doubt, power belongs to the sovereign state and not to one of its corporate subdivisions. The result has been that the state legislature—in the past dominated by small-town merchants and lawyers who were inexperienced in city social patterns—has often not given the city the power needed to deal with local problems.

Picayunish control over local matters has been carried to such an extent by many state legislatures that cities have sometimes been given almost no opportunity to decide any important matters for themselves. This type of action by the lawmakers turns the legislature into an *administrative* overseer of city government. This practice gives the citizen the impression that the really important decisions are made, not in the city hall, but in the state capital and that, therefore, city government is not of sufficient consequence to rate much attention. Such supervision by the state government has also had its adverse effect upon municipal officeholders, whose creativity becomes dulled and discouraged by being constantly told that they are in danger of exceeding their authority. When their powers are interpreted narrowly by the courts and they must go to the legislature whenever they wish to make a departure from customary policy, city officials begin to orient their jobs toward the annotated statutes and the opinions of the attorney general instead of toward economic and sociological demands. Ordinary citizens, impatient with legalism, are likely to view the plight of the harassed official without sympathy. The explanations they hear will sound to them like excuses for inaction.

The politically atomized pattern of contemporary American suburbia results from the fact that this was a rural nation in the days when laws of annexation and attitudes toward large cities were developed by the state. In those days, rural and urban life-styles were sharply distinguished. Legislatures have for the most part kept the traditional legal separation unchanged. As a consequence, the boundaries of a city are almost always artificial and arbitrary and have nothing to do with economic and social realities. In some states, even the forms of governmental structure a city may choose are closely circumscribed by the state.

5. Financial Weakness State-imposed limitiations upon the power of the city to tax have especially restricted the actions of city governments. American cities have been, and still are, overwhelmingly dependent upon a levy that was designed to fit the needs of a frontier society—the general property tax. Because legislatures have not been anxious to allow cities to use other types of taxes, municipalities often have found that their limit of services renderable comes at whatever point the property tax seems to reach a psychological saturation point. Again, the impatient and annoyed citizen is likely to turn to the state or national government for a service for which the city "has no money." The story of bankrupt cities in the Great Depression of the 1930s has passed into American folklore. It does not enhance the prestige of our cities. The almost continuous financial crises of the 1970s have not helped to improve the image, especially when New York, Yonkers, Oakland, and other cities literally faced bankruptcy.

6. Apathy Finally, however, whenever our cities have not been governed in a fashion that satisfies the high expectations of most citizens, the cause may be found in general public apathy. Ordinary citizens are busy persons with many demands upon their time. As a consequence, they must budget their interests—and municipal government has rated a low priority. This has been true in part because city dwellers have viewed local government as one that performs primarily routine service functions. Who, they want to know, can become interested in such prosaic problems as the supplying of water, the maintenance of streets, the disposal of sewage? Are these not routine matters to be handled by civil servants? Why should they concern themselves? Many advocates of the reform movement of a few decades ago advanced the misconception that municipal government is nothing more than the application of the principles of "good business management" from which the politician ought properly to be excluded. Undoubtedly, city governments exist primarily to render services to patron-citizens. These services, however, are often far from routine, and the existence of alternative approaches to public policy offers the basis for lively citizen participation in genuine political issues. In recent years, issues of fluoridation, annexation, segregation in housing, bussing of students, and the unionization of local employees have destroyed the image of city governments as being unconcerned with public policy matters. Much of this book will be taken up with the consideration of nonroutine political issues in urban functions.

Until recent decades, citizen interest was often at low ebb because middle-class citizens thought they could not be connected (or at least not openly) with city administrations that were often under the control of a boss or a machine or were cooperating with professional criminals. It was uncommon for a representative of the community elite to become involved in municipal politics prior to the advent of the reform movement in the 1880s, which helped to make that sort of thing respectable. Even today, many persons still believe that city politics is corrupt and hence to be shunned by good citizens. Such viewpoints severely cripple the efforts of city governments.

The high-mobility characteristic of contemporary American city dwellers, combined with their extreme heterogeneity, has militated against most people's having a sense of belongingness in the community. This in turn has resulted in a low degree of civic pride and morale, which produces lack of interest in the local political process. Irvin S. Cobb once said, "There is this to be said for New York City: it is the one densely inhabited locality—with the possible exception of Hell—that has absolutely not a trace of local pride." Mr. Cobb to the contrary notwithstanding, the same problem exists in most large cities.

Many factors have, therefore, combined to produce the cultural image of municipal government that exists today. Of all of them, however, the most important is the failure of lay citizens to take an interest in the government that is the most intimate, the most observable, and the closest to them of all the coercive agents of society.

URBAN SETTLEMENT PATTERNS

The settlement pattern of urban areas has largely been a response to economic forces. The industrial revolution made possible the city clustered densely around a downtown industrialized and commercial center. Steam provided power, including that of the factories, railroads, and steamboats. The development of electric power and the invention of the gasoline-powered auto made possible the pattern of urban sprawl that has characterized American urbanized areas since roughly the period of the Great Depression. Modern methods of communication also contributed. With the effective, inexpensive telephone service of today, few individuals or industries would isolate themselves from the core city.

But change in response to technology is continuous. The rise in the price of petroleum and the recognition that other fuel resources are limited may bring about yet other patterns of urban settlement. In the mid-1970s, there was some movement of people away from urban areas to the country. In some suburbs and outer fringes of metropolitan areas, people who had already arrived in a pleasant community were sometimes seeking to keep others from following, and they were getting support from city ordinances and the courts. Some suburbs and few core cities (notably San Diego) were following a slow-growth or no-growth policy. Such a policy would, if effective, discriminate against lower-income persons in housing, and the decline in economic growth would deprive people of needed jobs.

In the five years following the 1970 census, metropolitan areas grew by 3.4 percent, other parts of the country by 5.5 percent. In 1974, 155 million people lived in metropolitan areas (an increase of 5 million since 1970), as compared with 56.4 million in small communities (an increase of 2.9 million).

The growth rate of 1.2 percent annually in the 1960s had dropped to 0.8 percent in the mid-decade. Much of the growth occurred in Arizona, Florida, and other retirement states, in the South generally, and in small towns elsewhere, for there people can live more cheaply.

Urbanization of the Western World

The city in western civilization is primarily a product of the industrial revolution. To be sure, cities existed in Europe before 1770 (roughly the time of the beginning of the revolution), but they were chiefly capital or trading centers. In 1550, Paris, both a trading center and a great seat of government, was, according to William B. Munro, the largest city in Europe, and its population did not exceed 300,000. Mighty London was a village during the Middle Ages, having only about 40,000 people as that period came to an end. It grew very rapidly in the sixteenth and seventeenth centuries as Britain became the trading center of the rising new economic world. By the time of the American Revolution, it had become the largest city in Europe, with a population of around three-quarters of a million people.

The Great City of the Nineteenth Century

With the rise of a machine technology, steam power, and the factory system, cities grew at phenomenal rates. In the United States, there were only small towns at the time of the Revolution. They were growing, however, and they continued to grow. From the turn of the nineteenth century, cities expanded at an ever increasing pace. Between 1820 and 1840, the number of people engaged in manufacturing increased by 127 percent. Between 1840 and 1850 alone, America's urban population increased by nearly 50 percent.

After the construction of railroads, the heavy influx of foreign investment and the Civil War (1861–1865), urban growth, which earlier had occurred on the East Coast and especially in New England, spread into the Middle West. The rise of the great corporations and the never-ending developments in technological knowledge continued to raise the American *standard* of living even as it changed the American *mode* of living. Immigrants who before had hurried to the rich clay loams of the Middle Western farm belt now remained in New York, or Cincinnati, or Chicago to become a commodity called "labor" in the factory, the steel mill, or the stockyard. The children of country bumpkins yearned to become city slickers and hurried off at the earliest opportunity to what was often their disillusionment. And they continue to do so today. The urban form of the nineteenth century was the densely settled city with a commercial and industrial center at its core.

The population of cities doubled between the begining of the Civil War and 1900. In the next quarter of a century, it doubled again. By 1920, over one-half (51.2 percent) of the American people were living in cities.[1] The percentage in 1970 was around 75 and continues to climb. We live in an urban nation. American farmers are no longer members of the dominant group in our society. Their cultural patterns and sets of values are rapidly being replaced by new ones more in keeping with our own, rather than our parents' or grandparents' world.

The population of the United States reached 205 million by census-counting time in 1970 and 220 million in 1976. This represented an increase of about 25 million in a ten-year period. All of that increase was urban, for the population that earns its livelihood from working the soil declines each year as it has—interrupted only by the years of the Great Depression—since shortly after the beginning of the century.

Urban Sprawl and Metropolitan Areas

In 1970, nearly two-thirds of the American population lived not merely in urban but in the 243 *metropolitan* communities. Approximately one-fourth of it lived in the twelve largest metropolitan areas. Nonmetropolitan America, with roughly a third of the population, has 90 percent of the land area.[2]

Suburbs sprang up along the railroad and "interurban" lines (the Main Line suburbs of Philadelphia) as long ago as the midnineteenth century. But these were residences of the very wealthy. Suburbanization by the masses had to await Henry Ford's "poor man's car," the Model T. As auto ownership became widespread, suburbanization began in earnest. By the Great Depression, middle-class migration was common. At the end of World War II, suburbanization became a mass movement. Such moves were helped by federal government loan guarantees

[1] For statistical purposes, the U.S. Bureau of the Census classifies cities as incorporated places with 2,500 or more inhabitants. Legal definitions differ from this in the various states.

In the censuses of 1960 and 1970, the Bureau defined urban, as distinguished from rural, areas as (1) places of 2,500 inhabitants or more incorporated as cities, boroughs, or villages; (2) the densely settled urban fringe, whether incorporated or unincorporated, around cities of 25,000 or more (the limits of this area determined more or less arbitrarily, based upon physical features); (3) unincorporated areas of 2,500 inhabitants or more outside the urban fringes; and (4) towns of 2,500 or more except in New England, New York, and Wisconsin.

The Bureau has also undertaken to define large urban places. "Standard metropolitan statistical areas" contain at least one city of 50,000 or more population. The nucleus of the area is the county or counties containing the core city or cities. Contiguous counties are included in the area if they are densely settled by nonagricultural workers and are socially and economically integrated with the core city. For technical criteria, see U.S. Bureau of the Census, *Standard Metropolitan Statistical Areas,* 1959.

[2] For an interesting discussion of this segment of society and its problems see Marion Clawson, "The Future of Nonmetropolitan America," *The American Scholar,* Winter, 1972–73, pp. 102–109.

under the Federal Housing Authority and later the Veterans' Administration, making low-interest loans available to the middle- and upper-working classes.

Truck transportation freed industry from the railroad sidings and allowed them to build new facilities in the cheaper land of the suburbs. In the 1960s and 1970s, commercial establishments abandoned the downtown central business district as one large-scale suburban mall was followed by an even larger and more striking one. The metropolitan area, composed of a core city, suburban cities and villages, and unincorporated area, replaced the Great City as the common form of American urbanized settlement.

By 1970, for the first time in American history, more Americans lived in suburbs than in core cities or in nonmetropolitan areas. The figures respectively were 76 million, 59 million, and 71 million.

The very largest metropolitan areas now generate the greatest suburban population increases, but the moderate-sized metropolitan areas (those between one-half million and one million people) grew more rapidly than did any other size community. In 1970, the huge core cities (except Los Angeles) generally lost population as people continued to show a preference for suburban life-styles. New York remained the nation's largest city, although its population declined as it had a decade earlier. So did Chicago's. The Los Angeles metropolitan area remained the second largest in the nation, having passed the Chicago area in 1960, and it remained so in the mid-1970s. The greatest increases, as had been the case a decade earlier, took place along the Pacific and Gulf of Mexico Coasts and in the areas near the Great Lakes. In the mid-1970s, the population center continued to move westward, not so much because of California's growth, but because of that of Arizona, Oregon, and other western states.

This migration has differed by race, with the core cities becoming increasingly black and brown, while suburbs are overwhelmingly white. Still, during the 1960s, some 800,000 blacks became suburbanites. If blacks had moved into suburbia at the same rate as whites, the figure would have been twice as large, but it indicates that blacks are following the same pattern as have earlier ethnic groups. It is no longer accurate to speak of the "lily-white suburbs."

One can overstate other differences between suburbs and core cities. The stereotype of metropolitan America, sometimes reflected in careless writing by social scientists and journalists, is of a decaying core city, occupied largely by lower-status persons, with a middle-class and upper-class suburbia of the affluent. While this is generally the pattern around the largest cities and some of moderate size, it is by no means always the case. In the South and Southwest, in particular, the relatively new core cities will likely contain most of the more expensive housing, with low-quality housing being found mostly in the unincorporated fringe area. In California and Arizona, this tendency is accentuated by the practice of cities to annex large areas of undeveloped land in order to control its eventual use and to make it a buffer against the working-class suburbs. In the nation as a whole, suburbs differ from core cities significantly only in percentage of nonwhites (the difference is less in the South and West), proportion of families with children at home, proportion of broken families with children, and proportion of single persons not living at home (except in the West).[3] Some of the other socioeconomic measurements show no locational differences. One should not overlook the fact, however, that differences may be sharp among individual suburbs, each of which is a legally independent municipality if it is incorporated.

Another stereotype that needs to be exploded is that of a continuing baby boom in the suburbs; while Bassinet Hills continues to attract families, the number of children lessens as the national birthrate continues the decline begun in the mid-1960s with the birth-control pill and the changes in abortion laws. Empty classrooms are found in the mammoth Vertigo Heights consolidated school, not yet fully paid for. A few facts about population: The absolute number of five-year-olds dropped 15 percent between 1960 and 1970. Actual births dropped 3 percent between 1970 and 1971 and 9 percent between 1971 and 1972, so that by 1973 the American birthrate was the lowest in history.

The Urban Region and Megalopolis

Only seven of the fifty states contain no metropolitan areas. These are Alaska, Idaho, Montana, Nevada (which is, however, 70 percent urban), North Dakota (the least urban state, with about 35 percent), Vermont, and Wyoming. Elsewhere, of course, it is around the metropolises that the population continues to cluster. In fact, these areas are growing into one another, so that Charlton F. Chute as early as 1956 found it advantageous to define "urban regions."[4] These consist of two or more contiguous standard metropolitan statistical areas. The greatest of these is the eastern seaboard region, which stretches for 600 miles from the vicinity of Haverhill, north of Boston near the New Hampshire border, to the southernmost suburbs of Washington, in Virginia, from the Atlantic Ocean to the Appalachian foothills. Forty-one million people, about 20 percent of the national total were concentrated in this vast region in 1970. A French geographer has called the area a "megalopolis"—seeing it as a new kind of densely urbanized and suburbanized area containing a dozen or more metropolitan areas with two focal points, Boston and New York. This kind of gigantic urbanized region, he believes, will become the characteristic type of settlement in the late twentieth century.[5] Other megalopises are well developed already, one from Milwaukee to Pittsburgh, and another in the West running from Santa Barbara to south of the Mexican border.

In all, eighteen urban regions contain about 40 percent of the nation's population. Because the complexity as well as the cost of government increases disproportionately with density, it can be expected that these will be the areas where governmental problems will continue to make their greatest challenge.

[3] Advisory Commission on Intergovernmental Relations, *Metropolitan Social and Economic Disparities,* report no. A-25, 1965.

[4] See Charlton F. Chute, "Today's Urban Regions," *National Municipal Review,* vol. 45, June and July, 1956.

[5] Jean Gottman, *Megalopolis: The Urbanized Northeastern Seaboard of the United States,* The M.I.T. Press, Cambridge, Mass., 1961.

The Future

How would continued high gasoline prices or a fuel shortage affect patterns of urban settlement? One has only a few clues. Everywhere interest is being revived in mass transportation. Cars are being reduced in size. Developers are finding it advantageous to build luxury apartments in the central city. But the impact of new technological constraints has hardly yet been felt. Some planners envision urban corridors along which a dense urban settlement would form, as is presently occurring at expressway exits. Railroads or rapid electric lines or monorails might follow this route. But as yet, no pattern is clearly evident. It seems certain, however, that Americans of all classes and ages are less willing to give up their automobiles than are professional planners and some politicians. This is so not merely for matters of convenience or because the auto is a status symbol, but perhaps, most importantly, because it provides for a privacy that cannot be matched by public transportation or car pool. In the unknown future, a new type of engine rather than a new type of basic transportation may be the key to the shape of the metropolis.

THE POLITICAL IMPLICATIONS OF URBAN SETTLEMENT PATTERNS

Cities are based on a money economy, and citizens are largely drawn to them to find better paying jobs. If these jobs are also more interesting or if urban living itself has innate attractions and excitements, so much the better for the individual. But economic opportunity is the magnet.

What, then, are the social characteristics of this economic mecca? It is a smoky, grimy sea of television aerials, noisome slums, bright neon signs, impatient traffic, mammoth factories and fantastic productive capacity, manicured suburbs desperately seeking to imitate a fond memory of a county-seat town in grandfather's day. It is a Champaigne fair of conflicting cultures where thousands of human beings live in close proximity to other thousands whom they dislike in one degree or another because—though they would not so state it—their values and cultural habits do not coincide. For human beings dislike what they fear, they fear much that they do not understand, and there is much in the modern city that they do not understand. It is a land of coolness in a nation of supposedly friendly people, where *émigrés* from rural places find an absence of the primary social relationships to which they are accustomed, and where people, in the midst of the greatest possible variety of activities, may lead basically dull lives, although they seek to hide that fact from their own consciousness.

We note next how urban citizens try to overcome some of these negative aspects of the big city by doing what human beings have always done: seek out their own kind. They seek people who share at least some of their own interests and values, even if many still remain strangers or only nodding acquaintances. We then examine the political effects of the settlement patterns that result.

The Rootlessness of Urban Life

Ours is a nation of seminomadic people. Opportunity for advancement, the necessity for going to the job that will not come to the individual, the practice of businesses and industries that operate over the entire nation or over even larger areas, to send men from assignment in one city to assignment in another while moving up the origanizational ladder—all contribute to this mobility. Some people move to escape unemployment. Some shuttle back and forth between their childhood town or farm and the city several times during a lifetime as it suits their momentary needs or whims. But, for the most part, moves are made as the result of, or in search of, economic advancement. Whether it is the Southern sharecropper moving into the Northern city to become a factory worker or the son or daughter of a clerk becoming an organization person and a middle-class suburbanite, the result is viewed by the migrant as another step toward the fulfillment of the great American dream of continued opportunity. As William H. Whyte, Jr., has said, "The man who leaves home is not the exception in American society, but the key to it."[6]

In the years after World War II, one-fifth of the population has changed place of residence each year. Some people move more often than the average, of course, and there are still Americans who are born, live, and die in the same house; but every five years, about one-half of the people in the United States change their places of residence. Most of these moves are within the same county, although about 5 percent of the total population annually moves to a different county within the same state and another 5 percent moves to a different state. Whyte paints a rather poignant picture of the uprooted and their nostalgia for what they left behind.[7]

> Are the transients a rootless people? If by roots we mean the complex of geographical and family ties that has historically knitted Americans to local society, these young transients are almost entirely rootless. They are very much aware of the fact; surprisingly often they will bring up the hometown, and though they have no intention whatsoever of going back, they dwell on what they left behind.

Like most urban Americans they continue to romanticize the life-styles of the communities from which they or their parents came. In 1966, 49 percent of the persons interviewed in one survey indicated that they would prefer to live in a small town or on a farm if they could choose to live anywhere they wanted to in the United States.[8] Even in cities of one-half million people or more, nearly 50 percent of the residents would prefer to live somewhere else: in the suburbs, in a small town, or on a farm. Of those interviewed, only 22 percent thought a city the best place to live. Not surprisingly, vast numbers of urban Americans feel a sense of rootlessness.

The factory workers, like the middle-class organization types, have also been faced with the problem of establishing some kind of roots in lieu of the traditional type. They, too, are accommodating to the new American way of life. A study of Detroit automobile workers, for example, found that the great bulk of them (82 percent) were American-born, in contrast to the factory worker in An-

[6] William H. Whyte, Jr., *The Organization Man,* Anchor Books, Doubleday & Company, Inc., Garden City, N.Y., 1956, p. 297.

[7] *Ibid.,* 318.

[8] Gallup Poll, published Mar. 23, 1966.

drew Carnegie's steel mills or to Jurgis Rudkus, the Lithuanian who slaved in the stockyards of Chicago at the beginning of the present century.[9] Over one-half (52 percent) had immigrant fathers, however. Most automobile workers are living in towns where they did not grow up, and they are to some degree culturally marginal. Actually one-fifth of Detroit automobile workers grew up on farms, another one-fourth in small towns. Only 44 percent were raised in large cities.[10]

Black Migration

The largest recent uprooting of whole communities has been among blacks. After the Civil War, most remained in the deep South, becoming sharecroppers on land subdivided when the great plantations were broken up. Their number increased with each census, but a lower economic standard, leading to a higher death rate, combined with an almost all-white immigration, caused the percentage of the population, which had been nearly 20 percent black in 1790, to drop to 14 percent in 1860 and to about 10 percent in 1930. The percentage rose to about 12 percent in 1970.

Even before slavery was abolished, some movement of Blacks out of the South took place. However, as late as 1900, only 10 percent of the black population lived in the North. The big change, the one that brought economic opportunity to poverty-ridden black sharecroppers, was the demand for their labor in the urban factory. The first great demand for this purpose came during World War I, when a shortage of factory hands caused an imbalance in supply and demand of labor. It was the younger, more adventuresome who first made the long trek to Chicago, Detroit, or New York. The word they sent back was that one could make far more money in less time under better conditions of labor in a factory than in the almost hopeless atmosphere of the tenant farm. As early as 1914, Henry Ford created a sensation when he offered a $5-a-day minimum wage. He also established a quota for black employees.

The young man in a Chicago rooming house, listening to the words of encouragement offered by the precinct worker for Mayor "Big Bill" Thompson's machine, did not write home about the terrible housing conditions, what would happen when employment dropped off, or the unscrupulous gougers who often acted as real estate men or retail merchants in the burgeoning South Side "Black Belt." Nor did he emphasize the bitter loneliness of the culturally marginal man—the man who was reared according to the values of one culture, in this case, that of the Southern black tenant farmer, but who moves to an area applying a different set of cultural values, in this case, those of a Northern industrial urban community. To him, a job in the city meant, for the first time, the possibility of entering into the competitive struggle for upward mobility and an increase in status position that had long been a typical pattern of activity for other Americans.

After World War I, only the Great Depression served temporarily to stop the

[9] In the novel by Upton Sinclair, *The Jungle,* The Viking Press, Inc., New York, 1906.

[10] Arthur Kornhauser, H. L. Sheppard, and A. J. Mayer, *When Labor Votes,* University Books, Inc., New York, 1956, pp. 26–28.

urbanization of the black. Every other important economic and political consideration—the closing of the gates to immigrants (1924), the mechanization of agriculture (after about 1920), World War II (1941–1945), and the prosperous years after 1945—encouraged the movement to cities. In the decade following 1940, 3 million blacks made the rural-to-urban change. By 1950, 27.6 percent of the black population lived in the North and nearly 60 percent of the total was urban, for Southern blacks also moved into Southern cities.

By 1970, the percentage of the black population located in urban areas was very nearly as large as that of the white population. In the years following the beginning of war preparations about 1940, the nonwhite growth in urban population was far greater than that on the farm. In cities of over 50,000, the nonwhite population increased at a rate five times that of the white population.

Politics and Mobility

High mobility is of political consequence in that large numbers of migrants find it difficult to identify themselves with their adopted communities.[11] Their civic pride is likely to be low. There is little loyalty to the city as an institution or as "home." If the migrant happens to live in a suburb, he or she may not even know whether it is actually an independent unit of government. Politically, this means that elections will be ignored. Government will be left in the hands of others—and the others may be grossly unrepresentative of the interest of the newer arrivals.

Yet one student found the reverse also taking place. Citizens who knew their companies would move them in a few years involved themselves just to lessen their sense of rootlessness.[12] Whyte, in his study of Park Forest, Illinois, found that there was indeed a good deal of apathy toward community problems in a new town made up entirely of persons who were rootless in the traditional sense. But he also found that some residents took up the real issues of providing for schools and public services because of a feeling of a need for "ties more meaningful than those of bridge and canasta and bowling."[13] Politics provided some sense of community roots.

Impersonality and Loneliness in Cities

To the newly arrived in the city, it is the feeling of "with all these people, no one really cares what happens to me" that is hard to bear. Everyone seems cold and calculating. Urban business relationships are impersonal and devoid of sentiment, in contrast with these same activities in rural and small-town situations. In the apartment-house areas of the city, one is lost in anonymity, having casual contacts with many persons rather than intimate contracts with a relatively few. People are judged by what they can do, not by what they are—by reputation

[11] See Robert C. Angell, "The Moral Integration of American Cities," *American Journal of Sociology,* vol. 57, July, 1951, part 2; Basil G. Zimmer, "Participation of Migrants in Urban Structures," *American Sociological Review,* 20:218–224, April, 1955; Basil G. Zimmer, "Farm Backgrounds and Urban Participation," *American Journal of Sociology,* 61:470–475, March, 1956.

[12] Whyte, *op. cit.,* pp. 325–327.

[13] Ibid.

rather than by character. So relationships among people are brief and stylized. People are cool toward one another, quick to take advantage, and, in the view of many ruralites, callous and hardhearted.

In the small town and on the farm, society is subjected to social controls characterized by primary—that is to say, close and personal—relationships. Some of these exist in crowded portions of cities, too, but to a much smaller degree. Secondary relationships and controls predominate there, and these are impersonal, fragmentary, and ephemeral. Social distance—the degree of relative lack of intimacy that one person has with another—is much greater. Urban society, therefore, becomes organized more formally, through more laws, than is the case in rural areas. The political process becomes more important in the city.

Urban behavior patterns have immediate effects upon the political institutions of the community. The rural society (and, to a considerable extent, suburbia) is policed largely by its system of primary social controls. Gossip and community opinion strongly discourage deviations from accepted values. The back-fence tattler may be a nuisance, but he or she also protects. Crime rates are low, and there may not be a professional law-enforcement officer within 30 miles or more. This is not so in the heart of the city. The near absence of most primary controls means that crime rates in cities are higher: mores must be enforced by police officers and by more laws instead of by gossips and community opinion; the courts are kept busier settling civil disputes; bigger government is necessary to reach more people in a more formalized, institutionalized manner.

Citizens seek to overcome this feeling of impersonality by attempting to recapture, at least in part, some of the intimacy of small-town life with its sense of community.

The Search for Community

At one time, sociologists viewed the big city as cold and depersonalized, with individuals moving about like so many programmed atoms. Clearly this pattern did not hold for the European immigrant to the nineteenth-century city, nor is it wholly true today. Likes tend to cluster with likes to create some semblance of community feeling. The clustering today is found to be related to three factors: social status or rank, generally defined by occupation, education, and income; ethnic and racial background, including especially the ties to near relatives; and life-style, which is based on whether the person is married or not and the age and number of children in the family.[14]

Thus, in suburbia, neighbors and business peers are the mainstays of social relationships, since organization families are often forced to live far from any of their relatives. However, residents of the core city, including factory workers, find that relatives are more important than are next-door neighbors or formal organizations.

Half of suburban residents are church members, but factory workers seem to

[14] For a summary of these studies based on the Shevky-Bell index, see Scott Greer, *The Urbane View*, Oxford University Press, New York, 1972.

be quite inactive in church groups, fraternal organizations, veterans' groups, neighborhood associations, and parent-teacher associations—a matter of considerable importance so far as social and political representation of interests is concerned. Unskilled workers, belonging to the working classes where the extended family remains important, probably migrate more to areas where relatives have already located than do middle-class persons. The latter have less of a choice of destination, being required to go where their skills are demanded. In Detroit, 89 percent of core-city working-class couples have relatives living in the same neighborhood. Two-thirds of the couples see their relatives once or twice a week at least, and over one-fourth see some relative nearly every day. Family gatherings at weddings, funerals, birthdays, and holidays are important. Of the people who see relatives once or twice a week, more than one-half see neighbors less than once a month.[15]

Core-city residents are thus less neighborhood-oriented than are suburbanites, though they seek to maintain primary relationships of some kind. When relatives live within driving distances, they are likely to concentrate their social activities upon them (and upon the impersonal aspects of urban recreational activities), thus emphasizing traditional family ties in preference to amalgamation into the impersonal community and its activities. This difference between core-city and suburban dwellers may have important effects upon the pattern of politics in the community and upon political participation. It should be noted, however, that persons with family ties are probably more likely to develop an interest in the community than are isolated persons.

Lack of skills and advanced education among most blacks and Puerto Ricans, resulting in low-income status, has meant that, like all new immigrants to the city, they have been drawn to the rental housing in the crowded core city. In their communities there is some sense of solidarity which finds its political expression in the election of black mayors and council members. Yet, the fact that those elected are primarily from the middle classes, the social disorganization of the ghetto, discrimination and low income that discourages movement to the suburb also have a fracturing effect on that sense of community.

The Suburban Seekers

Studies of how suburbanites select their neighborhoods highlight the process of seeking out similar types in an attempt to recapture a sense of community. It is not unlike what people have always done, even in the Great City, in trying to find "a nice neighborhood to bring up the children." In suburbia the possibilities are widened, and distinctions based on life-style and housing value can be more nicely defined.[16]

This out-movement follows what might be called the "homogeneity princi-

[15] Survey Research Center, University of Michigan, 1955, report of the Detroit Area Study. See also Joel Smith and others, "Local Intimacy in a Middle-sized City," *American Journal of Sociology,* 60:276–284, November, 1954.

[16] *Governor's Study Commission on Metropolitan Area Problems,* State of Michigan, Final Report, Lansing, Mich., 1960. The senior author served as chairman of the commission.

ple," that is, like kinds of people tend to segregate themselves: the rich, religious or ethnic groups, white-collar workers, etc. This tendency is reinforced by the practice of building houses in large blocs within a fairly narrow price range, which results in economic segregation.

Also, institutions locate or relocate in certain areas. For instance, the building of a synagogue in an already Jewish residential area multiplies the attraction of this area for more Jewish people. The suburban parish does the same for Catholics—even more so when the church buys up considerable residential land around its new church structure and sells it largly to Catholic home builders.

The objective of minimizing social conflict within the suburb threatens America's traditional emphasis upon fair play and equality. How, then, do suburbanites rationalize their practices of segregation? They do so in two ways, principally: (1) by arguing that nearly all persons are happier if they live among people like themselves and if there is as little friction as possible of the sort that results from a clash of values and (2) by arguing that the "ghettoization" of the suburbs "protects property values."

A sensation was caused in 1960 when the attorney general of Michigan—with one eye on reelection prospects, perhaps—publicly revealed the techniques used in the wealthy Grosse Pointe suburbs of Detroit in order to control the land use, life-styles, and ethnic composition of the area. For each person who wanted to buy in one of the suburbs involved, the local property owner's association and the realty board had an investigation conducted by a private detective. The detective filled out a standard form; for most people, 50 percent was a passing grade. The questions asked dealt with such things as level of education, place of birth, and church membership. But the realtors also inquired into whether the family's life-style fitted that of the four Grosse Pointes or perhaps more closely resembled that of some cultural subgroup—in particular, whether the applicant spoke English without an accent, whether his friends were primarily from the mainstream of American culture rather than from an ethnic group, whether the men of the family dressed in conservative or flashy style, and whether they were swarthy or fair-skinned. Persons of, or descended from, certain cultural subgroups had to have more than 50 points: Italian-Americans, for example, had to have 65, and Jews 85. Blacks and Americans of Oriental descent apparently could not qualify at all.

This technique for segregation is probably more formalized and elaborate than one would find in most suburbs, but the process takes place through one means or another. When asked how the system could be justified, one broker explained that the "fears and prejudices" of the *buyers* made the system necessary. He said they "prefer congenial neighborhoods where their investment is likely to be secure."[17]

The standard argument that homogeneity protects property values requires some examination, and it has received this in a study of 10,000 real estate sales in

[17] Norman C. Thomas, *Rule 9: Politics, Administration and Civil Rights,* Random House, Inc., New York, 1966.

areas that were changing from all-white to mixed black and white.[18] The findings indicate that the odds were 4 to 1 against property values declining when blacks began to buy into an area. Even when values did go down, as they did in 15 percent of the cases studied, the decline was modest, nearly always less than 9 percent.

The reason, thus, for restrictive land-use and realty practices is not usually just to guard against a perceived threat to property values but also to maintain the social homogeneity of the area—and for this purpose local control, that is, suburban rather than metropolitan-wide government, is a powerful aid. Regardless of the statistical data, many a suburbanite would agree with the businessman in the Chicago suburb of Deerfield who said, "I've put everything I have into my home here and I don't want to lose it to a bunch of do-gooders."

The metropolis thus may be viewed as a collection of half-formed neighborhood communities, some still trying to be born. The sorting out process is one of like attracting like, given the constraints of finance, and for blacks and some other minorities, one of race. People seek neighbors who will act in what seem to them reasonable, predictable ways they can understand. Joe Swinger does not mix well in a suburb of young-married housing or in Retirement Village, and neither he nor they want to mix that closely.

These patterns are reinforced by the differential prices of housing. In the suburbs, residents often try to cement them in further by incorporating cities around the communities and walling them off legally from neighbors. These little governments of suburbia that try to preserve values and life-styles on a parochial basis are hence a source of political conflict by the very techniques they use in seeking to minimize conflict. The Balkanized pattern of suburban America is not designed to help solve the national problem of racial and group conflict.[19]

The Battle of the Suburbs

The politics of protecting neighborhood communities is not a new one to the core city. For many years, sociologists have charted out what they call the "invasion" of a neighborhood by residents of a different type, usually a different class or ethnic or racial group. There is what Samuel Lubell has called "The Old Tenement Trail," a ladder of neighborhoods through which immigrant groups moved on their way from the slums outward and eventually to the suburbs.[20]

This kind of tension and conflict still occurs in the core city. The pitched battles over bussing in the mid-1970s in Irish South Boston provide one example. The question sometimes takes the form of policy toward proposed public housing units. Should they be built only where existing slums have been torn down, or should vacant areas be used where there may be alterations of the character of

[18] Luigi Laurenti, *Property Values and Race,* University of California Press, Berkeley, Calif., 1960.

[19] Robert C. Wood, *Suburbia, Its People and Their Politics,* Houghton Mifflin Company, Boston, 1959. See Part III. On the general topic of location and politics, Kevin R. Cox, *Conflict, Power and Politics in the City,* McGraw-Hill Book Company, New York, 1973.

[20] Samuel Lubell. *The Future of American Politics,* Harper & Brothers, New York, 1951.

existing communities? A related question has been over the building of multiunit apartments or duplexes in what has been single-dwelling neighborhoods.

Tensions may also result from counterinvasions, as in the cases of the reexpansion of Boston's Beacon Hill into the surrounding slums or the white "colonial restoration" of the largely black Georgetown section of Washington, D.C., in the 1930s. Residential areas may be invaded by commerce and industry, which also causes resentment and political strife, because it, too, threatens neighborhood life-styles as well as property values. So-called "improvement associations" have been established in many urban neighborhoods, chiefly to protect property values. Often these organizations exist primarily to keep lower-status groups out of the area. In the past, they and subdivision developers have had legal assistance in the form of "restrictive covenants" in deeds to property. Such covenants prohibited conveyance of the land to specified groups of persons (e.g., blacks, Jews, persons of the yellow race) for a certain number of years, or permanently. In 1948, however, the United States Supreme Court, taking note of the fact that the United States Constitution prohibits a state from denying "to any person within its jurisdiction the equal protection of the laws," declared all such provisions unenforceable.[21]

Hearings before city councils or appeal boards on the rezoning of an area often conceal interclass or interracial conflicts behind ostensible arguments concerning property values. A public or cooperative multifamily housing project which is to be nonsegregated is likely to become a political issue. Opponents may not state their real objection but may advance other arguments, such as a complaint that the proposed project will destroy the single-family-homes character of the neighborhood. If the apartments were designed to rent to restricted clientele, the community attitude might be much different.

The legal tactics of exclusion using zoning laws, building codes, and subdivision regulation are many:[22]

> . . . besides raising the prices of developing land, many suburbs impose so-called "Cadillac requirements." For example, building codes may call for relatively expensive housing materials, thus barring cheaper, factory-produced units; or they may require the construction of costly sidewalks, water lines and sewers before a house or apartment can be built. But the ultimate weapon of the exclusionists is what the open-door forces call "snob zoning." These are ordinances that permit only single-family homes to be built—and then only on relatively large 1- or 2-acre plots.

In 1969, the National Association for the Advancement of Colored People (NAACP) began an attack in the courts against such practices on the basis that they preserved a suburban white noose around core cities. In 1975, it lost an important case. A Rochester, New York, suburb, Penfield, had zoning restrictions that made the community 98 percent single-family dwellings, houses

[21] *Shelly v. Kraemer,* 334 U.S. 1 (1948).

[22] See Roger Babcock and F. P. Bosselman, *Exclusionary Zoning: Land-Use Regulation and Housing in the 1970s,* Praeger Publishers, New York, 1973; quotation from "The Battle of the Suburbs," *Newsweek,* Nov. 15, 1971, p. 64. See also Cox, *op. cit.*; and Martin E. Sloane (ed.), *Fair Housing and Exclusionary Land Use,* Urban Land Institute and National Committee Against Discrimination in Housing, Washington, 1974.

whose minimum cost to build was $30,000 and increasing daily. The Supreme Court held 5 to 4 that the appellants, who included Penfield residents and nonresidents, builders as well as civil rights groups, had not shown sufficient personal injury to rule in their favor.[23] The year before, the Court held that a municipality could limit "single-family" occupancy to traditional families or groups of not more than two unrelated persons.[24] Other cases were on the docket.

At about the same time, officials of the Department of Housing and Urban Development (HUD) persuaded Dayton, Ohio, to establish a housing agency that would make a study of low-income housing and develop a plan for quotas of public housing units throughout the five counties and twenty-nine municipalities. Though suburban participation would be voluntary, this fair-share plan has had some success, and some housing proponents seek to tie future federal housing aid to the adoption of such low-income housing dispersion plans throughout all of the nation's cities. Such a plan is viewed with suspicion by middle-class persons who fear that low-income housing would bring with it life-styles with which their own would be incompatible.

To summarize: Racial integration of suburbs has been largely on a voluntary basis. In the courts, the bussing decision in the Detroit suburban case stated that bussing could not be required across school district lines as a device for bringing about racial integration. Restrictive zoning, when not absolute or obviously discriminatory on racial grounds specifically, has been upheld. The issue continues to be a lively one in the politics of core cities and suburbia.

A Closing Statement

American population has been steadily on the move since the rapid industrialization that followed the Civil War. Early experiences of failure in the governing of the new Great Cities of the nineteenth century have left lingering negative attitudes in respect to cities and their government. The most recent pattern of settlement has been one resulting in urban "sprawl," encouraged by the versatility of the private auto. Enclaves of persons of like social, ethnic, and familial status have, as in the past, developed. But many of today's social communities also have independent local governments, better able to protect their communities from settlement by those unlike themselves. The legal and political battles over such practices form an important theme of local politics of the late 1970s.

SELECTED READINGS

(For further bibliography, see earlier editions of this volume.)

Adrian, Charles R., and Ernest S. Griffith: *A History of American City Government, 1775–1870,* Praeger Publishers, New York, 1976.

Berry, Brian J. L.: *The Human Consequences of Urbanization,* St Martin's Press, Inc., New York, 1973. (Analysis by a geographer of differing paths of urbanization based on the degree of planning and control applied in different nations.)

Burgess, E. W., R. E. Park, and R. D. McKenzie: *The City,* The University of Chicago

[23] *Warth v. Seldin,* No. 73–2024, decided June 25, 1975.

[24] *Belle Terre v. Boraas,* No. 73–191, decided April 1, 1974.

Press, Chicago, 1925. (A classic study.)

Casstevens, Thomas, and Lynn Eley: *Politics of Fair Housing Legislation,* Chandler Publishing Company, San Francisco, 1968.

Clawson, Marion (ed.): *Modernizing Urban Land Policy,* Johns Hopkins Press, Baltimore, 1973.

Cox, Kevin R: *Conflict, Power and Politics in the City, A Geographic View,* McGraw-Hill Book Company, New York, 1973. (How public policy determines accessibility to urban land.)

Downs, Anthony: *Opening Up the Suburbs: An Urban Strategy for America,* Yale University Press, New Haven, Conn., 1973. (An argument for the racial and social integration of American urban areas.)

Edmonston, Barry: *Population Distribution in American Cities,* Lexington Books, Lexington, Mass., 1975.

Esslinger, Dean: *Ethnicity and Mobility in a Nineteenth Century Midwestern City,* Kennikat Press, Port Washington, N.Y., 1975. (An analysis of population movement in South Bend, Ind.)

Glazer, Nathan, and Daniel Patrick Moynihan: *Beyond the Melting Pot, The Negroes, Puerto Ricans, Jews, Italians and Irish of New York City,* The M.I.T. Press, Cambridge, Mass., 1963. (Argues ethnic groups continue their identification in third-generation Americans and beyond.)

Gottmann, Jean: *Megalopolis,* The M.I.T. Press, Cambridge, Mass., 1961. (A study of the Northeastern seaboard urban region by a famous French geographer.)

Green, Constance McLaughlin: *The Rise of Urban America,* Harper & Row, Publishers, Incorporated, New York, 1965. (History of sixteen cities in various parts of the nation.

Greer, Scott: *The Urbane View,* Oxford University Press, New York, 1972. (An urban sociologist's review of his own research from after World War II to the 1970s. Gives good insight into changing concerns.)

Griffith, Ernest S.: *A History of American City Government,* Praeger Publishers, New York, 1974, 2 vols., 1870–1900, and 1900–1920.

Hirsch, Werner Z. (ed.): *Urban Life and Form,* Holt, Rinehart and Winston, Inc., New York, 1963. (Nine papers by outstanding urbanists of various disciplines.)

Laurenti, Luigi: *Property Values and Race,* University of California Press, Berkeley, Calif., 1960. (Traces effects of black movement into previously all-white areas.)

Long, Norton, E.: "Have Cities a Future?" *Public Administration Review,* 33: 543–552, November, 1973. ("Once we have freed ourselves from the dogma" of the city's powerlessness, it could become "the instrument of a good and noble life.")

Lubell, Samuel: *The Future of American Politics,* Harper & Brothers, New York, 1951. (Excellent chapters on immigrant groups that made up the FDR New Deal condition.)

Mumford, Lewis: *The City in History,* Harcourt, Brace & World, Inc., New York, 1961. (Reviews the place of the city in human society through 5,000 years. Highly opinionated but brilliant.)

Orleans, Peter, and W. R. Ellis, Jr. (eds.): *Race, Change, and Urban Society,* Sage Publications, Inc., Beverly Hills, Calif., 1971. (Includes bibliography on race and cities.)

Roberts, E. F.: *A Basic Introduction to Land Use Control Law and Doctrine,* Northeast Regional Center for Rural Development, Cornell University, Ithaca, N.Y., 1975. (Zoning and its alternatives.)

Rossi, Peter H.: *Why Families Move,* The Free Press of Glencoe, New York, 1956. (A study of inducements for the suburban movement.)

Schlesinger, Arthur M.: *The Rise of the City,* The Macmillan Company, New York, 1933.

Schlesinger, Arthur M., Jr.: *The Age of Jackson,* Little, Brown and Company, Boston, 1945. (An account of the coming of industrial society to America.)

Schmandt, Henry L., and Warren Bloomberg, Jr. (eds): *The Quality of Urban Life,* Sage Publications, Inc., Beverly Hills, Calif., 1969. (Emphasizes current conditions and trends.)

Scientific American Editors: *Cities, Their Origin, Growth and Human Impact,* W. M. Freeman and Co., San Francisco, 1973.

Teaford, Jon C.: *The Municipal Revolution in America,* The University of Chicago Press, Chicago, 1975. (Development of city governments, 1650–1825.)

Van der Slik, Jack R. (ed.): *Black Conflict with White America,* Charles E. Merrill Publishing Co., Columbus, Ohio, 1970.

Warner, Sam B.: *Street Car Suburbs,* Harvard University and The M.I.T. Press, Cambridge, Mass., 1962. (The early suburban movement was made possible by public transportation.)

Weber, Adna F.: *The Growth of Cities in the Nineteenth Century,* Columbia University Press, New York, 1899. (A famous analysis of census data.)

Willbern, York: *The Withering Away of the City,* University of Alabama Press, University, Ala., 1964. (Explores various political implications of the urbanization movement.)

Williams, Oliver P.: *Metropolitan Political Analysis,* Free Press, New York, 1971. (How local-government land-use regulations are used for exclusionary and restrictive purposes to the advantage of those who control the rules.)

Wirth, Louis: "Urbanism as a Way of Life," *American Journal of Sociology,* 44:1–24, July, 1938. (A seminal statement, although no longer fully accepted by social scientists, of urban life-styles as unique compared with rural.)

Zehner, Robert F., Stuart Chapin, Jr., and Joseph T. Howell: *Across the City Line, A White Community in Transition,* Lexington Books, Lexington, Mass., 1974. (Invasion of white working-class suburbs by blacks.)

Chapter 2

The Urban Panorama

Cities come in all sizes and shapes. Some are large, some are small. Some are homogeneous and some are the home of many racial, ethnic, and class groupings. Some are parts of metropolitan areas, and others, similar in population size, lie out on the plains of Nebraska west of Omaha, without another city of comparable size nearby. No two are exactly alike. We can speak of statistical patterns and "typical" cities, but we can only approximate what we would find if we were to give an intensive examination to any one city. An impressionistic glance may, however, furnish a few generalizations which can be examined in greater detail as we proceed farther on in this text.

URBAN PERSONALITY

American cities, for the most part, have a dull monotony about them. To be sure, there are exceptions. There is only one Boston, New Orleans, New York, Atlantic City, San Francisco, or Washington.[1] New England towns are greatly different from those of Wyoming. New York's slums, externally, look not at all like those of Los Angeles. The smaller cities of northern California look "western," those of Southern California, "Mexican" or "Mediterranean." But the typical city has

[1] Constance McLaughlin Green, *American Cities in the Growth of the Nation* (Harper Colophon Books, Harper & Row, Publishers, Incorporated, New York, 1965), looks at the history of sixteen cities; Anselm Strauss, *Images of the American City* (The Free Press of Glencoe, New York, 1961), looks at American opinions regarding rapid urbanization.

little to distinguish it as a personality. It has failed to develop its own individuality, to exploit latent traditions, to use its every opportunity to make the community a place where life is richer because of its own particular attributes. In the past, the local politicians and most pillars of the community have been too busy in a frenetic world to concern themselves with such an expendable as local color.

The drift to sameness has been accelerated by the nationalization of the American culture. The same deep-fry carbohydrate processing vendors can be found in Portland, Maine, and Portland, Oregon. The sometimes confusing four- or six-lane expressways with their green direction signs warning of an impending interchange are the same; and when the traveller corkscrews off, there to greet one and all are the Golden Arches of McDonalds, a bustling K Mart, or the Pickwick-like figure of a Ramada Inn. Inside the motel is the same Walter Cronkite giving forth with the evening news about the latest satellite shot or the cash crisis in New York City or a garbage strike in some other large city.

One journalist set out to find out if there were really any differences among America's fifty largest cities below their surface sameness, differences that would make one "more livable" than another. He tabulated the statistics on such things as crime, health, wealth, housing, education and professional achievement, population density, and amenities. In all he made twenty-four statistical comparisons which gave him overall city ratings that varied from 14.0 to 41.6. At the high end of the scale he found America's most newly formed cities: Seattle, Tulsa, San Diego, San Jose, and Honolulu. At the other end were those whose major population settlement in the core city was in the nineteenth century: Baltimore, Detroit (somewhat later), Chicago, St. Louis, and at the very bottom, Newark. New York ranked thirty-second.[2]

Some cities, such as Tulsa, Indianapolis, Nashville, and Oklahoma City, had clearly improved their 1970 ranking by large-scale annexation of suburban areas. Cities ranked differently on individual measures as well. But what is perhaps most startling about the tabulations is that there seems to be a migration of livability qualities from the old manufacturing cities of the Northeast to the newer cities of the West and Southwest, a pattern that has overtones of the original migration from core city to suburb.

Bearing these differences in mind, we describe a series of impressionistic types of cities found both in metropolitan areas and elsewhere. No such generalizations of social composition or politics can precisely fit any one city, but such rough guidelines may at least bring some semblance of order for the reader out of the confusion of American cities.

THE SMALL TOWN: URBAN ANOMALY

Village and small-town life has been a traditional part of America, honored in memory and song and satirized in novel and poem. The town has its origins as a

[2] Arthur M. Lewis, "The Worst American City," *Harpers Magazine,* January, 1975, pp. 67–71. Studies like this are fun to read but should not be taken too seriously, for the writer may have left out important variables. One wonders if Lewis has ever spent a season in the continuous, depressing drizzle of a Seattle winter or experienced years of parochial isolation on the flatlands of Tulsa.

service center for a small rural area. Throughout much of the nation, shopping villages were originally spaced close enough together to allow any farmer to reach one by horseback or buggy within a reasonable length of time, perhaps an hour. County seats were generally situated so that they were not more than a day's buggy ride from the farthest farmer. They were larger than ordinary trading places, since they contained the incipient bureaucracy of government, the offices of lawyers who dealt with that bureaucracy on behalf of clients, livery stables, hotels, and other establishments catering to the citizenry that found it necessary or desirable to visit the seat of government.

The ordinary country town contained a general store, repair shops, a physician and a veterinarian, a weekly newspaper, a bank, a school, and a church or two. If the community was large enough, it also served as a market. With the coming of the automobile and telephone, this pattern began to change. By the 1950s, the general store had come more to resemble the corner grocery of the city or, in larger towns, had become a supermarket. Physicians found they could make more money and serve more people by moving into the nearby city. The weekly newspaper, in the face of high labor and newsprint costs, was beginning to change in character and purpose. The bank had become a branch of a city institution or had disappeared. The school now represented the consolidation of a great many formerly rural districts with an elaborate system of school bus routes. The churches continued to perform some, though not all, of their traditional functions. The population was made up of locally employed persons, a considerable number of retired farmers, and a new element—commuters. Many persons, either because of preference for the small-town life or because of shortages in low-cost housing in the cities, have taken up residence in the town but may drive up to 25 miles and more each day to their jobs in the city. Townspeople themselves commute to city jobs.

One small town after another is being engulfed by the metropolis as it sends its highways, television, and demand for housing out to the surrounding countryside. This is not universally the case, however. Much of the nation remains outside of metropolitan areas. Let us view small-town politics in a relatively pure and uncontaminated form, the way it might be on the prairie, 60 miles west of Fargo, North Dakota.

Small-Town Politics

Politically, the villages and towns have been, throughout the nation, centers of conservatism. Most of them are one-party communities, either Democratic or Republican, depending upon local traditions. Although their governments provide some basic community services in the areas of water, sewage disposal, police and fire protection, the small community remains a center of skepticism about the social-service state. Lacking experience in the social problems of large cities or in living together with cultural groups having different values from their own, its citizens used to be intolerant of proposed state or municipal legislation dealing with problems that do not exist or exist in minor ways in their communities. To them, the fact that such problems exist in large cities is taken to be evidence of the degeneracy or moral inferiority of urban life. This attitude cannot be ignored as quaint but harmless, however. Representatives from small towns, until the mid-1960s, dominated most state legislatures, which are the agencies that control the powers exercised by large city governments.[3]

Yet the town is itself becoming a political, economic, and social problem. Its difficulties stem from several things: the declining farm populations, which produces a declining market; the preference of many farmers for the more specialized and hence more expert services in the nearby city, now easily available by modern auto and good roads; the lack of opportunity in the town, while our culture emphasizes the desirability of opportunity, with the resultant draining off of the most able young people; extreme conservatism in a day when many attitudes which this produces do not fit into the value systems learned in the consolidated schools and on television by young people; and finally, current highway department practices of bypassing practically all towns, thus cutting off the transient business that had earlier helped to sustain them. The isolated small town is an urban place and its life-style is no longer as different from that of the large city as it once was, but it is still different—as its governmental and social problems are different.

Consensus and Inaction in Springdale

"Springdale," a rural village in upstate New York, was studied by two sociologists who wanted to see how the villagers were accommodating to life in mass society. The community offers some not atypical examples of small-town life. Its politics differs radically from that of the metropolis. The large city is often the scene of strident and undisguised political conflict, but in the village:[4]

> . . . Politics is conducted on the principle of unanimity of decision. In two years of observation of village board meetings in Springdale, all decisions brought to a vote were passed unanimously. The dissent, disagreement, and factionalism which exist in the community are not expressed at board meetings. Through a process of consultation prior to an official meeting and by extended discussion involving the entire group during the meeting itself, a point is reached when it seems reasonable to assume that everyone will go along with the proposed action. Only then, as a final parry, will someone suggest that a motion be made to propose the action.

Although the large city is the scene of constant experimentation, the arena in which new social-service activities of government are launched and in which a highly professional bureaucracy administers complex programs, the pattern in the village is totally different:

> Although the principle of unanimity of decision is almost a requirement in Springdale politics, few items of business outside of routine and legally required action ever reach the decision-making stage. It is an outstanding characteristic of village govern-

[3] Charles Press and Charles R. Adrian, "Why Our State Governments Are Sick," *Antioch Review*, 53:100–120, June, 1964.

[4] Arthur J. Vidich and Joseph Bensman, *Small Town in Mass Society*, Princeton University Press, Princeton, N.J., 1958.

ment that it does not initiate new undertakings and new projects. . . . It is a common complaint among all groups in the community that the village board does nothing.

The authors note that many community projects, whether new park benches or band concerts, are initiated and carried through by private individuals or groups.

This is the kind of low tax–low service local government called by Williams and Adrian, "caretaker."[5] It is favored by those in communities with static or declining commercial enterprises and those whose residents are on fixed incomes, such as the retired. The novelist Max Shulman in *Rally Round the Flag Boys* mentions a handsewn sampler hanging in the office of a small-town official which read:[6]

MAKE IT DO
WEAR IT OUT
USE IT UP
DO WITHOUT

But such small towns are more and more being engulfed by urbanization, if not the metropolis, and by the mass society that surrounds them. The old ways of doing things in social life and politics change. Williamston, Michigan (population 2,600), 10 miles east of Lansing, Michigan, recalled two members of its school board in 1974, ostensibly because their opposition to the welfare state's federal school-lunch program was seen by voters as a threat to its local continuance. Ironically, the very next year, California's urbane governor, Edmund G. (Jerry) Brown, was gaining political support from his urging of the sampler credo cited by Shulman, and one northern California county in 1975 attracted much attention when its Board of Supervisors refused to pay state-mandated local welfare charges.

THE CORE CITY

Although in the nineteenth century nearly all people in an urban area lived within the core city, the present-day pattern is very different. Suburban movement has tended to leave the core with little but specialized governmental, business, and professional activities—and the poor. Some large cities have virtually no middle-class residents left within their boundaries. Even many of the better-paid members of the working class (particularly the "hard hats") have moved to suburbia. Indeed, at the beginning of the 1970s, a majority of suburban residents in metropolitan areas were blue-collar rather than white-collar workers.

Note that these generalizations are most true about the nation's largest and oldest core cities. The tendencies are clearly present, however, in many middle-

[5] Oliver P. Williams and Charles R. Adrian, *Four Cities,* University of Pennsylvania Press, Philadelphia, 1963.

[6] Max Shulman, *Rally Round the Flag Boys,* Doubleday & Company, Inc., Garden City, N.Y., 1954.

sized core cities, including some in the 50,000 to 100,000 population range. Because these older core cities fit the image most Americans hold, we will fit our generalizations to them.

Problems of the Core City

At the heart of the core city in many of the nation's metropolitan areas lies the poverty of its hard-core ghetto. Around this area swirl all the problems of social disorganization associated with urbanization. Racial discrimination exacerbates the situation, as some blacks are denied the residential location to which their skills and income entitle them. All other core-city problems are to some degree related to this central one of the ghetto and its poverty.

The Problems of Bigness

Suburbanites have always regarded the size of core-city government as one of its greatest political problems ("You can't fight city hall"), and some students of organization are coming to agree with them.[7] Within the big city there are experiments in decentralization, the reasons for which are clear. What citizens see are large-scale bureaucracies able to defy mayor, council, and often the citizenry as well. Most are protected by civil service tenure rules and many, in addition, by unionization or the power of professional associations. A political scientist turned journalist notes:[8]

> In 1974, an illegal nine-day strike won for San Francisco's municipal employes a wage increase approximately twice the size of the one originally offered to them. A crucial strike weapon was the closing of three sewage treatment plants, which poured 100 million gallons of raw sewage into the fragrant bay each day.
>
> Recently, New York Mayor Abraham Beame pretended to be planning to include some garbagemen in the layoffs . . . to cope with the city's financial crisis. So the garbagemen launched an illegal strike.
>
> After less than three July days, with about 60,000 tons of garbage on the steaming streets, Beame capitulated, cutting back the payroll cutbacks. To underscore the lesson that crime pays, he paid the garbagemen $713,500 in time-and-a-half over time wages to clean up the mess they caused.

Are large-scale administrative organizations always more efficient in all crucial aspects than smaller ones? Some recent studies suggest conventional wisdom may need revision. In Indianapolis, suburbs were matched with core-city neighborhoods they bordered so that both had similar racial and socioeconomic characteristics. Police services were then compared. Costs per capita were found less in the suburbs, mainly because of absence of core-city ghetto crime. When the cost of this was subtracted, they were slightly more in the suburbs. When citizens

[7] A basic discussion is Gordon Tullock, *The Politics of Bureaucracy,* Public Affairs Press, Washington, D.C., p. 156. Vincent Ostrom, *The Intellectual Crisis in American Public Administration,* University of Alabama Press, University, Ala., 1974, discusses the assumptions of the centralists. For an argument for the decentralization of big cities with block and neighborhoods having political powers, see Alan A. Altshuler, *Community Control,* Pegasus Books, The Bobbs-Merrill Comapny, Inc., Indianapolis, 1970.

[8] George Will, syndicated column, July 15, 1975.

were polled it was found:[9]

> While the Indianapolis force received evaluations as an excellent department, there is no single indicator on which the Indianapolis police force was rated higher by citizens in Indianapolis when compared to citizen experience and evaluations of the smaller suburban departments. Residents in smaller jurisdictions consistently rated police higher on response time and police-community relations, had lower victimization rates and were more likely to have received assistance from a policeman.

The study has to date been repeated in six metropolitan areas with similar findings. Students are beginning to rethink the questions: are some types of large-scale organizations politically unmanageable? Are large organizations more efficient in all respects than smaller ones? The evidence to date is still inconclusive, but it raises questions about assumptions largely unchallenged until recently.

Declining Tax Base, Rising Costs

Money has been a major problem to the core cities of metropolitan areas in all the years following World War II. Even after the exodus of many middle-class residents and of much of business and industry, the core city continued to have a solid base of tax support in the valuable businesses and industries that could not or, because of sunk costs, chose not to move outside the core. But even though these cities retained sources of taxable wealth, the problems confronting them were greater than the taxable resources permitted them by suburban- and rural-oriented legislatures. At the same time, many large cities undertook expensive programs aimed at relieving the social ills that their ghetto residents faced. Because these programs involved largely payroll expense, they have continued to increase in costs irrespective of their efficacy. As a result, every large city in the United States has now for decades suffered from a serious shortage in financial resources. Mayors of such cities have been faced with the problem of trying to secure from reluctant legislatures, or from an often unenthusiastic Congress, the funds needed to try to cope with the ever-expanding problems of an aging city with a largely impoverished population.[10]

Threats to the Central Business District

The traditional "downtown" areas of cities, the central business district (CBD), has been undergoing a steady decline in value and social usefulness in the years since 1945. Its streets are congested, it has inadequate and expensive parking facilities, it lacks off-street loading facilities, it is not compactly organized for

[9] Robert L. Bish and Vincent Ostrom, *Understanding Urban Government,* American Enterprise Institute for Public Policy Research, Washington, D.C., 1973, p. 44. For a full discussion, see Elinor Ostrom and others, *Community Organization and the Provision of Police Services,* Sage Professional Papers in Administrative and Policy Studies, 01–001, Sage Publications, Inc., Beverly Hills, Calif., 1973.

[10] This trend was anticipated many years ago. See Harvey E. Brazer, "The Role of Major Metropolitan Centers in State and Local Finance," *American Economic Review,* 48:305–316, May, 1958.

shopper convenience, its land remains highly valued—often, perhaps, overvalued—and is hence difficult to redevelop, it is usually owned by a great many persons—many of them nonresidents—who often cannot agree on policies of renovation. And the area is generally old in appearance, unattractive, and lacking in an architectually integrated design. [11]

The importance of the central business district has changed rapidly with the coming of the automobile as a family car and with the great expansion of population in metropolitan areas. One of the most dramatic movements away from dependence upon the central business district has been seen in Los Angeles, where the pattern is perhaps only slightly more exaggerated than is the case in the typical community. In 1930, about three-fourths of the retail sales for the metropolitan area took place in downtown Los Angeles. By the end of World War II, this figure had been cut to one-half. After that, it dropped precipitously. It was down to 18 percent in 1960, and was still falling. By that date, Los Angeles had no central business district worthy of that name. Neither did many communities of moderately large size, despite desperate efforts to create downtown malls.

Yet the CBD is an area carrying an enormous investment. The Cleveland CBD, for example, is estimated to be worth at least 750 million dollars in land and buildings. Many of the "metropolitan-area studies" that have been so popular in the postwar years have probably been inspired by those who fear the results of the pattern of decline that is evident in the CBD. They wish to put a stop to this trend and hope that an integrated government and area-wide land-use controls will lend them a hand. In many cases, city fathers have sought to correct the CBD situations that are making suburban living and trading alternatives so much more attractive. At best they could hope only to diminish the rate of decentralization.

Subsidization of the Suburbs

In addition to its decreasing tax base, the core city has been forced in most states to subsidize the suburbs. As the tax base declines, the amount and number of subsidies increase. There are at least two ways in which the core city is forced to help suburbanites pay for their governmental services: by furnishing services of the city free or below cost; and by paying a disproportionately large share of state and county taxes in return for a disproportionately small share of their services.

The core city, whether it likes it or not, builds streets to carry people into the city each morning and back to the dormitory towns each evening. The city pays for the repairs on the highways that deteriorate rapidly under the pounding of an ever increasing traffic load. The city hires extra police officers to handle the nonresident traffic. It provides parks, ice rinks, ball fields, libraries, museums, botanical gardens, and zoos, all of which may often be used by suburbanites without cost.

Some core cities are required by state law to furnish fire protection, water, sewage disposal, or other facilities to the suburbs at less than cost. Chicago has

[11] John Rannels, *The Core of the City,* Columbia University Press, New York, 1956.

tried unsuccessfully since 1904 to get permission from the legislature to charge a differential rate to suburbs, for example, even though some suburbs sell the water to others at a profit.

The core city also subsidizes the urban fringe through the payment of a disproportionate share of county taxes. The county was traditionally a rural unit of government. In many urban communities it still performs few functions within the core city. There are some important exceptions to this, but for the most part the county collects most of its taxes within the city and spends them outside, particularly in unincorporated areas. The inequity is increased by the fact that core-city properties are sometimes assessed at a higher rate than are those in suburbs.

The large cities also pay a great deal in state taxes. Yet the state often spends money on services in the rural and suburban areas, expecting the large cities to finance most of their functions themselves. The state police, for example, will often lend assistance to the amateurish efforts of suburban police but seldom operate within the core city. Health, education, highway, welfare, and other state functions may be provided more generously outside the large cities than inside them. State governments have done little in the past to assist core cities with the problems of housing, public transportation, jobs for the poor, or area-wide planning and land-use controls. Possibly, this pattern is changing, though states in the late 1970s were experiencing serious financial problems of their own.

Race Relations

The issue of racial relations is one of the most important facing core-city government. Whites who remain poor continue to be among those who are prejudiced against the newer and darker migrants to the city. Blacks and browns, in turn, have basic areas of conflict between themselves. As the core city becomes increasingly dominated by new types of political leaders—with black mayors and a black majority of the council soon to become commonplace in many of them—relationships between the core city and the suburbs will become increasingly sensitive. Although there is no research evidence on the subject, it seems very likely that the deterioration of the core city has resulted at least in part from the tragic failure in the first quarter of a century after World War II to work out a satisfactory relationship between or among the races.

Ghetto Problems

The ghetto (or slum, to use the older word) is a study in contrast. There is the warm support of a sense of community and the terror of a police raid. There are delightful ethnic foods combined with the too frequent use of every type of dangerous drug. There is fear, hate, joy, and despair.

Throughout American history, the ghetto has been occupied by the most recent urban arrivals, so that almost every ethnic group has served its time in the ghetto. Some fine books have been written by persons who began in the slums, became successful, and as older persons recall the pains and pleasures of their youthful ghetto life.[12] That life and its concerns have always been far different from that of the well-off person living on the fringe of the city or in the suburbs. The black sociologist, St. Clair Drake, has given us a bit of the character of the black slum portrayed in the following word picture.[13]

> The character of the Black Ghetto is not set by the newer "gilded," not-yet rundown portions of it, but by the older sections where unemployment rates are high and the masses of people work with the hands—where the median level of education is just above graduation from grade school and many of the people are likely to be recent migrants from rural areas.
>
> The "ghettoization" of the Negro has resulted in the emergence of a ghetto subculture with a distinctive ethos, most pronounced, perhaps, in Harlem, but recognizable in all Negro neighborhoods. For the average Negro who walks the streets of any American Black Ghetto, the smell of barbecued ribs, fried shrimps, and chicken emanating from numerous restaurants gives olfactory reinforcement to a feeling of "at homeness." The beat of "gut music" spilling into the street from ubiquitous tavern jukeboxes and the sound of tambourines and rich harmony behind the crude folk art on the windows of store-front churches give auditory confirmation to the universal belief that "we Negroes have 'soul.' " The bedlam of an occasional brawl, the shouted obscenities of street corner "foulmouths" and the whine of police sirens break the monotony of waiting for the number that never "falls," the horses that neither win, place, nor show, and the "good job" that never materializes. . . . The spontaneous vigor of the children who crowd streets and playgrounds . . . and the cheerful rushing about of adults, free from the occupational pressures of the "white world" in which they work, create an atmosphere of warmth and superficial intimacy which obscures the unpleasant facts of life in the overcrowded rooms behind the doors, the lack of adequate maintenance standards, and the too prevalent vermin and rats.

The relationship of the people to their local government and their public policy concerns are very much different in the ghetto from those elsewhere. An inquiry among ghetto residents would surely indicate that many of them are concerned about such things as welfare policies preeminently. Most city governments have only a limited welfare function today, and changes that seem to be needed in welfare policies probably will have to come at the federal government level. But certainly the inquiring, "bossy" social caseworker has become increasingly a symbol of scorn and hatred which probably carries over to other government workers.

Slum dwellers are also concerned about police policies. Most middle-class citizens had no contact with the police before the coming of the automobile age, excepting perhaps to ask directions. But such is not the case in the ghetto where police officers (many white) with working-class backgrounds are called upon to enforce laws reflecting middle-class values upon people, many of whom do not

[12] For example, Harry Roskolenko, *The Time that Was Then: The Lower East Side, 1900–1914,* Dial Press, New York, 1970.

[13] St. Clair Drake, "The 'Ghettoization' of Urban Life," *Daedalus,* 94:1168–1193, Fall, 1965.

accept the middle-class notion of the legitimacy of the law and of the police officer's activities.[14] But, contrary to a popular notion, ghetto residents do worry about crime quite as much as do middle-class citizens, and they are anxious to be protected by the police. Ghetto residents also worry about their health and that of their children, even though they may not inform themselves of available facilities. Some slum dwellers are concerned about the quality of education their children are getting in the ghetto schools, accepting the traditional American emphasis upon education as a way toward upward mobility; but others seem to place little emphasis upon education, and the drop-out rate in the ghetto is high.[15] Many residents cannot afford automobiles and hence are concerned about public transportation facilities. Factories have moved to the suburbs, which is convenient for the white-collar workers but not for the unskilled worker living in the old core city. As transportation facilities decline, so do the prospects for the slum dweller of getting to work. As a result, welfare rolls increase and morale in the ghetto declines still further.

Many of the governmental concerns of other urbanites are of little or no importance in the ghetto. The former worry about such things as taxes, commuter highways, school curriculum, smog, the environment, the fluoridation of water, and the aesthetics of city and suburb. Although schools are a mutual interest, the concerns about them are vastly different. The others are often seen as irrelevant or beyond the poor person's ability to influence.[16] Even as to taxes, there may be little concern in the ghetto. Persons with little education also tend to have little information about the tax system, and it is probable that the typical slum dweller pays far more in taxes than he realizes, for the relative burden upon him is heavy, particularly in the case of the retail sales tax and the general property tax (which the slum landowner passes on to him as a part of his costs in calculating his rent).

The middle-class suburbanite and the ghetto dweller are both very much concerned about one aspect of urban government policy, which is that of land uses and controls. Suburbanites are interested in protecting the value of property, and both they and ghetto dwellers share in concerns about possible changes in the character of their neighborhoods. The breaking up of a neighborhood by running a limited-access highway through it or by construction of an urban-renewal project can have serious economic and psychological consequences for slum dwellers. Such changes may break up important neighborhood patterns, force changes in school attendance, or make it more difficult or impossible to get to work. Throughout its history, urban renewal has resulted in few homes, homes that the poor cannot afford to rent. Some urban-renewal projects may have been undertaken in order to discourage black residency in that particular city, but the main reasons blacks are so much affected by it is that they usually occupy the poorest housing in the city.

[14] Burton Levy, "Cops in the Ghetto: A Problem of the Police System," in Louis H. Masotti and Don K. Bowen (eds.), *Riots and Rebellion,* Sage Publications, Inc., Beverly Hills, Calif., 1968, pp. 347–358.

[15] Marilyn Gittell (ed.), *Educating an Urban Population,* Sage Publications, Inc., Beverly Hills, Calif., 1967.

[16] *Ibid.*

A few final observations about the ghetto should be made:

1 The most obvious indication of a ghetto is to be found in the low quality of its housing. Much of it consists of overcrowded apartment houses, called tenements, or of what were once large family homes that have now been broken up into many apartments. Not all ghettos give one the initial impression of being what they are. The Watts area of Los Angeles, for example, requires further investigation before one can be certain that it is, in fact, a ghetto. But housing in all such areas of our cities shares one important characteristic: it declines in quality through time. This is partly so because of the continuing migration of rural people into the ghettos, assuring the landlord of customers and hence no need to make his property more attractive to prevent it from standing vacant. Another important reason is to be found in the characteristics of the general property tax. Since the tax is based upon the value of the land and building rather than upon its income-producing ability, any improvements by landlords—by logic of the tax—should result in an increase in their tax assessments. It is therefore to their advantage to let the property run down, though not to the point where the building might be condemned for occupancy. But even if threatened with that, slum landlords can usually count on their own tenants coming to their support; for if they were forced to move out, they might have no suitable place to which to move, at least at the same amount of rent. Much of the American middle class is relatively unconcerned about slums and ghetto life. Americans are accustomed to ghettos, for they have existed throughout the history of the nation.

2 Not only is the ghetto an area of low income but its retail prices tend to be higher than are those in suburbia. The resident is thus at a double disadvantage. This pattern prevails for at least three reasons. One is that the ghetto dweller typically has less transportation mobility than does the suburbanite. The slum shopkeeper has something of a captive customer. Secondly, shoplifting and other forms of petty thievery are common and probably occur much more often than they do in the suburban shopping center, thus raising costs of business which are passed on to the consumer. Finally, vandalism and riots are more common in the ghetto than elsewhere, and as a result insurance rates may be ten or more times higher than in a middle-class area.

3 The ghetto of today is generally in a weaker political position than it was two or three generations ago. During the time of the political bosses and machines, the ghetto was organized on a ward, precinct, and even block basis, often with a professional block or precinct worker serving as a connecting link between the needs of the ghetto dweller and the political organization. The changes that have taken place in the years especially since the Great Depression have further alienated the ghetto dweller from urban government. Few professional political workers exist any longer in the ghettos. Political organization between elections may be almost nonexistent. The reform movement desire for small city councils, preferably elected at large, often has resulted in no ghetto representation on the council at all and with that body reflecting overwhelmingly middle-class values. In the 1880s and 1890s, city councils were typically much larger than they are today and were almost always, in large cities, elected by wards. This guaranteed that each ghetto area would have some direct representation on the council; and, to further reinforce this, ward boundaries were often drawn along ethnic and racial lines. Furthermore, although the bosses and machines cooperated closely with business people, they were dependent for votes primarily in the ghetto areas; and they had means for making certain that the vote was turned out on election day. Today, with no such spur, the ghetto resident is likely to be apathetic about municipal elections unless some salient event has given them extraordinary visibility in some particular year.

The general isolation of the urban poor from their local government was recognized in the Economic Opportunity Act of 1964. That act provided that, in carrying out its various programs, the Office of Economic Opportunity should involve the "maximum feasible participation" of the poor. Although most members of Congress probably thought this was no more than a homily, some of the supporters of the bill intended it to be taken literally. Since the act coincided with the emergence of a new type of young black and brown leadership in many ghetto areas, this provision was given an unusual amount of attention. But political participation is a complex matter; and a group of essentially apolitical people cannot be molded and integrated into a political system simply by holding public meetings or establishing advisory boards, or even through well planned confrontation politics. The effect of this provision concerning participation appears to have been minimal. In cases where more radical activists have sought to invoke it, their activities have probably been dysfunctional for the causes of the poor.[17] Furthermore, as soon as the program got under way, local political leaders took steps to prevent political control from slipping out of their hands into those of the ghetto leadership. Indeed, the net result was to reinforce prevailing political patterns rather than to bring about major changes.[18]

The ghetto is the home of millions of Americans and of almost as many social and economic problems. Many, perhaps most of the issues of domestic social policy in the 1970s, will center on this part of the metropolis. Many of the problems that have been overlooked or ignored since the time when ghetto residents became virtually excluded from the urban political process (with the decline of the political machine) will confront decision makers. How the nation will cope with them cannot accurately be predicted, but it is safe to say that the issues can never again be entirely dropped from the agendas of national, state, and local governments.[19]

Core-City Politics

Only in Albany, New York, and in Chicago are there survivals of the old-style, turn-of-the-century political machine. These are increasingly facing the criticism of reform and minority group leaders and seem to survive primarily because of the personality of their leaders.

[17] See J. David Greenstone and Paul E. Peterson, "Reformers, Machines, and the War on Poverty," in James Q. Wilson (ed.), *City Politics and Public Policy,* John Wiley and Sons, Inc., New York, 1968, pp. 267–292; Donald Von Eschen, Jerome Kirk, and Maurice Pinard, "The Conditions of Direct Action in a Democratic Society," *Western Political Quarterly,* 22:309–325, June, 1969; Harlan Hahn, "Ghetto Sentiments on Violence," *Science and Society,* 33:197–208, Spring, 1969.

[18] Greenstone and Peterson, *op. cit.*

[19] For further reading, see Jack R. Van der Slik (ed.), *Black Conflict with White America,* Charles E. Merrill Publishing Co., Columbus, Ohio, 1970; and Alan Shank (ed.), *Political Power and the Urban Crisis,* Holbrook Press, Inc., Boston, 1969.

In most of the other older core cities, after World War II, the reformers won and have elected bright, energetic mayors out of the third generation of the immigrant groups. As time has gone by, an increasing number of these mayors have been blacks: Stokes of Cleveland, Hatcher of Gary, Jackson of Atlanta, Young of Detroit, and Bradley of Los Angeles.

While the caliber of these mayors has been generally high, they have met with limited success in their attempts to bring some semblance of order and justice to urban politics. They do not have the power necessary for what is expected of them, and often the outcome has been a stalemate.[20]

Newark: Politics and Poverty

Newark, New Jersey (population 400,000), is a near neighbor of New York City. It was described in a previously cited study as the nation's worst city in which to live. Here are mixed the elements of poverty and despair with perhaps some hope attached to a black reform administration headed by Mayor Kenneth Gibson.[21]

In 1970, Gibson narrowly defeated the former mayor, a white who was subsequently jailed as charges of corruption made against him were substantiated. In 1974, Gibson was reelected over four contenders.

Ironically the Newark metropolitan area is one of the richest in the nation, ranking fourth in per capita income. Yet one-third of the core-city residents are on some form of welfare, one quarter are below the poverty level as defined by the federal government, and in 1975, 20 percent were unemployed, twice the national level.

During the day, one-half the workers in the busy downtown Newark area are whites. Yet of the core-city's residents, 60 percent are black, 10 percent Puerto Rican, 9 percent Cape Verde Portuguese, and only 21 percent white.

Financially the city government is and has been in desperate straits. It has the lowest bond rating given municipalities by Moody's Investment Service, which means interest rates to borrow are high. Its property-tax rate is among the highest anywhere nationally, and two-thirds of city acreage is built upon by tax-exempt enterprises, such as public housing, the county and state colleges with relatively high white enrollments, and hospital and transportation facilities, including the new airport. Faced with a $36-million-dollar potential deficit in 1975, the city dismissed 900 employees and sent out termination notices to 1,600 school employees, a little over one-half of whom could hope to be retained in the fall.

As one would anticipate, unemployment among Newark youth is very high—estimated at 60 percent—and the crime rate is among the highest in the nation, as is the percentage of substandard housing and the infant mortality rates.

What had the mayor accomplished in four years? A great deal but hardly enough. The city government is now virtually free of corruption. Racial tensions

[20] On the many factors making it difficult for black mayors to effect rapid change, see Edward Greer, "The New Mayors: Black Power in the Big Cities," *Nation,* 219:525–529, Nov. 23, 1974.

[21] This section is based on Bryant Collins, "Across the River: Another Big City in Trouble," *New York Times,* June 29, 1975. For a study of Newark in depth, see a series of four articles, "The Nation of Newark," *Society,* Sept.–Oct., 1972, pp. 20–59.

had decreased markedly from the times of the massive burning of the inner city by blacks in the late 1960s. The city's first recreation department had been created and there were clear-cut improvements in health care. To ameliorate some of the basic problems of poverty and unemployment, Mayor Gibson could only hope for more aid from state and federal governments and more investment by private enterprise in the core-city's downtown area. Operation Bootstrap is not easy to pull off.

A Closing Note

In the frontier tradition of America, we have developed an urban area, used it for individual and social profit, and then, as the efficiency of the area has declined, we have abandoned it with its problems and moved on to newer, more promising places. Such, to a considerable degree, has been the fate of the core of our metropolitan areas. Yet, the core cities with their housing areas for the poor and their central business districts still serve a useful social purpose and therefore cannot be abandoned. Neither can their people.

THE SUBURB: AN AMERICAN DREAM

What is behind the centrifugal force that is pushing our urban population toward the periphery of the community? No doubt the increasing size of the urban population is itself a factor, for additional population is likely to require increasing area. But this, as we have already seen, is far from a sufficient reason to explain the great suburban movement since the end of World War II.

Rather we should ask: What do most American people want out of life? Where, and under what conditions, can their desires best be fulfilled?

A summary of the findings of social-psychological research into these questions has been reported as follows:[22]

> The goal which, if reached or reasonably approximated, will fulfill the basic needs of the urbanite is a community that will combine some qualities of both small town and large city. Neither, in its present form and at the current stage of cultural development, satisfies all of the fundamental human requirements. The small town provides ample opportunity for companionship and friendship, for easy access to local services, and for certain forms of security. On the other hand, it may fall short of fulfilling man's need for recognition and variety of experience. The large city does provide insurance against boredom, affords wider opportunity for choice of occupation, freedom from unwanted interference with one's personal life, and permits one to identify himself with the city's greatness or, at least, bigness. Nevertheless, it may fail to meet other basic social needs of man. The city can be a very lonesome place. It can thwart natural human friendliness. It can breed suspicion and misunderstanding. It often has dissolved long-established values as to behavior while putting nothing comparable in their place.

[22] William L. Slayton and Richard Dewey, "Urban Redevelopment and the Urbanite," in Coleman Woodbury (ed.), *The Future of Cities and Urban Redevelopment,* The University of Chicago Press, Chicago, 1953, p. 367. By permission of The University of Chicago Press.

The suburb, many urbanites believe, is the best available compromise, especially if the medium-sized city is not a possible choice. In addition to allowing the urbanite to keep *some* of the best of both the large city and the small town, there are other subjectively determined values held by Americans today that add to the attractiveness of the suburb. Studies show that people want to own their homes, that they want single-family dwellings, and that they want more space than is available within built-up cities, at a cost they can afford. They want to avoid, or at least reduce, dirt, noise, congestion, traffic, and taxes. They want vegetable gardens and rosebushes. They want a private play yard for the children.

People want better government than they think they are getting in the core city. They want "services without politics." The middle-class suburbanite talks of the desirability of a council-manager government, which the large city, as a rule, does not have. A "better, more honest" government is something that many think is available in the suburb, although this is much less important than are many other factors. Neighborliness, the reestablishment of some of the primary controls of the rural and small-town society, is something that many yearn for. A suburban address is also a symbol of higher prestige than the typical core-city address, and this fact does not escape many urbanites, for social climbing is very important as a source of recognition in an impersonal society.

The suburb keeps within hailing distance of the variety of scene and activity, of job opportunities, and of accessibility to multiple and specialized services that people want from the large city. Most people would like to have nearby a corner grocery for last-minute shopping (the supermarket for the large weekly shopping list may be some distance away), a drugstore, a playground, and a grade school. Other services, entertainment media, and places of work may be considerable distances away, for the automobile, people believe, will take them there within the limits of a tolerable amount of sacrifice. The commuting time and effort, within present value systems, is not too great a price to pay for the advantages of not living near the manufacturing or business districts.[23]

The Intellectual Image of Suburbia

Although suburbia has been the sought-after home of Americans now for a generation and hence must meet many social and psychic needs of people in numerous social categories, it has also been one of the most criticized aspects of America. The criticism has come chiefly from intellectuals, many of whom nevertheless choose suburbia for their residences. Scott Donaldson has concluded that the suburb "has been the victim of a critical onslaught of monumental, and largely nonsensical, proportions."[24] Some of this criticism has tended to ignore the longtime characteristic of the general American culture. Some of the criticisms have

[23] This section draws heavily upon Slayton and Dewey, *op. cit.,* part III. The empirical research justifying the above statements is there summarized and cited. See also William Dobriner (ed.), *The Suburban Community,* G. P. Putnam's Sons, New York, 1958.

[24] Scott Donaldson, *The Suburban Myth,* Columbia University Press, New York, 1969, p. 1. Donaldson offers a critical review of the literature on suburbia, drawing upon both the social sciences and fiction.

been made by persons emotionally committed to a rural society and are really directed against a metropolitan-industrial society rather than simply suburbia, which is the symbolic villain. Donaldson suggests, relying upon Freud, that perhaps the harsh criticism is the result of feelings of guilt and ambivalence. The suburb represents the pursuit of personal happiness and satisfaction, but our consciences tell us that we also have a responsibility to be concerned for all people, many of whom are not comfortable or secure. Suburbia is the symbol of America's cultural success and of her sense of guilt over it.

The Drive for Independence

Why do people want "their own" little suburban government? For two reasons: to protect their neighborhood communities from invasion by "strangers and outsiders" and to get the municipal services they want and are able to pay for.

For some whites, the unwanted invaders are those of lower-income status than themselves. These can be excluded by controlling what the zoning laws, building codes, and subdivision regulations require. High requirements mean high-quality homes and also high-cost homes. For other whites, the issue is one of race. The black or Oriental or Puerto Rican as a neighbor means a distinct loss of status in their own eyes, and they assume, in the eyes of others. Suburban governments must at all costs keep "them" out—a theme we will return to.

Local control also means that services are provided to suit the suburbanites' desires. Among the areas where local retention of control is most wanted would probably be land use, garbage and rubbish collection, police policies, maintenance of residential streets, and education.[25] Low-income neighborhoods may want to haul their own rubbish to the dump. Well-to-do people may prefer twice-a-week collection from the back door, while the core city offers only once-a-week service from the front curb. Local control of educational services is desired because of the great expense of this item, its importance to the future of their children, and the importance of the school plant as a status symbol. Low-income areas and areas of older people may want minimal services in education out of cost considerations. But the size and luxury of the school auditorium and, especially perhaps, of the swimming pool (if any) have become important symbols in contemporary suburbia. To have decisions about these policies left to the impersonal bureaucracy of a large-city school system would be undesirable to suburbanites of low and high income alike. Land-use policies, which by the logic of the planning profession are the most region-wide in character of all policies, are vitally important to suburbanites. The ethnic, industrial, and commercial balance is of the greatest concern to them. They want races, classes, and occupations segregated. They want to be personally acquainted with, or to feel that they can influence, those who sit on the planning commission so that they will not change

[25] Oliver P. Williams, Harold Herman, Charles S. Liebman, and Thomas R. Dye, *Suburban Differences and Metropolitan Policies,* University of Pennsylvania Press, Philadelphia, 1965, offers supporting data. See also three articles by Basil G. Zimmer and Amos H. Hawley, "Home Owners and Attitude toward Tax Increase," *Journal of the American Institute of Planners,* 21:65–74, Spring, 1956; "Property Taxes and Solutions to Fringe Problems," *Land Economics,* 32:369–376, November, 1956; "Approaches to the Solution of Fringe Problems," *Public Administration Review,* 16:258–268, Autumn, 1956.

the land use in their area (except to the suburbanite's advantage). The professional bureaucracy of the core city with its impersonal dedication to the principles of planning does not spell an improved community to them; it spells loss of control and potential disaster for them as homeowners.

What the suburbanite believes and what is at least in part borne out by the data[26] is that residents of smaller communities are more likely to have access to their political governors than do the same residents of a big city; government is more likely to be personal, the citizen is more likely to know an official, the official is more likely to be a person pretty much like herself or himself. All this adds up in the resident's mind to more influence with the political decision makers.

Problems of Suburbia

Where the problems facing the mayors of core cities at times seem overwhelming, those facing the managers, mayors, and councils of suburbia seem only challenging. When the downtown business districts were beginning their serious decline in the late 1950s, a number of metropolitan-area studies were undertaken. The solution generally proposed was to recreate the Great City of the nineteenth century with the downtown as its hub. To convince suburbanites of the wisdom of such a move, the problems noted below were often used. Many suburbanites remained unconvinced, though most are real problems. Nevertheless, next to the problems of the older core cities, these suburban problems leave one with the comfortable feeling that something can be done about them—something can be worked out.

Amateurism In the midst of specialists of every type, many of the suburbs try to get along with untrained amateurs. On the one hand, the governmental operations of suburbs are often simpler than are those of large cities, and fewer skills are required. But on occasion, amateurism can lead to costly mistakes or economies overlooked.

Lack of Services "Taxes are lower in Perambulator Park," the real estate advertisements proclaim; they are less likely to mention that they are lower in part because few services are provided. The absence of many urban services may be accounted for in a variety of ways. Suburbanites may think they cannot afford some services or may prefer to perform them individually. They may regard them as not worth the cost. Many services are more expensive in the suburbs than in the core city because of the lesser density of population. This applies particularly to sewerage, storm drainage, street paving and maintenance, street lighting, water supply, garbage collection, and sewage disposal.[27]

Lack of Cooperation Suburbs tend to become intensely jealous of their independence, and—encouraged by local officeholders—they attribute ulterior motives to all suggestions of cooperation with the core city or even with other

[26] Charles Press, *Main Street Politics,* Institute for Community Development, Michigan State University, East Lansing, Mich., 1962, pp. 84–85.

[27] John K. Galbraith, *The Affluent Society,* Houghton Mifflin Company, Boston, 1958, pp. 251–264.

suburbs. This attitude is likely to decrease coordination and lead to inefficient use of plant and equipment.

Unequal Tax Bases The accident of boundary lines contributes to the creation of suburbs with highly unequal financial facilities for supporting local government. There may be wealthy suburbs alongside a core city that is desperately in need of more taxable wealth to support its services—which are used by residents of that suburb. Other suburbs may be very poor, even though they are located in the heart of a prosperous urban area. This is true, for example, of middle- or lower-income suburbs with no industry. Often the suburbs most needing services are among those least able to afford them.

Some inequities are being partly relieved by the transfer of some functions to special districts, the county, or the state; by increasing use of state and federal grants-in-aid with built-in formulas to consider relative need; by state-shared taxes; by forcing commuters to pay some of the cost of their use of services of other local units of government through the application of earnings taxes or through their payment of state and local taxes; and by a broadening of the tax base so that even poor suburbs that have not attracted industry are having their property-tax income increased somewhat through the diversified location of offices, salesrooms, medical clinics, supermarkets, shopping centers, and other commercial establishments.[28] But these trends are being partially offset by the decline in the relative average value of new construction in suburbs as they become increasingly the home of all classes.

Rising Costs Fringe-area taxes may begin at what appears to be a much lower level than those of the core city, but the suburban buyer can be assured that they will increase at a rapid pace. The major portion of one's property-tax bill goes toward the support of schools, and in contemporary suburbia, one school-bond issue has followed another with little respite. Each issue raises taxes. As population density increases, furthermore, the need for other urban services increases. Each new service must be paid for by additional taxes.

Water and sewage systems must be installed. Soon neighbors want to have the street paved and a storm sewer laid. Street lights become desirable. Fire and police service may have to be expanded. The sewage-disposal problem, enormously expensive and nearly always ignored as long as possible, must be solved.

All these problems fall upon the mortgage- and debt-ridden suburbanite. Many of them were never faced by subdivision developers. They have, in any case, long since disappeared from the area. In desperation, the citizens seek solutions through special districts, incorporation, new state legislation, or, more rarely, annexation to an existing municipality.

[28] Robert Wood, "Metropolitan Government, 1957," *American Political Science Review,* 52:113–115, March, 1958.

Types of Suburbs

Suburbs are of many types to fit the tastes of many types of individuals. They are difficult to classify, and it is probable that most of them will include characteristics of more than one of the following types.[29]

Residential Suburbs The residential suburbs are primarily living places for persons who work within the core city or the industrial suburbs. They are also called dormitory suburbs. There may be very little community spirit and almost nothing to give the area a sense of community. Its boundaries may well be determined by following main traffic arteries.

Industrial Suburbs Industrial suburbs usually center on one or more large manufacturing establishments. They may have a relatively independent existence from the core city. Such industries leave the core cities, not primarily because of being squeezed out but rather in response to positive factors. Suburbs offer some hope of lower taxes; they offer cheaper land, a vital consideration since a properly laid-out, healthful, physically attractive factory needs a good deal of room; they offer better parking facilities for workers; they bring the factory nearer the workers' homes; they eliminate the need to bring large semitrailer trucks into the heart of the city, for the factory can be located near important highway intersections; and they aid in reducing congestion on the commuter highways and in the central portion of the core city.

Recreational Suburbs This type of suburb probably seldom exists by itself, and the term should be taken to mean places where people go to play, to escape. Sometimes there is a lake or the sea near the core city. Beaches, dance halls, and picnic places are built up, with perhaps a carnival or amusement-park area included.

Some suburbs become havens of gambling establishments and houses of prostitution.[30] This is sometimes the result of advance knowledge that these localities will not enforce the law strictly. They may be across a county or state line or, in the case of some, such as Tijuana and Windsor, across an international boundary. Racetracks, because they require a great deal of room for the physical plant and for parking space and because they cause dust and a good deal of noise both day and night, are nearly always located in a suburban area which is (at least at first) not heavily populated.

Enclaves Some American cities have grown so rapidly that they have quite literally swallowed up their suburbs. Independent suburbs on the urban fringe may remain approximately static in area for years. The core city may then sur-

[29] See Leo F. Schnore, "The Social and Economic Characteristics of American Suburbs," *Sociological Quarterly,* 4:122–134, Spring, 1963.

[30] See James A. Maxwell, "Kentucky's Open City," *The Saturday Evening Post,* Mar. 26, 1960, pp. 22ff. The story of Newport, Ky., recreational suburb to Cincinnati for three generations.

round them on all sides, making something of a mockery out of their independent legal status and their suburban appellation.

Formerly Autonomous Communities Not only does the core city sometimes swallow up its suburbs, but it draws into its economic and sociological (but rarely into its *political*) orbit communities that were once independent of it, that were created for, and developed as the result of, factors other than those that created the core city. Some small towns have gone through such an evolution from rural to an engulfing urban environment.

Residential Suburbs

Among the residential suburbs, certain patterns are evident. Although the wealthy were generally the first to move out of the central city, they were rivaled by the working people of some communities. In any case, all income levels of people are suburbanites today, and collectively they behave somewhat differently in relation to their governments than do their economic peers in the central city. We might note some of the types of residential suburbs here, keeping in mind, however, that a great many of them contain mixed groups. Although the goal of Americans seems to be to reduce social conflict by moving into a suburban area where people share one's income level, beliefs, and life-styles, it is not always possible to achieve complete homogeneity among the various groups.

The Wealthy Suburb Before the beginning of the present century, wealthy Americans began to move out to the fringe-area "estates" where they built large homes that were staffed by armies of servants. They reached their offices in the central city by using commuter trains. The early developments along the main line of the Pennsylvania Railroad outside of Philadelphia demonstrate this type of phenomenon. Today, the suburbs of the wealthy are likely to have smaller lots—perhaps half an acre—but 10-acre and larger areas are still to be found in many of them. The large lots required by zoning ordinance discourages efforts of lower-income people to move into the area and guarantees the pristine charm of quasi-rural living.

Here the homes are all individually designed by architects. Services may be of a luxury type—in one "estate" suburb of Cleveland, the police once delivered the milk. Many such suburbs have "city parks" that are exclusively for residents and are actually country clubs administered by the suburban government. In some cases, the wealthy do not want ordinary city services—street lights, curbs and gutters, paved streets—because these things remind them of urban life, not of the gentlemanly country living they seek to imitate. Around the largest cities, many of the wealthy seek to locate on the outer fringe, far from the core, where open land is still available and where the leisure implied by great distance from the hub assures high status. These people even have a special term for themselves—the *exurbanites.*

The government of these suburbs is often a triumph of amateurism of a sort that the business executives living there would never permit in their own firms.

Some wealthy suburbs have professional city managers, but the key administrator—the clerk, or supervisor, or mayor—may be a local resident who lives in one of the several modest enclaves that are likely—perhaps through historical accident—to exist. The necessary, full-time, nonprofessional, nonelective persons, such as clerical help and street-maintenance workers, may not live in the suburb at all. The people in the city hall are likely to be obsequious in their relationships with the people for whose homes they provide services.

The elected council and school board will probably be made up of both men and women from among the wealthy residents. They will seek to establish policies that fit their objectives: no invasion of lower-status families or groups, and a school system that will allow their children to gain admission to the most prestigious preparatory schools and universities. Some of them will be concerned about metropolitan-area government generally and about the pattern of change in the core city—after all, they are frequently landowners or members of the top bureaucracies of core-city business and manufacturing firms. As "organization persons" of corporations, they have been told that they have a responsibility to take part in public affairs, to be concerned about metropolitan-area problems, and to help make their organizations "good citizens." As a result:[31]

> An . . . executive will inveigh against the jurisdictional mess of his metropolitan area in a staff-ghosted speech that repeats uncomprehendingly the clichés of current municipal reform. This activity is good corporate citizenship, the more so as the executive hasn't the foggiest idea as to how the changes he advocates will help his company, though doubtless in all honesty he thinks they will. It is difficult for the corporation executive to avoid a kind of ritualistic do-gooding when he embarks on the unfamiliar role of city father.

Wealthy suburbanites are likely to play some kind of role in core-city politics as well as in the community where their home is situated. They are not so likely to be as concerned about suburban independence as are lower-income persons because they believe that they can probably influence core-city policy, should their area be annexed or a supergovernment created, while the more typical suburbanites fear that annexation means loss of influence over matters—particularly school and land-use policies—that they consider really important. Yet high-income suburbanites—perhaps especially the wives—will not approve of metropolitan-area changes that may result in significantly lessened influence over the policies of the government that serves their place of residence.

The Middle-Class Suburb This is the home of the average-income person, the white-collar worker, the picture window, the charcoal grill, and the power mower. It is here that preoccupation with property values and social acceptance has helped mold a distinctive contemporary American life-style. The homes here are mass-produced, the number of different models that the builder has to offer depending generally on the cost level of the area's homes. The people in the

[31] Norton E. Long, "The Corporation, Its Satellites, and the Local Community," in E. E. Mason (ed.), *The Corporation in Modern Society,* Harvard University Press, Cambridge, Mass., 1960, p. 210.

mass-produced houses follow the fashions in mass culture and mass leisure. They are not innovators; they do not want to solve the world's problems, or even those of their own metropolitan area. Social conflict is not, to them, a challenge to be met through the institutions of democratic government—they seek to avoid conflict by living in homogeneity with those who share their goals. There is no place in their lives for experimentation with the admission of lower-status ethnic or racial groups, with seeking meaning in life through a concentration on one's personal resources.[32]

These people have helped bring back a revival of interest and confidence in local grass-roots government, an interest that rarely exists in rural communities which are governed by consensus, low-tax ideologies, and the avoidance of innovation; and a confidence that is not often to be found in the government of the core city, with its impersonal professional bureaucracy and strife-ridden politics.

The middle-class suburbanites, then, have a life-style with a special view, including a special view of politics:[33]

> Deeply concerned with the quality of schools, conscious of their new status, suburbanites are inclined to "care" about local affairs—zoning regulations, recreational plans, garbage collection, school curricula, street paving—in an especially intense way. As the logical converse of their apathy toward strong party affiliations, suburbanites approach the politics of the community on the basis of individual preferences; they are, more and more frequently, nonpartisan, sharply distinguishing their local public preferences from their views of national and state affairs.

The Working-Class Suburb The suburb of the hourly rated unskilled or semiskilled worker usually consists of mass-produced single-family homes which have less variation than those of the middle-class types described above. They are built of siding that is less expensive than that of brick or stone, the lots are small—possibly no larger than the minimum established by law—and the traditional gridiron pattern of streets may be used rather than the loops, cul-de-sacs, and curves that typify the neighborhood of the organization person. Low cost, not aesthetics, is the concern of the developer. These are the homes that are often spoken of as American's next slums, but because of individual ownership and a concern for resale value, they have generally been well cared for and continue to have a satisfactory appearance.

There are other working-class suburbs, too, however. Many of these were first developed in the 1920s and were located at the end of the streetcar line. Some are built around amusement parks which the transit company built before World War I in order to attract customers and to give core-city dwellers somewhere to go on a summer Sunday. Others center around a lake or stream and consist largely of summer cottages that were converted for year-round living by desperate factory workers during the Great Depression. These tiny old homes, on lots now below the legal minimum size, create health and roadway problems.

[32] Robert C. Wood, *Suburbia: Its People and Their Politics,* Houghton Mifflin Company, Boston, 1959, p. 6.

[33] *Ibid.,* p. 153.

Many of them are occupied by retired factory workers. All the residents want to enjoy the status of home ownership and they imitate some, but not all, of the patterns of Babbittville, which is nearby. One would find breezeways and charcoal grills, for example, but also an ancient car under repair in the backyard—a situation that would generate a call to the police or the planning commission in a middle-class suburb—and a tavern on the corner. (The middle-class person does his or her drinking at home or in a private country club.)

The working-class suburb is occasionally unincorporated. It is cheaper that way, and the residents must look for ways to save money so as to preserve their status as homeowners in time of economic difficulties—and in order to spend money on luxuries in imitation of the middle class. If the county or township administers the area, part of the cost of governmental protection and services may, through the property tax, be transferred to residents in wealthier areas, and costly services are likely to be demanded of a more distant government than one's own municipal organization. If the area is incorporated as a separate municipality, less participation in government is likely than is the case in the middle-class suburb. The residents may be skeptical of the council-manager plan or other forms of professionalization, and they will expect taxes to be low. Services will be few: Septic tanks are preferred to sewage-disposal systems, state parks to municipal parks, inexpensive gravel to hard-surfaced roads, open ditches to curbs and gutters. Building codes will place few limitations on the builder and will probably, in any case, not be rigidly enforced. Many new residents may build their own homes. The educational system will probably have a pronounced vocational cast to its curriculum. The area as a whole will view with hostility potential annexation to the core city or the imposition of a metropolitan-area supergovernment. Both threaten to expand services, raise the caliber of the existing ones to a professional level (more expensive than what exists), and deprive the residents of such access to government as they may now have. These are marginal homeowners, and they do not want to fall below the margin. The great majority of them may have one or two parents who were born on a farm and have fond memories of childhood.[34]

Although many studies immediately after World War II seemed to confuse middle-class with working-class suburbs and often assumed that the working-class people who did move to the suburbs would take on the protective coloration of the middle class, we now have enough information to know that some of the early assumptions are incorrect. In general, suburbia is developing in the same general pattern as did the older core cities. That is, it has wealthy, middle-class, working-class, and industrial areas, but instead of being under a single government, each tends to be separately incorporated, although some life-styles may share a single government in the form of the county or special districts. In general, working-class people in suburbia tend to continue their older life-styles. They are still less interested in voluntary organizations than are members of the middle

[34] Charles Press and Clarence J. Hein, *Farmers and Urban Expansion,* U.S. Department of Agriculture, 1962.

class, they retain their Democratic political allegiance, are less interested in politics than are members of the middle class, and are relatively less interested in churches and civic activities. But they are conservative as to tax policies and less likely to support expanded local services if paid for by property-tax revenue.[35]

Suburban Politics

The American image of suburban government is of one run by a professional city manager for an upper-middle-class clientele. Many such suburbs exist, but instead of describing one we take a look at a less familiar style of governing, that of a middle-class–working-class suburb.[36]

Politics, to Orville L. Hubbard, is public relations. It is one long publicity stunt. It is neither graft nor corruption, nor is it service to the underprivileged or personal profit. For Hubbard represents a new, mid-twentieth-century style of political leader. He symbolizes the modern successor to the old boss and machine: the political leader of the suburbanite.

The Suburb Dearborn, Michigan (1970 population: 104,199), is a southwestern suburb of Detroit. With the exception of one slum area immediately adjacent to the mammoth River Rouge plant of the Ford Motor Company, it is made up of lower- and upper-middle-income residents, with several very expensive neighborhoods. It consists of single-family dwellings for the most part, although there are some expensive apartment buildings of the type known in the Detroit area as "terraces." Over 80 percent of the families living in Dearborn are homeowners. The population of the city has grown rapidly since World War II.

In 1941, three important things happened in Dearborn, things which were subsequently intertwined and confused in the minds of many of the voters. In the first place, the Ford Motor Company was unionized that year by the UAW-CIO after a long and at times bloody fight. In the second place, a grand-jury investigation uncovered officially the already well-known fact that Dearborn was a wide-open town for gambling and prostitution with little or no interference from the police, and the city was cleaned up. In the third place, Orville L. Hubbard, who had been a perennial candidate since 1933, was elected mayor. By 1974, he had been elected to his eighteenth consecutive term and had survived, in addition, a 1950 recall attempt and an attempt to unseat him in 1974, after he had undergone major surgery. Almost from the beginning he has been called a "boss" or "dictator" by his many opponents. He is hated by many, yet he wins elections easily. How does he do it?

The Middle-Class Appeal Hubbard does not have a machine in the traditional sense. He has almost no patronage appointments. There are no ward or precinct organizations. Nor does he have the support of the regular party organi-

[35] Bennett Berger, *Working-Class Suburb: A Study of Auto Workers in Suburbia,* University of California Press, Berkeley, Calif., 1960; and E. E. LeMasters, *Blue-Collar Aristocrats,* University of Wisconsin Press, Madison, Wisc. 1976.

[36] This section is based in large part upon personal interviews and observations by the senior author. Two newspaper feature serials are helpful: *The Detroit Free Press,* Nov. 16–17, 1949; *The Detroit News,* Apr. 17–19, 1950. There is also an article in *Time,* Aug. 21, 1950.

zations, for Dearborn has a nonpartisan city ballot. Instead he depends upon personal contacts, professional public relations activities, municipal services of good quality, and trouble-shooting department heads. Each department head is assigned a district within the city. He or she is expected to cover that area constantly, looking for things to be done, anticipating complaints of residents, keeping the service departments on the alert.

Hubbard is aware of the continuing value of some of the techniques of the old-time machines. The personal touch is a good vote getter, he knows, and sometimes he will appear in person at the home of a complainer to say that the problem has been taken care of—and to the satisfaction of the resident, he hopes. He knows that the propaganda technique of *transfer* is especially useful in connection with religious activities. Hubbard attends many different churches within the city. Can he help it if the members of each congregation receive the impression that he is a member? Under his administration the city has erected two signs for each church in the city in locations selected by the pastor and pointing toward the church. Municipal parking lots are located with a mind to their use for free Sunday church parking.

Dearborn has some of the best municipal services in Detroit metropolitan area. It is a policy of Hubbard to start at least one new service before each election. In 1953 sidewalk snow removal and sweeping was introduced—a service that was then available only in the expensive Grosse Pointe suburbs. Camp Dearborn, a "private country club" for Dearborn residents and their guests only, was established in 1949.[37] Under Hubbard a "tot lot" was established in every subdivision. Dearborn has also a retirement village in Florida, reserved for ex-Dearborn residents only. He has provided for dozens of baseball diamonds, ice-skating rinks, hockey rinks, fireworks displays on the Fourth of July and Labor Day, thousands of trees and shrubs, and hundreds of new street lights and street signs.

All of this costs a great deal of money, for these services are normally available only in "millionaires' " suburbs. How does he do this without being driven from office as a spendthrift? Hubbard is fortunate, for he is mayor of an unusual city. It is tremendously wealthy, with most of its wealth held not by the homeowners who get the superior services, but rather by industry. Something like two-thirds of the assessed valuation of the area is in industrial property, about one-half of it in the hands of the Ford interests alone. Only this makes the unusual services budgetarily possible, but Hubbard gives the credit to Hubbard.

Techniques of Appeal Hubbard is a great campaigner, and he loves campaigning. His electoral support at the polls varies inversely with the income of the voter. In the slums of south Dearborn he gets nearly all of the votes; in the Springwells Park section, made up largely of Ford executives and engineers, he can expect to be defeated by as much as 10 to 1. His greatest support, numerically, comes from the lower middle class, and his campaign platform contains

[37] It has lakes, over 500 acres of timber, picnic areas, camping areas, a trout brook, a large beach, 100 aluminum rowboats usable without charge, but no canoes—a drowning would cause bad publicity and a loss of votes. Busses haul children the 35 miles to the camp, where they can stay at a charge far less than cost.

three *implicit* planks: better services for a cleaner Dearborn, a firm stand against the Ford interests, and a preservation of property values especially by keeping blacks out of the city. The platform is aimed directly at the hopes and fears, the aspirations and the insecurities, of the lower-middle-class property owner. It has proved greatly effective.

The better services have already been explained. He has delivered on his promises. When he talks of keeping Dearborn "clean," he means not only that he will keep the garbage and rubbish cleaned up and the alleys free of dead dogs, but that the area will be "spiritually clean," he will not tolerate organized gambling or prostitution. If a police officer seeks to line his pockets from this source, he ceases to be a police officer. Hubbard understands how to appeal to middle-class values.

The feud with the Ford company and family is largely window dressing, but with a symbolic purpose. Dearborn contains many skilled and some unskilled workers from the great River Rouge plant which dominates the life of the whole community. In the old days, before the plant was unionized, it was a common thing for the Dearborn police to be used for strikebreaking purposes and for the prevention of labor disturbances. Hubbard asserts that he is an "unbossed mayor," which in Dearborn means that he is independent of the Ford company, something that before he was elected was unusual in the history of that city. Many who remember the earlier days count on him to keep the city government from becoming "annexed" once again. (The Ford Motor Company operates under an entirely different philosophy today from that of 1939 so far as labor relations are concerned, but fear is a convenient tool for the politician.) He finds many ways to badger the company and the family, sometimes with resulting gifts to the city. Yet he named his youngest son Henry Ford Hubbard, and once when accused of driving Ford gifts out of the city and into Detroit, he ordered "Home Town of Henry Ford" printed on all city stationery.

There are few blacks in Dearborn, and few Japanese-Americans have moved in while Hubbard has been mayor. In an industrial area with an ever increasing black population, the lower middle class tends to become obsessed with a fear of invasion and of "lowering property values." Because this is so, some politicians in Detroit and many of its suburbs find it politically profitable to exploit this fear. Hubbard has found ways of using this gimmick effectively in irrelevant situations. In 1948, the John Hancock Mutual Life Insurance Company sought to build a multimillion-dollar private housing development in the city. There seemed to be no objection to the proposal until Hubbard decided to oppose it, probably on the theory that his stand would be popular with owners of single-family homes. Once he had spoken, it became necessary for him to win, since a defeat on a major issue can be disastrous for any politician. He called upon the voters to defend themselves against "an invasion of renters." He called the expensive units a "bunch of row houses" and a "*public* housing project" (which it was not). He attacked the Ford interests for selling the land for the project to the insurance company. But his trump card was played on the day of the referendum. He sent his department heads around to the polling places, distributing cards bearing the injunction: "Keep the Negroes out of Dearborn. Vote against the John Hancock Housing Project."[38] That did it. There had never been any special intention of renting the homes and apartments in the project to blacks, but that did not matter—Hubbard had won. In a later campaign for reelection, he emphasized that he had stopped a proposed Wayne County park from extending into Dearborn since it would have "attracted all types of undesirables." One of the greatest attractions of Camp Dearborn to prejudiced whites is that it, unlike other public parks, is open only to Dearborn residents—which means few blacks. If you ask a Hubbard man about the administration's racial policy, he will explain that the city does nothing to keep anyone out. It just so happens that there are no homes for sale if a black wishes to buy.

Politics as Showmanship Like many of the bosses of old, Hubbard is an expert in public relations and is an excellent judge of public opinion. For sheer color and campaigning skill, he is on a par with "Big Bill" Thompson of Chicago of the 1920s. He keeps a dossier of his contacts with every constituent. He thus not only knows who is indebted to him, but can also give his correspondence a personal touch. He sends a letter or makes a personal call whenever there is a birth, death, wedding, house fire, or the arrival of a new resident in Dearborn. He signs his name in green ink with a special pen and in letters up to an inch high. His name and picture appear almost everywhere in the city. He was at the station to say good-by to every Dearborn inductee during World War II and was there to greet him on his return as a civilian. He created the Dearborn Navy during World War II to protect the city from the German submarine menace. (When city employees began to use the boats for pleasure cruises, the navy was scuttled.) He takes the city directory with him on vacations and sends home hundreds of postcards to citizens—who are flattered by the mayor's thoughtfulness. He sees to it that some department head is a member of every club or organization of any size in the city. He himself belongs to as many as possible. (In the 1951 campaign he listed membership in twenty-five, including everything from the National Sojourners to the Michigan Academy of Science, Arts and Letters.) Like so many of his constituents, he started from the bottom of the social ladder, and, again like so many of them, he was born and raised on a farm before coming to the big city. He is an expert at substituting irrelevancies for issues and in covering up embarrassing situations with confusion.

The final stage of an election campaign is completely professionalized. A meeting is likely to be held at Fordson High School, with a professional master of ceremonies, a professional show, and professional chorus girls. All of the good sign spots, parking places near voting booths, and auditoriums are taken up well in advance of the campaign—and usually well in advance of the less alert opposition.

In 1945 a jealous council (often he elects enough members of his slate to control the council, but before the next election he is usually feuding with many

[38] *Detroit News,* Apr. 19, 1950.

of them) passed an ordinance prohibiting the mayor from talking business with his constituents either personally or by telephone. Through the newspapers he received national attention. After having milked the publicity possibilities dry, he had himself arrested for deliberately violating the ordinance (more publicity) and then had the whole thing declared unconstitutional. An embarrassed council repealed the ordinance.

In facing his enemies—and they are many—Hubbard can be as merciless as any old-time boss. His path is strewn with the political bodies of those who have opposed him. He will do whatever is necessary, his opponents say, to destroy a man whom he has turned against. He has triumphed over all opponents and has dismissed some of his department heads (including his own law partner) even though they had been instumental in his own advancement. After the *Dearborn Press* turned against him, the publisher's personal property assessment was increased 50 percent.[39] Hubbard's opponents do not think it a mere coincidence. They claim that other property assessments have taken sudden, unexplained dips and increases while Hubbard has been mayor. But there has been no graft or corruption. The worst charge that a one-man grand jury investigation into the Hubbard administration could levy was that after the 1950 tax assessments of a large Dearborn retail store were reduced by $120,000, Hubbard was offered and accepted a television set as a gift from the company.[40] But Hubbard, like many old-time bosses, has no interest in money. He wants power and publicity.

Interpretation Hubbard seems to represent a new trend in urban political organization. He is a characteristic leader, appealing to the working class and the middle class of a metropolitan suburb with things they want to hear, a leader with little interest in patronage or personal financial gain, but with a desire to give effective, professionalized services that the voters demand.

Allowing for local environmental and personality differences, this pattern is likely to become more and more in evidence. The Republican organization in Nassau County on Long Island is similarly an efficient political organization. It receives its support from upper-middle-class New York commuters—business executives, bankers, and lawyers. The county is organized with a county manager. J. Russel Sprague served for years as both the manager and county Republican chairman. His department heads were also leaders in the organization. His organization was efficient, disciplined, and honest.

Urban Problems: A Closing Note

The problems discussed in this chapter are matters of concern to metropolitan areas as a whole and some are of concern to the nation. Unsafe sewage-disposal practices in any part of a metropolitan area may endanger health in another part. Economics may dictate a collective effort to secure additional water supplies from a distant lake or mountain stream. Traffic-flow patterns are necessarily interrelated. Land-use practices in any one section will affect those in other sec-

[39] *Time,* Aug. 21, 1950.
[40] Wayne County, Mich., Circuit Court, Misc. 78616 (1953).

tions. Smoke and noise nuisances pay no more attention to legal boundaries than do disease germs. Ghetto problems affect all Americans as they spread social disorganization in their own and other communities, and they are also a moral burden affecting all Americans.

These are some of the collective problems. But the greatest problem of all, perhaps, is "the inability of metropolitan residents to reach any substantial degree of consensus as to what should be done . . . about the generally recognized issues of their common life—government organization, finance, blight and redevelopment, school, race relations, land-use control, and so on."[41] The same might be said of all American urbanized places.

SELECTED READINGS

Altschuler, Alan A.: *Community Control, The Black Demand for Participation in Large American Cities,* Pegasus Books, The Bobbs-Merrill Company, Inc., Indianapolis, 1970. (An argument for neighborhood control and decentralization of large-city government.)

Banfield, Edward C.: *The Unheavenly City Revisited,* Little, Brown and Company, Boston, revised edition, 1974. (A critical examination of the assumptions concerning urban blight and poverty.)

Berger, Bennett: *Working-Class Suburb,* University of California Press, Berkeley, Calif., 1960. (Auto workers in California.)

Bish, Robert L., and Vincent Ostrom: *Understanding Urban Government,* American Enterprise Institute for Public Policy Research, Washington, D.C., 1973. (A basic argument against assuming that large-scale organization is superior to smaller units in all respects.)

Donaldson, Scott: *The Suburban Myth,* Columbia University Press, New York, 1969. (Argues that suburbia has been "grossly and unfairly maligned." A review of works on suburbia.)

Downs, Anthony: *Urban Problems and Prospects,* Markham, Chicago, 1970.

——: *Who Are the Urban Poor?* Committee for Economic Development, Supplementary Paper No. 26, revised edition, 1970. (Dispels a number of common myths.)

Drake, St. Clair, and H. R. Cayton: *Black Metropolis,* Harcourt, Brace & World, Inc., New York, 1945. (A classic study of Chicago's black community.)

Eisinger, Peter K.: *Patterns of Interracial Politics: Conflict and Cooperation in the City,* Academic Press, New York, 1976. (Political beliefs of ordinary citizens as they affect the behavior of elites.)

Gans, Herbert J.: *The Levittowners: Ways of Life and Politics in a New Suburban Community,* Pantheon Books, Random House, Inc., New York, 1967.

Green, Constance McLaughlin: *American Cities in the Growth of the Nation,* Colophon Books, Harper and Row, Publishers, Incorporated, 1965.

Haar, Charles M. (ed.): *The End of Innocence, A Suburban Reader,* Scott, Foresman and Company, Glenview, Ill., 1972.

Handlin, Oscar: *The Newcomers: Negroes and Puerto Ricans in a Changing Metropolis,* Harvard University Press, Cambridge, Mass., 1959.

[41] Coleman Woodbury, "Great Cities, Great Problems, Great Possibilities?" *Public Administration Review,* 18:332–340, Autumn, 1958. Quote from p. 339.

Howard, Ebenezer: *Garden Cities of Tomorrow,* The M.I.T. Press, Cambridge, Mass., 1965. Originally published, 1898, as *Tomorrow: The Peaceful Path of Reform.*

Johnson, Keith, and others: "Suburbia: The New American Plurality," *Time,* Mar. 15, 1971. (A questioning of stereotypic assessments. Includes the findings in a Louis Harris opinion poll of suburban attitudes.)

Kornblum, William: *Blue Collar Community,* The University of Chicago Press, Chicago, 1974.

Krickus, Richard: *Pursuing the American Dream: White Ethnics and the New Populism,* Anchor Books, Doubleday & Company, Inc., Garden City, N.Y., 1976. (Examines an often-neglected group in core cities and suburbs.)

Long, Norton: *The Unwalled City, Reconstructing the Urban Community,* Basic Books, Inc., Publishers, New York, 1972. (Argues that the cure for ghetto problems is not to create a reservation of welfare recipients but to create jobs in the core city.)

Masotti, Louis, and Jeffrey Hadden (eds.): *Suburbia in Transition,* New Viewpoints Publishing Co., New York, 1974.

Novak, Michael: *The Rise of the Unmeltable Ethnics,* The Macmillan Company, New York, 1972. (By an eloquent defender of the values and goals of members of white ethnic groups.)

Ostrom, Vincent: *The Intellectual Crisis in American Public Administration,* University of Alabama Press, University, Ala., 1974. (A reexamination of the principles of public administration that argue in all cases centralization is more efficient than *competing administrative units.*)

Petersen, E. T. (ed.): *Cities Are Abnormal,* University of Oklahoma Press, Norman, Okla., 1946. (Unfavorable criticisms of cities as social institutions.)

Robson, William A., and D. E. Regan (eds.): *Great Cities of the World, Their Government, Politics and Planning,* 3d ed., Sage Publications, Inc., Beverly Hills, Calif., 1974. (Essays by a variety of scholars describing government of specific cities.)

Schnore, Leo F.: "The Socio-economic Status of Cities and Suburbs," *American Sociological Review,* 28:76–85, February, 1963. (Suburbs have higher socioeconomic status in larger and older urban areas than do core cities, but the opposite is the case in newer, smaller urban areas.)

Seeley, John R., and others: *Crestwood Heights: The Culture of Suburban Life,* Basic Books, Inc., Publishers, New York, 1956.

Slayton, William L., and Richard Dewey: "Urban Redevelopment and the Urbanite," in Coleman Woodbury (ed.), *The Future of Cities and Urban Redevelopment,* The University of Chicago Press, Chicago, 1953. (A major early study of slum redevelopment problems and prospects.)

Vidich, A. J., and Joseph Bensman: *Small Town in Mass Society,* Princeton University Press, Princeton, N.J., 1958.

White, Morton, and Lucia White: *The Intellectual Versus the City,* Harvard University and The M.I.T. Press, Cambridge, Mass., 1964. (A review of criticism of American cities from Thomas Jefferson to Frank Lloyd Wright.)

Whyte, William H. Jr.: *The Organization Man,* Anchor Books, Doubleday & Company, Inc., Garden City, N.Y., 1956. (Contains a vigorous criticism of suburbia.)

Williams, Oliver P., Harold Herman, Charles S. Liebman, and Thomas Dye: *Suburban Differences and Metropolitan Policies,* University of Pennsylvania Press, Philadelphia, 1965. (An application of analysis of community characteristics to facts of suburban cooperation in the Philadelphia metropolitan area.)

Wirt, Frederick, Benjamin Walter, Francine Rabinovitz, and Deborah R. Hensler: *On the*

City's Rim, Politics and Policy in Suburbia, D. C. Heath and Company, Lexington, Mass., 1972.

Wood, Robert C.: *Suburbia: Its People and Their Politics,* Houghton Mifflin Company, Boston, 1959.

Zorbaugh, Harvey: *The Gold Coast and the Slum,* The University of Chicago Press, Chicago, 1929. (A classic study of Chicago's socially mixed near-North Side.)

B

The Political Machinery

Chapter 3

Elected Officials and Community Leaders

Politics is the catalyst that can change citizens into public officials and individual wishes into public policy. It is essential to democracy. On the local scene it operates largely in the same manner as it does for state and national governments. A chief difference has been that more of the local political actors do not make a full-time career of politics. Otherwise only the emphasis and the relative balances of forces are changed.

THE NATURE OF THE POLITICAL PROCESS

Politics as Demand and Supply

In order to have an understanding of the nature of the political process, it is necessary to be able to picture it not as the principal purpose of a certain type of human activity but rather as a *by-product.* Human life in Western culture is a struggle for power, prestige, and security. Some people, in their search, turn to politics and attempt to secure these values through governmental action. They become the relatively small group of politically active citizens. The general public, politically passive on most issues, may occasionally express itself on policy choices through elections or an aroused public debate that may spread out into community conflict. More frequently a collection of specialized publics or clientele groups seeks services from government in order to help themselves. Or, alternatively, they seek to *prevent* government from launching certain types of services if they feel that their goals can be reached by some other type of activity.[1]

The politician, then, is a person who in his or her pursuit of a successful political career seeks to determine what some portion of the public is asking of government and to make this available to them if possible. (As a leader, he or she may also seek to determine what the general public or specialized publics potentially may want and seek to "sell" it to the voters.) Because the individual normally has a certain amount of choice in selecting public officers and is free to join various groups that exert pressure upon government, government is to some degree responsible to the people—the essential characteristic of a democracy.

The Role of Ideology

The political process occurs within the boundaries set by the currently popular ideologies. For many years questions of water and air pollution were largely off the local agenda, since the ideology then current argued that such questions should be beyond the sphere of governmental policy. In the same way, questions which once might have been considered properly on the local agenda, such as the proper length of women's skirts or the wearing of shorts in public, are no longer considered by most citizens as within the sphere of governmental action. Decision makers thus largely choose policies consistent with current ideological beliefs, but this allows considerable latitude, particularly today when it is believed by many that pressing problems are subject to amelioration or solution if government applies scientific knowledge to them.

Politicians, Influentials and Citizens

In every city some public officials set the tax rate, decide which streets will be paved, how marijuana laws will be enforced, and who the new park will be named for. Such governmental decisions are controlled by political officeholders—those politicians who are successful in getting elected. In making such public policy, the political official allocates the scarce resources of power, prestige, and security to some citizens, often at the expense of others. Thus, the student of politics wants to know: how are these policy decisions made and what are the effects? This chapter begins the examination of the first question. Later chapters examine the second.

Sometimes public officials in making policy decisions follow largely their own policy or career goals. Often they are influenced and even may be coerced by others. It is the aspect of influence and power relations that properly has most concerned the students of local politics.

Democratic theory assumes the primary influence will be by the general public. We will examine in greater detail this influence in a later chapter. At this point we emphasize only that political participation involves both material and

[1] See the writings of Harold Lasswell, especially *Psychopathology and Politics,* The University of Chicago Press, Chicago, 1930; and *Power and Personality,* W. W. Norton and Company, Inc., New York, 1948.

psychic costs, and this fact is related to the degree and type of political activity that one can expect from any citizen. Citizens have other matters to concern themselves with rather than whether an expressway will be built and, if so, where and how it will be constructed. Just the costs of gaining the information required to make an intelligent decision are often greater than most citizens wish to pay. Note also that some citizens are clearly advantaged in that because of education or position in the community, the costs of getting information about the proposed expressway are less. Also some are advantaged by being better able to pay the costs of participation or may actually have to pay less. Not everyone can take off from work and attend a daytime civic meeting or even take time off to vote when lines before the polling booth may be shortest. Not everyone can afford the risks of running for office, or being elected, or taking the time off from a regular job that such election may require.

General citizens thus are limited in how much and when they will wish to participate in influencing the policy decisions officials make. The whole body of citizens cannot sit as a continuous town meeting to discuss every issue as it arises. The individual must depend on representatives, knowing that the cost even of influencing these very often may be high. But the citizens as a whole do reserve for themselves judgment of the results of official decision making (that is the power to throw the rascals out and possibly throw new rascals in) and the right to intervene as individuals or groups where they feel their own interests are directly affected.

Thus, commonly, officials face a united and aroused general public rather rarely. More frequently they deal with a number of specialized constituencies and interest groups. In this chapter we are concerned with the political officials, and then with those citizens whose social or economic status may give them such control over political resources that officials will consult them on major policy. Such citizens are seen by some as a local political elite or power structure. In the chapters that follow, we examine urban interest groups and then the influence of the general public.

THE URBAN ELECTED OFFICIAL

Urban politics differs most markedly from national politics in the degree to which it is unprofessionalized. In large cities, a few offices, notably that of the mayor and sometimes the city council, are held by persons who make politics a full-time career. Here one finds such pros as Mayor Abraham Beame of New York, who worked his way up through the ranks over decades. More commonly the mayor, even in middle-sized cities, and councilors, even in large cities, are filling their public offices at the same time that they are running a local shoe store or are a middle-level executive at the local Thingemabob plant. The overwhelming number of urban elected officials are political amateurs. They seek no career in politics.

In American folklore, in newspaper editorials, in magazine articles, in political campaigns, and in suburban gossip, it has been common to picture the nineteenth-century city boss and machine as if they were a contemporary phenomenon. To many citizens, the boss and his ward heelers are the epitome of the professional politician. It is thus perhaps appropriate to begin a discussion of political officeholders by examining this type of political professional.

The Machine Type of Political Professional of the Past

It is not uncommon even today to hear the phrase "boss-ridden cities." Actually, the boss and machine performed a necessary social function in their day, but they have outlived their usefulness and have been disappearing from the American scene. William Marcy Tweed of New York, "Ed" Flynn of the Bronx, "Big Bill" Thompson of Chicago, "Doc" Ames of Minneapolis, "Abe" Ruef of San Francisco, and a host of others left the front pages of the newspapers and have taken their place in the history books, where they have become a romantic, if not exactly an honored, memory.

There is probably no need to describe in detail the method of operation of the old-time machine. A few points should be made concerning it, however.

In the first place, the machine did not exist *in spite* of society. It existed because it filled a real need. It served as a highly effective, if inefficient, system of social welfare. To the poor in the slums of cities, the machine provided needed services: It found jobs, or tided the family over during periods of unemployment; it buried the dead; it cared for widows and orphans; it organized youth activities; it provided a multitude of neighborhood social functions; it contributed to the churches of poor neighborhoods; it provided bail bonds and legal advice; it furnished assistance in finding housing and tried to help tenants talk their landlords out of rent increases. It provided literally hundreds of services, the need for which was not recognized by much of the middle class.

Secondly, the machine was a product of universal suffrage, perhaps its first important manifestation. The services provided were offered in the expectation that the recipients would cast their ballots in support of the machine. If the ordinary male worker in the slum had not been enfranchised, as he was in the 1830s and 1840s, the pattern of urban politics during the remainder of the nineteenth century would have been quite different from what it was.

Thirdly, the machine raised the great amounts of money that were needed for the services it provided (and often for the personal profit of its leaders) by acting as a broker for the city's services. It raised most of its money from businesses and industry, and owing to the then-current belief that it was cheaper to buy off the machine than to fight it, businesses often worked hand in glove with the machine.

The organization raised its money in a great variety of ways. It made available, for a price, building permits, all types of licenses, utilities franchises, and ordinances that might be helpful to a business. Sometimes it resorted to simple blackmail or the shakedown racket. Much money was made through contract rebates. Contracts were granted to a firm that was working cosely with the machine with the understanding that part of the profit would be returned to the machine. Municipal employees were very commonly assessed part of their pay, and other funds could be raised from the purchase of land by inside members of the organization for resale to the city. It was this type of profiteering that was made famous as "honest graft" by George Washington Plunkitt of Tammany Hall. It was Plunkitt who stated the code of the more sincere organization worker when he said, "If my worst enemy was given the job of writin' my epitaph when I'm gone, he couldn't do more than write 'George W. Plunkitt. He Seen His Opportunities, and He Took 'Em.' "[2]

The Decline of Bossism

Opportunities, as seen by Plunkitt, began to fade away as the effects of the reform movement came to be felt. The decline of the boss and machine began to accelerate after World War II, in particular, and by 1950, the boss and machine in almost every American city had been either destroyed, badly mangled, or profoundly modified in its pattern of behavior.

There were many reasons for this. Since World War I, there has been a steady decline in the percentage of foreign-born in American cities, and it had been to the needs of this group that machines had particularly appealed. Blacks and other rural-to-urban migrants likewise became less subject to machine control after they became more sophisticated in urban ways. Another factor was the high employment after 1940, which allowed large numbers of people to escape the extreme poverty that had forced them to be partly dependent upon the machine.

The general adoption of the officially printed secret ballot made it more difficult for the machine to stuff ballot boxes, falsify election returns, or conduct other election frauds. Lincoln Steffens tells us that the voting lists of Philadelphia at the beginning of the century were padded "with the names of dead dogs, children and non-existent persons." Success in such practices has become increasingly difficult in recent years. Yet it was only two generations ago—in 1936—that the *St. Louis Post-Dispatch* won a Pulitzer prize for uncovering 45,000 false registrations in that city. In 1975, it was revealed that large numbers of persons, primarily municipal employees, not living within the city were voting in San Francisco elections. Charges that the candidate of the party or faction not in power has been "counted out" in close election contests because the in-group controlled the election machinery continue to be heard today, and it is reasonable to expect that not all of them are unfounded.

The reform movement in general damaged machine government by helping to arouse potential members of opposition groups and by rallying businesses to fight the machine instead of buying it off. The rise to power of organized labor and the growing independence of black leaders have upset the traditional balance of control in many cities.

Lastly, and perhaps of greatest importance, a modern and professionalized approach to the problems of social welfare has taken away from the political

[2] See the fascinating profile by William L. Riordon, *Plunkitt of Tammany Hall,* Doubleday & Company, Inc., Garden City, N.Y., 1905; reprinted by Alfred A. Knopf, Inc., New York, 1948.

machine its principal means for achieving loyalty and support. Government administration of such functions as workmen's compensation, unemployment compensation, old-age pensions, old-age insurance, aid to dependent children, Medicare, and their administration by professionally trained civil servants proved a mortal wound to the old-time machine.

Machines in Decay

Beginning with the reform movement around the beginning of the century, an entire procession of machine defeats has paraded across the front pages of the newspapers of the nation. The one-time organizations in St. Louis, Minneapolis, and San Francisco are long dead. The once-powerful Republican machine in Cincinnati was defeated and permanently modified by reform efforts in the elections of 1924 and those that followed. The castle of Thomas J. Pendergast and his Democratic machine in Kansas City came crashing down in 1939.[3] Tammany Hall in New York began losing ground with the 1932 Seabury investigation of the James J. Walker administration. It was greatly weakened during the long period when its enemy, Fiorello H. La Guardia, served as mayor.[4] Today, despite the fact that reformers still denounce it in each campaign, Tammany is only a shadow of its old self.

By the time of World War II, bosses and machines were thoroughly outmoded. Nearly all those that remained were liquidated during the period of postwar readjustment. The Republican machine of Philadelphia, which had enjoyed uninterrupted control of that city since shortly after the Civil War, lost important ground in the election of 1949 and was thoroughly routed in 1951, when it lost control of the mayor's office and of a majority of the council to a reform Democratic group.[5] The old Democratic Kelly-Nash machine, now under Mayor Richard J. Daley, still held control of the city of Chicago in 1976. Despite much criticism from many sources, several serious scandals in the police department, and harsh criticism during the 1968 Democratic National Convention, the Kelly-Nash organization is regarded as having brought Chicago politics closer to prevailing urban patterns in the years after World War II. Mayor Daley appeared to be more popular than ever.

James Michael Curley of Boston was defeated by reformers in 1949 and never recovered.[6]

[3] Miniature portraits of some of the more recent city machines are painted in John Gunther, *Inside U.S.A.*, Harper & Row, Publishers, Incorporated, New York, 1947.

[4] See the views of La Guardia in his article, "Bosses Are Bunk," *The Atlantic Monthly,* 180:21–24, July, 1947. On New York, see Wallace S. Sayre and Herbert Kaufman, *Governing New York City,* Russell Sage Foundation, New York, 1960.

[5] See James Reichley, *The Art of Government: Reform and Organization Politics in Philadelphia,* The Fund for the Republic, New York, 1959; Joseph D. Crumlish, *A City Finds Itself: The Philadelphia Home Rule Charter Movement,* Wayne State University Press, Detroit, Mich., 1959.

[6] Jerome S. Bruner and S. J. Korchin, "The Boss and the Vote, *Public Opinion Quarterly,* 10:1–23, Spring, 1946; J. M. Curley, *I'd Do It Again,* Prentice-Hall, Inc., Englewood Cliffs, N.J., 1957; Joseph Dinneen, *The Purple Shamrock,* W. W. Norton & Company, Inc., New York, 1949; and a fictionalized life of a Curley-like boss, Edward O'Conner, *The Last Hurrah,* Little, Brown and Company, Boston, 1956.

The Hague machine in Jersey City was defeated in 1950 and in succeeding elections, although the destruction of his machine did not signal the rise of a reform administration, as happened in many other cities.[7] In Memphis, Edward H. Crump managed to keep an effective machine together until his death in 1954. But like so many who exercise power for a long time, he had made no adequate provision for a successor, and in the following year his heirs were not even able to field a candidate for mayor.

There can be no doubt that the nineteenth-century machine system has outlived its usefulness. In some cities, party organization is still viable, though less effective than it once was. A study of New Jersey counties found party organization on the decline but still important as broker between citizens and government, particularly in black and Puerto Rican areas.[8] Some of the techniques of old-style machines have been adopted by a few organizations of a new suburban, middle-class type, such as those in Dearborn, Michigan, under Orville L. Hubbard and, for many years, in Nassau County, New York.[9]

The Political Professional of Today

The mayors of most large and a few middle-sized cities and sometimes a few of the councilmen devote full time to their professional political careers. Some, like former Mayor Carl Stokes of Cleveland, moved into the job from the state legislature. Some were members of the council, like Mayor Thomas Bradley of Los Angeles. Samuel Yorty of Los Angeles and John Lindsay of New York left Congress to take their jobs. A few like Jerome Cavanaugh of Detroit held no previous major office. In some large cities, ways are still found to make the job of council member a political sinecure in the style of the old-time machine. In most this is not the case.

Today's elected professionals depend on public relations more than on political organization. This has meant that they must be careful about their impact on public opinion through newspapers, radio, and television, being as concerned about their "image" as any presidential hopeful. At the same time, they are required to have a sophistication about urban policy problems. They are supposed to initiate programs to deal with such conditions as urban blight, racial conflict, crime, and pollution. No longer can they run on the good government platform of "I will manage the local sewage-disposal plant in a more efficient and businesslike way than Torkelson." More is expected of the new breed of urban political professionals.

In Chapters 8 and 9 we detail some of the characteristics of this modern type of urban official. Here let us only note a phenomenon increasingly associated with them. They are dependent on the civil service professional within city gov-

[7] Dayton D. McKean, *The Boss: The Hague Machine in Action,* Houghton Mifflin Company, Boston, 1940.

[8] Richard T. Frost, "Stability and Change in Local Party Politics," *Public Opinion Quarterly,* 25:221–235, Summer, 1961.

[9] E. E. Malkin, "Dearborn's Madcap Mayor," *Coronet,* 44:66–70, September, 1958; and a case study on Hubbard, above, pp. 49–54.

ernment as well as the expert outside. Through professional organizations and panels of national urban groups, the mayors and even council members meet technically trained experts including many from universities. It is common for even professional politicians viewed by the general public as close to the old boss system mold, such as Mayor Daley of Chicago, to have as their assistants university-trained aides or professors on loan from a nearby university. Governing a big city is no longer a task that can be wholly trusted to political appointees who are nonspecialists.

Amateur Politicians

Politics dominated by amateurs means participation by those who can afford to take time from their jobs, by the bored, and by those with free time on their hands. For these, costs of participation are relatively less. In suburbia, homemakers tired of the routine of diapers and chauffeuring may become active in politics and finally candidates for the council. The person retired from business is often attracted to the part-time political office and often makes a major contribution to the community through such service. But most of the amateur officials are likely to be local merchants or private organization employees who are particularly concerned with the decisions made by their local city councils since they may intimately affect business on Main Street and in the shopping center.

Running for local public office, even for those who can afford it, is not all gravy, however. A *Los Angeles Times* reporter drew this composite picture of Candidate X, based on interviews with a number of amateur civic-minded citizens running for office: Two men running for positions on the Board of Education had amateur staff members who passed out a press release with misspelled words. But most such candidates had few supporters to help their campaign. They had no one to drive them about, write statements for them, put up lawn signs, or collect money. Rather they went themselves door-to-door by foot. The reporter described one candidate's gripe: "After I walked up the longest driveway in the world, the woman of the house said, 'I'm busy, can't you come back tomorrow?' " But that was the least of his trouble. "The dogs are terrible. Walk up to the door, ring, and the dogs start barking." Sometimes citizens have their own messages. "I handed one guy a brochure and he gave me a Bible," said Candidate X. Publicity was also a big problem. There were 122 candidates for council and television does not have enough time for them all. One candidate wanted to make a major statement. A small, local radio station offered him 15 seconds. He pleaded with the manager, saying the statement was complex and he needed more time. The manager relented, boosted it up to 40 seconds but would run it only once during the day. Getting money was difficult, the best sources being hardheaded, unemotional contributors who did not want to waste a dime. Persons in business and city employee groups, for example, usually give only to the incumbents because they usually win. The reporter summed it up: "It all adds up to a difficult task. 'It's like swimming the Pacific Ocean' said Candidate X."[10]

[10] Bill Boyarsky, "Race for Local Office, A Job of Pure Drudgery," *Los Angeles Times,* Mar. 17, 1971.

A distinguishing feature of urban politics in cities where most politicians are pursuing other careers for their livelihood is the relative absence of the notion of conflict of interest. Local suburban merchants may sit on the Board of Review (which reviews grievances on local assessment of property for tax purposes) and see nothing wrong with participating in a decision concerning a bank or business with which they are associated. Not only is this not regarded as questionable but it may be positively defended on the basis that they have a greater knowledge about such matters than does the average citizen. Thus zoning boards may be dominated by the realtors, or councils deciding on parking lots and one-way streets may be controlled by local merchants.

But a politics by amateurs also has some advantages, particularly if combined with professional civil service management of the day-to-day administration. The amateur does occasionally raise new issues and does often identify with the consumer of government services. Many such citizens have rendered great service for what are basically minimal returns. Chapters 8 and 9 on urban executives and the city council further discuss these contributions.

LOCAL COMMUNITY LEADERS: A POWER STRUCTURE?

Not enough is as yet known about those who are viewed by their fellow citizens as "leaders" of the community. Leadership is an intrinsic part of group existence, and community leaders may through their influence with political officials actually make the decisions. Furthermore, group action generates power. Those who take a positive interest in any problem are likely to have a considerable advantage over those who are passive and apathetic. And, of course, those who feel they have the most at stake are also likely to be the ones who become the most active in political decision making.[11]

But it is also possible that persons who appear to be policy leaders, even to the extent of seemingly dominating the decisions of those holding public office, are really only verbalizers. That is, they merely say, as symbolic leaders of the community, the things that are already widely believed in the community. If this is the case, the same policies might have resulted whether or not these persons had taken any action in seeking to have policies developed. Leading bankers, merchants, realtors, and chamber of commerce secretaries in small towns or middle-sized cities are certain to have their remarks given considerable publicity through newspapers, radio, and television, and may thus seem to be real leaders. Merchant princes and bankers are sometimes listened to because they are natural leaders or because of the deference they receive as a result of their prestigeful

[11] A good bibliography of power-structure studies may be found in Robert O. Schulze and Leonard U. Blumberg, "The Determination of Local Power Elites," *American Journal of Sociology,* 63:290–296, November, 1957; Charles Press, *Main Street Politics,* Institute for Community Development, Michigan State University, East Lansing, Mich., 1962; and Geoffrey Debnam, "Nondecisions and Power," *American Political Science Review,* 69:889–899, September, 1975. Some 240 studies are listed in Willis D. Hawley and Frederick M. Wirt (eds.), *The Search for Community Power,* Prentice-Hall, Inc., Englewood Cliffs, N.J., 1968.

positions. But their preferences as to public policy may be forestalled, for example, by implacable resistance from workers responding to a labor leader. This leader's own status position will probably be a modest one, and his or her technique not one of oppressive coercion but merely of pointing out to the union membership the consequences for them of a proposed line of action.

If community leaders had nearly absolute control, there would probably be consensus and little community conflict—only a disgruntled few would resist. In many cases, however, leaders have to do more than take a position. They must launch a selling campaign and must overcome opposition from competing leaders. A small amount of knowledge and drive—with a purpose—can sometimes project a relatively low-status person into a leadership position. One finds power in the community unused and seeks to exploit it. When one does so, the action spurs dominant leaders into counterattack. A conflict ensues that may not only get out of control for the initiators of action but may bring back memories of countless old (and often irrelevant) conflicts from the community's past.

Power Elites or Pluralism

The most continuous debate that has concerned students of local governmental decision making is whether the elected public officials respond primarily to the actions of a few persons of wealth and status or whether a pluralist situation exists in which political decision makers compete with each other as well as responding to a variety of specialized group pressures.

The boss and the political machine became a local governmental prototype of elite rule. Enterprising journalists, like the turn-of-the-century muckraker Lincoln Steffens, showed that the boss was often part of or cooperated closely with an elite of wealth. As we have noted, however, some students have also argued that the boss was at the same time able to respond to citizen needs of immigrants so that the elitist view is an oversimplified one in this case.

In the 1920s, the first notable sociological study of community decision making, that of Robert and Helen Lynd, argued that in Middletown (Muncie, Indiana) the pattern of elite influence was somewhat less crude than boss rule but just as effective. Local government was viewed as dominated by the owners of the major local industry, and its officials were encouraged to do nothing about issues of concern to the public. Students of today holding this view argue that questions important to the average citizen are excluded from the local government's agenda in many communities, so that what these city governments do is largely inconsequential. Thus, it is argued that when city councils do not take action on such pressing problems as local air and water pollution, residential segregation of blacks, or the conditions of housing in the local slums, it is because an elite behind the scenes does not want them to and stops them either by direct action or by its control over the opinions being expressed in the local newspaper, church pulpits, etc. Such latter control is described as the mobilization of bias in the community.

Other students examining specific public decisions, as for example Robert Dahl in his study of New Haven, Connecticut, found that the members of the local economic elite had not participated greatly in shaping decisions which made major changes in the community and spent considerable amounts of local tax funds. Among such actions examined were those on urban renewal and public education. His study suggests that significant political action was being taken on major problems because political officeholders hoped to make a reputation and to carve out a further career in politics. Lack of political action of local government, where it occurs, is explained by students sharing Dahl's views less as the result of elite influence as of the absence of a structured political competition, the influence of specialized interests, or even the acquiescence or concurrence of local majorities which are not concerned with the problems of local air and water pollution, the effects of residential segregation of blacks, or the conditions of housing in local slums.

An additional explanation of the pattern, a view from which our own analysis has borrowed heavily, is that of Norton Long. He argues that local politics and policy is less the result of conspiracy or plan on the part of either community influentials or officeholders than it is a by-product of the uncoordinated activities of many persons. He sees it resulting from many individuals each pursuing private interests and no one concerned about what the overall result will be.[12]

At this point the battle among scholars is joined. The major agreement is on two facts: that relatively few citizens participate actively in local politics and this is particularly true of those who earn substandard wages or have low educational attainment, and secondly, that different patterns of elite or pluralist influence may exist in different types of communities. No student espousing one view, however, has ever found a community operating as those of the other would claim it does. (Perhaps this is because of a difference in unarticulated assumptions about power. Those using an elitist analysis assume that the elites rule strictly in their own interests and "exploit" nonelites. Pluralists make no such assumption.)

Whatever the merits of the above arguments, political scientists are not as interested in identifying community power holders as they once were. This is so for several reasons: (1) Important decisions in urban areas now almost always involve persons at more than one level of government. Powerful persons locally may be overruled by decision makers at the state or national level over whom they may have little or no influence. (2) Absentee ownership of business and industry has made local executives less important than they were when firms were owner-managed by persons who also lived permanently in the city. (3) Core cities that once included within their limits persons of every job and status level are now largely abandoned by the politically active and powerful middle classes, leaving power widely dispersed over metropolitan areas. (4) Power studies tend too often to find what researchers expect to find. Their assumptions become self-fulfilling prophecies. (5) Much of the elitist-pluralist controversy centers around the *motives* of the top power holders, something always difficult to de-

[12] Norton E. Long, "The Local Community as a Ecology of Games," *The Polity,* Rand McNally, Chicago, 1962.

termine. Do they act selfishly for themselves and their class (elitists think so) or more generally as community-regarding citizens (pluralists say so)? If we could have a disinterested answer to this question, community-power analysis might be worth pursuing further.

Major Findings of Community Studies

Students examining their own urban area might keep in mind the following points in regard to the political power structure as it exists or is supposed to exist:

1 Some economically powerful leaders, in particular the managers and top executives of local plants of nationwide corporations, may refuse to become involved in community activities of any kind not directly affecting the company, lest enemies be unnecessarily made. Thus some of the persons who, because of great economic power, might be expected to be important decision makers exert little or no influence on decisions regarding community public policy. Heads of locally owned firms, on the other hand, are likely to be both active and powerful locally.[13]

2 Power structures may not necessarily be constructed in the shape of pyramids, although some studies have found such shapes.[14] It is quite possible to have power structures that do not lead to a few top leaders but instead have a polynucleated structure with various leaders, each of whom is powerful in some particular area of public policy but not in all such areas. In other words, there may be functional specialization, so that a person who is very influential in deciding questions dealing with, say, traffic-flow patterns, may have much less to say about housing policies and may not be consulted at all relative to the introduction of a new recreation program.

3 Some studies show that there are a few people who are very much interested in, and influential over, virtually all important decisions made in regard to public policy. These are the top members of the power elite. It is possible, even probable, that no such small clique of general leaders exists in the largest cities simply because of the great complexity of social organization that exists in such large governmental units. In such cities, the leaders in various areas of community policy making seek their own goals, with imperfect coordination of their efforts with those of other leaders seeking other goals. Communication—keeping other leaders and the public informed—becomes increasingly imperfect as the size of community increases. To the public, interest groups, as such, become more visible than the individual leaders as the size of the city increases.

Some evidence indicates that community power complexes were once more nearly monolithic than they are today. With the decline of home-owned industry and the entrance into political activity on an effective basis of racial, ethnic, and labor groups, the community power complex has become increasingly competitive in character.[15]

[13] See city "Alpha" in Oliver P. Williams, *Four Cities,* University of Pennsylvania Press, Philadelphia, 1963, as an example.

[14] See the Mills and Hunter studies, *op. cit.*

[15] Ruth McQuown, William R. Hamilton, and Michael P. Schneider. *The Political Restructuring of a Community,* Public Administration Clearing Service, University of Florida, Gainesville, Fla., 1964.

4 Policy leadership should not be confused with policy invention. The studies made so far tend to show that leaders need not themselves be creative in finding solutions to social needs. Their job is to assess proposals as to their degree of adequacy as solutions and then to push for the adoption of those found most acceptable. New ideas in meeting problems are most likely to come from persons with exceptional technical knowledge of a particular subject, persons who may be in the bureaucracies of private business, government, the universities, or elsewhere. Their names are commonly little known to the general public and sometimes even to the person who serves as symbolic leader for the promotion of the ideas they have put forth. Thus, when the headlines read "Banker Lauded in Presenting New Parking Plan" or "Mayor Torkelson Announces Plan to Renew Business District," the prestigeful persons mentioned in the stories are merely playing out their particular social roles. The anonymous persons who actually thought up the plans in the first place will probably not even be mentioned in the story.[16]

5 Governmental officials may once have been tools of the economic leadership group, but they are becoming increasingly important centers of power in their own right, and this is especially true as government plays an ever greater role in the lives of citizens.[17] In earlier times, government was simple and performed few functions. With business institutions overwhelmingly important by comparison, business leaders sometimes used officeholders as their front. This is less likely to happen today, and many important community leaders themselves now become council members and mayors. Local politicians today generate demand, mobilize support, and otherwise serve as leaders, as power centers.

6 The top members of the power structure may be powerful because they come from high-status families to whom deference has always been paid by other residents of the community or because they are newspaper editors. But they are most likely to be powerful because they speak for interest groups and have ability to bring some of the weight of the group to bear upon political institutions. One's place in the power structure reflects (except perhaps in small cities and towns where individuality remains especially important) the relative overall strength of the group for whom the leader is a representative.

7 Members of what has been called the community power complex do not necessarily make up a monolithic power group.[18] They may, in fact, be badly divided internally into two or more factions. In some cases, the editor of the local newspaper, the real estate board, and commercial and industrial leaders may be arrayed against racial, ethnic-group, and organized-labor leaders. As the middle class moves out of the core city into the suburbs, the latter grouping is likely to increase in power, thus encouraging a split between the community economic and political leadership.

The exodus of the middle class to the suburbs in the last generation has altered the power structure of core cities. In one city:[19]

[16] See Peter H. Clark, *The Businessman as a Civic Leader,* The Free Press of Glencoe, New York, 1960.

[17] See Talcott Parsons, *Structure and Process in Modern Societies,* The Free Press, New York, 1960, chap. 6, on this point.

[18] Delbert Miller and William H. Form, *Industry, Labor and the Community,* Harper & Row, Publishers, Incorporated, New York, 1960.

[19] David A. Booth and Charles R. Adrian, "Power Structure and Community Change," *Midwest*

> The top leaders of 1954 or their immediate successors in the same positions continued to dominate decision-making in 1961. However, the top group was no longer monolithic, but more variegated than was the case seven years before. Also, given roles appeared, in some cases to be more important than the particular incumbent. . . .
>
> A further conclusion is that decision-making in the community is shared between two antagonistic groups, neither in complete control. The dominant group in the power structure cannot legitimize its decisions on public policy without the approval of an electorate-based veto group in the council, a group with only small membership in the top power complex.

8 Community power cannot be considered independently of power at the state and national levels. The important decisions affecting communities are not made in the community alone. All three of the traditional levels of government and all three of the traditional branches of government are involved in policy development. A prosperous community in which most persons are employed in locally owned industry may be relatively more independent than is the community which has most of its labor force employed in absentee-owned industry and business.[20]

9 Many vital decisions are not made by government at any level. Furthermore, "a comparatively small portion of the attention and involvement of most Americans" is devoted to governmental activities.[21] This means not only that many decisions are made by power structures of nongovernmental social insitutions but also that those who feel strongly enough about the desirability of achieving a particular public policy and who are willing to invest time, money, social capital, and other resources are likely to find that they are not challenged by other citizens.

In a study by Robert V. Presthus, 52 percent of the organizations identified in one community and 28 percent of those in another participated in the major decisions of the community; however, 90 percent of these organizations had been active in only one decision each.[22]

In a small industrial city, politics was commonly viewed as being of less importance than other activities, particularly business. Political leaders were found to be selected from the middle level of economic positions. Persons of higher economic status felt that the political game was not worthwhile, and persons in lower positions did not possess enough information to play the game effectively.[23]

10 Professional administrative specialists and "influentials" are both necessary for decision making. In a study contrasting professional administrators

---

Journal of Political Science, 6:277–296, August, 1962.

[20] See Robert V. Presthus, *Men at the Top,* Oxford University Press, Fair Lawn, N.J., 1964; and city "Alpha" in Williams and Adrian, *op. cit.*

[21] York Willbern, *The Withering Away of the City,* University of Alabama Press, University, Ala., 1964, chap. 5; Robert A. Dahl, *Who Governs?* Yale University Press, New Haven, Conn., 1961, chaps. 24–26.

[22] Presthus, *op. cit.,* pp. 432–433.

[23] Paul A. Smith, "The Games of Community Politics," *Midwest Journal of Political Science,* 9:37–60, February, 1965.

with members of the community power structure not associated with bureaucratic positions in city government (influentials), the influentials ranked higher in socioeconomic status, were involved in more policy issues, and were far more willing to be involved in taking positions in local elections. Even so, the two groups were frequently involved in close working relationships and hence were interdependent to a considerable degree.[24]

11 In early community power studies, the assumption seemed to be made implicitly that power was inexhaustible in the hands of those who, for one reason or another, held it. More recent studies seem to imply that the use of power is costly, that is, that power is one form of social capital and can be exhausted if used improvidently. Because power is exhaustible, those who hold it probably choose not to make use of it unless they believe that the input-output ratio is efficient, that is, unless they believe the payoffs are worth the costs.

12 One of the difficulties in identifying a power structure results from the fact that participants in community decision making may be involved either overtly or covertly. Those who are openly involved are relatively easy to identify, but some may be powerful figures, even though they are not actors on the community stage. These may be individuals who enjoy high status in the community or who, because of their economic or political positions, are feared by others. This results in *anticipatory behavior.* That is, the decision makers *assume* that these persons are potentially actors in the decision-making process and that it is necessary to accommodate to their particular interests, as the other leaders view them, if they are not to become active in the process and veto proposed policies of other actors. The "richest man in town," or a leading banker, or a major manufacturer, or any other persons viewed as potentially powerful may, hence, remain out of the political arena by having their expectations discounted in advance. The possibility always exists that they are overdiscounted, and, for the researcher, it is extremely difficult to determine who such actors are and whether the allowance made for their potential power is exaggerated or not.

13 The community roles that are viewed by the culture as being important and hence deserving of a place in the community power complex are well known as the result of the large number of studies by sociologists and political scientists. Almost all power structure studies include the following leaders: the editor or the publisher of the local newspaper, a leading banker or two, the heads of the two or three largest manufacturing firms, the heads of the major central business district retail firms, the manager of the local chamber of commerce, the mayor, and one or possibly two council members, but never a majority of the council. In addition, the head of the realty firm that handles most of the central business district property will often be included.

Among those who are seldom mentioned in a study of reputational elites are ethnic and racial leaders, the manager of the leading television or radio station, and labor leaders. These persons probably are not included in the reputational power elite because they lack legitimacy; that is, the respondents do not view them as having a *right* to be included in the community power structure and hence they are not listed.

In an attempt both to simplify the determination of local power elites and to

[24] M. Kent Jennings. "Public Administrators and Community Decision Making," *Administrative Science Quarterly,* 8:18–43, June, 1963.

overcome the prejudice against persons who are not viewed by the upper middle class as having a right to a place in the power structure, two sociologists have developed a simplified method of determining the local power leaders.[25] They have assumed that the actual leaders in a community cannot be hidden from knowledgeable people, an assumption also made by the political scientist Robert A. Dahl. Using this assumption, they have found it possible to construct a profile of the local power elite by asking any two leaders in the following seven areas to list the persons whom they regard as having most power and influence: persons from business, the clergy, the communications media, education, financial institutions, organized labor, and the black community.

14 An important aspect of political power lies in the ability of the powerful to control the community agenda. Leaders may decide not to act relative to an issue that some people in the community would like to have placed on the agenda, or they may decide not to decide. That is, they may implicitly accept some item of social concern as having at least a marginally legitimate place on the agenda, but they may decide to do nothing about it. Even beyond this, they may decide to engage in nondecision making. Thus, "When the dominant values, the accepted rules of the game, the existing power relations among groups, and the instruments of force, singly or in combination, effectively prevent certain grievances from developing into fullfledged issues which call for decisions, it can be said that a nondecision-making situation exists."[26] Thus, community leaders may decide not to develop a new municipal park, or they may decide not to make a decision this year concerning the imposition of a municipal income tax, or the school superintendent may decide not to call to the attention of civic leaders the fact that certain practices in the school system do not represent sound professional practice. (The costs resulting from the conflict that would follow might do the school system more harm than good.)

Closing Statement

In this chapter we have examined two aspects of the local policy-making process: the impact of the elected public official and of the community leader and influential. Both have important parts in the drama of community decision making, and they will reappear in the later chapters on the functions of government.

SELECTED READINGS

Agger, Robert E., Daniel Goldrich, and Bert E. Swanson: *The Rulers and the Ruled,* John Wiley & Sons, Inc., New York, 1964. (A major empirical and theoretical study of community power.)

Bachrach, Peter: *The Theory of Democratic Elitism, A Critique,* Little, Brown and Company, Boston, 1967. (A critique of pluralist theory as found in the writings of Dahl and Polsby.)

Bachrach, Peter, and Morton S. Baratz: *Power and Poverty, Theory and Practices,* Oxford University Press, New York, 1970.

[25] Miller and Form, *op. cit.*

[26] Peter Bachrach and Morton S. Baratz, "Decisions and Nondecisions," *American Political Science Review,* 57:632–642, September, 1963. For a rigorous criticism of the Bachrach-Baratz approach, see Debnam, *op. cit.*

Clark, Terry (ed.): *Community Structure and Decision Making, Comparative Analysis,* Chandler Publishing Company, San Francisco, 1968.

Dahl, Robert A.: *Who Governs?* Yale University Press, New Haven, Conn., 1961. (Includes a criticism of the reputational approach to power and concentrates upon decision-making participants. This study strongly influenced community politics research.)

Debnam, Geoffrey: "Nondecisions and Power: The Two Faces of Bachrach and Baratz," *American Political Science Review,* 69:889–899, Sept., 1975. (A criticism of the "non-decision" concept.)

Gosnell, Harold F.: *Machine Politics: Chicago Model,* The University of Chicago Press, Chicago, 1937.

Greene, Lee S. (ed.): "City Bosses and Political Machines," *The Annals of the American Academy of Political and Social Science,* 353: entire issue, May, 1964. (An appraisal, by several authors, of contemporary municipal politics.)

Hunter, Floyd: *Community Power Structure: A Study of Decision-Makers,* The University of North Carolina Press, Chapel Hill, N.C., 1963. (A watershed in the study of communities.)

Jennings, M. Kent: *Community Influentials: The Elites of Atlanta,* The Free Press of Glencoe, New York, 1964. (Atlanta, about a decade after Hunter, is not found to be homogeneous in its goals or structure.)

Kaufman, Herbert, and Victor Jones: "The Mystery of Power," *Public Administration Review,* 14:205–212, Summer, 1954. (Criticism of Hunter. This review article had a strong impact on urban politics research.)

Long, Norton E.: *The Polity,* Rand McNally & Company, Chicago, 1962. (See especially, "The Local Community as an Ecology of Games.")

McKean, Dayton D.: *The Boss: The Hague Machine in Action,* Houghton Mifflin Company, Boston, 1940.

McQuown, Ruth, William R. Hamilton, and Michael P. Schneider: *The Political Restructuring of a Community,* Public Administration Clearing Service, University of Florida, Gainesville, Fla., 1964. (Especially important for its examination of the influence of university faculty members upon a community.)

Merriam, Charles E.: *Chicago: A More Intimate View of Urban Politics,* The Macmillan Company, New York, 1929.

Meyerson, Martin, and Edward C. Banfield: *Politics, Planning and the Public Interest,* The Free Press of Glencoe, New York, 1955. (A study of politics and group activity in housing policy development for Chicago.)

Miller, Delbert, and William H. Form: *Industry, Labor and the Community,* Harper & Row, Publishers, Incorporated, New York, 1960. (Sees the "community power complex" as being frequently competitive and lacking in shared values. A major study by sociologists.)

Polsby, Nelson W.: *Community Power and Political Theory,* Yale University Press, New Haven, Conn., 1963. (Statement of pluralist position.)

Press, Charles: *Main Street Politics,* Institute for Community Development, Michigan State University, East Lansing, Mich., 1962. (A summary and evaluation of power analysis; digests many articles.)

Presthus, Robert V: *Men at the Top,* Oxford University Press, Fair Lawn, N.J., 1964. (A comparative study of two small cities, using both reputational and decision-making research techniques.)

Vidich, A. J., and Joseph Bensman: *Small Town in Mass Society,* Princeton University Press, Princeton, N.J., 1958. (An anthropological study of a New York village.)

Wildavsky, Aaron: *Leadership in a Small Town,* The Bedminster Press, Englewood Cliffs, N.J., 1964. (A study of Oberlin, Ohio, finds a pluralistic pattern of leadership and greatest influence with those who specialize in a functional area.)

Williams, Oliver P., and Charles R. Adrian: *Four Cities,* University of Pennsylvania Press, Philadelphia, 1963. (A comparative study of community politics in four middle-sized cities.)

Wood, Robert C.: *Suburbia: Its People and Their Politics,* Houghton Mifflin Company, Boston, 1959. (A theory of suburban politics.)

Chapter 4

Urban Interest Groups

Public policy affects different segments of the general public in differing ways. Those whose ways of making a living are most intimately affected are most likely to band together in an attempt to shape such policy. In an urban setting, groups formed for other purposes, particularly those related to business and professional concerns, move readily into the political arena in an attempt to influence policy makers.

An interest group differs from a political party chiefly in that it does not seek to capture offices for its members but rather attempts to influence public policy. It also differs from most political parties in the United States in that it is made up of persons with basically the same interests and viewpoints—it is normally much more ideologically cohesive than is a political party in this country.

It is these specialized and relatively well-organized interests that we examine in this chapter, noting their potential effect on urban policy making.[1] We also examine those potential groups whose interests are also affected but who are generally disorganized because they have few resources for influencing the local

[1] A basic discussion of interest groups is David B. Truman, *The Governmental Process,* Alfred A. Knopf, New York, 1951. See also Mancur Olson, Jr., *The Logic of Collective Action,* Harvard University Press, Cambridge, Mass., 1965.

policy maker. They may turn to protest activity since conventional channels to policy making seem closed. We conclude with a discussion of community conflict.

Is Group Action Democratic?

Much has been said of the evil influences and dangers of pressure groups in politics. It has even been suggested by some critics that they be legally abolished or stringently controlled. Most such suggestions are, however, naïve. If we had a system of two or more political parties, each standing upon a definite platform of proposed action to which the parties could be held, interest groups, or at least their lobbying activities, could be greatly reduced. Such is not the case in the United States, however, and especially not so in cities, many of which are nonpartisan or have long been dominated by one major party. Neither is it practical to say that public officials can determine the viewpoints of a cross section of the citizenry simply by noting the comments of those they happen to contact personally—not in any but the smallest villages, at any rate. And only the naïve or foolhardy would suggest that officeholders should be elected with no promises to the public and then be entrusted to use their own free will and best judgment in doing as they see best "for all the people" while in office. They must constantly be reminded of the nature of the shifting viewpoints of their constituents.

Another criticism of interest groups is that they are organized primarily by, and for the benefit of, middle-class and upper-working-class persons. Such organization further weakens the already nearly powerless position of those who lack the skills, knowledge, or incentive to form interest groups of their own, primarily the poor. One of the goals of the antipovery program, through the "maximum feasible participation" of the poor, was to help organize the poor and to seek indigenous leaders from among its membership. It is true that the poor lack effective organization for the most part, but it is also true that they are less able to benefit from democracy generally than are members of the dominant working and middle classes. Their condition does not logically lead to a condemnation of interest groups as a method of marshaling and presenting ideas and concerns to government.[2]

Interest groups are not only not evil, they are an absolute necessity in a democracy. They serve the purpose of marshaling individual opinions, organizing them, and presenting them in a skillful way to the proper governmental officials. Individual interest groups no doubt do sometimes go beyond the bounds of the mores of society, do fail to give an accurate picture of the interests, desires, and aspirations of their individual members, and do act otherwise irresponsibly. But they also face some checks on their activities.

The Effectiveness of Groups It is a mistake to visualize all groups as operating with machinelike efficiency in influencing policy. Some groups are kept in check by counterpressure groups. For example, the local radio stations and news-

[2] On the political advantages of "Middle Americans," see Charles R. Adrian and Charles Press, *American Politics Reappraised,* McGraw-Hill Book Company, New York, 1974.

papers compete for the same advertising dollars and are apt to be skeptical of each other's claims. In this fashion, some of the potential dangers of the organized power of one group is neutralized by the watchful eye of the opposing group. And each watcher is also watched. But for some groups, few organized counter groups are active. The radio station and newspaper may be owned by the same corporation. No general interest group representing the consumer's interest exists and none is likely to despite the popular talk of a "consumers' movement" in the 1970s. Thus groups often are only held in check by such counterforces as community ideology, public officials and political candidates, and public opinion as guided by the news media.

Interest groups are also kept in check by their own ineptness and the lack of full support of their membership. Group members sometimes belong to opposing groups and are cross pressured. The business people who are members of the Methodist Church may find the local Chamber of Commerce to which they belong backing an enterprising person wanting to put in a deep-fry chicken and hamburger stand next to the house of worship. One of their groups or both are likely to receive their reduced support. But even in the absence of cross pressures, full mobilization of group membership is difficult.

Groups are made up of individuals seeking private goals. As soon as the group becomes larger than a dozen or so, and even sometimes in these small groups, the internal conflicts begin to handicap those wishing to act collectively. The most serious handicap is that individual members find it to their advantage to reduce their own costs by cutting down participation. Thus the business executive who does not make a financial contribution to the fund created to bring new industry to Pottsville benefits as much as other Pottsville merchants if the campaign is successful but at other people's expense. In this case, social pressure from other merchants, if the group of merchants is small, may force a contribution anyhow. Other groups, such as labor unions or the local bar or medical associations, can also force participation by coercion or by providing special side benefits. Without these techniques potential members would find they could get the benefits of the association without paying any of the cost.

This dodging of participation costs by members means groups seldom operate at peak efficiency and can probably never depend on the full support of their membership. The fund drive may flop, only a few dozen or so may appear for the massive rally at city hall after the rumor goes out that trouble is expected, or only a handful of the total membership turns out for the mass meeting even if door prizes and entertainment are provided.

Action on behalf of the group is thus most probable where special benefits accrue to the group leader. A common method of achieving success is by hiring a professional to act on behalf of the group (the Urban League director or the Chamber of Commerce secretary). It also occurs when individual members are crucially affected by the decisions and find it worth their while to pay the costs of leadership (for example, the realtor whose proposed new subdivision is under fire by the newspaper). Also a relatively unknown citizen with political ambitions may seize leadership of a group on an issue and pay the costs in order to advance his or her own political career. Other such leaders have emerged when their ideological commitment was unusually high as for example the relatively little known minister who became leader of the Birmingham bus strike—Martin Luther King, Jr. Thus while groups may not act at 100-percent efficiency, their impact on specific policies may be high because of an active leadership.

Characteristics of Groups Several things should be kept in mind in classifying these interest groups. Some of them are especially created for the single purpose of lobbying; to others, indeed to most groups, lobbying is only a sideline. Some are temporary organizations created because of a special problem; others are permanent groups. Some, in large cities and in state and nation at any rate, are always present and lobbying at the seat of government; others do not lobby except when a matter of particular importance to the group is under consideration.

Interest groups are constantly realigning their forces as expediency demands. It should not be assumed that politics is simply business versus labor, or that business people always work together, or that various groups operate in fairly permanent alignments. The *fluidity* of the pressure-group system is one of its most prominent characteristics.

Business people often line up on opposite sides of an issue, for example. Downtown merchants might lobby before a city council for one-way streets, since this would help hurry traffic to the place where their stores are located, but neighborhood-shopping-area merchants oppose one-way streets, since these reduce accessibility to their locations. Downtown and neighborhood-shopping-area merchants alike may favor municipally owned parking lots, but realtors are quite likely to oppose them. Labor unions frequently come into conflict with one another before legislative or administrative bodies. Jurisdictional disputes and the long-standing conflict of interests between the railroad brotherhoods and the teamsters' (truckers') union are examples. Business and labor leaders work together on many matters. Ours is a dynamic system. (See Figure 4-1.)

Organized and Unorganized Groups

If all groups in society were equally well organized and equally effective in presenting their sides of issues, the process of determining public policy through compromise among the various interests involved would be highly satisfactory, indeed, nearly as perfect a device for democratic policy making as human society could achieve. Not all groups have their interests equally well protected, however. The less verbal members of the working class are not so likely to have their views expressed before councils as are members of the most prestigeful groups in society. They are certain to be accorded less deference when they speak. The sub-working-class poor, with few skills and little or no training and chronically on welfare, are not, even if organized, likely to be given serious or sympathetic attention in the political area. In terms of status, inside connections, funds for spreading propaganda, and other factors, there are vast differences in the relative power of groups.

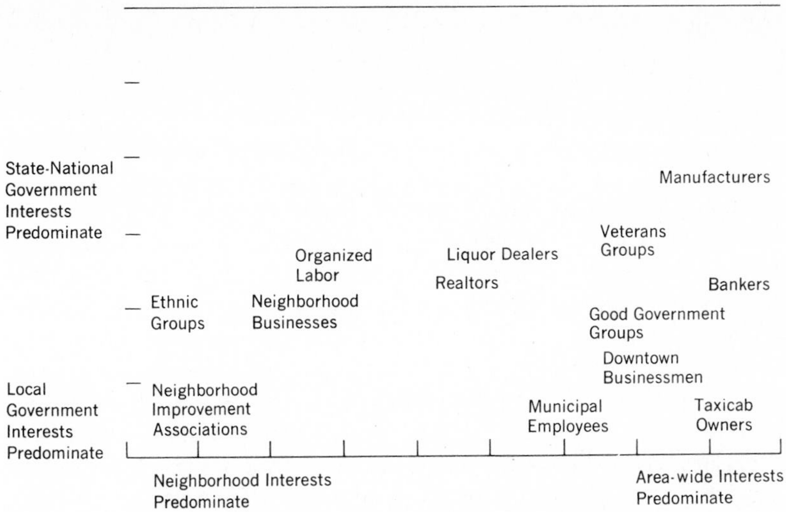

Figure 4-1 Group interests are multidimensional. Two aspects are shown here.

It should not be assumed, however, that a group is necessarily strong because it is well organized or weak because it is unorganized. A well-organized and vigorously active group may, for example, have its relative strength reduced through the gerrymandering of the city council. Some unorganized groups are very weak politically (e.g., ex-convicts); others are strong (e.g., the elderly). In a democracy, virtually all groups are free to organize and to lobby, but the ability of the members of a group to understand the techniques of doing this varies greatly, and their political resources also vary widely. The result is a weakening of the representativeness of a politics based upon the summation of vector forces.

The Techniques and Motivation of Groups

Not only do groups vary according to their degree of organization, but they also vary according to the techniques they use and the level of motivation they have for political participation.

Techniques might be said to vary according to the way in which the groups fit into the system of cultural values. One group may be able to "get away" with something that would produce highly unfavorable publicity for another. The medical association feels impelled to act within the public image of dignity which it has created for itself; a labor union can safely be more free-swinging in its behavior. A conservative group may be able to make recommendations concerning the election of nonpartisan judges with newspaper approval; a liberal group may be criticized by the same newspaper for "interfering" if it does the same thing.

There are various bases for the political motivation of groups. Many organizations, for example, seek to use the sanctions of the state to support their own battles against other interests. Either labor or management can benefit in their struggles by having governmental officials or legal provisions supporting one side. In other cases, one might make the generalization that *the political activity of any group is proportionate to its stake in the marginal definition of legality and of law-enforcement levels.* Thus, middle-management bureaucrats in private industry are not intensely involved in politics, except by choice, because their jobs and their way of life are well within the bounds of accepted behavior. They are not likely to be in trouble with the law, nor is their welfare especially dependent upon its decisions. Similarly, the professional bank robber is not politically active because his job is so far outside the law that he cannot possibly hope to secure governmental sanction for his activities. But those on the edge of legality, where economic survival depends on marginal definitions, are the ones with the greatest stake in political decisions, and they make the maximum investment in the political process. Thus, a racetrack owner must be politically active because that business is just barely acceptable as legitimate by American values. The electric-utilities executive is similarly highly motivated, because the rate structure is determined through the political process. The corner druggist is deeply concerned over traffic-flow patterns. A decision to prohibit parking near his or her store may wipe out the margin of profit.

The pattern of marginality varies over time. Blacks who once thought they could not make economic or social progress through political action now find that they can. As a result, they have changed their behavior pattern from almost total political apathy to intense activity. Americans vote, lobby, issue propaganda, or otherwise take part in the process of politics according to their level of motivation. This, in turn, varies according to whether the individual's activities are well within the norms of society and of established public policy or whether decisions on public policy that may affect the individual are of a sort that are unpredictable but of immense importance to her or his social or economic welfare.

Groups and the Public Interest

When any group announces a policy position, it seeks explicitly or implicitly to associate its stand with the public interest. In fact, virtually every politically active individual or group claims to be acting in the public interest. Critics of the stand taken by a particular group, on the other hand, not uncommonly complain that interest groups are selfish and that they ought to act in the public interest. With everyone thus borrowing the term, it becomes useless as an analytical tool. Yet it is a basic part of the folklore of democracy to say that public policies as they are adopted are, or ought to be, in the public interest. As such, the concept may serve a useful function in encouraging compliance with the law, which in turn is an important device for achieving a stable society. It is also useful as a symbol to remind legislators and administrators that no matter how many groups they may have listened to before making a decision, other groups and citizens who are unrepresented or underrepresented before them will also be affected by the decision.

As one writer on the subject has said:[3]

> Instead of being associated with substantive goals or policies, the public interest better survives identification with the process of group accommodation. The public interest rests not in some policy emerging from the settlement of conflict, but with the method of that settlement itself, with compromising in a peaceful, orderly, predictable way the demands put upon policy.

URBAN INTEREST GROUPS

Interest groups operate in basically the same pattern on the national, state, or local level. To be sure, there may be differences in the relative balance of power of the various groups. On the national and state level, for example, agricultural groups tend to be among the more powerful. Liquor lobbyists tend to be more powerful before state and local bodies than before the national government. Real estate groups and downtown merchants tend to be extraordinarily powerful in city politics.

Good-Government Groups

The so-called "good-government groups" are among the few that restrict most of their organized efforts to the local scene. These groups have been mentioned above in connection with the reform movement.[4] Examples of them include the Citizens League of Pawtucket, the Richmond Civic Association, the Municipal League of Spokane, the Cleveland Citizens League, the Citizens Union of New York City, Citizens Action of Grand Rapids, the New Boston Committee, the Worcester Citizens Plan "E" Association, and the Hartford Citizens Charter Committee. While many of these groups date back to the reform era, new ones continue to be formed and old ones become inactive. Most of them have been strongly influenced by the programmatic goals of the National Municipal League.

In general, these groups lobby for the lowest possible taxes and the greatest possible value from each tax dollar. They often seek to promulgate the basic aims of the reform movement, such as the council-manager plan, a professional civil service, performance budgeting, municipal home rule, and nonpartisan elections. They are interested in "good government" as such, usually with no immediate personal benefits expected except in the belief that the changes they advocate will save taxpayer dollars. Some members belong to these groups as something of a hobby; others consider it to be a civic obligation. The groups often work in close cooperation with municipal research bureaus (such as the Citizens' Research Bureau of Milwaukee, the St. Louis Governmental Research Institute, and the Cleveland Bureau of Governmental Research).

Because these groups are interested in keeping taxes low through keeping city expenses down, they often find themselves arrayed against labor unions in struggles for higher pay for city employees, the extension of old services, the

[3] Frank J. Sourauf, "The Public Interest Reconsidered," *Journal of Politics,* 19:616–639, November, 1957. Quotation from p. 638.

[4] See pp. 62.

assumption of responsibility for new services by the city, or a change or increase in the city tax structure. While these groups were considered "progressive" and forward-looking during the apogee of the reform movement in the 1920s, quite a few of them are today aligned with the largest taxpayers on the side of conservatism. Others, however, continue to be primarily interested in studying municipal issues and advancing rational attitudes toward them.

These "leagues" and "unions" often follow the practice of making recommendations concerning initiative and referendum propositions at each election and of endorsing a slate of candidates on a nonpartisan or bipartisan basis. These recommendations receive much newspaper publicity in many cities, including New York, Chicago, and Detroit, for the groups often enjoy the open support of at least some of the newspapers. The effect of these endorsements varies greatly, however, depending upon the degree of political organization, local traditions, and many other factors. The Detroit Citizens League is far more effective, for example, than the Municipal Voters League of Chicago. Some groups do not make recommendations for voting but do give their opinions as to whether or not each candidate is qualified for the office he or she seeks.

An example of a good-government group that has existed for a long time is the Citizens Association of Kansas City. It has dominated the recruitment and election of councilors in Kansas City from the time it was organized in 1941 until the present, with only the period between 1959 and 1963 as an exception. During the four-year interval, a group oriented much more toward working-class values and opposed to the council-manager plan controlled the city. This was a period of confusion and inaction in local politics, and it continued until a majority slate with Citizens Association backing regained control of the council. The association has been attempting to broaden its base through participation of a diversity of local group members and representatives of various life-styles. One of the difficulties that led to its temporary eclipse in 1959 was that it had been viewed as exclusively a middle-class, do-gooder organization.[5]

Related to the above type of group are various other middle-class clubs and endeavors. Women's groups, particularly the League of Women Voters, often work for good government per se. The League prepares a voter-information sheet in many cities. Being nonpartisan, the League usually has a prepared set of questions on current issues which it submits to candidates. The questions are generally not "loaded" (the League *does* sometimes endorse certain policies—for example, perhaps, the council-manager plan, or a four-year term for elective officials), and the answers are printed verbatim (unless, of course, the candidate is too long-winded). The Parent-Teachers Association (PTA) is also a powerful group, much more interested in the affairs of the school board, of course, but where its interests overlap with those of the city, the PTA may lobby before the council or the voters, if a referendum is involved.

Improvement Associations

In many cities, virtually every neighborhood shopping area has an association for the safeguarding and furthering of the interests of the businesses operating in that

[5] Stanley Gabis, "Leadership in a Large Manager City: The Case of Kansas City," *The Annals of the American Academy of Political and Social Science,* 353:52–63, May, 1964.

community. Likewise, in many sections of the city, similar groups will be found for the various residential subdivisions. These groups serve many purposes. If the city is growing or shrinking in size, they fight to keep property values high. If the city or neighborhood is losing population, the slackening of demand for homes demands diligence in order to save as much as possible of the homeowners' investment. If the city is increasing in size, older neighborhoods are constantly undergoing transition in character. In this case the association fights—usually without ultimate success if there is real demand for space—to keep Jews or blacks or Chicanos or some other socially unwanted group out of the area.

These groups often appear before the council or administrative officers of the city, for they have almost countless bases for making such contacts. They are interested in every proposed rezoning of the area, since this has a direct effect upon property values. They do not want commercial or industrial areas nearby; they want the factory eight blocks upwind to stop making all that smoke and noise; they want more stop signs in the neighborhood ("Trucks are using our street for a through street."); they want the chuckholes repaired immediately (though this must not result in a tax increase); they want the patrol car to drive past the house more often at night (but "Look at all the money the police want to run that lousy department for next year!"); and they want only single-family dwellings in the neighborhood if such has been the previous character of the area.

The improvement associations also serve other functions. Americans seek to lessen insecurity by joining together with others who feel as they do, and the neighborhood civic association gives individuals another club to add to their list. There are also offices to be filled, and Americans like to be presidents or vice-presidents of almost anything. They will appoint a committee at the first excuse, and neighborhood associations present a multitude of reasons for appointing committees: to "investigate the situation on 81st Street," or to "see the police chief." The associations also help to satisfy the urban dweller's longing to restore the primary relationships characteristic of the small town and rural community, for most of these groups are limited to a fairly small, truly neighborly area. If the group is made up primarily of homeowners, as a suburban group is, or if it is a business person's association, the organization also affords an opportunity to identify oneself more closely with these socially honorific classes. Members of neighborhood associations are fond of talking about the rights and responsibilities of homeowners and taxpayers, and members of a business person's group remind one another that they are indeed business people and hence the mainstays of the American economy. In fulfilling these psychological needs for prestige, the improvement associations, like many other pressure groups, serve a useful social function beyond that of exerting political pressure alone.

Taxpayers' Groups

As something of a cross between the good-government groups and the business groups in the community, there are often organized "taxpayers' leagues" of one title or another. In general, they stand for lower taxes and fewer government activities and services and have their support in the more conservative business community—the large taxpayers. They often publish propaganda based upon either real or pseudo research on taxation, budgeting, and borrowing policies.

Their membership is normally not large, and their influence on government varies greatly from place to place. Some of these groups have broader interests, more in the nature of the good-government groups.

Business Groups

So many business groups exert pressure upon government that they would probably overshadow and overpower all the others if it were not that they spend so much of their time opposing one another. There is an organization equipped to lobby for every business interest in the city. To name only some of them: there is often an association of downtown merchants, representing the owners, or in a large city probably the managers, of the large stores downtown. These people would obviously have numerous interests. They pay much of the general property tax of the city and so have an interest in tax rates; they want ample parking spaces, paid for, if possible, from taxes and not from their own pockets; they want freeways that will bring people downtown to shop and will discourage the development of competing neighborhood shopping areas.

The small businesses, especially in the village or small city, see their gross income as fairly fixed. Their expansion prospects are poor. For this reason, they think in terms of cutting costs and see taxes as one of their fixed costs. To them, additional taxes will not produce commensurate benefits but will only diminish their possible profits. They become, therefore, a supporter of a low-tax ideology.[6] In middle- and large-sized cities, the more prosperous, expansion-minded merchants of the central business district are likely to be advocates of boosterism—and of tax levies to support its aims of a bigger and better city—but the neighborhood small merchants are likely to have views similar to those of the village merchant and to see the large downtown businesses with their ideas of constant growth as a threat.

The large retailers have political problems, too. They must constantly be on the alert against all kinds of threats to their profits, many of which the ordinary citizen would not even think of as being political in character. For example, the mighty and prestigeful Fifth Avenue Association of New York City once took a large advertisement in the *New York Times* in order to urge the mayor to veto an ordinance which would permit a Loyalty Day parade on a regular business day. The city council was anxious to oblige the veterans' groups, but the great shops along the avenue pointed out that this particular expression of patriotism would cost them 1 million dollars in sales.[7]

The downtown merchants and property owners are of tremendous influence both in determining the outcome of elections and in setting policy afterward. In middle-sized cities without political machines they are often the dominant group, and even in large cities they wield great power. In Detroit and Los Angeles, for example, their influence is pervasive, although it is kept unpublicized and *sub rosa* by choice.

If a political machine exists, these groups must use a somewhat different

[6] See A. J. Vidich and Joseph Bensman, *Small Town in Mass Society,* Princeton University Press, Princeton N.J., 1958, chap. 5.

[7] *The New York Times,* Apr. 22, 1958.

approach. The traditional arrangement was for the dominant merchants and manufacturers to permit the machine's politicians to operate the city government and to control its patronage, in return for guarantees of nonharassment and assistance in commercial and industrial expansion.

General Business Groups The chamber of commerce is interested at the local level, as at the state and national, in tax rates, labor legislation, and other matters that affect business activity and costs. In quite a few cities, the chamber serves as the principal surrogate for business before the council and city officials. Often it acts in lieu of a downtown property association and exerts the same type of pressure.

The so-called "service clubs," the Rotarians, Lions, and Kiwanians, are basically for business people, but their interests are primarily apolitical and they are not likely to act in this capacity, except perhaps in connection with a summer playground program or some such community service project.

Banks Banks and related financial institutions are important interest groups for several reasons. First, they are businesses and have the interests of business persons. Secondly, bankers being among the most respected of all business persons, their views are likely to be taken into the bosoms of others, who then present them as their own. Furthermore, because bankers decide who is to be permitted to borrow money and under what conditions, they may in dozens of subtle or open ways influence the thinking, or at least the behavior, of others. Thirdly, bankers always have a direct stake in local legislation affecting public utilities, in which banks have a pecuniary interest, and in bond issues and sinking funds, since banks act as brokers in servicing these. Banks are also interested in public policies that may affect businesses to which they have loaned money; hence they are interested in such matters as business regulation, taxation, zoning, and housing.

Utilities Public utility companies in a great majority of cities are today dependent upon a state body for determining rates and service, but they also have many local interests. They must guard against movements to place their utility under public ownership; they are often dependent upon the goodwill of the city administration in order to extend or restrict the area covered by their services; and since the city is responsible for the public safety, the city's interpretation of what is safe or adequate equipment is of vital interest.

Contractors The city has the power of inspection over all sorts of construction. The building, plumbing, lighting, and other codes are hence of great interest to contractors, as is the manner in which these are enforced.

Business executives who are particularly desirous of procuring public contracts are, of course, unusually interested in the political scene. Some businesses, such as road-grading and -surfacing companies, depend for most of their work upon public contracts, and they can be expected to seek to do their utmost to influence both elections and policy decisions.

Taxicabs Taxicab owners (and their drivers' unions) also play an important role in municipal politics. The city council normally determines the number of taxi licenses to be issued and decides the question of who is to get them. The council can thus make or break any given company. Furthermore, both the owners and the drivers are interested in *restricting* the number of licenses below that of actual need—so that they may charge monopoly rates. Drivers and their union are as interested in keeping down competition as is the company itself.

In almost every American city, taxicab rates are high (especially if one includes the tip, which is really a hidden portion of the charge), and the number of cabs available is greatly restricted. This is a direct result of pressure-group activity upon the council and is an illustration of the council acting in the interest of the organized few rather than the unorganized many.

Taxicab companies, and often their drivers, find it necessary to pick candidates and support them in municipal campaigns. Those who bet on the winning candidates will have the lion's share of the licenses for the next term of office, while those who are wrong will get the crumbs. Taxicab companies also seek ordinances against "jitneys" and urge strict enforcement of these ordinances.

The Professions Professional organizations have a stake in government. Some of them, such as medical and dental groups, are more important as lobbyists before state and national governments, but others, and particularly the city or county bar association, are also active locally. The bar association is interested in city government for a variety of reasons. Lawyers make up a large portion of the candidates for public office and are likely to view this field as a private hunting ground. Lawyers and their organizations look upon themselves as singularly responsible for guarding the law and its traditions. They are particularly concerned over the modern tendency to use administrative tribunals rather than law courts in the settlement of many public matters, since the former need not always be made up of lawyers and do not necessarily use the traditional processes of the courts of law. Lawyers, furthermore, often consider themselves to be trained in the problems of public policy formulation and peculiarly qualified to comment upon them, even though the law is not a social science and most lawyers have had very little training in sociology, economics, psychology, or even political science.

Real Estate Groups The local real estate board and other similar groups have a special interest in local government. The city zoning ordinance and building code are of the greatest interest to them; the city tax rate is important, because the general property tax is the major source of city revenue; the cost of paving streets, curbs, gutters, and sidewalks is a factor in the selling of homes; public housing is anathema to them. Builders and real estate speculators are often among the most influential groups before a city government, and this is particularly true in suburban areas in a period of expansive home building. Builders may often contribute to the campaign funds of *all* candidates for office in a modest-sized suburb, especially if they are the large assembly-line type of "project" builder. There are often conflicts before the city council between project builders and improvement associations representing subdivisions of individually built homes, and also between homeowners and large real estate companies interested in the development of commercial and industrial properties.

Liquor Interests Time was, near the beginning of the century, when the two most powerful groups in most cities were the public utilities and the liquor interests. Since then, there has been a considerable decline in the power of the liquor and beer industries. Prior to prohibition, licensing of beer and liquor stores was largely a local function, making the interests of these occupations in city government obvious. Of course, there was also the question of the attitude the local police would take toward laws dealing with closing hours, selling to minors, selling on Sunday, engaging in such socially disapproved but financially profitable sidelines as the narcotics trade and prostitution, and the like. During prohibition, the liquor industry continued (with public approval) quite unabated. In order to do so, it was necessary for purveyors to buy off local governments whose officials were in a position to work an easy shakedown racket. Bootleggers in many instances virtually captured whole city governments, even in very large cities, as when the Capone gang dominated Chicago in the 1920s. Today liquor interests are less powerful in most cities, but they still exercise considerable influence, especially where the law and local mores are not in accord. The policing of the liquor industry, now largely in the hands of state government, has relieved city officials of some of the problems and temptations that existed before prohibition.

Illegal Occupations The gambling, prostitution, and narcotics businesses are almost everywhere illegal, but they operate to some degree in most of our larger cities, as well as in many smaller places. They may be beset by peace officers from all three levels of government, but they persist because they are profitable, and they are profitable because of the highly inelastic character of the demand for their services. Because they are illegal, they must be particularly concerned with politics. Where they cannot purchase protection, they seek to establish a pale wherein their operations are allowed by either tacit or explicit arrangement. Failing this, or as a preferable substitute, they may seek to operate in a suburb if the core-city administration is especially hostile. The narcotics trade is probably the least thriving of these businesses, for, despite the cravings suffered by the drug addict that will make him go to any extreme in order to obtain supplies, federal-government officers have long sought to exterminate the trade, usually, although not always, with the cooperation of state and local peace officers. On the other hand, gambling and prostitution are likely to be with us for some time to come, for there is seldom strong opposition to them.

Newspapers

As has often been pointed out, newspapers tend to be conservative influences in the community because big business is conservative and newspaper publishing, at least of the large-city dailies, is big business. It is also true that newspapers which are moderate on national and international questions may become much more conservative, or even reactionary, on matters of local politics. A daily which accepts the existence of labor unions when discussing national labor law may speak of unions in the same terms it might have used in the nineteenth century when discussing local politics. Physical proximity and the immediacy of the economic interest involved may be factors in producing this phenomenon. A further consideration is that business executives are dependent on the city government for all types of permits, licenses, favors, and sympathies, in order to operate freely and successfully. A government controlled by labor or by unsympathetic liberals is a frightening specter to most business persons and hence to newspaper editors.

Newspapers often work together with good-government groups and give them much free publicity. They may even print their press releases on the front page as news stories and not mention that it is partisan propaganda of an interest group. In many cities, newspapers have been important forces in support of local governments that reflect middle-class values.

Reasons for the Importance of Newspapers The overall effect of the opinion of a newspaper editorial board would probably not be great if the publication's effect were limited to its editorial opinions. Probably only a tiny percentage of newspaper readers pay any attention to the editorials, and those who do for the most part agree with them already. Yet a newspaper can be very influential in many different ways. It can influence individual opinion by emphasizing or burying an item; by distorting the relative importance of the various facts involved in a story; by choice of location for the story; by choice of adjectives and adverbs; by phrasing of headlines; by its use of cartoons (picture editorials that reach far more people than do the ordinary ones). A newspaper that would not permit the "loading" of a story on a national matter may make its stories during a local election into veritable editorials. It may play up the speeches and pictures of Candidate Twitingham and bury those of Candidate Torkelson on page 37. Individual newspapers may vary greatly in their use of these available weapons. Some seek to give balanced attention to all events. Others, for example, the Hearst newspapers, normally pay relatively little attention to local issues, being more concerned with the national and international scene. A locally owned newspaper is more likely to give space to local issues (and to take sides) than is one that is chain-owned or one whose editorial policy is determined by a person who lives elsewhere.

In many cities, especially large ones, limited-circulation weekly newspapers may be of more influence in elections than are the large downtown dailies. These newspapers are usually aimed at a definite clientele: residents of a suburb or of a neighborhood area in the core city, foreign-language-reading members of an ethnic group, members of a labor union, blacks, Catholics, or Jews. Since they emphasize the interests of particular groups, they are able to call specific candidates or issues to the attention of the voter and to discuss them in terms of his or her interests.

The suburban and neighborhood newspapers are especially influential since they are not viewed as "commercial" or "partisan." Because they reflect the interests and values of the neighborhood, they are thought of rather as agents of "community welfare and progress."[8]

Radio and TV

Radio and television are important media in large cities for reaching voters and people to be propagandized over local issues. In the days before television, radio was not too successful for conveying ideas concerning local matters. People would listen to the President, but not to the mayor, and almost certainly not to a local labor leader or the president of the local chamber of commerce, unless the issue were of the most unusual importance. Television, with a hypnotic quality lacking in radio, is able to catch the eye and thought of citizens where radio failed, but it is too expensive for most local candidates. Radio and television managers offer editorials on local issues but do not appear to have great influence.

Organized Labor

Probably no event in the present century is likely to have so great an effect upon the future pattern of urban government as the coming to power of organized labor. Especially important as a long-range factor was the rise after 1937 of the Congress of Industrial Organizations (CIO) with its organization of the unskilled and semiskilled workers and its fresh supply of imaginative, able, and ambitious leaders. By the mid-1970s, about one-fourth of the American labor force held union membership. The full effect of organized labor as a political-action group has never been felt at the local level because labor leaders have preferred to devote their resources to the election of governors and members of the two houses of Congress. Labor-union leadership and membership, furthermore, is less united on local issues than it is on those at the state and national levels. Ethnic and racial jealousies and status strivings are most clearly manifested at the local level and sometimes involve loyalties stronger than those of the union. Although the leaders deliver the votes quite well on national, and even state, matters where they can convince members that they have a real and immediate stake, there has been less success in convincing them that local politics is of equal importance to the labor movement. Many union members are home buyers, and the impact of the property tax upon themselves is obvious and painful. (At state and national levels the relationship between payments and benefits is generally more obscure.)

It is still true that "unions have a long way to go before they achieve a community position equal to that of older and better established groups."[9] To date, they have not been willing to devote a major share of their political-action

[8] Morris Janowitz, *The Community Press in an Urban Setting,* The Free Press of Glencoe, New York, 1952.

[9] For a case study of one union local (of the United Steelworkers) in one city (probably Gary), see Joel Seidman, Jack London, and Bernard Karsh, "Political Consciousness of a Local Union," *Public Opinion Quarterly,* 15:692–702, Winter, 1952. The quotation is from this study. See also William Form, "Organized Labor's Place in the Community Power Structure," *Industrial and Labor Relations Review,* 12:526–539, July, 1959.

funds to the local level. In addition, labor efforts to win local elections are quickly criticized as "partisan" and "aimed at the advantage of a small minority" in the conservative press. This makes the task the more difficult.

Labor groups have always had some effect upon urban politics in the largest cities, but the coming of the CIO with its definite social consciousness made a great difference. The older craft unions of the AFL were interested primarily in what is called "business unionism"—the highest possible wages, best possible working conditions, shortest possible hours. Few of them had developed a social ideology. The AFL sought essentially to achieve a monopoly of skilled labor and to make its people better and more prosperous members of the middle class. The CIO, on the other hand, sought to inculcate into its members the idea that the working class has a set of interests to pursue that are different from those of the business-oriented middle class. It was therefore to be expected that they would seek to challenge the business community for control of city government. After the merger of the two great unions into the AFL-CIO in 1955 and the establishment of a political arm—the Committee on Political Education (COPE)—the CIO ideology of political action came to dominate the new organization, and vigorous action in municipal politics was made a part of its program.

The Goals of Labor Organized labor has a whole list of wants it desires from government, and a large number of them result in a conflict with other interest groups. Labor expects that the many services it demands be financed on an ability-to-pay theory of taxation, rather than on a benefit theory. This brings labor into conflict with those who are expected to foot the bill. Labor is more interested in services than in the tax rate. Many workers do feel that the burden of the general property tax is of no concern to them because they do not own homes. This assumption is fallacious, since renters pay the property tax as part of their rent. It does, however, affect their attitude.

The considerable increase in the rate of ownership of homes by members of the working classes since the end of World War II, as a result of liberal financing provisions of the Veterans Administration and the Federal Housing Authority, is likely to change their attitude in time. Many workers, especially in the skilled trades, have today become members of a new working class of suburbanites quite different from the traditional. They are sometimes called the "blue-collar" class. Though these people tend to be Democratic in state and national politics, they are likely to assume the conservative characteristics of homeowners in the nonpartisan politics at the local level. Some students of politics see such an emerging "hard-hat," blue-collar constituency as exerting great future influence.

Labor is also interested in such things as a subsidized public transportation system—in contrast to the business person's views on a pay-as-you-ride system, preferably privately owned. It wants public housing with low rentals, perhaps an FEPC ordinance (although some of its members will oppose the leadership on this), and high wages for city employees, all of which are likely to run it into various conflicts with business, good-government, and other middle-class groups. Labor leaders also want to control the city administration, if possible, partly in order to ensure a sympathetic police force in the event of strikes or other labor disturbances. They well remember the time, not long ago, when the local police department was often considered available to any manufacturer for strikebreaking purposes.

The flight to the suburbs, led by members of the middle class, is changing the position of organized labor in core cities. In a larger and larger number of cities, labor will elect mayors and a majority of the council in future years; in many it already does so. Labor is also serving a special function as the social institution that is providing members of various ethnic groups with a base for political action. In the Ohio steel-manufacturing city of Lorain, for example, the multiplicity of ethnic groups had long produced mutual jealousy and suspicion, which prevented effective political action. As a result, middle-class residents controlled the town, though they were a small minority. After 1937 and the unionization of the steel mills, the United Steelworkers of America succeeded in bringing the ethnic groups together by superimposing a sense of labor identity upon the ethnic sense that had long prevailed. The result was political control of the community by the combined groups.[10]

Municipal Employees

Employees themselves are organized into pressure groups and can exert influence on the administration and council for matters that interest them, particularly wages, hours, and conditions of labor. Because many employees belong to labor unions that have close association with the other AFL-CIO unions of the city, they are in a position to bring up reinforcements from these other unions at important times.

Municipal unions have grown rapidly since about 1960. They have enjoyed support from political leaders at the state level, who find local-government employees an important source of potential votes. Often a governor or legislators can freely support unionizations or wage increases locally, knowing that the local governing body will have to find the money to pay for them.

During the rapid monetary inflation of the 1970s, unions gained many converts and increased their militancy. Strikes among teachers, police, and fire fighters became much more common than they had ever been before. Police, who had been very active politically in the days of bosses and machines, returned to the political wars with strikes (some of them clearly illegal), referendum proposals, and (through their unions) candidate support. Other groups followed this same pattern.

City employees may also be members of professional organizations such as the International City Management Association, the Civil Service Assembly of the United States and Canada, and the American Society of Municipal Engineers. Purely local unions also commonly exist, either because they are old, respected, and powerful, or because unions with national affiliations are discour-

[10] James B. McKee, "Status and Power in the Industrial Community," *American Journal of Sociology,* 58:364–370, January, 1953. See also, Richard Krickus, *Pursuing the American Dream,* Indiana University Press, Bloomington, 1976.

aged by local public policy. Examples include the Milwaukee Government Service League and the Detroit Police Officers' Association. These groups occasionally compete when new groups of employees begin to organize. Unionization has advanced particularly rapidly among school teachers where competition between the NEA (National Education Association), a professional group, and AFT (American Federation of Teachers), affiliated with the AFL-CIO, has been intense in some communities.

In some cities, the municipal employees band together for political action, seeking to eliminate from the council members who will not support their demands regarding wages, hours, and conditions of labor. If they have the aid of the regular labor unions of the city, and if other organized political activity is not strong, municipal-employee unions may even succeed in electing a slate of councilors that constitutes a majority of the council.[11]

The Politics of Equality

Although there is no logic from a theoretical standpoint in having democratic representation on the basis of racial or ethnic groups and no particular reason why such groups should be separated from one another in such a manner as to require them to act as interest groups, such is nonetheless the case. Minority groups find that they are beleaguered and feel the need to protect themselves from further encroachment by an unsympathetic dominant group in society.

A study that examined municipal elections in Newark and compared these nonpartisan elections with the partisan elections for the state legislature found that party identification was unimportant to the typical voters as they considered candidates for office. Ethnic affiliation, on the other hand, was extremely important; hence, social cleavages were accentuated by the viewpoints of the voters. This was, of course, in contrast to the goal of municipal reformers who, by the adoption of the nonpartisan ballot, hoped to eliminate party, ethnic, and class considerations in municipal elections.[12]

Minority groups are interested in such things as FEPC, the protection of their equal right to civil service jobs, equal police protection and treatment, and a fair share of housing. Minorities often vote in blocs in political campaigns, resulting in such situations as that in New York where the mayor, the controller, and the president of the council must always be of different ethnic or racial groups. For a well-balanced city-wide ticket, these positions must be apportioned with no more than one each to an Italian, an Irishman, a Jew, or a black. A similar recognition of political realities may be found in many cities where identifiable groups are important.

For pressure purposes, many organizations represent these people. Blacks, for example, may be represented at council hearings by the National Association for the Advancement of Colored People as well as by the local Urban League.

[11] For one example, see city "Delta" in Oliver P. Williams and Charles R. Adrian, *Four Cities,* University of Pennsylvania Press, Philadelphia, 1963.

[12] Gerard Pomper, "Ethnic and Group Voting in Nonpartisan Municipal Elections," *Public Opinion Quarterly,* 30:79–87, Spring, 1966.

The NAACP has been more active politically than has the League, which has been interested mainly in making more jobs, more economic opportunities, available to blacks. Both are potent organizations, especially in large cities, even though they are now considered by many blacks to reflect an old-fashioned approach. Many blacks now respond to an appeal quite different from that of these groups.

The effectiveness of the new type of leadership is reflected in the way that it has made a subculture, suffering under a tradition almost totally lacking in a concept of political participation, suddenly and significantly aware of the identity of white-supremacy candidates as against those who are more favorably disposed toward black interests. Black sophistication in politics is growing both in the South and in the Northern industrial cities where, in earlier years, blacks were often pawns completely manipulated by the adroit politician and almost totally without their own political leadership.

Some research[13] seems to indicate that attitudes toward direct black participation in the political process are not merely a function of economic concern, but may vary according to different cultural values within the same economic framework. These values, of course, tend to change with time. This offers the possibility that Southern values which seemingly have been changing over recent decades may, through further movement in the direction of permissiveness and tolerance, change enough to permit the development of a genuine universal system of suffrage in the relatively near future.

In every community that has more than a few blacks, a black leadership and power pattern develops, just as is the case in cities which continue to have identifiable ethnic groups. In a study of one Southern city, blacks rated themselves and were rated by others along a radical-conservative continuum. Black leaders, as rated by other black leaders, were predominantly liberal in their views on public policy questions. There were more conservatives than radicals, but the conservatives, although still considered powerful, were no longer important in decision making. Relative to the issue of school desegregation, liberal leaders were found to predominate by a 6 to 1 ratio over conservatives, and by 3 to 1 over moderates. The most powerful black leaders, in the view of both minority leaders and the general citizenry, were rated as liberals and were active in all phases of desegregation.[14] (See Table 4-1.)

The pattern of black leadership has changed greatly since about 1950:[15]

> Conservatives are no longer powerful leaders in Crescent City. In the past these compromise leaders often held their positions because they were acceptable to the white community. They believed that the interests of the Negro could best be served by adjusting to the authority of the whites. Some may have feared reprisals if they failed to cooperate with white leaders in controlling the minority community.

[13] See John H. Fenton and Kenneth N. Vines, "Negro Registration in Louisiana," *American Political Science Review,* 51:704–713, September, 1957.

[14] M. Elaine Burgess, *Negro Leadership in a Southern City,* The University of North Carolina Press, Chapel Hill, N.C., 1962, chap. 7.

[15] *Ibid.,* pp. 180–181.

> They were acceptable to other Negroes, not only because accommodation was regarded as the most practical policy, but because they also had prestige in their own right within the Negro social structure. This type of race leader was powerful in Crescent City through the 1930s and early 1940s. . . .
>
> Today the suggestion that a Negro is unduly susceptible to white influence has meant loss of power. . . .
>
> Conservative leaders still remain the most acceptable to a segment of Crescent City's white leadership. By and large, however, the white leaders by-pass the conservative leader, for they know he no longer wields power in the Negro community.

In a period of rapid economic, political, and social change, blacks are badly divided concerning the question of desirable techniques. Older black leaders fear that irresponsible individuals may gain power and thus weaken the entire movement toward equality of opportunity and status. Younger blacks fear that the movement may lose its militant spirit. Similarly, there is no agreement on tactics. Younger activists prefer use of the economic boycott and the sit-in; older, more conservative blacks prefer private negotiations, the traditional approach to relations with the dominant whites.[16] Chicanos in the Southwest and Puerto Ricans in New York and, to a lesser extent, elsewhere face the same kinds of problems as do blacks. Other permanent ethnic groups do, too.

In the 1970s, the U.S. Department of Health, Education, and Welfare, relying upon general authorization by civil rights acts, called upon local governments to establish "affirmative action" plans, a euphemism for programs to increase the hiring and promotion rates of persons of certain minority groups and of women. The ultimate effects of these plans remain unknown. They seem certain to have increased the political awareness of the pressures to hire and promote more persons who fall within the "affirmative action" categories. Women's groups seemed to be best organized to present their demand. Minority groups also moved to take advantage of the new public awareness in the 1970s.[17]

[16] Jack L. Walker, "Protest and Negotiation," *Midwest Journal of Political Science,* 7:99–124, May, 1963.

[17] *The Municipal Year Book, 1975,* International City Management Association, Washington, 1975, p. 164, shows employees by sex, minority grouping, and occupation.

TABLE 4-1. Race-leader Peer-group Classification

Type of Leader	Radical Percent	Liberal Percent	Moderate Percent	Conservative Percent
Power nominees*	6.5	54.8	19.4	19.3
Power leaders*	9.1	72.7	18.2	

* Power nominees were persons believed by three groups of informants to be the most powerful or influential. Power leaders were those individuals who actually played the most active role in community issues.

Source: M. Elaine Burgess, *Negro Leadership in a Southern City,* The University of North Carolina Press, Chapel Hill, N.C., 1962, p. 178.

Religious Groups

Virtually all religious and church-related organizations represent political forces. Perhaps the only exception would be those sects that are opposed to political action. Since a religion—any religion—is based upon some kind of faith or set of beliefs, it is to be expected that political and social questions will be interpreted in the light of these moral value scales and viewpoints taken in accord with them.

In almost any important councilmanic hearing, ministers, priests, rabbis, or leaders of religious lay groups will be found testifying for their members. Because Catholics tend to be concentrated in cities and because the Church is disciplined and dogmatic, its views are often particularly powerful and effective. The Church has dozens of lay organizations that act as pressure groups. Protestants are less well organized, but may be equally active, especially through local ministerial associations. Methodist groups may work for a policy of restricting the number of retail liquor permits; Quakers may be interested in the humane treatment of prisoners in the local workhouse; a group of ministers may lobby for a human rights commission.

Ministerial associations may be interested in matters related to public health, welfare, housing, and other matters. They are especially likely to be concerned with public policies relative to vice, racetracks, liquor sales, and juvenile delinquency. In Underwood's "Paper City," Catholic priests were concerned about policies that affected the parochial schools, religious practices in public schools, public health clinics if they provided birth-control information, gambling, and problems related to alcoholism. The politicians, he found, "tend to look upon either Roman Catholic or Protestant moral interests chiefly as those of one more organized group to be anticipated, managed, and met."[18]

Veterans

After each war, veterans—at least many of them—organize themselves into interest groups. They are particularly powerful because, unlike ordinary groups, they have no organized opposition, no counterpressure group. It is not easy for a politician or another interest group to oppose the interests and demands of a well-known veterans' group. In local politics, returned servicemen are interested in such things as tax exemptions, civil service preferences on job certification, "patriotism," taxicab licensing, liquor permits for their clubhouses, and all other types of licensing, with an eye toward privileges for veterans.

The largest and most powerful veterans' groups on the local as well as the national scene are the American Legion and the Veterans of Foreign Wars, both of which have members who served in the two world wars and in the Korean and Vietnamese conflicts. Products of World War II, such as the Amvets and the AVC, are smaller and less powerful. There are also groups that represent two special interests simultaneously, such as the Catholic War Veterans and the Jewish War Veterans.

[18] For more on churches and local politics, see Kenneth W. Underwood, *Protestant and Catholic,* Beacon Press, Boston, 1957, especially chaps. 18–20. Quotation is from pp. 319–320.

Low-Income Groups and Protest

Until the 1960s, no efforts were made to politicize large-city impoverished groups as such. Federal administrators then began seeking to activate the poor through participation in poverty-board elections, in keeping with requirements of federal "antipoverty" legislation, much of which was later eliminated or curtailed.[19] Their efforts were not notably successful, with sometimes less than 3 percent of the potential voters participating. Social workers and other professionals have, with perhaps greater success, worked with such groups. Saul Alinsky and his Industrial Areas Foundation developed specific techniques for organizing in low-income areas.[20]

The problem of organizing the poor is complicated first by their lack of political resources such as wealth, political information, organizational skills, or leadership experience.[21] Their major resource is in effect threats of violent action or of peaceful disruption. Thus instead of going through the conventional channels of influence, they may have a greater probability of influencing public officials through militant protest activity, including rioting, sit-ins, "trashing," or picketing. In doing this successfully, the leaders of low-income groups must concentrate on three constituencies.

Their first constituency is the low-income citizenry itself. We have already noted the problems of mobilizing and keeping a group together. These problems are maximized when individual members see the costs and risks of participation as high and the probability of success low. This is the case for low-income citizens, for they must come to meetings in their limited free time. They lose work time to engage in protest activities and sometimes may risk losing their jobs as well. Those who have no jobs but are chronically on public welfare may not have a means of transportation to attend meetings. For many low-income persons the information costs merely of learning about groups or activities that are designed for their benefit may be too high for them to learn about them or to find out if participation seems worthwhile. They have few funds for even small group expenditures. Finally they have generally experienced failure in most other activities and have come to expect it to be the result of all activity.

The other constituencies are the communications media, and other groups within the community who, out of sympathy (especially the upper-middle class) or to end protests, may act on behalf of the low-income citizens. Placating and managing each of these three constituencies (including the public officials) involves the leader in tensions and unresolvable conflicts. Michael Lipsky concludes that the positive results of protest activity are likely to be some symbolic action by officials rather than material rewards that low-income citizens can directly experience. Such symbolication is taken to satisfy the third parties moti-

[19] See below on "Citizen Participation," pp. 121–123.

[20] Saul D. Alinsky, *Reveille for Radicals,* The University of Chicago Press, Chicago, 1945, is the story of one of the earliest and best-known poverty workers. See also Charles Silberman, *Crisis of Black and White,* Vintage Books, Random House, Inc., New York, 1964, chap. 10.

[21] See especially Michael Lipsky, "Protest as a Political Resource," *American Political Science Review,* 62:1144–1158, December, 1968.

vated on behalf of low-income groups and because basic changes require large-scale costs for the community. The negative results of symbolic payoffs are disillusionment by low-income persons and their reaching the conclusion that the benefits of protest are not worth the cost. The most rational course for individuals such as themselves, they may decide, is to lapse into political apathy or perhaps criminal activity.

Given symbolic responses that result in few perceived changes, low-income groups are also likely to turn from militant to moderate political leaders and from public to private goals. They will settle for leaders and acts that at the very best promise only small incremental gains. The result overall is that low-income persons are likely to be unrepresented or poorly represented in the local group struggle, despite bootstrap organizing.

COMMUNITY CONFLICT[22]

Controversy occasionally divides a community so sharply that its citizens behave like two warring factions in open conflict. Groups within the community are pressured by contestants to join one side or the other on an emotionally charged issue, and bitterness permeates much of the decision-making process. In recent years, such conflicts have developed over any number of events: civil rights (school integration, restaurant sit-ins, and other demonstrations, or a riot over the movement of a black family into a previously all-white neighborhood); the conduct of the school system; a change in zoning practices; the status of the city manager; charges of communism, generally directed at libraries or schools; a strike, or threat of one, in a local industry. A long series of smoldering bad feelings may suddenly burst aflame, as when permanent residents of a resort community vent their dislike of summer transients. Most commonly a feeling of suspicion, resentment, or frustration precedes the conflict. Citizens already feel some degree of discontent. This discontent need not be over local issues. The conduct of the war in Vietnam may be as significant as the threat of large-scale local apartment building. The issue that erupts is generally one that persons can see as symbolic of a radical change in the life-style of the community. Its symbolic nature makes it one to which extremist groups of the right or left are readily attracted.

Serious and prolonged conflicts most commonly occur in small- or medium-sized cities or suburbs; few sweep big cities, though, as the Watts riots indicated, they may occur in a section of the metropolis. It appears that a relatively high level of community identification is necessary. Persons must feel deeply and be willing to act passionately for an issue to catch fire. In suburbia, particularly, conditions are often ideal for such strife, because many residents hold images of the ideal community. When one set of images clashes with another, conflict may become serious.

The way a community handles a traumatic struggle seems to affect its han-

[22] James Coleman, *Community Conflict,* The Free Press of Glencoe, New York, 1957.

dling of future controversy. In some cities, the conflict leaves the community divided into antagonistic groups for many years, and every new controversy is likely to follow the old cleavage lines. In other cities, the clash may have been resolved by a massive show of force, and there is evidence that other controversies that follow are handled the same way. Likewise, those communities that resolve their conflict by discussion, compromise, and adjustments are likely to handle other conflicts the same way. Communities thus seem to create patterns of handling frustrations, just as individuals do.

Community conflicts often follow similar patterns. An event touches the lives of groups of citizens in different ways. It poses an issue which citizens see as potentially resolvable at the community level if some community action is taken. It may well be a national issue. (One community, for example, decided to bar all books mentioning the Communist leader Lenin from its library.) The kinds of cleavages that form within the community are naturally related to the kind of battle lines that potentially exist. The issue may divide along economic, racial, ethnic, or religious group lines, or simply pit old against new residents; or subdivision against rural-life-style residents. A public housing or private development in an older neighborhood is capable of creating a sharp feeling of cleavage.

In a number of cases, conflict has been touched off by outsiders who either visit the community, as did civil rights and some anti-civil rights demonstrators, or who write widely circulated publications which activate local residents. The latter technique has been widely used by radical right groups. Where city or school administrators have few contacts with citizens or where a segment of the community is alienated from what they see as "the establishment," an issue can be easily found. At the beginning, the sides are likely to be composed of a small group of activists against those who defend the status quo, with the large majority of the community neutral and largely uninterested in getting involved. When suspicion among groups or general feelings of frustration already exist, the conflict can most easily spread. If it does, specific issues give way to general ones, new and different issues are introduced, and disagreement changes to antagonism. Associations between factions wither and, within factions, intensify. New leaders emerge, many of whom have only tenuous ties to the community. Lack of previous community involvement is an advantage at this stage since it permits greater freedom of action. These leaders often try to intensify the battle, drive out moderates, and draw established organizations to their side. As the controversy proceeds, more dependence is placed on word-of-mouth communication, and an insatiable demand for news develops. Rumors and the air of conspiracy abound (for example, the rumors of police beatings of blacks or black killings of whites during ghetto riots).

The way the conflict is resolved depends on the political and social arrangements that previously existed. A tradition of tolerance of diverse views may permit a community to ride out the issue. Individuals tend to respond in terms of their previous group associations, but group-association leaders frequently want to resolve the difficulty with compromise, lest the conflict tear apart their groups, for group memberships often overlap. Thus, the leaders of a church group with both strikers and nonstrikers in its membership will attempt to dampen open conflict and seek compromise in a labor-management clash. Those who least have attachments to community groups are most likely to want to release aggressions, often through violent action. Prestigeful groups and persons become important in determining the course of the conflict at this stage.

Closing Statement

Struggles like those described above are relatively rare in most communities. More generally, an occasional controversy occurs, but less than one-quarter of the citizens become very intimately involved, and differences are settled by some form of compromise. For most communities, it appears that officials make most decisions with the acquiescence of the large body of citizens. Desires of the more important interest groupings are anticipated; lobbying tends to occur on minor points, such as zoning changes; and the policy that results is a blend of administrative and political points of view. Political parties are weak or absent. The same description might fit the politics of larger cities, except that parties and interest groupings are frequently better organized and more active, though ordinary citizens are themselves, if anything, less active.

SELECTED READINGS

Alinsky, Saul: *Reveille for Radicals,* The University of Chicago Press, Chicago, 1945.

Banfield, Edward C.: *Big City Politics,* Random House, Inc., New York, 1965. (A study of many of the nation's largest cities.)

Coleman, James: *Community Conflict,* The Free Press of Glencoe, New York, 1957. (A monograph of 26 pages that is incisive in its analysis.)

Crain, Robert, and others: *The Politics of Community Conflict, The Fluoridation Decision,* The Bobbs-Merrill Company, Inc., Indianapolis, 1969.

Holtzman, Abraham: *Interest Groups and Lobbying,* The Macmillan Company, New York, 1966.

Lipsky, Michael: *Protest in City Politics, Rent Strikes, Housing and the Power of the Poor,* Rand McNally & Company, Chicago, 1970.

Lowi, Theodore J.: *At the Pleasure of the Mayor,* The Free Press of Glencoe, New York, 1964. (The patronage decisions of the mayor of New York are influenced both by clients directly and by interest groups.)

Olson, Mancur: *The Logic of Collective Action,* Harvard University Press, Cambridge, Mass., 1965. (An economist views interest-group behavior.)

Pennock, J. Roland, and John Chapman (eds.): *Voluntary Associations,* Atherton Press, Inc., New York, 1969.

Rogers, David: *The Management of Big Cities,* Sage Publications, Inc., Beverly Hills, Calif., 1971. (Looks at political power, intergovernmental relations, and, especially, urban interest groups as they affect policy.)

Salisbury, Robert H. (ed.): *Interest Group Politics in America,* Harper & Row, Publishers, Incorporated, New York, 1970.

Sayre, Wallace S., and Herbert Kaufman: *Governing New York City,* Russell Sage Foundation, New York, 1960. (An analysis of the groups that are important in New York policy making.)

Truman, David B.: *The Governmental Process,* Alfred A. Knopf, Inc., New York, 1951. (The principal work on interest-group theory.)

Zisk, Betty H.: *Local Interest Politics: A One-way Street,* The Bobbs-Merrill Company, Inc., Indianapolis, 1973. (The relationship of lobbyists to council members in the San Francisco Bay area.)

Chapter 5

Voters and Elections

Probably the simplest, most common, and ultimately most important *direct* contact typical citizens have with their city or village takes place when they step into the booth and exercise their privilege of voting. Unlike voting in national-government elections, the local suffrage offers a chance to make a choice for many offices (in most cities), in addition to numerous proposed charter amendments, bond issues, and referred and initiated municipal ordinances.

THE ELECTORATE

Who Is Eligible?

Time was when more persons were eligible to vote in state than in municipal contests. As a matter of fact, some American cities in the colonial period were "close corporations" where no one at all, not even the wealthiest enjoyed the suffrage. Rhode Island required ownership of some property in order to vote in municipal elections until 1928, even though there was no such requirement in state elections.

Today, with but a few exceptions, the right to vote in American municipal elections is determined by eligibility to participate in state elections. The usual prerequisites include American citizenship, a minimum age of eighteen, a minimum period of residence in the state, county, and polling district, and registration. Other requirements are sometimes added.

Special Local Requirements

During the Great Depression, Arizona, Michigan, Montana, Nevada, Texas, and Utah provided that only property-tax payers could vote on questions of direct appropriation of public money or the issuance of bonds. By property-tax payers are meant property owners, of course. Contrary to popular misunderstanding, a renter pays just as much in property taxes as an owner, although it is hidden in the rent. There may well be a *psychological* difference between owner and renter when it comes to taxation, but there is no *economic* difference. One study indicated that the Michigan law prevented more than one-half of the Detroit electorate from voting on such issues during the Great Depression.[1] A very few states make, or are constitutionally permitted to make, an actual distinction between eligibility for municipal, as against general, elections. But all these provisions are unusual, are seldom resorted to, and are far off the course being steered by contemporary democratic theory. The almost universal rule is that persons who are eligible to vote in national and state elections may also vote in municipal elections.

VOTING AND NONVOTING

Political scientists have considerable information as to the kinds of people who vote, those who do not, and why they do not. Reasonably confident generalizations can be made.

Apathy on Election Day

In comparison with the people of such democracies as Great Britain and the Scandinavian countries, Americans do not feel any overwhelming need to vote. Only about one-third of the eligible voters are in the habit of going to the polls regularly. The turnout for state elections is ordinarily much smaller than that when the nation chooses a chief executive, and local elections usually produce the smallest of all. It is not uncommon for the vote in municipal elections to drop to less than one-fourth of the qualified voters. Even the New England town meeting does not appear to inspire citizens to participation. In one study, a town meeting was analyzed in which 700 citizens were qualified to take part. Only 110 did so, a participation figure of 15.7 percent.[2]

The extent of voting varies in different sections of the country, and even between different governmental units in the same section. Each community has its own tradition of participation or nonparticipation. Sometimes a matter of particular interest will bring out a larger vote for a local election than was the

[1] Donald S. Hecock and Harry A. Trevelyan, *Detroit Voters and Recent Elections,* Detroit Bureau of Municipal Research, Detroit, Mich., 1938.

[2] From an article by Andrew Nuquist, reported in Roscoe C. Martin, *Grass Roots,* University of Alabama Press, University, Ala., 1957, pp 60–61.

case in the preceding presidential vote. The degree to which the electorate is organized, or to which organized groups are active in campaigns, influences the size of the turnout. In almost all jurisdictions and at all levels of government, the primary election is of considerably less interest than the general election. (Exceptions are to be found in one-party areas.)

One voter-participation study found that in the average city of Los Angeles County between 1935 and 1952, voter turnout at the average state and national election amounted to 77.2 percent of the registered voters. For the average municipal election, however, the figure was only 41.1 percent of those registered.[3]

The study indicated that participation did *not* vary inversely with the size of the municipality. The city of Los Angeles ranked twenty-sixth out of the forty-five cities in local elections but ranked lower in state and national contests. Tiny Avalon had a very good record, but San Marino, only slightly larger, had the poorest of all records in local elections. Some cities had good records in state and national elections but poor ones in local elections, and vice versa.

The study found that there was no correlation between distance from the core city and amount of voter participation. It was found, however, that predominantly Republican cities had better voting records than did those that were predominantly Democratic. (The municipal elections themselves are nonpartisan in California.) But wealthy communities did not necessarily have good records in *local* elections. Beverly Hills, for example, had next to the poorest record.

Among the important conclusions of the study were these:[4]

> **1** . . . People tend to vote *against* candidates and propositions rather than for them. . . . People attend city council meetings more often to protest than to affirm some proposed action.
>
> **2** . . . Voter turnout is dependent upon the degree of *opposition* that can be generated in the minds of voters.
>
> **3** . . . There is a sizable number of citizens who consistently participate in state and national elections, but *never vote* in municipal elections.
>
> **4** . . . Percentages of the registered electorates remain fairly *constant* in each city for almost all municipal elections. This may be contrasted with the somewhat more erratic percentages found in voting for state and nation offices. . . . *There is a small core of citizens in each city who sustain municipal government.*

Apathy and the Duty to Participate

Although the doctrine of grass-roots democracy calls for vigorously active participation in the political process and in the assumption of public office as a duty to the community, the fact is that in America there is frequently a great deal of difficulty in getting public positions filled. Not only may no competition exist for the jobs, but sometimes no one will even allow himself or herself to be drafted.

The small town, the suburb, and the school district often present scenes, not of strident conflict, but of citizens urging other citizens to accept jobs that need

[3] L. W. O'Rourke, *Voting Behavior in the Forty-five Cities of Los Angeles County,* Bureau of Governmental Research, University of California, Los Angeles, 1953.

[4] *Ibid.,* chap. 2. Italics added.

to be done. These are positions that carry considerable prestige but involve the budgeting of much of what would otherwise be leisure time for the individual.[5]

In the case of bond-issue referendums, genuine disagreement may be generated, and hence more interest, but even when money is involved, the community may be essentially agreed as to how it should be used. The principal reason for apathy in municipal elections, in fact, is likely to be a pervasive consensus; that is, there may be widespread agreement in the community as to the kinds of persons who are wanted in public office, as to expenditure levels, and as to public policies. Under such circumstances, little incentive exists for any but the most conscientious voter or the chronic dissenter to go to the polls.

Many other reasons are to be found, of course, for the absence of a contest in a local election, and hence for low interest levels. Some of them include:

1 Incumbents are sometimes so popular that other potential candidates have little or no chance to unseat them. They are hence unopposed.

2 In strongly one-party cities with partisan elections, there may be a contest in the primary election of the major party, but the second party can expect to have difficulty in getting candidates to run.

3 The formal political process may not be the effective process of decision making. That is, the important decisions affecting the community may be made outside of government, and public offices are therefore of little importance in the view of the ordinary citizen. A long-standing tradition in America advocates keeping as many issues as possible "out of politics," because the political process is not trusted. Furthermore, community leaders may prefer to negotiate privately among the various interests centering around a controversy, keeping control out of public officials' hands—and outside the reach of the voter. Thus business leaders may agree among themselves on the amount of money to be devoted to port development and present a packaged plan to the council for its ratification. Land-use policies may be controlled in a similar way.

4 The ruling political group may be so strong (as in Chicago over many decades) that no one thinks it worthwhile to oppose it.

Lack of competition for office reduces the importance of both the primary election or other nominating device and the final election. Absence of genuine conflict contributes to apathy. Where there is little to be decided, most voters consider it rational to stay away from the polls.

Futility and Nonvoting

Even so, we may ask why voter turnout is so low. Why should 28 percent of the interviewees in a representative sample in the 1952 presidential campaign—one in which interest was generally regarded as having been high by American standards—be willing to state openly that they were "not much interested" in the contest?[6] Why should 32 percent of those interviewed say that it would make no

[5] See Martin, *op. cit.*, pp. 60–62.

[6] Angus Campbell and others, *The Voter Decides*, Harper & Row, Publishers, Incorporated, 1954, p. 34.

difference whether the Democrats or Republicans won the election and another 40 percent think it would make only a small difference?[7]

Part of the answer seems to be furnished by a study made in Detroit[8] A representative sample of persons was asked these questions: Do you feel that there is anything you can do to improve the way the city is run? What do you feel you can do? *More than one-half the people declared that they can do nothing.* One-third could suggest only voting. Only one person in twelve believed that one could exert influence by means of personal criticism or by joining in group action.

In another study, one-third of the members of the United Automobile Workers agreed that "people like me don't have any say about government does."[9] These sentiments were especially strong among persons who had feelings of estrangement from society, or feelings of personal futility, or who were generally pessimistic. Persons who felt they could not influence governmental policy also, not surprisingly, tended to be nonvoters. On an authoritarian-democratic scale, they tended more toward the authoritarian position in personal values. A similar attitude of futility was to be found before the 1945 election in the city of New York when one-third of those eligible to vote told pollster Elmo Roper that "no matter which of the candidates is elected, the city will be run about the same."[10] Similar findings have been reported in Philadelphia and Boston.[11] In the latter city, the favorite in the 1959 mayoralty election apparently was defeated because he was perceived by many voters as the leader of a group of powerful politicians, business leaders, and others who wanted to run the city in their own interest. This reaction "was particularly strong because many voters in Boston felt politically powerless."[12] His opponent won, not for the positive qualities in his personality, record of experience, or campaign promises, but because people wanted to vote *against* the favorite. Furthermore, of those who helped elect John F. Collins as mayor, 57 percent thought he would be "no better than his opponent." They could only *hope* that he would come closer to the wanted image. Furthermore, they did not expect Collins's policies to differ fundamentally from those of the man he defeated.

They may have been quite right. Elections do not usually decide issues in America; the interaction of interest groups and their leaders does that, and the election is only one part—perhaps a relatively minor part—of the political process.

[7] *Ibid.,* p. 38.

[8] Arthur Kornhauser, *Attitudes of Detroit People toward Detroit,* Wayne State University Press, Detroit, Mich., 1952, p. 28.

[9] Arthur Kornhauser, H. L. Sheppard, and A. J. Mayer, *When Labor Votes,* University Books, Inc., New York, 1956, pp. 198–200.

[10] Elmo Roper, "New York Elects O'Dwyer," *Public Opinion Quarterly,* 10:53–56, Spring, 1946. For a later study reporting similar findings, see the impressionistic reporting in F. J. Cook and Gene Gleason, "The Shame of New York," *The Nation,* Oct. 31, 1959, entire issue.

[11] James Reichley, *The Art of Government: Reform and Organization Politics in Philadelphia.* The Fund for the Republic, New York, 1958: Murray B. Levin, *The Alienated Voter: Politics in Boston,* Holt, Rinehart and Winston, Inc., New York, 1960.

[12] Levin, *op. cit.,* p. 28.

Just how serious is our high percentage of nonvoting anyway? The chances are that its dangers have been greatly exaggerated. Although feelings of voter "alienation"—of frustration and impotence—are reported in studies of large-city politics, these feelings seem much less common in middle-sized cities. Furthermore, even in large cities, the cynicism reported may be more of a culturally expected response—traditionally almost everybody damns the politics of large cities—than of an actual abandonment of faith in a democracy. The person who says "both candidates were no good" or "voting was a waste of time" may also give strong support for political action through interest groups, such as the union, trade association, neighborhood improvement association, or church. Elections may leave individuals unmoved, but they may see the interaction of groups in lobbying rather than elections as the key to policy making. An elaborate study of New York City politics found that "anyone can fight city hall," that most groups do, and that many are very successful.[13]

Most people who stay away from the polls do so deliberately and by their own choice. They are not interested, and they feel that voting in the particular instance will avail them nothing. Except where cynicism is pervasive, the important question is not whether people *do* vote but rather whether they *may* vote if they so choose. Studies made of why people do not vote show that, outside of illness or a broken fan belt on the way to the voting booth, most people stay home because of lack of interest. To most people, choice of candidates is of marginal interest. When something they consider to be truly important comes up, they will vote. (Of course, with the typically low information levels of voters, they may seriously underestimate the significance of many political events and issues.) Americans are more interested in voting against candidates than for them.[14] They become excited about elections when they are determined to register a protest. The ballot box is the safety valve of democracy.

Political Participation

Not only do a large number of Americans not vote in elections, and particularly state and local elections, but another huge bloc of citizens does nothing politically except vote. In the 1952 presidential contest, 27 percent of the eligible voters said that they talked politics and tried to persuade others to vote for their candidates, and 11 percent engaged in some kind of organized party activity. In this category, 3 percent said they did some party work such as stuffing envelopes; 7 percent said they attended political meetings, rallies, picnics, and the like; only 4 percent contributed money or bought fund-raising tickets. Some people, of course, were active in all three types of positive activity; and some did not vote because of ineligibility or for some other reason.[15] In a postelection survey in the same year, 9 percent of the United Automobile Workers' membership claimed (in

[13] Wallace S. Sayre and Herbert Kaufman, *Governing New York City,* Russell Sage Foundation, New York, 1960. Alienation studies to date do not show whether or not the alienated regard all possible roads to political influence as equally blockaded. Indeed, the precise meaning and significance of "alienation" remains unknown.

[14] For more data, see Charles R. Adrian and Charles Press, *The American Political Process,* 2d ed., McGraw-Hill Book Company, New York, 1969, chap. 8.

[15] Campbell and others, *op. cit.,* p. 30.

a sample study) to have been active in the campaign in such things as handing out leaflets, displaying posters, and the like. Another 17 percent said they had talked politics during the campaign, and 73 percent stated that they had done nothing active.[16]

Who Goes to the Polls?

Certain generalizations can be hazarded concerning the qualitative makeup of our voting population. We know that, in terms of percentages, more men vote than do women, more whites vote than do blacks (there is some evidence to indicate that blacks in some Northern urban areas vote in higher percentages than do whites in the same economic category),[17] more people who are property-tax payers vote than do those who are not, and more conservatives vote than do liberals. Except for persons who must stay at home because of the infirmities of old age, people vote in larger proportions as they grow older. Almost twice as many vote at the age of fifty-one as vote at twenty-one. This seems to support the general theory that people do not vote because they theoretically ought to or because they feel it is a duty or a great privilege, but rather they vote when they feel that they have a direct stake in the outcome.

There is a direct relationship between size of income and participation in elections and between amount of education and participation. Since World War II, at least, urbanites have voted in greater proportion than have farmers. The white-collar middle-class votes in greater proportion than do nonunion members of the working class.

It is not known whether these state and national voting-population characteristics generally fit municipal voting, too. One study has addressed itself to the question.[18] In a Midwestern state, it found that the above characteristic patterns generally applied. There was one significant modification: The evidence indicated that, in municipal elections, voter turnout tended to be greatest among the groups that were normally most influential in controlling municipal politics. In three cities where Republican-conservative groups dominated, voters of these interests had the highest voter-turnout habits. In one other city, where Democratic-labor groups controlled, the wards dominated by Democratic labor-union members had the superior voting record. Apparently, the prospects for victory encouraged participation—and helped to ensure it.

All of these patterns affect the balance of forces in the political arena. Apathy or a sense of futility within any given category can have the effect of further weakening the particular interest involved. Each group in society, therefore, has a stake in getting its supporters to the polls, for the vote may be a genuine force in affecting the content of public policy. And, in fact, cities with issue cleavages tend to have higher voter turnout.[19]

[16] Kornhauser, Sheppard, and Mayer, *When Labor Votes,* chap. 1.

[17] *Ibid.,* pp. 49–50.

[18] Oliver P. Williams and Charles R. Adrian, "The Insulation of Local Politics under the Nonpartisan Ballot," *American Political Science Review,* 53:1052–1063, December, 1959.

[19] Robert R. Alford and Eugene C. Lee, "Voting Turnout in American Cities," *Americal Political Science Review,* 62:796–813, September, 1968.

An alert public is probably a prerequisite to progress in the art of democratic government. But cheerful homilies about the obligations of the citizen will not serve to inspire the individual who believes that the outcome of the elections will have no effect upon the conditions of his or her existence. Far more effective than sermons would be serious campaigns to remove the factors that have tended to create a sense of futility in the nonvoter, in other words, to make public officials more accessible and more representative of a cross section of the public.

BALLOTS, NOMINATIONS, AND ELECTIONS

American cities use both partisan and nonpartisan ballots in their municipal elections. The ballot itself may take several forms.

General Parties on the Local Scene

From necessity, the basic strength and organization of a political party is in the local community. Until nonpartisan elections came into use around 1910, municipal election campaigns were invariably conducted by the local party organizations. In that earlier day, many large cities were dominated by well-organized political machines. The minority party was usually less well organized and often had very little chance for success at the polls. In most cities the ward was, and is today, the basic unit of party organization. It was often subdivided into precincts.

Today few political machines remain, and partisan elections are used in only about 40 percent of American cities. Despite the trend away from partisan municipal elections, some political activists argue that such elections are desirable, at least for large cities, because the strength of state and national parties depends upon effective local organization and because public policy today is executed simultaneously on all levels of government. The functions performed by cities are interdependent parts of the whole process of government. Politics and politicians on the local level do not differ fundamentally from their counterparts on the higher levels. Charles A. Beard once asserted that many local problems can be solved only by cooperation with either the state or the national government or both. Today this is surely true of such functions as public health, welfare, highways, safety, housing, and unemployment. Since political parties serve as a liaison between politicians and since a party approach toward a public problem may include plans that require action at all levels of government, partisanship on the local scene may be desirable.[20] Despite the expansion of nonpartisanship and the decomposition of political parties generally, some political scientists still argue for the resuscitation of parties and their use for social reform at all levels of government.[21]

Opponents of partisanship, on the other hand, argue that running a city is not a matter of skillful politics but rather one of efficient business management.

[20] See Charles A. Beard, "Politics and City Government," *National Municipal Review,* 6:201–205, March 1917.

[21] See Willis D. Hawley, *Nonpartisan Elections and the Case for Party Politics,* John Wiley & Sons, Inc., New York, 1973, for such an argument, empirically bolstered.

The editors of the *National Civic Review,* for example, have argued in the following vein:[22]

> There is, after all, no valid reason for national and state parties to be involved and every reason why they should not.
>
> It has been amply demonstrated that, to be effective and self-reliant cities must be emancipated from the tyranny of the national and state political parties. Good citizens who agree on vital local issues should not be divided by blind loyalties that serve only to confuse these issues.
>
> The way to decency and honesty in national as well as local politics is to eliminate parties from the local scene and thus make all voters "independent."

The arguments on both sides are doubtless exaggerated. Many municipal officers elected on a nonpartisan ballot do cooperate successfully with partisan state and national officers. Our general parties have not proved to be very effective in a liaison role, neither do they stand on definite principles or policies.

Local organizations of the national and state parties, on the other hand, are often quite independent of the higher party structure, especially on local questions. The "blind loyalties" of party exist, without doubt, even though party loyalties have declined sharply in the last generation; but this phenomenon may be exaggerated, too. Devoted members of a political party in national and state elections may well vote quite independently in municipal elections. This is especially true if city and general elections are held at different times.

Certainly, party leaders often try to inject state or national issues into local campaigns. Sometimes they are successful, sometimes not. However, it is a fallacy in logic to say that local campaigns in which candidates run as Republicans or Democrats cannot be conducted on local issues. The real question is one of how often any kind of a campaign on any kind of ballot can be conducted on issues.

Whatever the merits of the conflicting arguments presented, there remains one very serious obstacle to the effective use of national parties for city elections: Most of our cities, instead of having two well-balanced parties where one stands ready at all times to take control away from the other, actually have only one strong party. This is highly undesirable, for our political system is conceived of as one of an in-party–out-party relationship. Where one party dominates almost to the total exclusion of the other, there is no effective criticism, there is no control of the party in power, and there is no real responsibility to the electorate. The city with a working two-party system is rare. The pattern in New York, where the Democratic party is almost never defeated except by its own dissidents, or in Philadelphia, where the Republicans once controlled the city government for over eighty consecutive years, is a common one. It is this situation, and not some of the more often-cited objections, that forms the greatest weakness of partisanship in municipal affairs.

Wherever partisan elections are used, however, the political party label provides an important cue to a large number of voters. In a great many cases, the

[22] The Editors, "Revolt of the 'Independents,'" *National Municipal Review* (now *National Civic Review*), 40:564–565, December, 1951.

voter need not be concerned about positions on issues or other types of information. In elections in which one feels a relatively low stake, one simply decides how to vote according to the party label. In the absence of that label, one is forced to find other cues. These may stem from the personality or perceived life-style of the candidate, the recommendations of newspaper editors in whom one has confidence, or the suggestions of opinion leaders, such as chamber of commerce secretaries or labor-union shop stewards.

Two studies have found that party affiliation is more important than class or any other factor in partisan elections and that it remains the best indicator of voting tendencies in nonpartisan elections, although of less importance there than in partisan.[23]

In the South, a somewhat different pattern has been found. In Democratic primary elections, race has been a better indication of voting tendency than party, although for a nonpartisan mayoralty election, these two have been about of equal importance. Party seems to be relatively unimportant in Atlanta, because of the importance of coalitions within the Democratic party. Elections in that city tend to be dominated by an alliance among professional political leaders, the civic elite, and the black leadership.[24] Perhaps in all cities using a nonpartisan ballot but with political parties that now have, or are perceived as having, potentially competitive party systems, a latent partisanship can be found in the voting patterns.[25]

Nonpartisan Elections: The Prevailing Urban Pattern

Early in the twentieth century, many members of the reform movement began to advocate the use of nonpartisan elections. They argued that city government was a matter of efficient business administration and that state and national politics had nothing in common with local politics.

The nonpartisan ballot is used in over 60 percent of the American cities of over 5,000 population. It is especially popular in council-manager cities, over 85 percent of which use it. A nonpartisan ballot does not, of course, in itself eliminate party activity from local politics, though it certainly appears to encourage such a development. To the extent that partisanship is removed, the goals of the reformers of two or three generations ago are achieved.

Many patterns appear to result from a nonpartisan ballot. The principal ones are the following:[26]

[23] Robert Salisbury and Gordon Black, "Classes and Party in Partisan and Nonpartisan Elections," *American Political Science Review,* 57:584–592, September, 1963; and Oliver P. Williams and Charles R. Adrian, *Four Cities,* University of Pennsylvania Press, Philadelphia, 1963, chap. 4.

[24] M. Kent Jennings and Harmon Zeigler, "Class, Party, and Race in Four Types of Elections," *Journal of Politics,* 28:391–407, May, 1966.

[25] Heinz Eulau, Betty H. Zisk, and Kenneth Prewitt, "Latent Partisanship in Nonpartisan Elections," in M. Kent Jennings and Harmon Zeigler (eds.), *The Electoral Process,* Prentice-Hall, Inc., Englewood Cliffs, N.J., 1966, chap. 10.

[26] Charles R. Adrian, "A Typology for Nonpartisan Elections," *Western Political Quarterly,* 12:449–458, June, 1959, and citations.

1 A system of elections in which the only candidates who normally have any chance to win are those supported by a major political party organization. In these cities, a short ballot is used, candidates are easily identifiable by party, and the result is not much different from partisan elections. Chicago is an example of this type of "nonpartisan" city; Jersey City was another during the time of the powerful machine of Frank Hague.

2 A system of elections in which slates of candidates are supported by various groups, including political party organizations. Here the voters perceive nonpartisan elections as being a distinctive type, but the political party groups are able to compete against slates of candidates presented by nonparty groups.

3 A system of elections in which slates of candidates are supported by various interest groups, but political party organizations have little or no part in campaigns. In these cities, candidates may have no party affiliation, or it may be unknown, or the voters may consider it to be irrelevant. This pattern appears to be far more common than the two listed above. Kansas City (since the fall of the Pendergast machine), Dallas, Fort Worth, and many California and Michigan cities appear to fit this category.[27]

4 A system of elections in which neither political parties nor slates of candidates are important. This type appears to be very common, possibly even more so than the third type. It is especially important in small cities, for in these communities what Eugene Lee has called the "politics of acquaintance" is often the decisive factor.[28] Under this system, according to Lee, the typical pattern is "the development of support, organization and funds by the individual candidate himself on an ad hoc basis. Rather than being recruited by a group and assuming its apparatus, the average candidate must build his own campaign from the ground up."

The Effects of Nonpartisanship In small cities and villages, where government is largely on an informal personal basis, nonpartisanship has worked satisfactorily. In the largest cities, however, nonpartisanship has not aided in producing a broad spectrum of representation in government. Without a guiding label on the ballot, the large-city voter has difficulty in identifying candidates, especially for council. The most important thing for the candidate is, therefore, not to have a platform but rather to have a name that rings a bell in the voter's mind. Publicity becomes all important, and the election is normally won by those who can control the media of mass communication, the newspapers in particular. This has been largely the pattern, for example, in Dallas, Detroit, Fort Worth, Los Angeles, San Diego, and San Francisco.

In large cities, nonpartisanship makes it difficult for voters to cast a protest vote for members of the council. The discontented will normally vote against the in-party and for the out-party. They cannot do this under nonpartisanship. The incumbent is thus given an advantage in a campaign, for his or her name is commonly the best known to the voter.[29]

[27] See Eugene C. Lee, *The Politics of Nonpartisanship: A Study of California City Elections,* University of California Press, Berkeley, Calif., 1960; Williams and Adrian, *Four Cities,* chap. 4.

[28] See Lee, *op. cit.;* and Richard S. Childs, *Civic Victories,* Harper & Row, Publishers, Incorporated, New York, 1952, appendix C.

[29] See Charles R. Adrian, "Some General Characteristics of Nonpartisan Elections," *American Political Science Review,* 46:766–776, September, 1952. For examples of professional public relations

Some evidence indicates that partisan and nonpartisan politicians are not to be found in two insulated compartments. If this was once true, as seems to have been the case,[30] it is probably becoming less so.[31] In such cities as Minneapolis and Detroit, as well as some cities in California, persons who begin their careers in the nonpartisan arena move into candidature for offices on partisan ballots. In a few cases, the opposite career pattern has appeared. It seems likely that the following generalization is valid: The more visible the office, the greater the options available to the incumbent officeholder who seeks career advancement, regardless of whether the office is partisan or nonpartisan.

A study of nonpartisan municipal elections in California in 1960 indicated a notable degree of competition for office and considerable opportunity for dissent and for casting a protest vote. On the other hand, Republicans were found to have a decided advantage in nonpartisan elections in the state, which has a majority of Democratic voters. Councilmanic elections were found to be as competitive as the partisan elections for the state legislature, although the latter were pale imitations of traditional party contests in the East. The two major political parties had little formal relationship to local nonpartisan campaigns, but nonpartisan officeholders were found quite commonly to compete for partisan office, often successfully. Most incumbents and most Republican county chairpersons wanted to continue nonpartisan elections, but 60 percent of the Democratic chairpersons favored a change to the partisan ballot. In elections, Republicans and conservatives exercised greater influence because of their higher propensity to vote. The larger the city, the more likely the political party organizations were to be formally involved in campaigns; the larger the city, the more influential the role of the local press was considered to be in influencing voter decisions.[32]

Evidence that the type of ballot does not segregate careers in large cities to either a partisan or nonpartisan pattern is found in a study of Milwaukee politics, where the recruitment of candidates for nonpartisan office was not found to be sharply separated from that for partisan office. Nonpartisan officeholders were not found to have any particular incumbency advantage, in comparison with partisan officeholders, when seeking reelection.[33] It is also doubtful if nonpartisanship aids conservative policies in large cities, as was once believed.[34] Factors other than formal structure of the electoral system, particularly state government policies and metropolitan population patterns, are probably more important influences upon public policy.[35] Furthermore, the general decline of political par-

---

work through the mass media of communication in communities with little political structure, see Irwin Ross, "The Supersalesmen of California Politics," *Harper's Magazine,* July, 1959, pp. 55–61; and more generally, Dan Nimmo, *The Political Persuaders: The Techniques of Modern Election Campaigns,* Prentice-Hall, Inc., Englewood Cliffs, N.J., 1970.

30 Adrian, "Some General Characteristics of Nonpartisan Elections."

31 A. Clarke Hagensick, "Influences of Partisanship and Incumbency on a Nonpartisan Elections System," *Western Political Quarterly,* 17:117–124, March, 1964.

32 Lee, *op. cit.*

33 Hagensick, *op. cit.*

34 John H. Kessel, "Governmental Structure and Political Environment," *American Political Science Review,* 56:615–620, September, 1962.

35 Charles E. Gilbert, "Some Aspects of Nonpartisan Elections in Large Cities," *Midwest Journal of Political Science,* 6:345–362, November, 1962.

ties as *organizations* and their relegation to symbolic roles has diminished the once-important distinction between partisan and nonpartisan contests. The more visible contests for public office at all levels—for President, senator, governor, or mayor—are increasingly being conducted by professional campaign management firms which prefer to operate without help or interference of party organizations.[36]

Local Parties: The Exception[37]

Numerous examples of local parties exist in municipal politics, although they have in no way become an integral part of the American political system. Americans in overwhelming numbers have taken the attitude that efforts toward third parties are a waste of time, and this viewpoint probably spills over into local politics. Local parties for the most part consist of small-town parties and reform parties.

Local Parties for Small Towns Local parties are to be found in many villages, and in small and even middle-sized cities where politics is on a personal basis, national parties are not desired, and yet for one reason or another (perhaps local custom, or state laws which do not permit nonpartisanship), a party label must be used. A small Iowa city, for example, may have a municipal contest between members of the People's party and the Citizen's party, or the Liberal party and the Temperance party, or the Progressive party and the Conservative party. These labels are most often nothing more than collective terms for slates of candidates having no organization, platform, or treasury. Politics is on a personal basis, and the label is meaningless.

Reform Parties Reform parties have been organized from time to time in various cities chiefly for purposes of driving out existing machines or corrupt politicians, or for establishing some of the principles of "efficiency and economy." Most of these parties have been short-lived, and their general failure has encouraged reform groups to organize themselves as *interest groups* rather than political parties, endorsing candidates and policies, but not putting people of their own into the field. This is true today of the New York Citizens' Union, the Chicago Municipal Voters' League, and the Detroit Citizens' League, for example.

Some of these groups, such as the one in New York, began as local parties but found this impractical for one reason or another (the Citizens' Union was nearly taken over by a Tammany Hall fifth column). They then proceeded to work toward their goals on a bipartisan or nonpartisan basis.

New York City saw a genuine local party created during the Great Depression in the form of the Fusion party with Fiorello H. LaGuardia as its principal driving force. The organization was made up of Citizens' Unionists, many Re-

36 For one interpretation, see Walter Dean Burnham, *Critical Elections and the Mainsprings of American Politics,* W. W. Norton & Company, Inc., New York, 1970.

37 See J. Leiper Freeman, "Local Party Systems: Theoretical Considerations and a Case Analysis," *American Journal of Sociology,* 64:282–289, November, 1958.

publicans (including LaGuardia), sundry persons not usually politically active, and antimachine Democrats.

The Charter Party Perhaps the best-known and most successful local party in the United States is the City Charter Committee of Cincinnati, often referred to as the "Charter party." Although the organization does not formally call itself a party and although its name does not appear on the Cincinnati nonpartisan ballot following the names of its candidates, it is organized in the general pattern of urban parties and functions as a local party.

Groups in several smaller cities, especially with council-manager forms of government, have sought to imitate the Cincinnati type of local party with varying degrees of success. Generally they fail to solve the problem of how to establish themselves as a party if no labels are on the ballot, or of maintaining a permanent organization, or both. In many cities, however, reform or business groups put candidates into the field and help finance their campaigns. These groups often have the backing of the local press. They should perhaps be classified as interest groups rather than local parties, although the line between the two is not easy to draw in this case.

Local Parties: An Appraisal Local parties suffer from serious handicaps that make the Charter party or even the Fusion party rare successes in America. It is often argued that such parties would quickly become mere adjuncts of national parties—the same old parties under different names. This does not necessarily follow and it would be quite possible to maintain these parties as separate entities; however, some very real problems do confront local parties.

In the first place, local parties require constant attention and interest from a large part of the public. This is difficult to secure, and the normal result is that shortly after "the rascals" are thrown out, the party begins to disintegrate. This has happened many times in the United States. A permanent organization with permanent electioneering on the Cincinnati model is imperative for longevity of local parties. Secondly, local parties are difficult to organize in any case. Political party structures are complex and require much coordinated effort. It is virtually impossible to organize a successful local party except under unusual circumstances (a deep economic depression, a particularly corrupt administration), and even then it is not easy. Thirdly, attempts to organize local parties, as such, are likely to be resisted by the informal ruling group of business leaders who put up candidates, finance them, and—in lieu of having an organized party structure—control the media of communication. Lastly, local parties have a great deal of difficulty in securing enough funds for survival. People will not make contributions unless they believe in the cause to begin with and further believe that a particular organization is capable of advancing that cause. The Cincinnati Charter party has been successful because it has been able both to develop an effective money-raising organization and to get the confidence and support of business leaders and others who have funds that can be tapped. The American Labor and later the Liberal party could survive in New York because they had a firm financial base in labor-union support. A poorly financed party has no chance of survival.

Methods of Nomination

Before there can be an election, the individuals who are going to make the race must first be chosen. There are numerous ways of placing candidates in nomination. The overwhelming majority of nominations on the local (or any other) level made in the United States today are by way of either the partisan or the nonpartisan direct primary election. There are, or have been, however, numerous other techniques, including caucus or convention nomination, sponsorship, and petition.

Early Nomination Devices The *caucus,* the oldest form of nomination in the United States, consisted originally of an informal meeting to choose candidates deserving of support for the various public offices becoming vacant. In America's early days, the caucus members could print a ballot and distribute it themselves.

With the development of cities, the caucus system degenerated. A more formal method and one that would make known the desires of the common voter, rather than those of the organized few, was demanded. The *convention* method called for nominations at a formal gathering whose membership was chosen by caucus at the precinct level. With the organization of nineteenth-century political machines, both the caucus and the convention tended to be dominated by a few people, with the general public having little actual choice in the nomination—and in most cities nomination by the dominant party was tantamount to election.

Reforms in Nomination Beginning early in the present century, the reform movement produced a change in nomination procedure. The *direct primary election* was substituted for the caucus and convention. It is now almost universal in the United States, although a few states do not use it for some important state offices and there are cities in such populous states as California, Texas, New Jersey, and Massachusetts that do not use it.

Strictly speaking, a primary election is nothing more than a *nonassembled* caucus. In an earlier day all eligible voters were entitled to take part in the selection of candidates. Later, part of this job had to be turned over to what were theoretically their representatives acting at a *convention.* When the convention proved to be unrepresentative and boss-ridden, the primary election was devised to return nominations "to the people." The plan in large measure transferred control of the nomination machinery from the party to the state, all parties choosing their candidates on the same day under the supervision of public election officials, with ballots standardized and printed at public expense, and with a secret ballot (in contrast with most caucus and convention systems).

The primary election has never been understood by the vast majority of American voters. They are annoyed by the fantastically long "bedsheet" ballot with which they are confronted; they resent the fact that they must usually reveal their party preference in order to vote; and even when the open primary is used, they become incensed when they discover that splitting the ticket is not permitted.

Types of Primaries Primary elections are of two types, nonpartisan and partisan. The latter is subdivided into two classes, open and closed. The *nonpartisan* primary is actually an elimination contest. Names appear on the ballot without party designation. The first election, popularly and sometimes legally called a primary, serves to eliminate all candidates except twice the number to be elected. Hence, if seven file for the office of mayor, only two will survive the primary—the two with the highest number of votes. If seven council members are to be elected, the fourteen highest at the primary are nominated. In some cases, such as in many California cities and in elections for the Chicago council, all candidates receiving a majority of the vote cast in the primary are declared elected, and the taxpayer is saved the cost of placing their names on the final ballot.

In nonpartisan as well as partisan primaries, one is listed on the ballot in the first place in one of three ways: by a simple formal declaration, by signature petition (in either of these two, a small filing fee to defray part of the expense of putting the name on the ballot may be charged), or by filing a forfeitable deposit. In some states, any fee may be avoided by filing a pauper's oath.

The *partisan* primary may be open or closed. An open primary is open to any eligible voter, regardless of party or whether one is a party member or a confirmed independent. One need not demonstrate or declare anything other than that one is a qualified voter in order to receive a ballot. A closed primary, on the other hand, is closed to everyone except members of the political party concerned.

Other Nomination Devices Some cities in a number of states make use of nomination by *petition* directly onto the final ballot. This method saves the expense of a primary election and usually has satisfactory results in small cities. But when the plan was used in Boston, the mayor was often a plurality rather than a majority choice, for there were nearly always more than two major candidates. (A *plurality* is more votes than any other candidate receives. A *majority* is at least one vote more than one-half of the number cast.) Boss James Michael Curley, as the best-known mayoralty candidate, sometimes found this plan to be of considerable personal advantage.

The *Model City Charter* of the National Municipal League recommends a plan, especially in connection with proportional representation, called the *sponsor system.* It is used in some California cities. It requires a petition to be signed by ten persons who are listed as "sponsors" of the candidate, and the filing of a sum of money, to be returned under certain conditions.

EXPERIMENTS IN DIRECT DEMOCRACY

The Initiative and Referendum

With the decline in the prestige of governing bodies in the last half of the nineteenth century came also a decline in citizen faith in representative democracy.

As a consequence, reformers proposed what were then considered radical solutions. They renovated and reorganized some old American institutions, introduced some new ones, and hopefully presented us with techniques for direct democracy as a check upon excesses and incompetence. The *initiative* permits a legally defined number of voters to propose changes in the city charter or ordinances which are then accepted or rejected by the voters at the polls. This device permits legislation to be effected with no recourse at all to the legislative body. The *referendum* permits the voters to accept or reject at the polls council-proposed changes in the city charter or ordinances. The referendum differs from the initiative in that it *follows* favorable action by the legislative body, whereas such an institutional device as the initiative takes place independently of the legislative body.

The Procedure An initiated proposal is normally drafted by the attorneys for the particular interest group seeking the legislation. Petitions to put the proposal on the ballot are then circulated by volunteers or by persons hired for the purpose, often at the price of a certain amount per signature. The quantity of signatures required may be a specific numerical total or be those of a certain percentage of voters (registered, or voting for a certain office at the last general election, or some other formula). Where such a percentage is used, it is generally from 5 to 10 percent, but may be higher. In most instances, the proposal is adopted if a majority of those voting on the proposal vote in its favor, although in some cases a majority of those voting *in the election* is required (this means that if voters ignore the proposal they are in effect voting "no"), or some special formula may be used. It is often provided that an initiated ordinance may not be amended or repealed by the city council, at least within a certain prescribed time limit.

The initiative and referendum (I. and R.), particularly the latter, have ancient origins in America and elsewhere. Antecedents are to be found in the direct democracy of ancient Greece, the ancient tribal governments of Germany, the right to petition the king in medieval England, the town meeting of colonial New England, and the direct democracy of Switzerland.[38] As early as 1825, the Maryland legislature provided for a referendum on the question of establishing a public school system. It later became very common to hold referendums on liquor questions, charter amendments, public utility franchises, bond issues, and other matters. California, Iowa, and Nebraska in the late nineteenth century authorized municipal use of the initiative and referendum. The San Francisco home rule charter of 1898 was the first such document to provide for them. From then the movement spread rapidly, and it is today widely authorized for municipal governments.

Around the beginning of the century, when many cities adopted the initiative and referendum, proponents made greatly exaggerated claims of their merits. Opponents were equally vociferous, viewing with alarm the potentiality for

[38] See William Munro (ed.), *The Initiative, Referendum, and Recall,* The Macmillan Company, New York, 1913, chap. 1. Also Ralph M. Goldman, "The Advisory Referendum in America," *Public Opinion Quarterly,* 14:303–315, Summer, 1950.

hamstringing the governmental process by their use. The results have not borne out the claims of either side.

Arguments concerning I. and R. Proponents of direct democracy argued that corrupt and low-quality city councils made it necessary for people to have a check upon the government. Reformers also took note of the trend toward a concentration of authority in government and a breakdown of the traditional check-and-balance system. The initiative and referendum could serve to replace some of these disappearing checks. It was argued that the use of these devices strengthened popular control over city government by giving the people "a gun behind the door" which could serve as a means of requiring greater alertness, honesty, and responsiveness on the part of council members.

It was believed that I. and R. would protect the people from political tricks and thefts from the public treasury. Some argued that it would encourage voters to become better informed on issues, since they would have to vote on so many of them directly and since they could not feel that they had a real chance to get things done in local affairs.

Opponents of the system argued that it confused legislative responsibility, lengthened an already overly long ballot, created a bad psychological effect upon the city council, expected more than was reasonable from an uninformed and uninterested electorate, would promote radicalism and a disrespect for property rights, was opposed to the best principles of Americanism (since the Constitution is based upon *representative,* and not *direct,* democracy), and would allow well-organized interest groups representing a minority of the population to exercise an inordinate advantage.[39]

I. and R.: An Appraisal The debate over the use of I. and R. has subsided in recent years, though the use of these devices is, if anything, increasing. Perhaps it is necessary here to make only two points, without discussing the merits of the arguments briefly outlined above.

First, the I. and R. seem to carry the implicit assumption that voters are always informed and rational in their choices. Actually, of course, this assumption is false. Furthermore, democracy as we know it does not require such an assumption. In an ordinary election, voters are merely asked whether or not they are relatively satisfied with things as they are. According to the state of their satisfactions, they vote for those in power or cast a protest vote. Their reasons are their own, and they need not be rational, logical, or informed. They are not asked to rule but merely to choose those who are to rule. But the I. and R. ask more than this of voters. They ask them to help rule themselves and to make policy decisions on questions that are often complex, technical, and minutely detailed.

Where the law permits or requires complex questions to be submitted to the general public for direct action, the results are sometimes humorous—or would be if government were not such a serious business. In the November, 1952, elec-

[39] Extensive arguments on the pros and cons are presented in Munro, chaps. 1–11.

tion, the voters of Waldwick, New Jersey (1950 population: 3,963), on the edge of the New York metropolitan area, voted to establish a full-time police force; but on another question, refused to appropriate the additional $10,000 a year to finance the project; and on a third question, voted to retain the existing part-time system. And all this at the same election.

Second, opponents of the I. and R. are wont to overlook the fact that the American political structure is pluralistic and not neatly integrated, and that the American political process is typically based upon the interaction of pressure groups. American cities, for the most part, do not have responsible political party structures, and few cities have a two-party system of any kind regularly competing for voter support. Furthermore, it is unlikely that this pattern will be changed much in the foreseeable future. Since this system may result in city councils that are not representative of a cross section of the population, the I. and R. may well be used as a check, "a gun behind the door."[40]

Although the original supporters of I. and R. thought that these devices would bring government "closer to the people," their actual operation has been complex and difficult. Organized interests, in most cases, are the only ones that can utilize them successfully. Getting the needed signatures is costly and it is difficult to get the volunteers needed to circulate petitions. It is possible to hire professional campaign management firms to get the needed signatures, but this is a costly procedure. In the Western cities, especially, I. and R. remain a popular method of seeking to influence public policy.

Most citizens probably favor the retention of the initiative and referendum, viewing them as safety measures, but they do not pay a great deal of attention to the typical issues. In Chicago, between 1924 and 1935, 85 of the 114 bond-issue referendums attracted less than one-half of the registered voters. This was true even though some of the proposed issues elicited campaigns involving a great deal of conflict.[41] A series of bond-issue referendums in DeKalb County, Georgia, which is suburban Atlanta, produced a turnout of only 24.2 percent in 1961. Higher-status individuals in all parts of the county were more likely to vote on the I. and R. questions than were lower-status individuals.[42] The greatest support for bond issues came from high-income persons to whom, of course, the additional cost meant the least. Support for the issues, which in general were designed to provide more of life's amenities of the type that are usually supplied by municipal governments, was highest among suburban voters. Least support came from persons in the outer fringe. Perhaps this was in part a reflection of the perceived needs for the various services. Support for the bonds was greatest among persons in the forty-to-sixty-year-old category.

A study of referendums in Michigan in the 1950s showed that voter interest

[40] In this connection, see Joseph La Palombara and Charles B. Hagan, "Direct Legislation: An Appraisal and a Suggestion," *American Political Science Review,* 45:400–421, June, 1951.

[41] Harold F. Gosnell, *Machine Politics: Chicago Model,* The University of Chicago Press, Chicago, 1937, p. 134.

[42] Alvin Boskoff and Harmon Zeigler, *Voting Patterns in a Local Election,* J. P. Lippincott Company, Philadelphia, 1964, chap. 6.

and support for proposals that had city-council support varied directly with socioeconomic status. Some evidence indicated that support for referendums tended to vary with the level of confidence that various groups of voters had in their city government.[43]

Another study, of defeated school-bond issues in two communities, indicated that persons with a strong sense of political alienation (powerlessness) tended to cast negative votes. To them, the referendum apparently served not as a device for indicating how the community could be improved, or even for casting a class-oriented protest, but rather as a generalized protest against personal feelings of helplessness in the face of political forces bigger than they could comprehend or hope to be able to influence.[44] The 1,512 bond and tax referendums held in the United States between 1948 and 1959 indicated that a high turnout of voters generally signals defeat for a proposal.[45]

The Recall

The third member of the triumvirate that was to produce popular control of city government was the *recall.* This is a device whereby any elective officers may be removed from office by a popular vote prior to the expiration of their term. Although it is often mentioned in connection with the initiative and referendum, the recall may exist independently of them. It was brought into extensive use by the same people, and for largely the same reasons. They argued that faithless or incompetent public servants should not be inflicted upon the people for the duration of their terms—that they should be removed as soon as their shortcomings were discovered. Again, Jacksonians who were not too happy with the increasing popularity of the four-year term, as against the traditional two years, found it easier to accept the longer term if "continuous responsibility" were maintained through the availability of the recall. The mechanism was probably first provided for in the Los Angeles home rule charter of 1903; unlike its two sisters, it has no direct precedents in American political practices.

The Procedure In order to recall an official, a petition must be circulated. Because a large number of signatures are usually required—such as 15 to 25 or even as high as 51 percent of the vote cast for the office of mayor in the last election—an organized group with a good deal of motivation and a sizable treasury is usually required. After enough signatures are certified by the city clerk or other appropriate election officer, an election becomes obligatory. There are several variants of the recall ballot, and its form may itself serve to either aid or discourage the prospects for removal of the official.

Arguments Pro and Con The principal argument for the recall is that it provides for continuous responsibility (especially important with the four-year

[43] Oliver P. Williams and Charles R. Adrian, *Four Cities,* University of Pennsylvania Press, Philadelphia, 1963, chap. 5.

[44] John E. Horton and Wayne E. Thompson, "Powerlessness and Political Negativism: A Study of Defeated Referendums," *American Journal of Sociology,* 67:485–493, March, 1962.

[45] Richard F. Carter and William G. Savard, *The Influence of Voter Turnout on School Bond and Tax Elections,* U.S. Department of Health, Education, and Welfare, 1961.

term), so that citizens need not wait in exasperation and frustration until the term comes to an end. It is similarly argued that, with a sword constantly hanging over the head of the public official, he or she will feel a need to remain alert at all times.

Opponents of the recall point to its costliness: A *special* election is imperative for its use, since it would be unfair to conduct such an election in connection with other questions (although this is sometimes done). A second objection to the recall is that it does not attempt to *prove charges* against an officeholder but merely to persuade the electorate, by whatever means, to remove the the incumbent. A third objection is that the recall is unnecessary. In all states, improper conduct by public officials is grounds for removal by other judicial, councilmanic, or sometimes gubernatorial action.[46]

A final objection to the recall centers is the assertion that it serves as a tool for well-organized interest groups and for political recrimination. Similarly, it is said that the threat of the recall is a constant and perfectly legal means for intimidation of public officials who must therefore slavishly follow public whims and sentimentality. A strong leader with a positive program may find that some interest group will stand in the way by threatening recall action if the plans are carried out.

The recall has never been widely used. Few new adoptions of it have taken place since about 1920. Yet it continues to be used especially by those who wish to emphasize a protest against the existing policy of a city council or school board.

The Public Hearing

A few words should be said about another important American device for involving the citizen in decision making, the public hearing. This institution is unusual in Europe but is well established in American tradition, which calls for the general public to be informed about every significant decision affecting public policy. Public hearings generally involve a rather informal procedure at which every citizen present is allowed to speak if she or he cares to do so. They are commonly used prior to the making of decisions concerning such matters as the zoning of land, the location of taverns, the moving of highways, the changing of public utilities rates, the exempting of certain property from the tax rolls (as in the granting of a permit for a cemetery), the location of a new school, and dozens of other purposes.

Political neophytes find the hearing procedure puzzling, because at a typical meeting nearly all persons expressing themselves are opposed to the proposal which is the subject of the hearing. The official or public body conducting the hearing does not, of course, take a vote at the time and dispose of the issue on that basis. Instead, the hearing is used as a safety-valve device for allowing disapproving persons to vent their feelings. These people thus gain a feeling of having had their "day in court," and they may succeed in having the proposed policy modified somewhat so as to meet, at least partially, some of their objections. The

[46] See chap. 9.

hearing also allows the responsible officials to judge in advance of decisions the political climate in which they will find themselves. They may also learn something that will suggest to them the language in which to couch the announcement of a decision so as to minimize the number and intensity of unfavorable responses.

Citizen Participation

The Economic Opportunity Act of 1964 had provided for the "maximum feasible participation" of the poor in programs designed to relieve poverty. This provision, probably not seriously intended by many members of Congress, coincided with the populistic revival of the period.[47] This combination of events, aided by the slogan of "participatory democracy" by the New Left, led to proposals of various kinds for increased citizen participation in local public policy making. Later, the State and Local Fiscal Assistance Act of 1972 (providing for "revenue sharing") encouraged such participation, and the Housing and Community Development Act of 1975 required it.[48] As early as 1972, two-thirds of all cities in a survey had some kind of citizen-involvement program.[49] Many other cities have since been added. Many advocates of participation plans had as a goal increasing the representation of the poor and minority groups, but most programs were devised, in theory at least, to involve all citizens.

Attempts to expand involvement included establishing "little city halls," neighborhood service centers (sometimes with officials from city hall paying regular visits), city hall "annexes," neighborhood councils, and other institutional devices.[50] The efforts involved many undemonstrated assumptions—guesswork—and one study concluded that advocates "neither possess nor can cite much hard evidence to support the various claims they make."[51] In many cases, citizen participation led to intense, prolonged, and bitter struggles with city hall. The greater the involvement, the greater the resulting conflict.[52] In some community-action-program elections, fewer than 3 percent of the eligible participated. Those who did participate in meetings were often from the higher-status groups in the neighborhood or ax grinders of the sort who have traditionally haunted city council meetings. Conflict arose between local leaders, who often saw "neighborhood participation" as an opportunity to build a political base, and city

[47] The anti-poverty program in general, and its failure, see Charles R. Adrian and Charles Press, *American Politics Reappraised,* McGraw-Hill Book Company, New York, 1974, esp. chaps. 1 and 12.

[48] See Howard Hallman, "Federally Financed Citizen Participation," *Public Administration Review,* 32:421–428, September, 1972. Also other articles on the subject in this issue.

[49] Carl Stenberg, *The New Grass Roots Government?* Advisory Commission on Intergovernmental Relations, Washington, 1972.

[50] See George Washnis, *Neighborhood Facilities and Municipal Decentralization,* Center for Governmental Studies, Washington, 1971; Douglas Yates, "Neighborhood Government," *Policy Sciences,* 8:209–219, July, 1972; Joseph Zimmerman, *The Federal City,* St. Martin's Press, Inc., New York, 1972.

[51] Peter K. Eisinger, "Community Control and Liberal Dilemmas," *Publius,* 5:130–134, Fall, 1972.

[52] See Edgar Cahn and Barry Passett (eds.), *Citizen Participation: Effecting Community Changes,* Praeger Publishers, New York, 1971; Paul Peterson, "Forms of Representation: Participation of the Poor in Community Action Programs," *American Political Science Review,* 64:491–508, June, 1970.

hall leaders. The former wanted to build new, strong decision structures; the latter often saw the process as a "relatively costless device to link disaffected citizens to the polity."[53] These two perspectives and goals were not necessarily imcompatible, however.

In general, moderate approaches seem to have worked best. Very weak programs provided apathetic responses. Those emphasizing neighborhood independence, hostility, radical change, patronage, and deliberate conflict generally resulted in lowered citizen morale and defeat in the hands of threatened public officials and the little-involved majority of citizens. Programs emphasizing cooperation, coordination of activities, joint planning between officials and citizens, moderate intensity of citizen involvement and modest program goals, with ultimate control remaining in city hall, seem to have worked best.[54]

One significant by-product of federal programs which require or encourage public hearings (possibly, but not necessarily, unintended) has been an increase in the patronage available to council members. The Housing and Community Development Act is especially valuable in this respect because the money is used for capital improvements—visible things like community recreation centers and mini-parks. Hearings are held in various sections of the city (in each ward if the council is so divided). Projects are carefully allocated for maximum political impact—and the federal government pays the bill while the council member takes the credit.

By the mid-1970s, the high hopes held by some for citizen-participation programs were already on the wane. City residents did not, of course, flock to neighborhood meetings or elections anymore than they traditionally have for city-wide events. Most citizens do not want to become involved, to be informed, to work through the difficult policy-development process.[55] Although citizens returned to (or never left) their normal apathy, some of these new institutions may become permanent fixtures in local government, for Americans have ambiguous feelings. They do not want to devote much time to government, but they do believe in the right of citizens to participate and to be involved in decision making. The appearance of things, the symbolism rather than the actual performance or results, may be the important function of "citizen participation."

Although mayors and council members have found it politically advantageous to favor "citizen participation" of some kind, it is significant that few of them seem to have supported a change that would quite surely have done much more to make city governments more representative of a cross section of the citizens—the considerable expansion in the size of city councils. In the typical council of today there are five to nine members, too few to be representative even

[53] Ira Katznelson, "Antagonistic Ambiguity: Notes on Reformism and Decentralization," *Politics and Society,* 3:329–330, Spring, 1972.

[54] Richard L. Cole, "Citizen Participation in Municipal Politics," *American Journal of Political Science,* 19:761–781, November, 1975. James Sundquest and David Davis, *Making Federalism Work,* Brookings Institution, Washington, 1969, a study of 29 programs.

[55] Pennsylvania charter commissions found their greatest disappointment in the lack of citizen participation and interest, for example. See Larry Gomm, "Pennsylvania Local Government Study," *National Civic Review,* 64:400–403, September, 1975.

in a city as small as 100,000 people. Council members generally dislike the idea of enlarging the membership because doing so would make them individually less important, would force them to learn new rules for campaigning and winning, and would raise the conflict level and hence the difficulties in reaching decisions in council meetings. Yet, America once had a strong tradition of large, representative councils (especially along the East Coast, less commonly elsewhere). When Boston was first incorporated in 1822 with a population of 40,000, the council consisted of 8 aldermen (the upper house) elected at large and 49 common councillors (the lower house), 4 for each ward. Tiny Bangor, Maine, in 1834 had 7 aldermen and 21 ward councillors. Even in the West, Cheyenne with a couple of thousand citizens in 1868 had 4 trustees elected by wards (perhaps 500 persons, or 170 eligible voters for each representative).[56]

SELECTED READINGS

Adrian, Charles R.: "Some General Characteristics of Nonpartisan Elections," *American Political Science Review,* 46:766–776, September, 1952.

——: "A Typology for Nonpartisan Elections," *Western Political Quarterly,* 12:449–458, June, 1959.

Boskoff, Alvin, and Harmon Zeigler: *Voting Patterns in a Local Election,* J. B. Lippincott Company, Philadelphia, 1964. (An analysis of voting on ten bond-issue referendums in DeKalb County, Georgia.)

Campbell, Angus, and others: *The American Voter,* John Wiley & Sons, Inc., New York, 1960. (A theory of voter behavior based on the empirical work of the Survey Research Center.)

Cole, Richard L.: *Citizen Participation and the Urban Policy Process,* D. C. Heath and Company, Lexington, Mass., 1974. (The effects of various participation programs.)

Fischer, Claude S.: "The City and Political Psychology," *American Political Science Review,* 69:559–571, June, 1975. (Does urbanization encourage or discourage political involvement?)

Harder, Marvin A.: *Nonpartisan Election: A Political Illusion?* Holt, Rinehart and Winston, Inc., New York, 1958. (A case study in Wichita, Kans.)

Hawley, Willis D.: *Nonpartisan Elections and the Case for Party Politics,* John Wiley & Sons, Inc., New York, 1973. (Reexamines the relationship of electoral institutions to community characteristics. Conclusions support earlier findings.)

Kotler, Milton: *Neighborhood Government,* The Bobbs-Merrill Company, Inc., Indianapolis, 1969. (Strongly supports this movement. For a more balanced view, see the Cole citation above.)

Lazarsfeld, Paul F., and others: *The People's Choice,* Columbia University Press, New York, 1948. (One of the first voter-behavior studies—by social psychologists.)

Lee, Eugene C.: *The Politics of Nonpartisanship: A Study of California City Elections,* University of California Press, Berkeley, Calif., 1960.

Munro, William B. (ed.): *The Initiative, Referendum, and Recall,* The Macmillan Company, New York, 1913. (Good study, written during reform era.)

Porter, Kirk H.: *A History of Suffrage in the United States,* The University of Chicago

[56] Charles R. Adrian and Ernest S. Griffith, *History of American City Government,* Praeger Publishers, New York, 1976, chap. 9.

Press, Chicago, 1918. (The principal historical source.)
Rosenberg, Morris: "Some Determinants of Voter Apathy," *Public Opinion Quarterly,* 18:349–366, Winter, 1954–1955.
Straetz, Ralph A.: *PR Politics in Cincinnati,* New York University Press, New York, 1958.
Williams, Oliver P., and Charles R. Adrian: *Four Cities,* University of Pennsylvania Press, Philadelphia, 1963. (Chapter 4 deals with voting behavior in four middle-sized Michigan cities.)
Yates, Douglas: *Neighborhood Democracy,* D. C. Heath and Company, Lexington, Mass., 1973. (Does decentralization of city government make it more responsive to common people and give them a greater sense of efficacy?)
Zimmerman, Joseph F.: "Electoral Reform Needed to End Political Alienation," *National Civic Review,* 60:6ff., January, 1971. (Changes in voting systems can improve minority-group representation.)

C

The Law

Chapter 6

The Law of Municipalities

Americans have a penchant for discussing problems of public policy in terms of constitutional law rather than in terms of public policy. This is particularly true in municipal affairs, for the legal position of the city is one of lowest priority: "The city is a political subdivision of the state, created as a convenient agency for the exercise of such of the governmental powers of the state as may be intrusted to it."[1]

May a city perform whatever functions a substantial proportion of its residents wants to have performed? Not at all. It may perform only those that the state legislature or the state courts allow it.

THE CITY AS A CORPORATION

The Problem of Sufficient Authority: A Case Study

Let us suppose that the city council wishes to eliminate a group of billboards that surround a city park. The council members believe that the billboards are destroying the natural beauty of the park and that people use the park in order to

[1] *Trenton v. New Jersey,* 262 U.S. 182 (1923). This is the standard rule, and its substance may be found repeated in dozens of cases.

get away from the prosaic, hurried, commercialized world of everyday. The council has had numerous complaints about the billboards, and a majority of the members promised in their campaigns for election to vote them out of existence. Is this sufficient justification for council action? Certainly not.

Before any action can be taken effectively, these questions, and perhaps many more, might have to be answered: Does the city charter authorize regulation of billboards? And because the legal mind is razor-sharp and hence capable of splitting hairs, the further question, perhaps: Does the city charter authorize regulation of billboards *on the periphery of public parks?* If the city charter does authorize regulation, is there a contravening general act of the legislature? Is such regulation, in any case, *reasonable?* Would it somehow violate the state or federal constitution? Would this particular regulation constitute, according to the common law, an *abuse of discretion* by the council? And is the proposed ordinance for a *public purpose?* Before World War I, regulation of billboards was considered by the courts an invasion of the rights of private property.[2] Then the courts began to allow regulation on the basis of the police power.[3]

In order for a city ordinance regulating billboards to be valid, it must be shown that such regulation is necessary to the safety and welfare of the people. The city must show that a rickety billboard might topple over on an unsuspecting pedestrian, or that a billboard might well be used as a place of ambush by a rapist, or that a billboard might serve to collect flammable newspapers and leaves.

It was not until 1935 that a high court was willing to allow regulation of billboards on a simple basis of aesthetics in the public interest. "Grandeur and beauty of scenery," the Supreme Judicial Court of Massachusetts said, "contribute highly important factors to the public welfare." This concept, although gaining in recognition, has not become the generally accepted rule.[4] Note the skepticism of an Illinois judge: "Authorities in general agree to the essentials of a public health program, while the public view as to what is necessary for aesthetic progress greatly varies. Certain legislatures might consider that it was more important to cultivate a taste for jazz than for Beethoven, for posters than for Rembrandt, and for limericks than for Keats. Successive city councils might never agree as to what the public needs from an aesthetic standpoint, and this fact makes the aesthetic standard impractical as a standard for use restriction upon property."[5] The judge said, in effect, that he can determine better than can

[2] *Massachusetts v. Boston Advertising Company,* 188 Mass. 348 (1905); *New York ex rel. Wineburgh v. Murphy,* 195 N.Y. 126 (1909); and other cases. See also Illinois Legislative Council, *Regulation of Billboards,* State of Illinois, Springfield, Ill., 1953, pp. 17–20.

[3] The *police power* is usually defined as the power of the state to "protect the health, safety, and morals" of society. See *St. Louis Gunning Advertising Company v. St. Louis,* 235 Mo. 99 (1911) and nearly all subsequent cases where billboard regulation was upheld.

[4] *General Outdoor Advertising Company v. Massachusetts Department of Public Works,* 193 N.E. 799 (1935). A more recent supporting case is *Berman v. Parker,* 348 U.S. 26 (1954).

[5] *Forbes v. Hubbard,* 180 N.E. 767 (1932). In accord with this more common opinion, see *Youngstown v. Kahn Brothers Building Company,* 148 N.E. 842 (1925); and *Wondrak v. Kelley,* 195 N.E. 65 (1935).

the council the point at which the public interest becomes more important than the private interest.

If all the many questions that may be raised can be answered in a satisfactory manner, the city may, perhaps after paying expensive court costs, proceed with its drive to eliminate the offensive billboards. Such are the limitations of authority under which city government must operate.

The Nature of a Corporation

The city, in lawyers' language, is a municipal corporation. A corporation, in turn, is an artificial *person* created by the state. In this sense, the city is something of a cross between the national or state governments on the one hand and the private corporation on the other. It differs from both, however. In theory, both the United States and the states are *sovereign,* or at least share sovereignty. A sovereign body is one possessing supreme temporal power, a state that owes allegiance to no one. Actually, of course, neither the United States nor any of the states possesses full and true sovereignty. The plenary powers of government are divided in a federal system in such a manner that the ancient concept becomes somewhat obscured. However, cities, villages, and other municipal corporations possess no sovereignty at all. They are children of the state, created usually by the action of the state legislature, and even in those states most dedicated to the principle of home rule, the *state* courts remain the final arbiters of what are local concerns.

The municipality, like any other corporation, derives its powers from the state, and those powers granted to it are expressed in a *charter.* A charter is the fundamental law of a corporation which establishes (1) the structure or form of government, (2) the powers that may be exercised by it, and (3) the general manner in which the powers granted may be exercised. The charter is almost never a single document, but includes all state laws and judicial opinions that affect the structure, powers, or manner of exercising the powers of the corporation.

The city, in some respects, has a legal position not unlike that of a private corporation. In fact, it has been only in the last two centuries or so that a definite distinction has developed. The two are still similar in that each has an existence independent of the members of the corporation, may own property, may make contracts, may exist, normally, in perpetuity, and may sue and be sued. They possess very important differences, too. A private corporation is created entirely by the *voluntary* request of a group of people who wish to form a corporation. They know the corporation law in advance and hence know the conditions under which they will operate. Furthermore, once the corporation charter is granted, it becomes a *contract* which cannot be altered or taken away (except under the rarest circumstances involving an overriding "public interest").[6] A public corporation, on the other hand, may be created with or without the consent of its

[6] The contract could be altered or taken away, of course, if provision for this existed in the contract itself.

membership (the persons living in the area), the terms of its charter may be quite different from what the people of the community desire, and, even more important, the charter is *not* a contract and is hence subject to constant, involuntary, and sometimes arbitrary changes. It can even be taken away without advance notice, unless the state constitution specifically prohibits this.

There are two other important differences between public and private corporations. A public corporation can act only in the legally described *public* interest and for a public purpose. A private corporation must always have the public interest in mind (one could not long exist, for example, if it were organized for the purpose of robbing banks), but it may also have private interests (such as profit making for the individual owners). The two also differ in the amount of control the state exercises over them. A private corporation can carry on any activities it wishes, so long as it does not violate some law; a public corporation can do only those things that it is authorized to do. A corporation producing cigarettes, for example, could take on a sideline of producing, say plowshares, without seeking an amendment to its charter or any other kind of permission from the state. (It could not, however, put in a sideline of marijuana cigarettes, since this would not be in the public interest and could be curbed by the state under its police powers.) A municipal, or public, corporation, on the other hand, could not decide to enter into such a sideline as, say, municipal parking lots or a municipal theater or to adopt a new form of taxation without having first the specific authority to do so.

The Elements of a Corporation What are the elements necessary in order to have a municipal corporation? Stated by McQuillin in the language of the law, they are:[7]

1 Incorporation as such pursuant to the constitution of the state or to a statute.

2 A charter.

3 A population and prescribed area within which the local civil government and corporate functions are exercised. However, the inhabitants of the municipality are not a separate legal entity and do not themselves constitute the municipality, and the common council or other governing body of the municipal officers does not constitute the corporation.

4 Consent of the inhabitants of the territory to the creation of the corporation, with certain exceptions [actually, the legislature in most states may act without consulting the local residents].

5 A corporate name.

6 The right of local self-government, although in most states this is held to be not an inherent right.[8] Unless otherwise provided by statute, a test as to whether an organization is a municipal corporation, using the term in its strict sense, is whether it has the power of local government as distinguished from merely possessing powers

[7] Reprinted from Eugene McQuillin, *The Law of Municipal Corporations,* 3d ed., vol. 1, sec. 2.07, published by Callaghan and Company, 6141 North Cicero Avenue, Chicago, Illinois, 60646.

[8] This is an example of the cautious legal mind. In *no* state is the concept of local self-government as an inherent right legally acceptable.

which are merely executive and administrative in their character. The characteristic feature of a municipal corporation beyond all others is the power and right of local self-government.

The Corporation and the Quasi Corporation In the above passage, McQuillin suggests that there may be local units of government that are not in the strict sense municipal corporations. He is referring to a legal distinction that is made between corporations and quasi corporations. The former include cities, villages, and the relatively few *incorporated* (under a separate written charter) counties and school districts. The latter include most of the counties, townships, unincorporated New England towns (even though any of these may have the same powers as cities), and the so-called "special districts" such as sewage-disposal, airport, drainage, mosquito-abatement, fire, and irrigation districts.[9]

So far as the lay citizen is concerned, the principal distinction between genuine corporations and quasi corporations is to be found in the fact that quasi corporations serve only as administrative agents of the state, but the true municipal corporation serves a dual purpose. It not only acts as a local agent for the state but also performs certain local functions exclusively in the interests of the people living within the corporate boundaries of the city.

In theory, the city acts as an agent of the state whenever it performs a function in which the state as a whole has a certain interest; for example, when it enforces the law, or maintains public health standards, or collects taxes. On the other hand, the city may perform some tasks purely for the comfort and convenience of the local inhabitants, in theory at least. This classification includes such things as the operation of a water-supply or public transportation system. Counties and school districts, in contrast, perform only such functions of statewide interest as the maintenance of records, the prosecution of crimes, the maintenance of roads, and the education of children.

Since the city acts in a dual capacity, it is said that the city performs two types of functions, *governmental* (as an agent of the state) and *proprietary* (as an agent of the local inhabitants and for their comfort and convenience). This distinction is less important for laymen than it is for lawyers. As will be seen later, the line of demarcation is in any event difficult to draw, is an artificial legalism, and has probably created more problems than it has solved. Property owned for carrying on governmental functions is in theory held for the state, which may dispose of it without consulting the city and without payment to it. On the other hand, property owned by the city for carrying on its proprietary functions cannot ordinarily be taken by the state without compensation, on the theory that constitutional guarantees of property rights extend to property held by the city in its proprietary capacity.[10] The same distinction is followed in the law of municipal-tort liability.[11]

[9] The special districts are discussed in chap. 10.

[10] See McQuillin, *op. cit.,* vol. II, sec. 4.132. The United States Supreme Court makes no such distinction so far as the United States Constitution is concerned. *Trenton v. New Jersey,* 262 U.S. 182 (1923).

[11] See below, pp. 144–145.

Powers of the Corporation The subordinate legal status of cities makes it necessary that the question of whether or not a particular city has the power to perform a particular function in a particular way be decided by the courts. Because the city is merely a creature of the state while the state itself is a sovereign body, the courts have established a rule of a narrow construction of municipal powers and a broad construction of state powers. To put it another way, the courts say that, if in doubt, the city does *not* have the power to do something it wishes to do. (In some home rule states, municipal powers are beginning to be more broadly interpreted. This is discussed below in the section on home rule.) The authority that is almost invariably cited by courts in support of this interpretation is *Dillon's rule.* John F. Dillon, a renowned Iowa judge and author, summarized the legal position of cities in the following words.[12]

> It is a general and undisputed proposition of law that a *municipal corporation possesses and can exercise the following powers and no others:* First, those granted in *express words;* second, those *necessarily or fairly implied* in or *incident* to the powers expressly granted; third, those essential to the accomplishment of the declared objects and purposes of the corporation—not simply convenient, but indispensable. Any fair, reasonable, substantial doubt concerning the existence of power is resolved by the courts against the corporation, and the power is denied.

It is this rule that explains why a city might have to spend weeks of time and thousands of dollars in actions before the state courts seeking to justify its decision to finance a municipal parking lot from the parking-meter fund rather than from the general-revenue fund, or seeking to find some theoretical justification for a planning or a smoke-abatement ordinance. That the community should demand them and that they should be adopted according to democratic procedures is not enough.

Dillon's rule allows the courts a good deal of leeway in determining what a city may or may not do. What are necessarily or fairly implied powers? What powers are essential to "the accomplishment of the declared objects and purposes" of the city? Only the judges know. They apply the principle of *stare decisis*—the rule of law in one case is the basis for the decision in later cases—but much is left to their discretion. It may be implied, for example, that a city may offer a reward for the arrest and conviction of someone who violates an ordinance (an act by the municipal governing body which, in theory, merely applies state law to local situations) but not for the violator of a state law, even for the murderer of the city's chief of police.[13] An implied power may vary greatly from one state to another. For example, it *cannot* be implied from anything in the Cleveland charter that the city has the right to spend its money in order to send council members to the state capital as lobbyists,[14] But it *can* be implied from the Minneapolis charter that aldermen may be sent to attend meetings of the Rivers and Harbors Congress in Washington.[15]

[12] John F. Dillon, *Commentaries on the Law of Municipal Corporations,* 5th ed., Little, Brown and Company, Boston, 1911.

[13] Compare *Choice v. Dallas,* 210 S.W. 753 (1919), and *Madry v. Scotland Neck,* 199 S.E. 618 (1938).

[14] *Cleveland v. Artl,* 23 N.E.2d 525 (1939).

[15] *Tousley v. Leach,* 230 N.W. 788 (1930).

Charters: General and Special Act

The concept of the city as a corporation dates back to Roman times, and noblemen granted charters of special privileges to unincorporated cities of Europe as early as the eleventh century, but the modern practice of incorporating urban communities and prescribing their powers did not appear in England until the fourteenth century.[16] Often these charters merely legalized the informal situations that already existed. In any case, the Crown (or an important lord or colonial governor) began to grant special charters wherein the specific city to be incorporated was named and its powers enumerated. This plan became the standard practice in England, on the continent of Europe, and in the British colonies of North America.

It was not until the French Revolution that the *general charter* came into use. As one of the reforms of 1789, the French established a general municipal code to apply to all communes, giving them equal status and powers. From that time on, the use of the general charter became standard in European democracies, although the pattern was somewhat modified in the United Kingdom, where the general laws were often supplemented by special laws and administrative orders granting special powers to particular municipalities.

The Special Act Charter The special charter plan, inherited from the mother country, was standard practice in America from colonial times and remained so until well past the middle of the nineteenth century. In 1851, Ohio, and a few months later, Indiana, outlawed special legislation, including special act charters of incorporation. (Special legislation for a particular municipality does not necessarily mean a formal amendment to a local charter, though it has precisely that effect.) The following century produced a series of attempts to eliminate or modify the use of the special act charter. The major objection to it was to be found in the tendency of legislators to substitute their preferences for those of a locally elected city council. In theory, the special act was useful: It provided a tailor-made charter to fit the special circumstances of the particular city. In practice, however, the legislature often permitted local governments little discretion concerning local affairs. Urban dwellers, therefore, sought to find ways of retaining or recapturing local control.

Where special legislation was not completely outlawed, an attempt was made after about 1870 to allow it only after formal notice had been given that the legislature was considering changes in the fundamental law of a city and after an open hearing at which interested persons and groups could testify. This plan was modeled on the British plan. It is in use in several states but has met with considerable success only in Massachusetts. Legislators will usually not cooperate with approaches that have the effect of restricting their powers, as this plan does.

In a few states, special legislation was permitted only if the proposed legislation received local approval. The New York constitution of 1894, for example, allowed special legislation if the proposal, after passage in the general assembly, was approved by the mayor in a first-class city (New York, Rochester, and Buffa-

[16] William B. Munro, *Municipal Government and Administration,* The Macmillan Company, New York, 1923, chap. 9.

lo) or by the mayor and council in other cities. The bill would then go to the governor for his consideration in the usual manner. If disapproved either locally or by the governor, it could be repassed by the legislature and become law nonetheless. The New York plan appears to have given considerable protection to localities, although quite a few bills continued to be passed despite local disapproval.[17] The adoption of home rule in 1923 made the plan obsolete.

An amendment to the Illinois constitution in 1904 sought to give Chicago some degree of local self-rule. It provided for a referendum on all special legislation applying to Chicago. The provision had the effect of protecting Chicago voters from what they did not want, but it established no method by which the city could obtain what it did want.[18] As a result, the provision has had little use, and the Chicago charter is seldom amended.

Some states permitted special acts only if no general act could "be made to apply" to the situation. This rule contained a loophole that could be discovered by even the dullest legislator. Since the courts are normally inclined to resolve doubts in favor of the action of the legislature, a pretense could almost always be found to argue that a given situation could not be met by general legislation.

Special legislation is not used only to prevent local policy making. In Iowa, when special act charters were used, "the people of the local community not only had in many instances a considerable share in formulating their charters in accordance with local needs, but they also had in effect authority to amend their charters. Special charter cities had little difficulty in securing amendments from the legislature. . . . While such charters and their amendments were subject to legislative control, the records do not show the existence of a meddlesome attitude on the part of the General Assembly."[19] But the picture was, and is, different in other states, and it has aroused considerable urban resentment.

Despite its unpopularity in urban communities, special legislation is still used, especially in New England and the South, and particularly in Alabama, Florida, Maryland, North Carolina, Tennessee, and Georgia. In Maryland, for example, 70 percent of the bills passed in some sessions of the legislature are local in character. About one-half of the states are constitutionally authorized to grant special charters or special acts, and a number of the states still employ this system either exclusively or predominantly. In more than one-half of the states, special act charters are still in existence, but no new ones are being created, either as a matter of policy or as a result of subsequent constitutional prohibition. About twelve states provide, at least in some instances, for a local referendum on new special act charters. This practice dates from the nineteenth century.

The General Act Charter The general act charter, designed to provide for uniform powers, privileges, and structures for every city in the state, has not met

[17] Howard L. McBain, *The Law and the Practice of Municipal Home Rule,* Columbia University Press, New York, 1916, gives a detailed account.

[18] As had been pointed out in Munro, *op. cit.,* pp. 180–181.

[19] George F. Robeson, *The Government of Special Charter Cities in Iowa,* Iowa State Historical Society, Iowa City, Iowa, 1923, p. 178.

with much success, except where it has been modified by home rule or local option. Because American towns vary from hamlets to empires of millions of people, it is unrealistic to expect that every city government should be exactly like every other in powers and structure. The failure of general acts to allow for an expansion of local autonomy is, however, more importantly attributable to the fact that legislators have been largely unwilling to relinquish traditional areas of authority over local government. They have sought loopholes of evasion and have met with considerable success.

Constitutionally required use of general legislation has been circumvented by three techniques, principally: by the passage of laws that purport to be general but are not in fact; by the establishment of special districts; and by prostituting the classification device. If special legislation is prohibited, the question arises: What *is* special legislation? The answer, of course, comes from the courts. Following the general rule of broad construction of state legislative powers, the courts have hesitated to rule against the legislature. Most of the state high courts have therefore been willing to allow as "general" any legislation that on the surface appears to be general, or any legislation that may potentially apply to another city, even though at the moment it affects only one. In one case,[20] the Ohio legislature, despite a constitutional prohibition against special legislation, passed an act applying to "any city having within its limits an avenue more than 100 feet wide known as Lincoln Avenue." Is this special legislation? Not at all. Practically any city could qualify if it chose to build such a street. If, however, the legislators had added "on January 1, 1900," or some such prohibitive qualification, the supreme court would almost have been forced to void it. In point of fact, however, it has been easy to achieve special legislation without judicial proscription.

Another method of avoiding the ban on special legislation has been by establishing special districts: for parks and recreation, sewage disposal, police, and the like. This has been possible because the prohibition on special legislation applied only against "municipal corporations" or "cities."

Some state constitutions, while outlawing special legislation, recognized that, say, the city of New York and the village of Au Sable Forks in the northern lakes country of the state could not be treated adequately with the same legislation, and therefore permitted the *classification* of cities. In some states the constitution established the classifications, in others it authorized the legislature to do so, and in a third group of states, where the constitution was silent, the courts permitted the legislature to classify, holding this to be general legislation. Whatever the source of authority for classification, the identical treatment of all cities, large and small, was generally recognized as being impractical. General acts did not allow for unique problems.

In some states, for example in Wisconsin, classification legislation has been used sparingly and for its intended purposes. In other states, however, legislators have sought to use the classification device as a disguise for special legislation.

[20] Munro, *op. cit.*, p. 178.

Sometimes the courts have insisted that classifications be reasonable, but in most cases they have been tolerant when the legislators have resorted to subterfuges. True, the courts have on occasion prohibited some types of classifications, especially those using a *geographical,* rather than a *population,* basis, but the lawmakers usually have had their way. Classification has made it particularly easy to pass special legislation for the largest cities.

In Pennsylvania, each of the three largest cities were once placed in separate classes, and in Ohio the *eleven* largest cities at one time each had its own class. [After classification had been reduced to an absurdity in Ohio, the Supreme Court outlawed *all* classification in *Ohio ex rel. Knisely v. Jones,* 64 N.E. 424 (1902). The legislature then unsuccessfully attempted to treat all cases alike. The problem was resolved in 1912 with the introduction into the state of municipal home rule.] Although some classification is necessary because the problems of large cities are not the same as those of small cities, state legislatures under the guise of classification have deprived the larger cities in many states of much of their power of local self-government.

General Act Charters: Cafeteria Style In those states without home rule or special act charters, it has been necessary to devise some way of meeting the particular needs of individual cities. Variations in needs occur in connection with both powers and forms of government. A large city might want the strong-mayor form, a middle-sized city the council-manager, and a village the traditional weak-mayor. In order to meet these variants, some states have adopted *optional charter laws.* Most states make use of this device, with about one-third using it as the principal source of city charters.

Under this plan, upon petition of a prescribed number of voters, or by resolution of the council, the council or the voters of a city may decide which *form* of government they wish to adopt. They are limited in choice, of course, to the type of options the legislature provides. A state may offer two or three basic charters; or five, as in Massachusetts; or as many as fourteen, as in New Jersey. The people of the city may go through the cafeteria line, picking from among the state's offerings. They may take only those things offered, however, and without variations or alterations. There can be no special orders to the kitchen. This plan is convenient for the state, and it offers some local choices as to type of government, although the powers that the city is authorized are normally much less variable. The plan is gaining in popularity in the United States. Of course, the legislature still determines the structure of government for each city, and *all* amendments to charters must still be obtained from the state, but the local population can determine whether it prefers to abandon the weak-mayor form, for example, or perhaps whether it wants the council-manager form with or without ward elections for council. A generous optional charter plan, such as that of New Jersey, may, to local residents, be a satisfactory method of bestowing charters.

Appraisal Efforts to prevent or reduce legislative domination over local government have been made through such devices as the constitutional control of classification of cities and the use of the optional charter plan. These efforts have met with limited success. The legislature remains paramount, and its members have found it relatively easy to legislate for specific cities whenever they have desired to do so.

But in seeking to grant independence to cities, advocates of general legislation tended to minimize the fact that cities do have unique requirements that must be met by specific legislation. As a matter of fact, no state today has a single general act to cover the powers, functions, and structure of all its cities.

Although legal restrictions on legislative control were circumvented by imaginative legislators, often with the cooperation of the courts, and while legislative participation is still common in several states, notably in the South, the legislatures of an increasing number of states have, as a matter of public policy, given the people of cities considerable autonomy in local affairs. In some states, home rule has provided for some local autonomy. This is especially true in California, Michigan, and Wisconsin, as well as perhaps Minnesota and Texas. Optional laws in many states enable cities to modify their forms of government as to details, and sometimes such laws establish permissive, as distinguished from mandatory, legislation which each locality may avail itself of as it sees fit. This is especially true in Wisconsin, Washington, and Nevada.

Some types of state control and supervision have been helpful to cities and not preemptive of local policy making. In many cases, city officials, instead of chafing under the existing degree of state controls, approve of this control or are unconcerned with it. Cities will always be subject to much legislative control. Nearly every function performed by cities affects the people of the state as a whole. In a day of large economic units and rapid means of transportation and communication, it is impossible for the cities to isolate themselves. Furthermore, there is no natural cleavage between state and local interests and functions. Because one tends to grow out of the other gradually, the state and its cities are under pressure to work together.

Charters: Municipal Home Rule

As towns were founded in colonial Rhode Island, "the local communities . . . organized and managed their own local affairs and services. Each town retained its own individuality and functioned to a great degree without reference to any higher authority, except for those few laws which were commonly accepted by all communities."[21] It was not until after the Revolutionary War that the general assembly of Rhode Island, together with the legislatures of other states, began to enforce claims of sovereign and plenary powers over matters of local concern. In the new United States, the earlier idea that local communities should be left alone as much as possible all but disappeared. Municipal home rule charters represent a somewhat romantic attempt to return to an earlier situation that is often pictured as ideal. The home rule movement was another device that won

[21] Robert J. M. O'Hare, "Cities Rush Home Rule Gate," *National Municipal Review* (now *National Civic Review*), 42:73–77, February, 1953.

the support of early-twentieth-century reformers in their drive to free the local community from the state legislature.

Municipal home rule, which is an indigenous Americanism, involves the power of municipal corporations to frame, adopt, and amend a charter for their government and to exercise all powers of local self-government, subject to the constitution and general laws of the state. Home rule may be provided for in the state constitution or by enabling acts of the state legislature. It may be available to all cities and villages (e.g., Oregon and Wisconsin), or only those of over a certain population (e.g., California and Colorado), or to a very limited number of cities (e.g., eleven in Washington, one in Pennsylvania). It may be a self-executing provision of the state constitution (e.g., Arizona and Nebraska), or it may require legislation before a city can adopt a charter (e.g., Texas and Wisconsin). It may be used by many municipalities in the state (e.g., in Oregon and Michigan), or by relatively few of them (e.g., in Ohio, Missouri, and West Virginia).

Home rule provides an important difference in the procedure for securing charters and subsequent amendments to them. Under the older system of special and general act charters, a charter is secured through the process of lobbying before the legislature, and every amendment to the charter requires the sending of city officials and other interested persons to the state capital to bargain with legislators. Under home rule, this is not necessary: The amendment is proposed (usually) by the council and is voted upon by the eligible voters. Under general act charters of either the classification or optional charter type, a city that lobbies for an amendment may find itself in the peculiar position of being opposed by another city in the same class or using the same option. This never happens under home rule.

Framing a Charter The procedural rules for writing a new charter or making major revisons in an old one vary, of course, from one state to another. In states having self-executing constitutional home rule, the procedures are outlined in the constitution itself. About one-half of them do not do this, however, but simply authorize the legislature to make the rules. The constitution of Wisconsin, for example, provides that "the method . . . shall be prescribed by the legislature." All states operating under legislative home rule, of course, use procedures established by the legislature.

The common procedure is for the voters of the city to elect a charter commission. In Minnesota, the commission is appointed by the local district judge; in Oregon, the city council acts as the charter commission, or a charter may be presented through the procedure of the initiative. The commission is usually given a certain length of time in which to draft a charter for submission to the voters, who must then approve (usually by a simple majority vote). It may sometimes be necessary to elect a second or third commission if the first cannot agree upon a charter or if its proposed charter is defeated at the polls. Sometimes state approval is required in addition to that of the voters.

Once a home rule charter is adopted, it may be amended from time to time. In some states the charter commission is a permanent body that can propose amendments at any time (e.g., Minnesota and West Virginia), but the most common system is to have the proposals for amendment come from the city council or through the use of the initiative. Ratification is normally by popular vote.

Because of the practical effects of Dillon's rule, city charters must be lengthy, complex, and technical in some sections. (The index to the Los Angeles charter alone contains more words than does the United States Constitution.) The result is that in many home rule cities the voters are frequently called upon to consider amendments to the charter. Many proposed amendments are of minor importance; others are highly technical. The voter is often either apathetic, confused, or both. In order to overcome this handicap to the effective operation of home rule, the New York constitution allows a city council to draft and adopt all charter amendments of a minor character without submitting them to a popular vote. If, however, organized opposition to the action of the council appears, a referendum can force a public vote: for certain types of amendments involving important questions of public policy, the conventional type of referendum is always required. A similar rule applies in Wisconsin, while Oregon and West Virginia (for third-class cities) allow charter amendment without popular vote under certain conditions. These methods reduce the length of the already crowded ballot and remove some of the technical amendments from decision by the voters.

The Origin and Spread of Home Rule Like many American political institutions, including the United States Constitution itself, municipal home rule had its origins in the expedient actions of practical politicians. The first state to establish a version of it was Iowa, which did so under an 1851 act of the legislature. After operating since territorial days under the special act charter system, the legislature in that year established a single method of charter adoption for newly incorporated communities or for towns desiring to become cities. If the inhabitants decided to incorporate, the law provided that an election would be held to choose persons to prepare a charter. The legislature provided the general limits of authority that could be granted by the charter, but these were broad. The charter, once written, was submitted to the voters for approval or disapproval.[22]

This unique and liberal law was not given a full opportunity to show its merit and hence was not actually the beginning of the home rule movement. Few uses seem to have been made of it. Most of Iowa's muncipalities had already been established by earlier special charters. In 1858 the law was repealed, for the new Iowa constitution adopted the preceding year followed the contemporary fashion and required the use of a general incorporation act. However, the new law allowed the already existing city charters to be amended locally, and the four remaining cities to which this applies still exercise this privilege.[23]

[22] State of Iowa, *Code of 1851,* chap. 42. See a research note, "Municipal Home Rule in Iowa," *Iowa Law Review,* 49:826–862, Spring, 1964. For even earlier antecedents for home rule, especially in New York, see Howard L. McBain, *American City Progress and the Law,* Columbia University Press, New York, 1918, pp. 22–29.

[23] Robeson, *op. cit.,* pp. 178–180.

The Missouri constitutional convention of 1875 furnished the stage for the first provision for *constitutional* home rule. The people and political leaders of St. Louis had long been dissatisfied with legislative oversight of the city government and the need to secure the approval of the legislature for any changes in the city charter. The St. Louis delegation, therefore, came to the convention with a set of proposals for the government of the city, including one for what is now known as home rule. This plan was included in the constitution and was adopted by the voters of the state, although home rule was restricted to St. Louis at that time. The reform period that followed helped to spread the idea of home rule throughout much of the nation.

The reformist National Municipal League first endorsed municipal home rule in 1900 and included it in its *Model City Charter* and, later, in its first *Model State Constitution* (1921). There have been three waves of adoptions of home rule: during the progressive reforms of the second decade of the century, immediately after World War II, and during the municipal difficulties of the 1960s and 1970s. A century after its first adoption in Missouri, a majority of states, twenty-eight, had some form of municipal home rule.[24]

The Practical Meaning of Home Rule Some reformers have incorrectly assumed that municipal home rule results in the granting of greater powers to cities, with more independence from the state legislature. The granting of home rule makes for changes in several aspects of the local political scene, but does it grant more power or greater independence to cities? The questions cannot be answered categorically. Home rule apparently gives cities their greatest freedom in choosing the form of government they are to employ and in exercising routine housekeeping functions (civil service rules, the fixing of salaries, the establishment of pension system, etc.). In these areas, non-home rule cities must nearly always accept or secure enabling legislation from the state. Home rule cities may *possibly* be freer on matters that are legally *local* in interest (the establishment of parks, the control of building regulations), but "their freedom is not measurably greater in matters of education, general police control and utility rates and services (except in Colorado)."[25] On financial matters, in which the state can always claim an interest, home rule cities have virtually no advantage over special and general act charter cities, except in California.

In many states, home rule has helped to give municipalities greater powers of discretion in making routine decisions. Cities without home rule often must go to the legislature in order to get authorization to perform some minor function or to exercise some power that most laymen would consider to be obviously a local responsibility. For example, a North Carolina town had to have the legislature pass an act in order that the council might declare it a misdemeanor to use roller skates on the public sidewalks. A Maryland city had to get special permission to increase the salary of a stenographer by $300 a year. A Nevada city had to get

[24] See William N. Cassella, Jr., "A Century of Home Rule," *National Civic Review,* 64:441–450, October, 1975.

[25] *State-Local Relations,* Council of State Governments, Chicago, 1946, pp. 164–166.

legislative permission in order to purchase a rotary pump for the fire department. An Iowa town discovered that it lacked power to purchase uniforms for the members of its police force.[26] Home rule is not a guarantee against such municipal impotence, but it has been helpful in overcoming it.

Although home rule cities often, in fact, enjoy greater powers than do nonhome rule cities, most of them are potentially subject to state control over their affairs. In most home rule states, the legislature enjoys concurrent or superior power to the city government in matters of local concern. And the legislature is, of course, supreme in those areas that the judges consider to be of state, rather than of local, concern. In most states, general acts of the legislature, or what purport to be general acts, take precedence over ordinances or charter provisions. Under these circumstances, the question of whether municipal home rule will promote greater local discretion, and the extent to which it will do so, is a question not of law but of public policy determined by the legislature, at whose sufferance home rule exists. To be sure, the enactment of a constitutional amendment providing for home rule places an implied moral obligation upon the legislature to carry out the spirit of its provisions, and this moral pressure appears to have had an effect upon the legislatures of several states.

In recent years, under increasing pressure from the National League of Cities, the National Municipal League, and the U.S. Advisory Commission on Intergovernmental Relations, constitutional provisions and judicial decisions have tended to resolve more doubtful powers in favor of cities. In eleven states (1975), the tendency now, under what is called the "Fordham Rule," is to grant cities powers not denied by constitution or statute and to give "liberal" interpretations of constitutional home rule provisions.[27] In this sense, home rule cities, since about 1960, are gradually beginning to gain greater legal flexibility than is granted by Dillon's rule, at least in some states. Even so, home rule cities operate under many restrictions, especially relative to financial matters.

Home Rule: An Appraisal Home rule allows charters to be tailor-made to suit the preferences of the particular community and permits them to be more flexible than the types provided by the legislature in allowing for changing exigencies and in taking advantage of new developments in administrative techniques. Home rule probably makes it easier to experiment with charter provisions, since the amendments are locally proposed and adopted.

Perhaps the greatest effect of home rule lies in its psychological value. To those interested in local government, it may give the impression of granting more independence to the city than is the actual case. This gives encouragement and incentive to those who would be active in local government and thus gives the reformer the feeling that if he fails, he has only himself to blame. The psychologi-

[26] Examples from among those cited in *Home Rule in Nevada,* Legislative Counsel Bureau, Carson City, Nev., 1952.

[27] See Casella, *op. cit.* For the original statement of the "Fordham Rule," see J. B. Fordham, *Model Constitutional Provisions for Municipal Home Rule,* American Municipal Association, Chicago, 1953.

cal effect upon legislators is also significant. Most legislators have been willing to accept the mandate of the voters when a home rule provision is written into a constitution and to permit home rule to operate even where legal authority to commit sabotage lies with the legislature. This is not always the case, but it often is. In home rule states, bills which would deal with local matters are sometimes opposed by legislators who wonder if they would not "interfere with the rights of local self-government" or "violate the principle of home rule." Home rule is hence more often an *attitude* toward local government than it is a legal injunction against legislative action.

THE CITY AND STATE

The state has been most unwilling to allow its child, the city, to grow up. A theory of perpetual infancy was adopted by nineteenth-century legislatures in their attitudes toward their offspring. Efforts at achieving independence for municipalities through the legal device of constitutional limitations were largely unsuccessful. Cities in most states did achieve more independence and less legislative supervision of their affairs after the first decade or so of the twentieth century, but the change seems to have been produced principally by a changing climate of opinion toward cities that accompanied the urbanization of the nation, together with a slight increase of public trust in the politician, both state and local.

Legislative oversight of local government declined in the twentieth century for another reason: Government became too complicated to be sufficiently understood by amateur legislators meeting for a few weeks annually or biannually as an interlude away from their principal occupations. City government became professionalized and technical; its complex details came to be understandable only to the professional, full-time technician. Flexibility, which legislatures did not possess, was needed. So was continuous, rather than sporadic, oversight. The twentieth century represented, therefore, a period during which state legislators were somewhat reluctantly, but inexorably, forced to transfer increasing amounts of local government supervision to the professional bureaucracies of the administrative branch of state government.

In addition to state legislative and administrative oversight of cities, the judicial branch also acts in a supervisory capacity. Some facets of this control require development.

State Judicial Oversight of Cities

Standing behind all city officials, looking over their shoulders, are judges. They are the individuals who settle all disputes between the city and the state, a taxpayer and the city, one local government and another. They are the umpires. Although they make a determination only when asked to do so, and then upon the basis of laws and ordinances made by other people, they are themselves lawmakers, for the judges decide ultimately what the law *means* and hence what the city can and cannot do.

Because the city is not a sovereign body, its standing at law is approximately the same as the standing of a private corporation, except when it is acting in the name of the sovereign (the state). Because of this legal position and because it enjoys only those powers granted to it under the principle of Dillon's rule, the city is constantly faced with the task of proving in court that it has the power to do what it seeks to do.

The Taxpayer's Action The court actions in which the municipality constantly finds itself embroiled may in some cases be brought by a state official, but most of them are brought by a taxpayer resident in the city, or by a corporation that is a taxpayer, for a corporation is an artificial person at law.

In Anglo-Saxon common law, "the King is the fountainhead of all power," and therefore "the King can do no wrong" and "the King cannot be sued without his own consent." This principle was transferred to the American republic, where the word "people" was substitued for "King" in the first quotation, but "state" was used in the last two. The United States Supreme Court has held that status as a taxpayer does not give one sufficient interest in the matter to test the legality of an act of Congress in a judicial action,[28] and this rule also applies in most of the states relative to legislative acts. The same protection does not extend to municipalities, however, for they are normally subject under the common law to taxpayers' suits even when there has been no statutory grant of the right.

Taxpayers' suits may be brought for three purposes: (1) to enjoin acts of the municipality that are unauthorized, unlawful, or *ultra vires;*[29] (2) to compel unfaithful officers, or even third persons, to repay into the treasury sums illegally paid out; and (3) to protect the interests of the municipality where its officers wrongfully refuse or neglect to perform their duties. This third type may involve legal actions by the taxpayer in the name of the city to protect municipal powers and rights that the officers of the city fail to protect.

In theory, taxpayer actions are analogous to the actions stockholders may bring against the officials of a private corporation (who are legally acting as their agents). The purpose is to stop acts that are allegedly illegal or to stop or remedy situations that give evidence of fraud, corruption, or other wrongdoing. The taxpayer suit has sometimes prevented the granting of fraudulent contracts, the issuing of improvident bonds, or the granting of illegal franchises.

The taxpayer action is often used as a weapon by interests that disagree with proposed municipal policies. Theoretically, an action cannot be brought simply because the taxpayer dislikes the judgment or doubts the wisdom of the city officials, or because their policies might damage the profits of the business. In practice, however, these are often the real reasons behind suits. Almost any public policy that deviates even slightly from traditional municipal behavior will result in action in which the policy is claimed to be *ultra vires.* The individuals or corporations in such a case may be seeking to protect their own economic interests or to impose their own personal ideology upon local policy making. The

[28] *Massachusetts v. Mellon,* 262 U.S. 447 (1923).

[29] *Ultra vires* actions are actions legally beyond the power of the municipal corporation or its officers.

courts are often the last resort of the obstructionist, and state court judges have often lent a sympathetic ear. City-government proposals have often been delayed by expensive, time-consuming legal actions.

A parking-lot owner may have a right to bring action to prevent a city from entering the parking-lot business on the ground that it is *ultra vires* to use money from the general-revenue fund (rather than the parking-meter fund) for the purpose. A home builder may be permitted legal action to stop a public housing project on the ground that such a project is not for a public purpose. A television station owner may be permitted legal action to prevent the city from operating a municipal television station on the ground that the city charter permits only a radio station. In such cases, the interests opposing the action are able to use the machinery of the law to support their positions, for the burden of proof is on the city government.

Taxpayer actions cause so much delay and are so nearly inevitable—that many cities, especially the larger ones, commonly arrange for a "friendly suit" to be instigated in order to clear away the legal cobwebs before launching into a new program or attempting to issue bonds under an untried procedure. Such actions not only save time and avoid the wasting of money in preparations that might otherwise later have to be abandoned, but they sometimes lead to the discovery of possible legal alternatives even when the original proposal does not survive the legal process. Middle-sized and small cities tend to allow the large municipalities to break legal ground; they are often slower in moving into a new area of activity, and by the time they do so, the court rulings may already have been made.

THE CITY AND THE CITIZEN

Because cities are corporations and not sovereignties, they are responsible for contract violations and torts. Almost every culture, even the most primitive, distinguishes between a *tort,* or wrong against an individual, and a *crime,* a wrong against society. A tort is a violation of a personal right established and protected by law. A violation of a contract is the violation of a personal right established by mutual agreement and protected by law. For purposes of this text, a tort is an injury to a person that is neither a crime nor a violation of a contract. Cities have much the same legal position as do private corporations. The basic rules of municipal liability are established in the common law, but they are subject, as is any part of the common law, to statutory modifications in the individual states.

Municipal-Contract Liability

Cities enter into countless contracts with individuals and corporations. In general, they are answerable for these contracts in the same manner as are private corporations. Even when there is no question of good faith involved in the carrying out of a contract, many other problems may arise—problems of interpretation of the contract, of determining when its conditions have been completed, of making settlement when performance of the conditions of the contract becomes impossible. Cities may therefore find themselves in court in the normal course of carrying out their activities.

The principal problem that faces the courts in the interpretation of contracts to which the city is a party is that of determining the conditions under which a contract is valid. In general, a valid contract is one that the city is authorized to make, that is made by the proper officer according to law, and that has been adopted according to proper procedures. (For example, the law may require that certain contracts be let only after advertising for bids, and then only to the lowest responsible bidder.) An *ultra vires* contract is normally invalid, but state courts sometimes order monetary settlements where the city has benefited from the contract. Similarly, a contract made by the wrong officer, or without following proper procedures, may sometimes, but not always, be validated, and the other party to the contract may have to assume any loss. Court practices vary from one state to another.[30]

Municipal-Tort Liability

It will be recalled that the city was earlier described as performing two different types of functions: those which it does involuntarily as an agent of the state, and those done at local option as a service to the immediate community. In performing the former type of activity, the city becomes a veritable department of the state government and, as such, becomes cloaked in the state's mantle of sovereignty. It is said to be performing a *governmental* (or public) function. In performing services of comfort and convenience to the immediate community, however, the city acts very much as if it were simply a private corporation doing the same job. It is said to be performing a *proprietary* (or corporate, or sometimes private) function.

Clearly a theoretical line could well be drawn between those functions where the city directly represents the sovereign, and hence cannot be sued without its own consent, as is the rule with the sovereign power; and where the city acts as an ordinary corporation, and hence could reasonably be expected to assume the same responsibilities as other corporations. The difficulty with such a legal fiction arises when an attempt is made to classify the multitudinous activities of a modern city. The theory requires a perfect bifurcation, with every function being either governmental or proprietary, and with no messy edges or leftover pieces. The functions themselves, however, are not very cooperative when a classification is attempted.

Is the parks and recreation function, for example, carried on only for the comfort and convenience of the community, or is it part of the sovereign's responsibility to protect the health, safety, and welfare of the inhabitants of the state? How about airports, hospitals, or garbage disposal? The answers to these questions are not easy to find. Furthermore, the law of municipal-tort liability is not the same in any two states of the union.

[30] Details of municipal-contract liability are developed by McQuillin, *op. cit.*, vol. X, secs. 29.01–29.04.

The classification of functions is done in the various states either by legislative statute or, in its absence, by the judges. The legislature is free to overrule the judges and can, if it chooses, make functions that are the most clearly governmental in character subject to tort action. The whole law of tort liability is based upon the judge-made common law, however, and most legislatures have been content to allow the judges to work their way through the problem on their own.

The courts almost invariably place certain functions in the governmental category, for which the city may not be sued. These include police, fire, education, libraries, traffic signals (they act in lieu of police officers), and public health. Functions that are nearly always held to be proprietary include city-owned public utilities, such as water, public transportation, gas, and electricity. Many functions vary considerably from state to state in their classification: parks and recreation (which tend to be governmental), hospitals (likewise), airports (which tend to be proprietary), street lighting, street cleaning, garbage collection and disposal, and the construction and maintenance of sewers.

Certain functions are generally recognized as being essentially governmental, but for which the municipalities must nonetheless maintain responsibility for torts. These are functions dealing with the *public ways.* Historically, the state has expected the municipal corporation to be responsible for torts committed in the maintenance (but usually not in the construction) of streets, sidewalks, bridges, culverts, and the like. Citizens have a right to expect that a bridge will not collapse under them or that they will not walk into an open manhole in the sidewalk. Even in these cases, however, doubts are resolved against the individual. It is always held, for example, that the city must be given a reasonable time in which to correct a fault or post a warning. (In the absence of statutes to the contrary, quasi corporations such as school districts, counties, and townships are not responsible for *any* torts. The theoretical reasoning holds that all of the functions of a quasi corporation are performed involuntarily as an agent of the state.)

The Rule on Discretion Regardless of whether a function is claimed to be governmental or proprietary, most courts will ask another question before deciding whether tort liability exists. That question deals with whether the action in litigation involved a *discretionary* or a *ministerial* act. That is to say, is damage claimed because the city decided to do or not to do something, or is it claimed because of the manner in which city officials or employees carried out established policy? Discretionary acts involve the making of public policy decisions, and they are *not* subject to tort action. Ministerial acts involve the carrying out of established policy, and they are normally the only type of acts that will allow for a legal action. For example, if the city council decides not to extend a water main or not to build a bridge across a stream, or if a police officer (acting in good faith and upon probable cause) decides to arrest a person who subsequently proves to be innocent of any crime, there could be no maintainable action, since these all involve decision making. On the other hand, once a bridge is built, the public has a right to expect the ministerial function of maintaining it to be carried out, and once the city decides to operate a bus line, the public has a right to expect that individuals will not be injured while riding on the buses.

The Rule of Respondeat Superior According to the common law, the master is responsible for the actions of the servant, providing that those actions may reasonably be said to follow from the orders given to the servant. This is the rule of *respondeat superior.* In municipal-tort liability, it means that the city must answer for the action of its officers and employees, providing that the city is suable for the particular function involved and that the officer or employee was acting in general compliance with the requirements of the job.

If a city official or employee does something not called for in the performance of duty, these actions are *ultra vires,* and the city bears no responsibility for them. Since individuals are responsible for their own actions where there is no master-servant relationship to protect them, this means that citizens who are wronged may sometimes be able to sue the *individual* city official or employee when they cannot sue the city itself. This may sometimes protect the injured person who may be wronged in the course of the city's performing a governmental function. But the individual, it must be remembered, is not responsible when the city cannot be sued—unless the actions are *ultra vires.* If a city police officer arrests an innocent person against whom a grudge is held, or if a fire-truck driver operates a vehicle in a grossly negligent manner, the individual who is harmed may be able to collect from the officer or employee as an individual. The chances are excellent, however, that even if he or she gets a court judgment, the city employee will not earn enough from his or her job to pay for such damages.

Recapitulation A tort is an injury to a person that is neither a crime nor a violation of a contract. Cities and villages are responsible for torts committed by their officers and employees (generally speaking) when the tort was committed in the performance of a ministerial act, by an employee who was not acting in an *ultra vires* fashion, in connection with the public ways, or in connection with a municipal function of a proprietary character, and not one of a government character. In most states, if any one of these conditions is not met, the city is not responsible in tort action.[31]

Closing Comment

The question of whether the municipality is or is not liable in tort action is controlled by state legislatures, which can overrule court decisions when they choose to do so. Legislatures do not act on the basis of equity or logic but rather, as with other legislation, on the basis of the balance of the pressures upon the membership. City attorneys, mayors, and managers, who must be concerned about their budgets, generally oppose expanding the city's responsibility. Lawyers who specialize in tort cases, persons who want to try making easy money through spurious suits, persons who have been injured on or by city property, logicians, and others would like to see municipal liability expanded. In contrast, some persons who are especially concerned about governmental expenditure levels would prefer that the municipality be made as immune as is the state.

The balance of interests seems to be such that the status quo is maintained,

[31] The basic material on municipal-tort liability is to be found in the treatises by McQuillin and Dillon.

by and large. In most cities, it remains less costly to the individual to be struck by a water-department truck than by a police-department patrol car.

SELECTED READINGS

Advisory Commission on Intergovernmental Relations: *State Constitutional and Statutory Restrictions upon the Structural, Functional and Personnel Powers of Local Government,* Advisory Commission on Intergovernmental Relations, Washington, 1962.

Council of State Governments: *State-Local Relations,* Council of State Governments, Chicago, 1946.

Dillon John F.: *Commentaries on the Law of Municipal Corporations,* 5th ed., Little, Brown and Company, Boston, 1911. (A classic study of local government law.)

Drury, James W.: *Home Rule in Kansas,* Governmental Research Center, University of Kansas, Lawrence, Kans., 1965. (A case study of adoption of constitutional home rule in 1960.)

Journal of Urban Law. (A quarterly, first published in 1966.)

McBain, Howard L.: *American City Progress and the Law,* Columbia University Press, New York, 1918. (A reform-era analysis of legal factors.)

——: *The Law and Practice of Municipal Home Rule,* Columbia University Press, New York, 1916. (Classic legal analysis.)

McCarthy, David J.: *Local Government Law in a Nutshell,* West Publishing Co., St. Paul, Minn., 1975. (A convenient summary by a law professor.)

McGoldrick, J. D.: *Law and Practice of Municipal Home Rule, 1916–1930,* Columbia University Press, New York, 1933.

McQuillin, Eugene: *The Law of Municipal Corporations,* 3d ed., Callaghan and Company, Chicago, 1949.

Model City Charter, 6th ed., National Municipal League, New York, 1964. (Incorporates structural features favored by contemporary reformers.)

"Municipal Home Rule in Iowa," *Iowa Law Review,* 49:826–862, Spring, 1964. (An example of legislative home rule.)

Rhyne, Charles S.: *Municipal Law,* National Institute of Municipal Law Officers, Washington, 1957.

Stauber, Richard L.: *New Cities in America,* Governmental Research Center, University of Kansas, Lawrence, Kans., 1965. (A study of municipal incorporations during the decade of the 1950s.)

Williams, J. D.: *The Defeat of Home Rule in Salt Lake City,* Eagleton Institute Case 2, McGraw-Hill Book Company, New York, 1960. (A case study of a referendum campaign.)

D

The Structure

Chapter 7

Forms of Government

A Minneapolis alderman once told one of us that forms of government have nothing at all to do with the effectiveness or honesty of government. He felt that Minneapolis, which has a nineteenth-century form, operates under a government as good as could be had under any of the newer forms which are so often advocated by supporters of reform. The viewpoint was scarcely new with him, however; similar expressions have come from Alexander Pope, Edmund Burke, and Lincoln Steffens.

It is true that Americans have been rather obsessed in recent decades with the idea of a relationship between structure and effectiveness of government. Many advocates of reform have been guilty of overstatement in this direction. Much literature may be found urging the commission or council-manager plan, for example, on the ground that these plans follow the organization form of the business world, the corporation. The implication is that the success of the one should ensure the success of the other.

The truth of the matter, it would seem, is that structural arrangements do have an effect upon the pattern of government, but they neither guarantee nor prevent the type of government a particular group of citizens might want. The forms of government are important because they affect the pattern of influence of various groups upon policy making. The specific structure in any given case helps to establish behavior patterns and attitudes toward power and the exercise of power that definitely affect the process whereby decisions are made.

A study of innovation relative to housing and urban renewal showed little relationship between policy making and structure.[1] On the other hand, a study of St. Louis government found that structure "plays an important role in determining the scope and intensity of political conflict in the community."[2] The mayor of that city is the dominant policy-making figure and, as such, groups interested in policy seek to influence his election and to secure access to him. Business leaders look to him for the development of programs affecting the location of industry, tax rates, adequate city services, and "the social climate of the community necessary to attract technical personnel for their businesses." If the mayor were not an effective policy leader, these groups might be disadvantaged.

Another set of interests—those of low-income people, of the small merchants and business persons, and of the black minority—seek to have their positions protected by the elective "county" officers (St. Louis is a city-county) and by the ward aldermen. These groups are interested, not in broad policy, but in such things as patronage jobs and individual favors of all kinds, such as the location of stop signs, parking regulations, help in getting an apartment in a public housing unit, and the other traditional types of political assistance to individuals. If the county officers were subject to the same rules as city officers—as could happen by elimination of the formal structural distinction—most of the patronage would disappear. If the council members were elected at large, they would have far less interest in doing favors for individuals than is the case under a ward system.

In another study of four Midwestern cities with about 50,000 population,[3] structural differences also seemed to be significantly related to the pattern of politics in the cities. The nonpartisan ballot, for example, appeared to weaken the potential influence of national parties in municipal elections. The level of education of council members was lower and the degree to which ethnic groups were represented was higher in cities using the ward system, as compared with those using at-large elections. The absence of a primary election in one city appeared to favor organized groups, or groups that had achieved a high degree of consensus on goals, as compared with independent candidates. The ward system militated against an aggressive annexation policy such as existed in the at-large cities. Why? Because aldermen feared that annexed territory might be added to their particular wards, thus upsetting the balance of forces that had, in the past, permitted them to secure election.

[1] Michael Aiken and Robert Alford, "Community Structure and Innovation: The Case of Public Housing," *American Political Science Review,* 64:843–864, September, 1970; and by the same authors, "The Case of Urban Renewal," *American Sociological Review,* 35:650–664, September, 1970.

[2] See Robert H. Salisbury, "St. Louis Politics: Relationships among Interests, Parties, and Governmental Structure," *Western Political Quarterly,* 13:498–506, June, 1960.

[3] Oliver P. Williams and Charles R. Adrian, *Four Cities,* University of Pennsylvania Press, Philadelphia, 1963.

In 1954, Indiana mayors, acting through the state municipal league, succeeded in killing a proposed home rule amendment to the state constitution. They feared that its passage might result in a spate of adoptions of the council-manager plan, which was not permitted in that state under existing law. The unwanted plan represented a threat to the mayors, in terms of both political power and compensation. In Indiana, St. Louis, and the four middle-sized cities, formal structure of government *did* make a difference in the making of policy and in determining which individuals and groups would be most influential in the process of making decisions.

Yet, one can overstate the impact of structure. For example while boss systems most frequently have existed in weak-mayor and strong-mayor cities, the commission system of Jersey City came under the boss control of Hague and that of Memphis under Crump, and the city manager system of Kansas City succumbed to Boss Pendergast. Also while the nonpartisan system generally has weakened national parties in local politics, the Chicago Democratic and Republican organizations continue effectively to control the outcome of its nonpartisan council member races. Structural reorganization is perhaps a necessary but not a sufficient condition for achieving political reform. The second, third, and other variables relate to characteristics of the citizens being governed.

The Basic Forms

There are three basic forms of city government in the United States: the mayor-council, commission, and council-manager plans. To this must be added the New England town meeting and its accommodation to modern urban conditions, the representative town meeting. There are many variations of these plans, and especially of the mayor-council plan. A 1968 tabulation of cities over 5,000 population shows 50.6 percent have the mayor-council plan, 43.0 percent the council-manager plan, and 6.4 percent the commission system.[4]

A word of caution should be given at the outset in examining forms of government: There are probably no two cities in the United States that have *exactly* the same structure of government. Very few fit the theoretical ideal of the general plan they follow. Nearly every charter commission or state legislature, in considering structure, finds it politically expedient to add its own improvisations on the given theme. For example, the strong-mayor–council system calls for the appointment of department heads by the mayor, yet many such cities have elective clerks and treasurers.

The mayor of New York has many administrative powers, a characteristic of strong-mayor cities, but the chief fiscal officer of the city reports to the board of estimate, rather than the mayor. Detroit clearly has a strong-mayor government, yet its organization chart is cluttered with a series of *advisory* boards and commissions that are vestiges of the old weak-mayor *administrative* boards and commissions.

[4] *Municipal Year Book, 1968,* International City Management Association, Chicago, 1968, pp. 52–63. The *Year Book* no longer publishes data on local government structure.

The manager plan calls for the manager to appoint all department heads, yet in most cities with this form some administrative officers are either elective or selected by the council. The variations are quite endless, and the structural descriptions that follow must be thought of as models which city charters tend to imitate. The difference between the weak- and strong-mayor systems, in particular, is a relative one. The models of each are at opposite ends of a continuum, and the various mayor-council cities must be thought as of being located somewhere along the continuum—rarely, if ever, at one of the extremities.

CITIES WITH A SEPARATION OF POWERS

The general historical context in which the structures of American city government developed has already been discussed. During nearly all of the nineteenth century, American cities were operated under the weak-mayor-council (or weak-mayor) system. Near the end of that century, what is now called the strong-mayor system gradually evolved. In recent years, a third principal derivative of the plan, a result of efforts to strengthen administratively the strong-mayor system in large cities, has evolved. For purposes of this text, it will be called the mayor-council plan with chief administrative officer (or mayor-council with CAO). This plan will be described later.

Taken collectively, the various types of mayor-council cities make up over one-half of all cities of the nation under any form of government.[5] Most smaller cities use this form, too, except in New England, where some variant of the town-meeting form is common. All but five of America's twenty-seven largest cities (over 500,000 population) use the mayor-council plan, usually of a strong-mayor type. Nearly two-thirds of the small cities of 5,000 to 10,000 people have the mayor-council form, usually of a weak-mayor type.

The Weak-Mayor–Council Plan

In the early decades of the nineteenth century, America's budding cities borrowed from rural government certain essential concepts. Today we call it the weak-mayor–council plan.

Characteristics The weak-mayor plan is a product of Jacksonian democracy. It reflects the spirit of the frontier, with a skepticism both of politicians and of government itself. It grew out of a time when the functions of city government were few, when the need for a single executive was not recognized, and when people were afraid to give powers to a single executive. Implicit in the weak-mayor plan are the beliefs that if politicians have few powers and many checks upon them, they can do relatively little damage and that if one politician becomes corrupt, he or she will not necessarily corrupt the whole city government.

The council is both a legislative and an executive organization under the weak-mayor plan. In small cities today, the council is small—five or seven mem-

[5] *Municipal Year Book, 1970,* International City Management Association, Chicago, 1970, pp. 76, 535.

bers—but in bigger cities it is usually a fairly large body of perhaps eleven to fifty members. At one time councils were as large as 200. Members are (except in small cities) ordinarily elected by wards on a partisan ballot. In the past, many councils, copying the state and federal systems, were bicameral (they had two houses). With the abandonment of the second house by Waterville, Maine, in 1968, only Everett, Massachusetts, retains the bicameral arrangement.

In addition to making policy, the council appoints several administrative officers, such as the city engineer and the city attorney. Council members (sometimes called aldermen if they represent wards) may serve on several ex officio boards and commissions.[6] A committee of the council usually prepares the budget and may even appoint the controller, who administers the expenditure of the budget.[7] (See Figure 7-1.)

The mayors are not "weak" because they lack policy-making power—they normally have a veto, can recommend legislation, and may even preside over the council. They are "weak" because they lack administrative power. There is, in fact, no single individual charged with the responsibility of seeing to it that the laws and ordinances are properly carried out or that the city administration proceeds in accord with an overall plan. Mayors have very restricted appointive powers; even when they are allowed to make appointments, they may not be able to remove those they place in office, so that they are deprived of any real control over them or responsibility for them.

Ordinarily several of the principal city offices are filled by direct election—the long ballot is a characteristic of the weak-mayor plan. Other offices, in addition to those filled by election and the council, may be of the ex officio type. Even the governor or some other state official may make some appointments, such as that of the police chief. Without a chief executive, the weak-mayor system is likely to be one in which the various departments are independent of one another and without coordinated effort.

The weak-mayor system requires the voters of the municipality to choose members of sundry boards plus such administrators as, perhaps, the clerk, treasurer, assessor, controller, and attorney. Two candidates for the park board might well offer differing platforms of policy (one might want a new park on the west side, while the other might prefer a new swimming pool on the east side), but will the voter have the time and inclination to look past the mayoralty contest as far as the council contests, much less to that for the park board?

In electing a clerk, treasurer, or assessor, the voter is even more sorely beset. Most of the voters will not know which candidate is best qualified to be the assessor, and they will not even know what functions are exercised by the clerk, treasurer, or, especially, the controller. In most cities, the clerk is a glorified file clerk, keeping the records of the city, while the treasurer is a bookkeeper, maintaining the financial records of the city. Both officers are important, but they are

[6] Ex officio boards and commissions have a membership of persons who hold office by right of holding another office. For example, the airports commission might be made up of the mayor, the clerk, the treasurer, and two aldermen.

[7] See chap. 13 on fiscal administration.

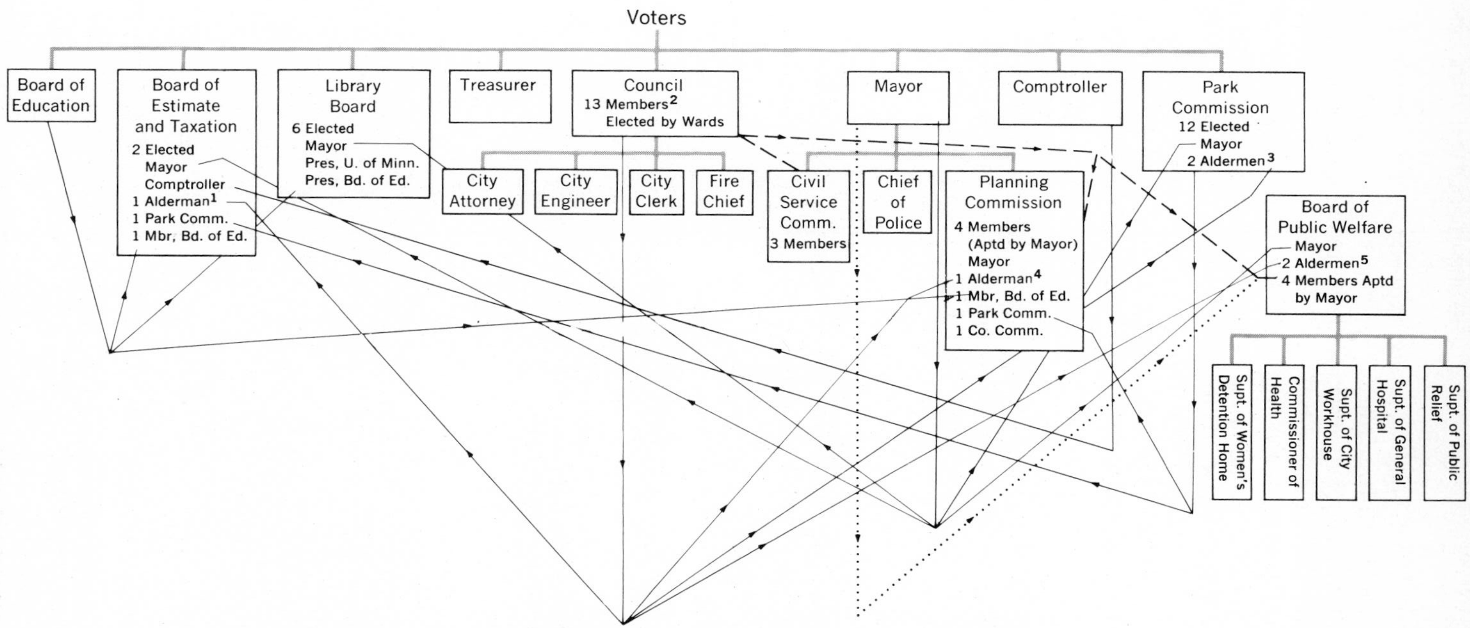

Appointment or Election
Ex Officio Membership
Council Approval Required

1 Chairman of Ways and Means Committee
2 Until 1953, the Council Consisted of 26 Members
3 Chairman of the Committee on Roads and Bridges and Chairman of the Committee on Public Grounds and Buildings
4 Council Elects One of its Membership
5 Council Elects Two of its Membership

Figure 7-1 An actual weak-mayor–council city: Minneapolis, Minnesota. *Note:* There are many other appointive and ex-officio boards and commissions which are not shown. Departmental subdivisions are also not shown. This plan was not substantially modified in Minneapolis until the mid-1970s.

ministerial rather than policy making. Theirs are normally routine jobs of an office-manager type that could well be performed by either appointive or merit-system personnel. The voter, unacquainted with criteria usable in selecting persons to serve in offices such as these, is likely, in a large city, to vote for the person whose name is best known to him—usually the incumbent—regardless of the candidate's qualifications. In small cities, the voter is likely to support a candidate on the basis of sympathy. A qualified person may be passed over in favor of an opponent who is a veteran, or a handicapped person, or one with a large family who needs the pay, but who is not qualified.

The number of elective offices in American cities, even under the weak-mayor plan, has been declining for many decades. In 1936, 70 percent of the cities of over 5,000 population elected one or more administrative officers other than the mayor. By 1966, this figure had dropped to 48 percent. In 1936, 240 cities elected their police chiefs. Despite a great increase in the number of cities since then, only 125 elected the chief in 1966.[8] (See Table 7-1.)

Appraisal The arguments for the weak-mayor plan are based upon the precepts of Jacksonianism. Many of these ideas are still popular with a large number of American people. For example, Americans may not know which officers are elected and which are appointed, but they are likely to insist that those who are

[8] See the current issue of the *Municipal Year Book,* International City Management Association, Chicago.

TABLE 7-1. Municipal Elective Offices In Cities over 5,000, Exclusive of the Mayor and Council

Title of Office	Percent of Cities Electing*	Number of Cities Electing
Treasurer	29	883
Clerk	24	713
Assessor	13	384
Auditor	10	304
Attorney	8	235
Controller	4	114
Police chief	4	125
Public works director	1	45
None of the above elective	52	1,554

*There were 158 cities not reporting and not included in the above. The list includes *all* forms of government. Percentages for mayor-council cities alone would be higher.

Source: Municipal Year Book, 1966, International City Management Association, Chicago, 1966, p. 97.

elected should continue to be elected. They may not know what tasks are performed by a particular officer or what the criteria are for choosing an officer for the post, but they want her or him elected.[9] The weak-mayor system encourages this frontier type of concept.

The weak-mayor plan was a product of a different world from that which Americans occupy today. It was never intended to serve large, impersonal urban communities. The plan does not encourage modern methods of housekeeping—budgeting, personnel, purchasing, and the like. In fact, with its resort to performance by amateurs acting without coordinated leadership, it fosters the use of the spoils plan. For example, the city engineer (in charge of maintenance of public ways) may well be appointed by the council in a weak-mayor city. If this is the case, the ward aldermen on the council may personally direct the activities of the engineer's office within each of their wards and will probably have considerable control over selection of the employees of the office. Street maintenance becomes not a matter of professional judgment and performance but one of doing repairs where they will be of the most help in the next election. The mending of political fences rather than of public ways becomes the first order of business.

Most of the great nineteenth-century machines operated under this plan, for it encourages the boss by its very clumsiness and lack of coordination. Under this plan, the voter can scarcely determine, after the most conscientious effort, who is responsible for what, or even what functions are being performed by whom. With no clear-cut locus of answerability to the voter, the boss has a real advantage. The weak-mayor plan is the most easily corrupted and bossed because of the confusing pattern or organization.

Probably the greatest criticism levied against the weak-mayor plan concerns its lack of provision for administrative leadership. The mayor, with very limited appointing powers and even more limited removal powers, is not a true chief executive. There is no officer to coordinate the various activities of the city. The mayor may not even make up the budget, which would serve at least to give an overall picture of the needs of the city and of someone's rank-ordering of the relative importance of proposed expenditures of departments. Suppose, for example, that the city is short of funds (and all cities are short of funds). In a form of city government in which one person is legally responsible for all administration, it would be possible for this person to determine that the parks and recreation department should spend less for the coming year so that more streets could be repaired. He or she might be opposed by interests, but the decisions would carry great weight. Under the weak-mayor plan, however, the park board is a law unto itself, not answerable to either the mayor or the council, especially if it has its own tax levy and hence funds independent of the council, as might well be the case. Each department is likely to move in its own direction with no one empowered to coordinate. The effect of all these independent agencies is to make city

[9] Donald S. Hecock, "Too Many Elective Officials?" *National Municipal Review* (now *National Civic Review*), 41:449-454, October, 1952, offers a case study of this phenomenon on the state level.

government into a series of many little governments rather than one. There is one city government for parks, another for libraries, another for airports, another for sewage disposal, and so on.

Despite the great amount of criticism that has been levied against the weak-mayor plan, modifications of it remain the most common form of municipal government in the United States today. This is so in large part because the traditional form of village government throughout the United States is that of the weak mayor. Of course, the form of government is less important in the smaller municipality because government is more personal, performs fewer functions, and has less elaborate machinery. It has therefore been less important for smaller cities to experiment with newer forms of government, and there has been less agitation for them to do so.

While the weak-mayor system is characteristically found in small cities and villages, quite a few cities of considerable size still have relatively weak mayors, especially in the South. Atlanta (1970 population: 498,973) is the largest city in the United States with what is clearly a weak-mayor system. Outside of the South, Chicago, with its huge council of fifty members elected by wards, retains many of the characteristics of the weak-mayor system, as do Los Angeles and San Francisco, where administrative boards and commissions are extensively used.

In Chicago, government is coordinated through the political party. The last effective large-city machine in the nation controls nearly all aldermanic seats and about 35,000 patronage jobs. In Los Angeles, with nonpartisanship and a strong merit system, the seventeen departments are largely independent under autonomous boards, and they play the mayor off against the council members. As a result, one newspaper reporter has noted, "We have Custer's Last Stand almost every week, with the mayor and the council taking turns playing Indian."[10] The system includes so many veto loci that policy development has become almost impossible in a city with a multitude of rapidly changing problems.

Rather extreme examples of the weak-mayor system may still be found in many places. Stevens Point, Wisconsin (1970 population: about 23,479), is an example. The voters select directly the mayor, controller, clerk, treasurer, assessor, city engineer, health officer, street superintendent, park superintendent, city attorney, and ward aldermen, in addition to school officials. The pattern is even more complicated, for control of the police and fire departments is vested in a commission separate from the council.

The structure of the weak-mayor–council plan is not regarded as being satisfactory for modern government. It is clumsy, uncoordinated, and has, for a long time, been declining in use for all but the smallest cities.

The Strong-Mayor–Council Plan

The development of a strong-mayor system of government in the last two decades of the nineteenth century was a gradual one. The new plan differed only in

[10] Quoted in Iola O. Hessler, *Twenty-nine Ways to Govern a City: A Comparative Analysis of the Governments of 29 of the Largest Cities in the United States,* Hamilton County Research Foundation, Cincinnati, 1966, p. 10.

degree from that of the weak mayor. It was not conceived of as a distinctly new form of government, nor was it one. Actually, the weak-mayor form resembled the structure of most state governments of that day and this. The strong-mayor system, on the other hand, was modeled on the national government, with its integrated administrative structure under the control of the President.

Few, if any, cities meet exactly all the conditions of the theoretical model for the strong-mayor system as it is described below. Most mayor-council cities represent a compromise between the very weak- and the very strong-mayor plan. The typical one is difficult to classify.

Characteristics In the strong-mayor–council city, administrative responsibility is concentrated in the hands of the mayor, and policy making is a joint function of the mayor and the council. (The strong-mayor plan is sometimes called the "federal" plan, because it follows roughly the plan of the federal government, but this term is confusing and will not be used in this text.) The plan calls for a short ballot with the mayor as the only elected administrative officer. He or she appoints and dismisses department heads, often without council approval. The mayor thus becomes the officer responsible for the carrying out of established policy and for coordinating the efforts of the various departments. The mayor also prepares the annual budget and controls its administration once it is adopted by the council. This allows the whole financial picture and the claims of the various departments to be compared in financial policy making, in contrast to the piecemeal methods by which these things are approached under the weak-mayor plan.

The mayor's legal position permits exerting strong political leadership. Not only does one have the veto power and the right to recommend legislative policy to the council, as is the case under the weak-mayor system, but the wide control over administration gives great power, which can be used in many ways as a weapon to overcome opposition, and furnishes a vantage point from which to recommend policy. Furthermore, this strong administrative position encourages the newspapers to give mayors credit or blame for events that take place within city government. The resultant publicity makes the public keenly aware of these activities and of recommendations to the council. As in the case of the President of the United States, when strong mayors speak, they receive far more attention than does even the most experienced or most respected member of the legislative branch. The fact that the mayor presents a comprehensive budget to the council for consideration also adds to the dominant political position, for by this very act public attention is focused on the mayor and the burden of proof for any changes in the budget is placed upon the council.

The council plays a highly subordinate role in a strong-mayor city. It does not, as in the weak-mayor city, share in the performance of administrative duties. Its functions are limited to the exercise of legislative policy making, and even this role must be shared with the mayor. If there is an aggressive member of the council, this body may seek to make policy for itself. But it is more likely that the mayor's recommendations, backed as they are by the greater focus of public attention, by constant oversight of the city administration, and by the veto power, will be dutifully enacted by the council, perhaps after insignificant changes or after a symbolic show of independence. Average citizens are not likely to have much knowledge of council activities in a strong-mayor city. In a large city they are unlikely even to know the names of more than one or two of the council members, especially if the council is elected at large, as is often the case.

Because the council is exclusively a policy-making body for the city as a whole, it is likely to be small (typically seven or nine members) and elected at large on either a partisan or a nonpartisan ballot. Unless the city is very large, members serve on a part-time basis, since they have no administrative duties to perform and are not expected, as they are in the weak-mayor system, to be errand runners for residents of their wards. When council members serve only part time, the effect is to give the mayor even greater powers, because of the advantage of spending the whole of the day studying the needs of the city. This may tend to place the council in an even more subordinate position. It will certainly put its members at a disadvantage in obtaining and evaluating information from the various departments and will place an even greater burden of proof upon the council when it disagrees with the proposed policies of the mayor. Terms of office for both mayor and council are likely to be four years in length. This is the result of the reform-movement attitude that public officials should be given time enough in office to prove themselves.

In addition to performing part of the legislative functions, the council is also entrusted with the important task of serving as critic. This is a function of all legislative bodies, of course, but it becomes unusually important where vast administrative power is vested in one official. The council is usually given full power to conduct investigations into any department or any phase of administration. In addition, an officer, usually called the auditor and responsible to the council, checks upon the way in which the administrative branch of the city has spent the moneys appropriated by the council.[11]

Appraisal Because of its provision for vigorous political leadership, the strong-mayor plan is especially desirable in large cities, where the complexities of government require someone to give firm leadership and direction. No other form of government in use in American cities makes an equal provision for leadership. Nearly all the nation's largest cities have some version of the strong-mayor plan. In smaller cities, where the functions performed are fewer and simpler and where government is more personal, the need for this type of leadership is somewhat less.

The strong-mayor plan, in comparison with the weak-mayor–council plan, permits use of the executive budget and merit-system personnel administration, overall executive planning, coordination of administrative activities, and greater public visibility for decision makers.

It has some problems, too. Perhaps the major one is that it expects too much of the mayor. In addition to serving as ceremonial head of the city, the mayor is supposed to be both an adroit politician and an expert administrator. This com-

[11] See Chap. 13 on fiscal administration.

bination is not easy to find. The able politician is likely to be either inexperienced with administration or bored by it, or both. The person whose training and interest are in administration, or some specialized phase of it, is very possibly a colorless campaigner or one who finds politics personally distasteful. Although the popular view that all politicians are extroverts and all public bureaucrats are introverts is not correct, it is true that skill in campaigning and administrative leadership are not often combined in the same person. The strong-mayor system expects that they will be.

Another problem in the strong-mayor systems is that of getting persons with the required qualifications to run for office. A person who can do all the things expected of a strong mayor is usually highly successful in business and industry and is ordinarily unwilling to give up a position which pays a high salary and in which there is reasonable security to conduct a political campaign for a position which carries far less salary and no security.

In selecting a mayor, many voters would no doubt like to consider the qualifications of each candidate as a capable administrator, but they are necessarily unable to do so. Judging whether or not a person is a good administrator is very difficult—more difficult than judging whether a person is technically qualified as an engineer or a physician. The candidates themselves are not of much help to the voter; the one who makes the greatest claims of administrative ability may be the one least qualified.

It has sometimes been said that the strong-mayor plan is undesirable because it "mixes politics with administration," but this is not a valid argument. As a matter of fact, this could be offered as an argument *for* the plan. The mayor is able to place administrative problems in their political context—where they must eventually be placed in a democracy—and can compromise between these two inseparable aspects of government.

Because it is based upon that American favorite, the separation of powers, in combination with its obverse, the checks-and-balances system, the possibility of a deadlock between the mayor and the council on the formulation of policy is always present. On the national level, where the same system exists, most students are aware of serious deadlocks that have taken place—during the last two years of Wilson's administration, the last two of Hoover's, almost the whole of Truman's after 1946, and much of the Nixon term. It is perhaps less common on the local level than on the national, however, because the strong mayor usually dominates the political scene and is in a position to keep the council subordinate. The threat is, however, inherent in the system.

The Mayor-Council Plan with Chief Administrative Officer

Chief executives in mayor-council cities may well recognize their own shortcomings as administrators and attempt to do something about it. The most common method of buttressing the position is to appoint an able, professionally experienced administrator to the position of chief fiscal officer, usually called the controller, who may act as something of a deputy mayor and attend to may details of administration.

The typical political mayor is not always willing to choose professional deputies, however. In order to provide some legal incentive to do so, a trend has been toward establishing by charter or ordinance officials known by various titles and here called chief administrative officers (CAO). Their powers vary considerably from one city to another, and sometimes they can scarcely be differentiated from the chief budget or fiscal officer, but according to the theory of the position, they should be appointed by the mayors and serve at their pleasure. That is to say, the mayor may dismiss the CAO without having to show cause or gain the council's permission for this action.

Chief Administrative Officers perform such functions as the supervision of heads of various departments, preparation of the budget (or supervision over the budget director), and personnel direction. It is their task to correlate the various departments in the important routines of day-to-day administration, to give technical and professional advice to the mayor, and hence to free the mayor for the other two major jobs of serving as ceremonial head of the city (greeting the governor, laying cornerstones, and issuing proclamations) and proposing and lauching broad overall policy.

The origins of the CAO are somewhat obscure, for the position grew out the garden-variety mayor-council plans, but the city and county of San Francisco appointed one in 1931 who must have been one of the earliest.[12] Many CAOs exist in California cities, but these all appear to be *managers* with reduced administrative authority. These so-called CAOs are appointed by the council, as is a manager, rather than by the mayor. In San Francisco, the CAO heads a group of city offices dealing only with public works and does not make up the budget or coordinate city departments.[13] In Los Angeles, the CAO has somewhat broader responsibility for the city's day-to-day operations.

Some authorities believe the CAO plan should be classified as a varation of the manager plan, rather than of the mayor-council plan; it combines some of the characteristics of each. Its classification is probably not too important. It is listed here in this book because it is a plan that continues the use of the separation-of-powers theory and places formal responsibility for administration in the hands of the mayor, rather than with the council as is the case with the manager plan. In states where cities have broad home rule powers, many of the characteristics of the council-manager plan can be incorporated under the strong-mayor form. As a result, there is no rigid dividing line between the two forms.

The Current Trend Large-city interest in strong-mayor plan with CAO has been increasing since the end of World War II. The Philadelphia charter of 1951

[12] John C. Bollens, *Appointed Executive Local Government: The California Experience,* University of California Press, Berkeley, Calif., 1952, pp. 12–14; John M. Selig, "The San Francisco Idea," *National Municipal Review* (now *National Civic Review*), 46:290–295, June, 1957. See Lent D. Upson, "A Proposal for an Administrative Assistant to the Mayor," reported in *The American City,* 44:93, June 1931; or, more generally, Wallace S. Sayre, "The General Manager Idea for Large Cities," *Public Administration Review,* 14:253–257, Autumn, 1954; and, for an argument that the council-manager plan may be more appropriate, even for large cities, John E. Bebout, "Management for Large Cities," *ibid.,* 15:188–195, Summer, 1955.

[13] See Bollens, *op. cit.,* pp. 9–11, 119–123; and Selig, *op. cit.*

provides for a CAO, as does the 1952 New Orleans charter. Both are home rule cities. The New Orleans charter, for example, calls for a council of seven, five elected by districts and two elected at large, for four-year terms. (See Figure 7-2.) The mayor has the usual powers in policy making and, in addition, appoints a CAO, who serves at pleasure. The CAO, with the approval of the mayor, appoints the heads of departments, except for those whose positions are filled according to state law. The CAO, of course, has supervisory and coordinative powers over the department whose heads he or she appoints.[14]

A CAO established by ordinance has served Louisville. St. Cloud, Minnesota, adopted the CAO plan in its 1952 charter. A director of administrative services, with some of the powers of a CAO, has been established in Boston. A 1951 charter amendment provides for an administrative officer for Los Angeles, appointed by the mayor with majority confirmation by the council and removable by the same process or by a two-thirds vote in the council. This officer is probably not a CAO, since Los Angeles is basically a weak-mayor city, and the administrative officer is principally the mayor's budget officer. In that city, the council has numerous administrative duties, and a score of departments are controlled by five-member commissions appointed by the mayor with the check of council approval and with a limited removal power. The city attorney and controller are elected officials.

The 1950 Faulkner Act in New Jersey provides for optional charters which may be adopted in the various cities after a local charter commission decides to present one of the options to the voters for approval. It makes the strong-mayor plan with CAO one of the options.

Abandonment in New York In 1953, two study groups recommended the CAO plan for use in the city of New York. After a three-year study which cost $2,200,000, the Mayor's Commission on Management Survey in its final report recommended against a general overhaul of the city's organizational structure and suggested the creation of a new office, that of a CAO to be called a "director of administration." It was also suggested that a "management cabinet," to consist of seven ex officio members, be appointed to aid the mayor. The director of administration would perform supervisory and coordinative functions over most of the city's departments and agencies. The deputy mayor would be assigned nearly all the ceremonial duties of the city.

Immediately after his election as mayor of the city, Robert F. Wagner, Jr., announced that he would appoint a CAO to the new post of "city administrator." For this task he selected a widely known student and practitioner of public administration, Luther H. Gulick.[15]

Mayor Robert F. Wagner, Jr., during his twelve years in office (1954–1966), gave formal support to the office and to the five persons who occupied it but

[14] See *National Municipal Review* (now *National Civic Review*), 41:250, May 1952; 41:570, December, 1952.

[15] Wallace S. Sayre and Herbert Kaufman, *Governing New York City,* Russell Sage Foundation, New York, 1960, pp. 665–666.

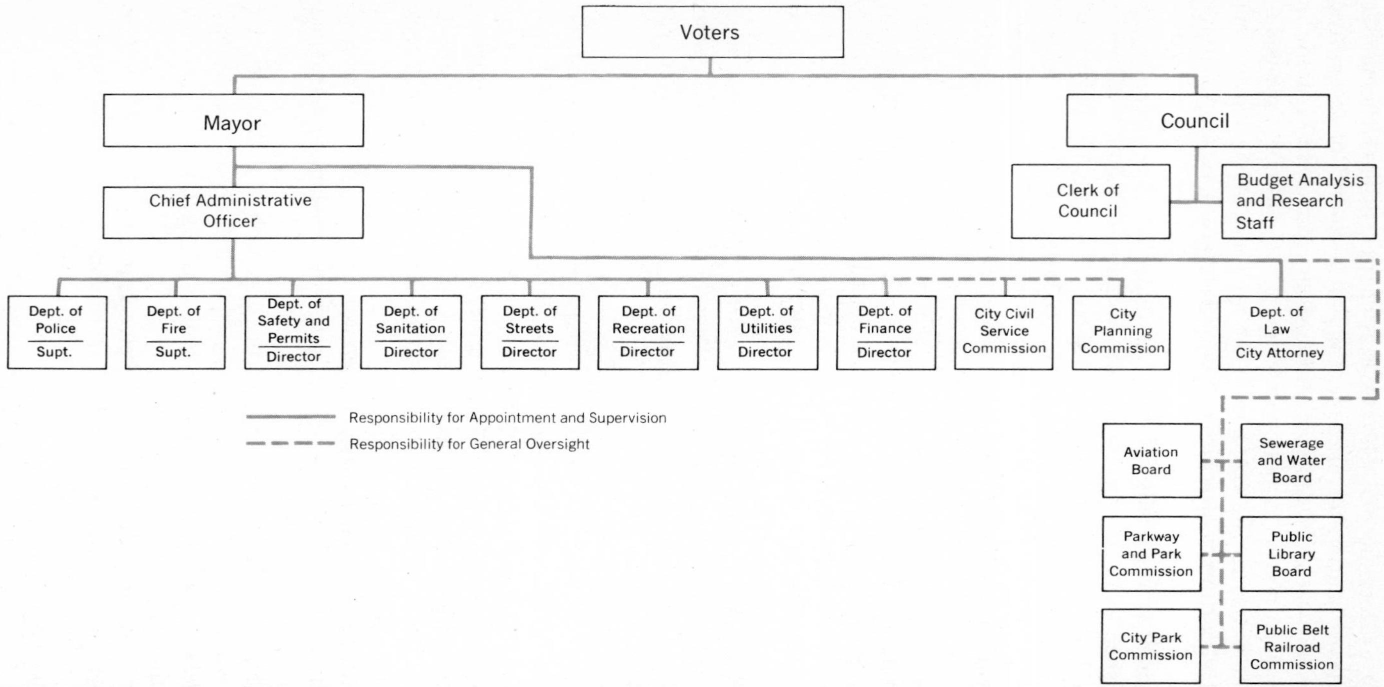

Figure 7-2 An actual strong-mayor–council city with chief administrative officer: New Orleans, Louisiana. *Note:* **Not all agencies are shown.** (*Adapted from* Annual Report of the Mayor, *City of New Orleans, Louisiana, 1953.*)

never clarified the incumbents' role. Their powers were gradually eroded. Mayor John V. Lindsay (1966–1974), immediately upon taking office, strengthened the formal powers of the office but appointed a leader of the local Liberal party to the position, thus raising suspicions of politicizing the office. (Lindsay was largely reliant upon the Liberal party for his election.) A study of the office shortly reported that it had "in fact very little power, mixed talents, a history of frustration, poor morale and an identity crisis."[16] It also faced the jealousy and suspicion of the other mayoral aides. In 1970, a city council committee called the office "irrelevant" to administrative activities and Mayor Lindsay began to dismantle it. One of the first acts of Mayor Abraham D. Beame in 1974 was to abolish the office. But Beame also established powers in the first deputy mayor which made that officer, in effect, a chief administrative officer responsible for supervising and coordinating the various departments with one another and with the budget bureau.[17] In effect, he reconstituted the office in another form.

Appraisal The strong-mayor plan with chief administrative officer seeks to free the mayor for policy making and give the city a professionally competent person to head administration. This variation on the old theme would appear to be especially acceptable in large cities, and these are the ones that, if fact, seem most interested in the development. The use of the strong-mayor plan with this modification would, however, leave that system still with at least one major potential defect: the continuing threat of a legislative-executive deadlock. It would appear, too, that there would be a great potential for jealous rivalry between the mayor and his assistants and the CAO, or for an uncooperative mayor to appropriate for himself the powers and function of the appointive CAO), especially if the mayor distrusted the professional outlook and administrative values of the CAO.

CITIES WITHOUT A SEPARATION OF POWERS

The Commission Plan

A hurricane in September, 1900, almost completely destroyed the city of Galveston, Texas, and in doing so, created the conditions under which the commission plan was produced. Actually, as Richard S. Childs has pointed out, the commission structure was not planned; it was the result of an accident.[18] During the period of rebuilding Galveston, the legislature suspended local self-government in the city and substituted a temporary government of five local businessmen, the Galveston *commission*—hence the name for the system. The commission, working with great zeal under extraordinary conditions, accomplished much more at less cost than had its almost bankrupt predecessor. A new charter in 1903 tried to

[16] Sigmund G. Ginsberg, "The New York City Administrator: A Critical Eulogy," *National Civic Review,* 64:451–458, October, 1975.

[17] *Ibid.*

[18] Richard S. Childs, *Civic Victories,* Harper & Row, Publishers, Incorporated, New York, 1952, pp. 134–136. Earlier precedents for the commission idea are cited in Ernst B. Schulz, *American City Government,* The Stackpole Company, Pittsburgh, 1949, pp. 319–321.

retain the sytem that had been working well and provided for a continuation of the commission, with three of its members appointed by the governor and two to be elected within the city. The courts held this unconstitutional, since an emergency no longer existed and, in ordinary circumstances, a city has a right to elect its council members. The legislature then made all five commissioners elective.

The success of the commission plan in Galveston soon attracted wide attention. Other Texas cities adopted the plan, and it quickly became popular in many parts of the nation. A Des Moines attorney, visiting Galveston, was impressed with the new "businessman's government" and proceeded to persuade the Iowa legislature to permit his city to adopt the plan. The legislature added other reform devices to the new charter—nonpartisan elections, and the initiative, referendum, and recall. It then became the "Des Moines plan."

The commission plan was adopted in Houston in 1905 and in Des Moines in 1907; by 1910, it had spread to some 108 cities. In 1917, at least 500 cities were using the plan. Then a reversal took place. The number of commission-governed cities began to diminish. Municipal reformers lost interest in the commission plan and began to advocate the council-manager plan as the true embodiment of a business form of organization. There have been almost no new adoptions since the 1930s, and the total number of commission cities has declined each year since World War I.

Characteristics The commission plan's outstanding feature is the dual role of the commissioners. Each of them serves individually as the head of one of the city's administrative departments, while collectively they serve as the policy-making council for the city. This plan, unlike the various mayor-council structures, provides for no separation of powers. The commission performs both legislative and executive functions.

The commission is always small, usually consisting of five members, as did the original Galveston model. Some cities, especially small ones, have only three members, and quite a number have seven. The mayor, in the theoretical model, has no powers beyond those of the other commissioners, except for performing the ceremonial duties for the city and presiding over the council. There is no veto power. In most cities the office of mayor is specifically named on the ballot and is hence filled by popular vote. In some cities, however, the council chooses one of its own members to serve; and in a few places, the person who receives the highest number of votes among all the candidates becomes mayor.

Because the plan is a product of the reform movement, the commissioners are usually elected on a nonpartisan ticket. This is the case in about three-quarters of the municipalities. The commissioners are usually expected to serve as full-time public servants, even in fairly small cities; and in the original plan it was hoped that they would possess business or engineering experience and not be "mere politicians." They are nearly always elected at large, and four-year terms are the most common.

The ballot is short. According to the original plan, only the commissioners are elected. Often staggered terms are used, so that only two or three members of a five-member commission are elected at one time.

Appraisal The commission plan was a radical departure from the prevailing weak-mayor system of the turn of the century, It concentrated power in the hands of a few, so that the decision makers became more visible to the voters. It greatly shortened the ballot from that which existed under the weak-mayor, or even most strong-mayor, systems. This gave the average voter a chance to know something about the candidates. Furthermore, only commissioners were chosen. Voters were not asked to select persons to fill routine offices (such as clerk or treasurer) or offices requiring technical skills (such as controller or assessor). Since the separation-of-powers doctrine was not used, there was no problem of the deadlock between the legislative and executive branches that is always a threat in a mayor-council city.

The commission plan, had, however, too many disadvantages to make it workable. It was supposed to provide for a city policy-making body on which business persons on leave from their ordinary pursuits would be willing to serve. Sometimes this was the case—for a few years. Actually, as a regular practice, it was not possible to select commissioners from among high-status business executives, or such persons from any walk of life, for they were unwilling to give up their own businesses and run for an office that paid a low salary.

Responsibility to the public was not definitely fixed; it was divided among the several commissioners. The plan did not eliminate amateur administrators as department heads. In this respect it was not much different from the weak-mayor plan. Local citizens might well be able to help make basic policy for the police department or for public ways, but they would be able to serve capably as *administrative* head of either department only as the result of political accident.

The commission was often too small to provide for the function of *criticism.* It is essential in a democracy that the actions of public officials be constantly subjected to critical evaluation. Although the mayor-council system might lead to deadlocks, it at least provided a mechanism for criticism. This was not true of the commission plan. With no separation of powers, only the commission members were left to criticize one another. In theory they could do so, but in a small group, people seeing one another day after day put their relationships on a personal basis. As politicians, they are certain to desire to avoid critcism. The commission very often, therefore, became a fraternity of tolerance.

Instead of watching one another, the commissioners would agree to mutual accommodation: "If you stay out of my department, I will stay out of yours." Criticism came to an end. No minority party watched the majority. No "backbenchers" eagerly awaited the chance to replace a member of the cabinet, as they do in the parliamentary system of government. There was no mayor with policy message and veto ready. The mutual hands-off policy went even further. In many cities it meant that several different city governments existed, each operating independently of the others, but with an occasional five-power conference being held to satisfy the demands of the charter.

Two further serious weaknesses affected the commission plan, both of them dealing with a lack of leadership. The plan did not provide for a chief executive. The strong-mayor and manager forms provide for administrative integration with a top official ultimately answerable for all administrative operations. No such person existed in the formal structure of the commission plan. And jealousy of the independence of one's department was likely to keep it from existing in practice. The top of the administrative pyramid was sawed off. Each department moved in its own administrative direction with no coordination at the top. This might be true to a degree even exceeding that found in the weak-mayor system.

No provision was made for top-policy leadership either, except fortuitously. The commissioners were equals and were likely to guard their equality zealously. There was no top policy maker, as under the strong-mayor system. An individual commissioner might by personality, experience, or skill at political organization come to dominate the council, but this was not common.

The plan attracted a great deal of attention for a brief period, but it was quickly outmoded by the invention of the manager plan and the development of a modern strong mayor. The inherent weaknesses of the commission plan then rapidly become manifest.

Present Status About 175 commission-governed cities remain in the United States today. The total number of cities under the plan has been on the decline since about 1917, and the drop has been especially sharp since 1946. Even so, about 8 percent of the cities with a population of more than 5,000 still use it, the largest city in 1967 being Memphis.

Abandonments, especially in larger cities, were frequent after 1945. The "Des Moines plan" was abandoned in Des Moines in 1949 in favor of the council-manager form. San Antonio, after thirty-seven years as a commission city, switched to the manager plan in 1951. The Hoboken, New Jersey, charter commission denounced the commission plan in that city as having been "a complete failure," and the city changed in 1952 to the strong-mayor plan with CAO. So did New Orleans. Inadequacy of policy leadership is felt most in the largest cities. Medium-sized and small cities, however, are also abandoning the commission plan. Cities as large as Portland, Oregon, St. Paul, and Tulsa still use the commission plan.

In the large and medium-sized cities that continue to use the commission plan, it has been made workable enough for its continued use through a number of modifications. The most important of these involve (1) the establishment of a modern budget office responsible to the commission as a whole and (2) the appointment of a professional administrator as the deputy head of each department, thus providing for a person to handle daily operational matters and providing the leadership and administrative skills that the commissioner assigned to the department often lacks.

Outmoded structures of government live beyond the time when they are needed, as do all human institutions which suffer the rigidity of formal organization. There is no future for the commission structure of government. Those commission cities that remain do so as a result of apathy or inertia.

The Council-Manager Plan

The origin of the idea for the council-manager plan is not known with certainty. It seems that one of the first instances in which it was urged was in an editorial in the August, 1899, issue of *California Municipalities.* Haven A. Mason, editor of the magazine, urged that there should be "a distinct profession of municipal managers." He listed desirable qualifications, saying that a manager should know something about engineering, street construction, sewers, building construction, water and lighting systems, personnel, accounting, municipal law, fire protection, and library management. "Every city that receives or expends $50,000 annually," he said, "ought to have a salaried business manager." He even went so far as to say that "when we require adepts to run our cities, our universities will establish a department to specially fit our young men to enter the new profession of conducting municipal business."[19]

The claim for having the first council-manager city is sometimes disputed between Staunton, Virginia, and Sumter, South Carolina. In 1908, Staunton, with a weak mayor and a bicameral council, sought a different form of city government. Getting a new charter from the legislature would not have been easy. It was decided, therefore, to hire a "general manager" for the city on the basis of an ordinance, who was to be a full-time employee in charge of administration, was to be hired by the council, and could be dismissed by it at any time.

While the Stauton experiment did not produce a neat organization chart and was not based upon a systematic theory, it may be said to have become a manager-plan city in that year. Richard S. Childs, a businessman, who was at that time secretary of the National Short Ballot Organization and who later was to become president of the National Municipal League, took a leading part in the development and popularizing of the plan. In 1911, he drew up a proposed city charter which was endorsed by the Board of Trade (chamber of commerce) of Lockport, New York, As it happened, the state general assembly refused to permit the city to use this model manager charter, but the charter attracted a good bit of attention and was adopted by Sumter, South Carolina, in the following year.

The manager-plan spread with great speed. During 1913, several small cities and towns adopted the Childs charter. At the same time, the Dayton Chamber of Commerce appointed a committee to study the need for a new charter in that city, for the state of Ohio had just granted to its municipalities the power of home rule. The committee, which was headed by John M. Patterson, president of the National Cash Register Company, came to favor the manager plan. While the group was pursuing its efforts, the Miami River, which passes through the city, overflowed its banks in spring flood. The ineptitude of the existing city government in meeting the problems that followed gave unanticipated support to the efforts of the charter-study committee. The voters adopted the proposed new charter in August. It went into effect on January 1, 1914, and the new council hired the city engineer of Cincinnati as manager, thus setting a precedent for the type of person who is still often preferred for the position.

The Dayton episode, partly because it occurred in a large city, partly because of the personal publicity efforts of Patterson, and partly because of the extraordinary drama connected with it, gave a tremendous boost to the council-

[19] The editorial is reprinted in Bollens, *op. cit.,* appendix III. For a history of city management, see Richard J. Stillman II, *The Rise of the City Manager,* University of New Mexico Press, Albuquerque, 1974.

manager plan. By 1915, there were 49 manager cities. Five years later, there were 158. The number has increased uninterruptedly ever since. On January 1, 1970, there were 2,289 manager cities and other local governments in the United States and Canada. Fifty percent of the cities between 10,000 and 500,000 population had managers.

The manager plan has enjoyed a rapid expansion in the period following World War II. Its growth has closely paralleled that of suburbia. It seems to be especially suited to the politics of consensus and the acceptance of professionalism that we find there.[20]

Characteristics[21] The outstanding identifying marks of the council-manager-plan model are a lay council responsible for policy making and a professional administration under a chief administrator responsible to the council. (See Figure 7-3.) The theoretical structure rivals that of the British parliamentary system in its simplicity.

The council is small, five to nine members, and is commonly elected at large, on a nonpartisan ballot, often for four-year staggered terms. It is responsible to the public for all policy making and ultimately for the overall character of administration. Under the model charter,[22] members of the council are the only officers who are popularly elected. The intended purpose of the short ballot is to concentrate responsibility upon these people and to ask the voters to fill only important policy-making positions in which they can reasonably be expected to take an interest.

There is no separation of powers, nor are there checks and balances. The mayor or president of the city or village, having no administrative powers, except in the case of an emergency, and no veto, normally performs only ceremonial functions and presides over the council. In almost one-half of the manager cities over 5,000 population, the council chooses the mayor from among its own membership. In most other cities, the mayor is directly elected; a few give the post to the person with the most votes in the council race.

The administration of the city is integrated under the control of a professional manager, who is hired by the council. In the model plan, the managers serve for no definite term of office but rather at the pleasure of a majority of the council. They are not subject to recall by the voters, for the voters did not select them and, furthermore, ultimate responsibility for municipal government belongs to the council. No manager may serve effectively who does not enjoy the confidence of a majority of the council, and therefore the credit or blame for what is done rests with the council.

The manager is a professional person and is expected to hire professionally

[20] See Robert C. Wood, *Suburbia: Its People and Their Politics,* Houghton Mifflin Company, Boston, 1959, pp. 183–186.

[21] The National Municipal League, New York, has issued several pamphlets and books in popular form. See especially Richard Childs, *The First 50 Years of the Council Manager Plan of Muncipal Government* (1969).

[22] See the *Model City Charter,* 6th ed., 1964, of the National Municipal League, New York. The manager plan has been endorsed by the League since 1916.

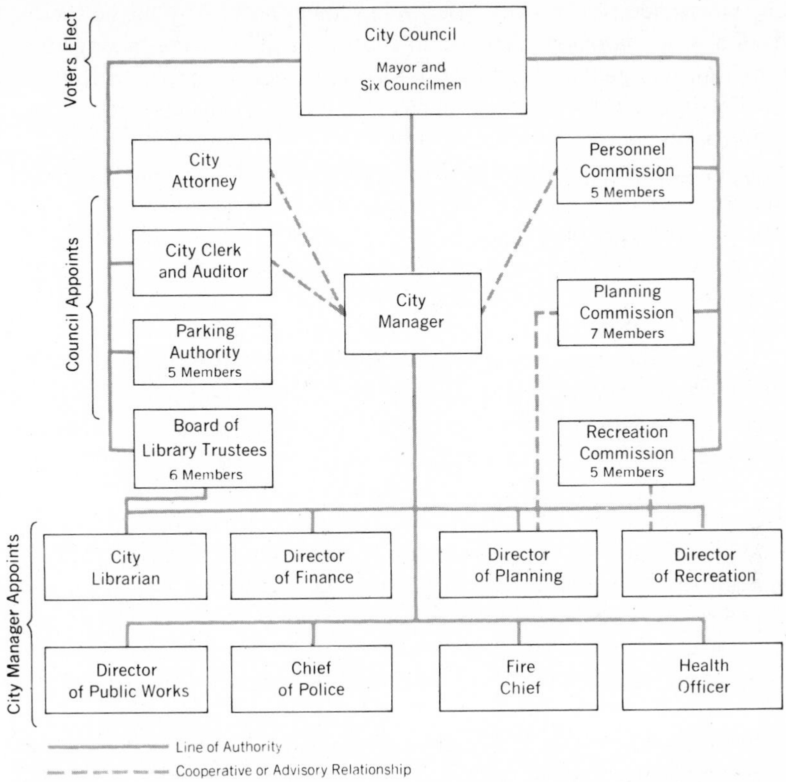

Figure 7-3 An actual council-manager city: Modesto, California. *(Adapted from* A Report of Progress, *City of Modesto, California, 1952.)*

competent technicians to operate the various departments of the city. The lower administrative positions, roughly those below the department heads, are also filled with persons who are technically competent. They are usually chosen by civil service merit examination.

Appraisal Municipal reformers have tended to accord to this plan inordinate praise, often attributing to it miraculous powers to bring about efficient and economical city administration, regardless of the traditions of city government, the kind of personnel which it employs, and whether the public understands and supports the basic principles of the plan. These exaggerated claims for the plan, as well as some of the specious arguments used against it, should be discounted by the sophisticated student of municipal affairs.

The council-manager plan calls for lay citizens, commonly political amateurs, to serve on the council and make public policy as representatives of the community. No professional politicians are expected to make a living from the positions, for the councilmanic jobs normally pay only a nominal salary or only a per meeting allowance. The execution of policy, as approved by the council, is in the hands of a professional staff of administrators headed by the manager. All administrators and technicians are supposed to be especially qualified for their jobs. The chief administrator can be selected by the council, not from among local politicians of one party, as would be the case if it were a patronage appointment, but rather from among trained persons anywhere in the nation. The choice is limited only by what the council believes it should offer as salary.

But while the manager plan emphasizes professional administration, it does not turn the city over to the whims of an independent bureaucracy. The manager and his or her subordinates are answerable to the council. They normally attend council sessions, where they are expected to answer questions, report on progress of various projects, and explain any of their actions that involve matters in which the council is interested. And there are none of the legislative-executive conflicts that arise from time to time in the mayor-council city, since, as in the parliamentary system, those who carry out policy serve at the pleasure of the legislative branch.

In contrast to the commission plan, however, criticism is provided for. Administrative spoils are not distributed among the council members, and hence there is less need for collusion against criticism. The legislative branch remains free to oversee the operation of administration, and the people who appropriate the funds are not the people who spend them. The council votes the funds and then checks upon the manager and the staff, both through its own supervision and through the receipt of auditors' reports.

Although the manager plan is a simple mechanism, it is not always understood by the general public. An important factor contributing to this is the carryover to the present day of many elements of Jacksonian ideology. For example, the plan is sometimes challenged as "dictatorial" or "un-American" because the chief administrator is not elected. To be sure, this fact violates a basic precept of Jacksonianism. But the argument is invalid, since responsibility for administration is clearly established. The manager plan also requires acceptance of the professional administrator. One study has found that where values of professionalism were in conflict with local value patterns, the plan was not accepted.[23]

Another study has found that council-manager cities are less responsive to cleavages than are cities with older-style governments. Reform tends to mute personal-interest or "private-regarding" demands. Efficiency-and-economy movement reformers wanted to minimize politics and emphasize professional administration. The results—the council-manager plan, nonpartisan elections, at-large elections—" are associated with a lessened responsiveness of cities to the enduring conflicts of political life."[24] Advocates of programs for the poor and minority groups, nearly all of them "private regarding," see reform structures as

[23] Garth N. Jones, "Integration of Political Ethos and Local Government Systems," *Human Organization,* 23:210–223, Fall, 1964.

[24] Robert L. Lineberry and Edmund P. Fowler, "Reformism and Public Policies in American Cities," *American Political Science Review,* 61:701–716, September, 1967. Quotation from p. 715.

diminishing their influence and hence tend to view the council-manager plan suspiciously.[25]

Some people argue that the manager plan is too expensive for small cities because the position of manager must command enough pay to attract competent personnel, or they say that the manager would not have enough work to keep busy in a small city. These arguments would seem invalid for most small places, however, for the plan is in operation in a large number of municipalities of under 5,000 population.[26]

There are more serious objections to the plan, however. The number of cities needing managers and professional department heads has increased rapidly in the last generation, and a shortage of able managers has been a chronic problem. The numerous positions in private business for administrators and engineers has also helped to reduce the number of persons available to cities. Some cities have tried the plan, only to complain that the manager was incompetent.

Managers are sometimes criticized on another ground. In the past many of them were engineers who had no education in the social sciences. As such, some of them tended to view issues of public policy as a series of engineering or budgeting problems rather than as matters of economics and sociology.

Some advocates of the manager plan have made the erroneous assumption that a sharp distinction can be made between politics and administration. No such line exists. One shades off into the other. Their idea is that managers are nonelective employees who should not make policy but should concern themselves only with the details of administration. Actually, it is almost a necessity for the lay, part-time council to look to the professional, full-time manager for recommendations concerning policy. If harmonious relations exist and the manager and the council are competent, the council will ordinarily not act on any policy matter without first getting the recommendations and a statement of the pertinent facts from the manager.[27] On some types of highly controversial issues, managers, if they are prudent, will avoid taking a stand, but apart from these, it is their job to make recommendations and, in fact, to initiate policy recommendations. They are nearly always in a better position to interpret policy demands than is the council. If the council accepts the recommendations of the manager with regularity, it does not necessarily mean that it is a rubber stamp; it may mean that the council has hired a competent manager and that recommendations accord nicely with the consensus of values in the community.

[25] Albert K. Karnig, "Private-regarding Policy, Civil Rights Groups, and the Mediating Impact of Municipal Reforms," *American Journal of Political Science,* 19:91–106, February, 1975.

[26] The pattern of managership in these cities is described in W. C. Busby, "The Small Council-Manager City," *Public Management,* 35:154–156, July, 1953.

[27] See Charles R. Adrian, "Leadership and Decision-making in Manager Cities: A Study of Three Communities," *Public Administration Review,* 18:208–213, Summer, 1958; Karl A. Bosworth, "The Manager *Is* a Politician," *ibid.,* pp. 216–222; Charles A. Harrell and D. G. Weiford, "The City Manager and the Policy Process," *ibid.,* Spring, 1959, and B. James Kweder, *The Roles of Manager, Mayor, and Councilmen in Policy Making: A Study of Twenty-one North Carolina Cities,* Institute of Government, The University of North Carolina, Chapel Hill, 1965.

Among managers themselves two ideologies (perhaps it is more a matter of two personality types) express the proper relationship of the manager to the council. Some managers center their attention on administrative operations and routine matters, avoiding taking a stand on any issue; others center their attention on policy matters and the development of the city. In some instances—Berkeley and East Cleveland at one time were examples—well-entrenched managers, long in office, may completely dominate a council. They may not only make it into a rubber stamp but may even have considerable influence in determining who is elected to the council.

Though the manager may tend to dominate the council in some cases, the policy-making arm may also tend to invade the area theoretically reserved for professional administrators. If the manager is weak, or if several members of the council do not accept the spirit of the manager plan, a good deal of "political" interference in administration may result. Council members may bypass the manager and deal directly with members of departments or seek to influence administrative decisions on the basis of short-range constituency considerations rather than professional standards and values. Hostile council members may even appoint a local politician to the post of manager. In cases such as these, the manager plan cannot operate according to the model plan.

It is not uncommon to find, especially where a modified manager plan leaves some administrative powers with the mayor, a disrupting power struggle between the mayor and the manager. One study has found manager tenure to be shorter where mayors were independently elected and where managers lacked political ties in the community.[28] This may also happen in cities where mayors do not understand or accept their role under the manager plan. If the public does not understand the principles of the plan, it is likely to support the mayor in such a fight, for the title of the mayor's office implies to many people that he or she ought to be the chief administrator. In some cities, certain officials, such as the city attorney, the city engineer, or the police chief, may be appointed by the mayor rather than by the manager. In such cases, there may in effect be two managers, one amateur and the other professional. It may follow that the council members are eventually forced to "choose up sides" if either the mayor or the manager launches into a policy of aggrandizement. The result is usually a dead, or at least badly wounded, manager plan.

Perhaps the greatest potential weakness in the plan is to be found in connection with the problem of policy leadership. No adequate provision for it is made in the model plan. The council is a body of equals. One of the members may emerge as a leader in policy making, but if this is so, it is the result of accident. More likely, the council will flounder about or turn to the manager. Managers have become such effective policy leaders that the plan appears to be working well even in large cities with their complex patterns of interests and conflicting ideologies. In 1970, managers were in office in six cities of over 400,000 popula-

[28] Gladys M. Kammerer and others, *City Managers in Politics,* University of Florida Press, Gainesville, Fla., 1962.

tion. The plan appeared to be working satisfactorily in all of them, and no movements for abandonment were underway.[29] (See Table 7-2.)

Some evidence indicates that the operation of the manager plan in a style somewhat approximating that of the model is dependent upon the existence of a fairly high degree of consensus in the community. When a city's politics produces a lineup of two fairly well balanced groups, each of which, when it comes to power, dismisses the manager hired by the opposition and finds one loyal to itself—as sometimes happens—the plan is in difficulties. Similarly, it apparently does not operate effectively in communities where the function of city government is viewed by a large number of citizens as that of an arbiter,[30] for this implies the need for a strong elective leader.[31]

The lack of a chief policy maker causes another problem. In large cities, especially, it is difficult for the general public to know much about the various candidates for the council or about the voting records of incumbents. The problem is especially great when the council is elected at large on a nonpartisan ballot, as is often the case. It is therefore not necessarily true that concentration

[29] Hessler, *op. cit.*, chap. 5 and *Municipal Year Book, 1968–1969–1970, op. cit.*
[30] See Williams and Adrian, *op. cit.*
[31] *Ibid.*

TABLE 7-2. Votes and Popular Action on Council-manager Government 1955–1965 Inclusive*

Population Class	Number of Cities in Class		Popular Action on Proposals to Change			
			To Adopt		To Abandon	
	Total	Council-manager	Yes	No	No	Yes
Over 500,000	21	4 (19%)	0†	0	0	0
250,000–500,000	30	12 (40%)	0	0	3	0
100,000–250,000	80	39 (48%)	2	2	8	0
50,000–100,000	192	96 (50%)	7	12	13	2
25,000–50,000	406	211 (52%)	24	25	27	13
10,000–25,000	1,033	447 (43%)	86	68	40	10
2,500–10,000	3,065	695 (23%)	191	109	57	31
Totals	4,827	1,504 (31%)	310	216	145	56

*Population classes based upon 1960 census.
† Dade County, Fla., adopted the county-manager plan in 1957, but this table does not include counties unless they provide general municipal services in the area.
Source: Edwin O. Stene, *The City Manager: Professional Training and Tenure,* Governmental Research Center, University of Kansas, Lawrence, Kans., 1966.

of responsibility in the council will result in informed voting. In cities small enough for candidates to be known by reputation, this is not likely to be as serious a problem, if indeed it is a problem at all.

Actual Results[32] The adoption of the council-manager plan has led to increased prestige for the council and in greater control by it over municipal affairs. Managers have generally been appointed by the council without regard to political activity, and tenure for the manager has, in most cases, not been interrupted by considerations other than administrative competence. Most managers have provided administration based upon professional values and standards and have brought far more coordination to the activities of their governments than had existed before. They have furthered long-range policy planning, and have encouraged the employment of specialists for advice on technical problems, have emphasized the merit principle in personnel administration, and have increased the interest of employees in their jobs. Managers have promoted coordinated, executive budgeting methods and have provided more financial information and better financial management than was afforded under the older forms of government.

The adoption of the council-manager form has not reduced the size of the total budget in most cities, but it has increased the public's confidence in municipal government, it has sometimes reduced *unit* costs by eliminating graft and waste and by utilizing personnel and methods of greater efficiency. There is some evidence that competent managers, regardless of the size of the cities, can save their own salaries many times over each year and that the plan has therefore been an economical one, even for small cities.

The council-manager plan, then, suffers from some weaknesses, as do all human institutions. It has, however, so satisfied the bulk of the voters in cities using it that, once adopted, abandonments are rare.

Prevalence of Manager Governments Studies of adoptions of the council-manager plan find an affinity between it and higher-income and more homogeneous communities. A study of seventy-four suburbs of more than 2,500 population found the plan to exist most frequently in suburbs with high housing values. However, after these suburbs adopted it, it also spread gradually to suburbs of lower housing values.[33] A second study of 300 suburbs in the nation's twenty-five most urbanized areas found council-manager government to be more frequent where (1) a greater number of heads-of-households worked fifty to fifty-two weeks a year; (2) heads-of-households held white-collar jobs; (3) more women in the household held outside jobs; (4) median family incomes and education levels were high; (5) new homes were being built; and (6) most homes were for single

[32] This section is based upon the findings reported in Harold A. Stone, Don K. Price, and Katherine H. Stone, *City Manager Government in the United States,* Public Administration Service, Chicago, 1940, which is a report on a three-year survey of fifty cities.

[33] Edgar L. Sherbenou, "Class, Participation, and the Council Manager Plan," *Public Administration Review,* 21:131–135, Summer, 1961.

TABLE 7-3. Largest Council-manager Cities—1970

City	1970 Population	Date in Effect	Size of Council	No. at Large	Type of Election*	Term	Other Elective Officers
Dallas	836,121	1931	9	9	NP	2	None
San Antonio	650,188	1952	9	9	NP	2	None
San Diego	675,788	1932	8	0	NP-s	4	Attorney
Kansas City	530,000	1926	13	6	NP	4	None
Phoenix	580,275	1914	7	7	NP	2	None
Cincinnati	495,000	1926	9	9	NP	2	None
Oklahoma City	380,000	1927	8	0	NP-s	4	None
Oakland	378,000	1931	9	9	NP-s	4	Auditor Controller
Long Beach	368,000	1921	9	9	NP	3	Auditor Attorney
Fort Worth	360,000	1925	9	9	NP	2	None

* "NP" refers to nonpartisan; "-s" means that council terms are staggered so that all do not expire at once.
Source: Municipal Year Book, 1970, International City Management Association, Chicago, 1970, Table XV.

families and were occupied by owners.[34] A third study found council-manager government to be most frequently adopted in middle-sized cities (25,000–250,000), in cities with native-born populations, cities with a primary economic activity concentrating on personal service, retail or finance, cities that were growing rapidly, and cities in one-party states.[35] But a number of large cities also have long experience with the plan. (See Table 7-3.)

Proponents and Opponents: The Politics of Reform The council-manager plan is often launched and supported by good-government and business groups, chambers of commerce, property owners' associations, taxpayers' associations, civic associations, citizens' action groups, women's clubs, and, very often, newspapers. Opposition to proposals for adoption frequently comes from organized labor, politicians in office (especially mayors who stand to lose both power and prestige in their offices by the employment of a manager), minority-group leaders, and political parties. Political leaders often dislike the manager plan because it offers little in the way of patronage and because it is often coupled with nonpartisan elections.

[34] Leo F. Schnore and Robert R. Alford, "Forms of Government and Socio-economic Characteristics of Suburbs," *Administrative Science Quarterly,* 8:1–17, June, 1963.

[35] John H. Kessel, "Government Structure and Political Environment: A Statistical Note about American Cities," *American Political Science Review,* 56:615–620, September, 1962.

In many cities, the two leading contenders in campaigns over manager charters have been the local chamber of commerce and local organized labor. The impression that the plan is antithetical to the best interests of organized labor is held by many, though not all, labor leaders in various parts of the country.

In contrast, the plan has been accepted with enthusiasm by business groups, for many reasons. It was the Board of Trade of Lockport that first endorsed the Childs plan, and the chamber of commerce in Dayton was responsible for the first large-city adoption. The plan is often lauded as a "businesslike government" in imitation of the corporate form of private business.

The upper-middle-class suburbs which are the homes of metropolitan business executives are characteristically administered by a manager. Many managers are engineers, and some are trained in schools of business administration. This means that they received much of their education in the more conservative colleges of our universities. They are likely to be personally conservative in political views. They are business-oriented in their social values. Many of them have had experience in private business before becoming managers; other may hope to move into good positions in private business after serving for a number of years in city government. Overwhelmingly, managers are male, white, native-born, and Protestant.[36]

Labor and minority-group leaders fear that the council-manager plan requires them to take an all-or-nothing plunge into local politics. The risk in this is especially great if elections are at large. Under such circumstances, these leaders are faced with getting a majority on the council in a city-wide contest. Failing this, the entire administration of the city may fall into opposition, or (at least from their viewpoint) undependable, unsympathetic, and unpredictable hands. In most core cities, the AFL-CIO works closely with the Democratic party which is likely to dominate partisan elections. The council-manager plan advocates nearly always favor nonpartisan elections, however, and this is a device that usually favors conservatives and weakens the effectiveness of labor-Democratic coalition or of minority-group activists.

Other reasons exist for labor's skepticism about the plan, too. Business leaders and chamber of commerce managers may be concerned with large issues of policy, but typical working people think of the machinery of government as something to be used for personal favors, to help them in an emergency. For their purposes, the ward aldermanic system is more effective than are the at-large elections which are the rule under the manager plan. Furthermore, at-large elections tend to select council members from middle-class ranks, persons who often have had little experience with the problems of low-income persons, minority-group members, the members of unions. Not only may they be unfamiliar with the concerns of these people, but they may be overtly hostile to unionism, especially if they are from small businesses. In cities where labor leaders have been active in municipal politics, working people are especially likely to be dissatisfied with the manager plan.[37]

[36] Richard J. Stillman, II, *The Modern City Manager,* International City Management Association, Washington, 1974.

[37] See Kenneth E. Beasley, *Attitudes of Labor toward City Government,* Governmental Research Center, University of Kansas, Lawrence, Kans., 1954.

In contrast to the general pattern, some unions have taken the lead in urging the manager plan. Furthermore, it would appear that labor usually supports the plan once it is well established in a city.

The manager plan enjoys labor support in Cincinnati, Kansas City, and Toledo. The AFL-CIO takes no national stand on forms of local government; it allows local organizations to decide positions in local campaigns for themselves. In 1950, union leaders in eighty cities where the plan had been in effect for twenty years or longer overwhelmingly approved of the plan. In only three of the cities was definite opposition expressed.[38] Labor is being somewhat reassured concerning the motives of those who favor the manager plan. It is likely, however, that the device will remain especially the favorite of chambers of commerce and middle-class good-government groups.

The Kerner Commission (National Advisory Commission on Civil Disorders) in its 1969 report stated that council-manager city governments played a significant if unintentional role in the eruption of racial disorders during 1967 by discouraging black ghetto participation in city government. Using the Commission's data, a study by Delbert Taebel showed a lower incidence of racial disorders for council-manager cities in every one of the commonly used seven population groups, except for cities in the 10,000–25,000 category where all three riots occurring in 1967 in that size of city occurred in council-manager cities.[39]

OTHER FORMS OF GOVERNMENT

The New England Town

The direct democracy of the town meeting characterized local government in New England until the urbanization of that area began to force the acceptance of modifications. In some urban areas, the town-government feature has been abandoned, while in others it has been made into a representative form.

The town makes no distinction between rural and urban places. As an area becomes more and more urbanized, it continues under the town system, sharing the same government with the neighboring rural area. The town is governed by a meeting of all the qualified voters, who choose officers and make basic policy. There is an annual meeting, traditionally in March, with as many other meetings as may be necessary. After making basic policy, the people choose a board of selectmen, usually three but in some places as many as nine, and a fairly large number of other officers. The selectmen and elective officers are then entrusted with carrying out the basic policies established by community action.

The urbanization of many towns has been accompanied by a sharp decrease in attendance at town meetings and a consequent decline in the effectiveness of this form of government. In many areas of New England, therefore, a *representative* town meeting plan has been developed. Under this plan, the voters choose a large number of citizens, perhaps a hundred or more, to attend the meeting, represent them, and vote. Any citizen can attend and take part in debates, but he

[38] See the pamphlet *Labor Unions and the Council-Manager Plan* (1950), issued by the National Municipal League, New York, and designed to be read by working people.

[39] Delbert A. Taebel, "Managers and Riots," *National Civic Review,* 57:554–555, September, 1968.

or she no longer has a direct vote. This plan is used in such large urban places as Brookline, Massachusetts (1970 population: 58,689).

Town government, outside of the meeting feature, resembles the weak-mayor or, more particularly, the American village form, except that there is no mayor, though the first selectman has some administrative powers. No one has a veto power. More and more commonly, the selectmen choose a manager to whom they assign routine administration. This is particularly the case in Maine and Vermont and is to be found in all New England states.

The New England legislatures have long been under pressure to alter the traditional town government in order to help meet contemporary needs. They have created new offices and commissions such as those of aviation commissioner, planning boards, civil service commissions, library trustees, and finance committees, the last in order to help provide for better planning in budget making so that this document is not pieced together in haphazard fashion at the public meeting. (Titles vary by states and even towns, of course.)

Other Meanings and Usages

Nothing much can be learned concerning the nature of an area simply because it is (or is not) called a city. The term itself derives from the Latin *civis* (citizen) and was restricted in England to application to cathedral towns. Other urban areas in England were known as boroughs—a term used today in the city of New York and to some extent in Connecticut, New Jersey, and Pennsylvania. The word *town* is from the Anglo-Saxon *tun,* a homestead surrounded by a hedge or other fence, from Old High German *zun,* a hedge. *Borough* is from the Anglo-Saxon *burh,* a fortified town. Today, in the states named above, it represents an incorporated area occupying a position between that of a city and a village. The five administrative subdivisions of New York are also called boroughs but are not separate corporations. *Village* is from the Italian and Latin *villa,* meaning originally a farm or country house. The term *municipality* is from the Latin *municipium,* which referred to certain Italian towns that enjoyed special privileges under Rome. In the United States today, and in this book, the term is popularly used interchangeably with *city* or *village.* A city in the United States is a legal, not a sociological, concept. City limits may be greater or smaller than the *de facto* urban area. In most states, a city may or may not be larger than the largest villages in the state. Villages may be tiny rural trading centers, or they may be sizable urban areas, as in the case of several of Chicago's large surburbs. The traditional village government in the United States is similar to that of the New England town, without the annual meeting, or the township elsewhere. Three to five trustees form the governing board. Usually they are elected at large. One is chosen president and is essentially a weak mayor. A clerk and treasurer are also often elected.

There may or may not be meaningful legal differences between cities and villages. In this text, what is said to apply to cities will generally apply to villages as well. As a matter of fact, the smaller urbanized areas of a state may legally be called villages (as in Minnesota) or towns (as in Iowa). The smallest rural unit of government is usually the township—except in New England, where it is a unique institution and is called a town. In Minnesota, townships are legally (although not popularly) known as towns. To add to the confusion, the township does not exist at all in most states, but in some metropolitan areas it has been permitted to become virtually a city. It constitutes virtually another form of city government in Michigan, New Jersey, and Pennsylvania. In states where this trend has not developed, the existing township—sometimes using its full 36 square miles—has often been the basis for an incorporated village or city.[40]

The largest urban communities are often popularly (although not legally) known as metropolitan areas (from the Greek *meter,* mother, and *polis,* city-state). These "mother-cities" are ordinarily made up of an agglomeration of counties,[41] cities, villages, townships, special districts, and other units that may total several hundred in number. In the United States, these sociologically cohesive units are virtually never treated as legal units; the metropolitan area is almost never a single city. (See Chapter 10 on metropolitan governments.)

Without a standard terminology, readers must be prepared to adapt their understanding of terms to conditions prevailing locally. For purposes of this text, an urban area is conceived of as a sociological community wherein the individuals are engaged primarily in diversified nonagricultural pursuits and where distinctive, nonrural patterns of behavior prevail. A county, city, village, borough, or (sometimes) town is a legally described region which seldom coincides with the actual urban area.

Closing Statement

Structures of government are tools. They make a difference as to how a community is governed and as to which groups and interests in the community are most influential. Local cultural circumstances help determine the type of structure that is wanted by politically dominant groups and the type of government that will be produced under any chosen form. Structure is significant, but it is only one of the factors that make up the particular characteristics of politics and community decision making in a city.

SELECTED READINGS

Abbott, Frank C.: "The Cambridge City Manager," in Harold Stein (ed.), *Public Administration and Policy Development,* Harcourt, Brace & World, Inc., New York, 1952, pp. 573–620. (A case study of a manager involved in controversy.)

Arnold, Davis S.: *Council-Manager Abandonment Referendums,* International City Management Association, Washington, 1964. (Evaluates ninety-seven referendums held in ninety cities.)

Banfield, Edward C: *Big City Politics,* Random House, Inc., New York, 1965. (Describes

[40] Thomas F. Hady and Clarence J. Hein, "Congressional Townships as Incorporated Municipalities," *Midwest Journal of Political Science,* 8:408–424, November, 1964.

[41] On counties as urban governments, see Chap. 10, below, or Charles R. Adrian, *State and Local Governments,* 4th ed., McGraw-Hill Book Company, New York, 1976, chaps. 8–9, for more detail.

the politics of several strong-mayor–council cities.)

Beasley, Kenneth E.: *Attitudes of Labor toward City Government,* Governmental Research Center, University of Kansas, Lawrence, Kans., 1954. (Examines attitudes of labor-union leaders toward the council-manager plan.)

Bollens, John C., and John C. Ries: *The City Manager Profession, Myths and Realities,* Public Administration Service, Chicago, 1969.

Booth, David A. (comp.): *Council-Manager Government, 1940–1964: An Annotated Bibliography,* International City Management Association, Chicago, 1965.

Bradford, E. S.: *Commission Government in American Cities,* The Macmillan Company, New York, 1911. (A study during the heyday of the commission plan.)

Bromage, Arthur W.: *Councilmen at Work,* George Wahr Publishing Company, Ann Arbor, Mich., 1954. (Bromage, a councilman–political scientist concludes that the weak-mayor plan can be made to work in a middle-sized city, but only at the cost of large investments of time and resources by amateur council members.)

——: *Urban Policy Making: The Council-Manager Partnership,* Public Administration Service, Chicago, 1971.

Brominz, Beverly C.: *North Kingdom Selects Two Town Managers,* Bureau of Governmental Research, University of Rhode Island, Kingston, R.I., 1962. (A case study of controversy over the manager plan.)

Carrell, Jeptha: *The Role of the City Manager,* Community Studies, Inc., Kansas City, Mo., 1962. (A study of council-manager conflict in Kansas City.)

Childs, Richard S.: *The First 50 Years of the Council-Manager Plan of Municipal Government,* National Municipal League, New York, 1965. (Statement by founder of the council-manager plan.)

East, John Porter: *Council-Manager Government: The Political Thought of Its Founder, Richard S. Childs,* The University of North Carolina Press, Chapel Hill, N.C., 1965. (A study of the ideas of the founder of the council-manager plan and of the way those views are now evaluated.)

Kammerer, Gladys M., and others: *City Managers in Politics,* University of Florida Press, Gainesville, Fla., 1962. (A study of manager tenure in Florida.)

Lopach, James J., and L. S. McKinsey: "Montana Local Government Review," *National Civic Review,* 64:393–399, Sept., 1975. (Montana's 1972 constitution requires every local government to weigh the merits of an alternative governmental structure at least once a decade.)

Mills, Werner E., and Harry R. Davis: *Small City Government,* Random House, Inc., New York, 1962. (Includes a study of a small city with a low-tax—caretaker—ideology and the council-manager structure.)

Nolting, Orin F.: *Progress and Impact of the Council-Manager Plan,* Public Administration Service, Chicago, 1969. (The history of the second 25 years of the International City Managers' Association by its former executive director. In 1969, the organization's name was changed to the International City Management Association to encourage membership by persons in general management positions with various titles.)

Presthus, Robert V: *Men at the Top,* Oxford University Press, Fair Lawn, N.J., 1964. (Officeholders were found to rival businesspersons in importance in small weak-mayor–council cities.)

Stene, Edwin O.: *The City Manager: Professional Training and Tenure,* Governmental Research Center, University of Kansas Press, Lawrence, Kans., 1966.

Stillman, Richard J., II: *The Rise of the City Manager,* University of New Mexico Press, Albuquerque, N.M., 1974.

Stinchcombe, Jean L.: *Reform and Reaction: City Politics in Toledo,* Wadsworth, Belmont, Calif., 1968.

Stone, Harold A., Don K. Price, and Katherine H. Stone: *City Manager Government in the United States,* Public Administration Service, Chicago, 1940.

Zimmerman, Joseph F.: *The Massachusetts Town Meeting: A Tenacious Institution,* Graduate School of Public Affairs, State University of New York, Albany, 1967.

Chapter 8

Executive Officers

The mayor of today's American small town is commonly a moderately successful small-business person, long active in local politics and civic affairs and well liked by the neighbors. In the large city of an earlier day, the mayor was often corrupt and incompetent—although there were outstanding exceptions. Today, our large cities seem to be producing an increasingly large number of capable chief executives. Still, many contemporary mayors are amiable mediocrities, lacking in ability and imagination and under obligation to a few interest groups that put them in office.

Cleveland, with a strong mayor elected on a partisan basis, has been an exceptional city so far as chief executives are concerned. It has not only had able reformers but has sent several men on to positions in state and national government. Tom L. Johnson (1901), a prominent businessman, became famous for fighting the "special interests." His campaigns were carried on by his successor, Newton D. Baker (1909), who was chosen a few years later to be President Wilson's Secretary of War. In 1935, Harold H. Burton was elected mayor of Cleveland. After being reelected for two more terms, he was elected to the United States Senate and later was appointed to the United States Supreme Court. Although he was not outstanding in these positions, his record is an indication that the mayor's office can be used as a step toward higher-status positions. Burton was succeeded as mayor in 1941 by Frank J. Lausche, a man of little administrative ability but with much political skill and ambition. He was reelected in 1943, receiving almost three-quarters of the votes cast. Later, he became Governor of Ohio and then United States Senator. In 1953, Lausche appointed his successor, Thomas A. Burke, to fill a vacancy in the United States Senate. Burke's successor, Anthony J. Celebrezze, became Secretary of Health, Education, and Welfare in 1962. In 1968, Carl B. Stokes, the first black mayor of a large city, took office and immediately assumed an important role in the national politics of the Democratic party. But the Cleveland system of consistent promotion to higher office is not typical.

The problem of securing able persons as mayors of large cities is complicated because persons who seek these offices are likely to have to place themselves under obligation to interest groups with specific political goals. This is so because someone must furnish the money for the expensive large-city campaign.

The need for forceful, imaginative leadership from the mayor has been emphasized in large cities as a result of concern about potential deterioration of property and economic obsolescence resulting from the flight of people, business, and industry to the suburbs.[1]

Strong mayors—the policy leaders of today's large cities—have great powers and many sanctions which they can apply in order to clear the path for the things they want to do. But they are also hemmed in by restrictions—they work in a glass house, prisoners to a considerable extent of the civil servants who serve them and of the rival boards and commissions that each have reserved some city policy making for themselves. The house is heavily mortgaged to the state and the fence around it is a barricade manned by earnest defenders of suburban independence.

Throughout American history, but especially in recent decades, mayors of large cities have found the job to be a "no win" situation. The problems of large cities are enormous and the mayors are expected to "solve" them. When they inevitably fail to do so, they leave office as unpopular figures and are not taken seriously for higher office. Furthermore, the large-city mayor is the symbol of the city, and people living elsewhere in the state, often distrustful of the largest city, refuse to support the mayor for governor or United States Senator. Thus, no mayor of New York City has gone to higher office since the Civil War. Only one Detroit mayor has moved on since the beginning of this century. Los Angeles mayors are talked about for other offices but are not chosen. Only one President, Grover Cleveland, has served as mayor of a large city—Buffalo, New York—and he was a desperate party's choice to clean up the corruption of his predecessors and save the party. (Andrew Johnson was mayor of a small Tennessee town.) Today, most big-city mayors are elected without important reliance upon any political party.

[1] See Leonard Ruchelman (ed.), *Big City Mayors,* Indiana University Press, Bloomington, 1970; Seymour Freedgood, "New Strength in City Hall," in Editors of *Fortune, The Exploding Metropolis,* Anchor Books, Doubleday & Company, Inc., Garden City, N.Y., 1958, pp. 63–64.

In the large cities, John Lindsay of New York, Carl B. Stokes of Cleveland, Joseph Alioto of San Francisco, Gerald Cavanaugh of Detroit, and Samuel Yorty of Los Angeles are all recent examples of mayors who have been consumed by the job. Only Richard J. Daley of Chicago, who is also political boss of the city, has been able to cope effectively as a manager of political conflict—and he never has ambitions beyond his own city.

POWERS OF THE MAYOR

The powers exercised by the mayor vary widely throughout the United States. The person called the mayor in a commission or council-manager city normally has few powers other than those of presiding over the council and performing the ceremonial role for the city. The mayor in a mayor-council city may have a great many powers, or he or she may be merely one of many virtually coordinate members of the city administration, as is the case in a weak-mayor city.

Legislative Powers

No difference necessarily exists between weak and strong mayors so far as their legislative powers are concerned. In virtually all instances, the mayor has the right to submit messages to the council and hence to recommend policy. These messages carry with them the prestige and the publicity potential of the mayor's office and must be considered by the council in light of this. Some mayors have the right to attend council sessions and to introduce measures. In those municipalities that have remained closest to English precedents, the mayor is actually a member of the council and presides over it. This is true in a common form of village government and is also the case in nearly all commission and council-manager cities.

Most mayors in mayor-council cities have a veto power. (See Table 8-1.)

TABLE 8-1. Veto Power of Mayors in Cities over 5,000 Population

	Percent of Mayors Who May		
Form of Government	Veto All Measures	Veto Selected Items	Not Veto Anything
Mayor-council	35.1	33.9	31.0
Commission	11.3	3.5	85.2
Council-manager	6.7	9.4	83.9
Town meeting			
Representative town meeting	0.0	0.0	100.0
All cities over 5,000	20.8	20.1	58.1

Source: Municipal Year Book, 1968, International City Management Association, Chicago, 1968, p. 57.

TABLE 8-2. Voting Power of Mayors in Cities over 5,000 Population, by Form of Government*

	Percent of Mayors Who May Vote	
Form of Government	On All Issues	In Case of Tie Only
Mayor-council	16.3	58.7
Commission	92.0	7.1
Council-manager	54.1	41.3
All cities over 5,000	31.7	50.7

* Statistics include only mayors directly elected by the people.
Source: Municipal Year Book, 1968, International City Management Association, Chicago, 1968, p. 56.

This is, of course, a substantial supporting weapon when the mayor recommends policy. The greatest power of the veto in the hands of a mayor, as of a president, is measured by its threatened use rather than by the number of times it is actually invoked. A veto may be overridden either by a simple majority or by some extraordinary vote such as two-thirds or three-fourths. In a few cities, notably Boston, a veto is absolute.

In strong-mayor cities, it is not uncommon to find mayors so powerful that the council does not attempt to make policy independently of them. Under such circumstances, they need rarely use the veto. The use to which the veto is put will depend, of course, on local custom, prevailing circumstances, and the personal ideology and political strategy of the incumbent mayor.

In some cities mayors have the power of casting a vote in case of a tie, even though they may not be a member of the council. If they presides over the council, they are quite certain to have this power. When the mayor is a member of the council, he or she, of course, has a vote. (See Table 8-2.)

Powers over Administration

The characteristic differences between the weak and strong mayors of America are to be found in their powers over administration. The strong mayors, unlike the weak mayor, are given powers to make them chief administrative officers. They have supervisory and coordinative powers over the activities of the various departments and are in charge of the preparation and administration of the budget. In a few cities they have so much power in budget preparation that the council is empowered to do no more than decrease or strike out items in the budget. The controller, who supervises expenditures by the operational departments, is normally an appointee of the chief executive in a strong-mayor city. At the opposite extreme, the budget is sometimes prepared by a committee of the council well out of the hands of the mayor, and the controller may be an elective official or a council appointee. When the mayor has control over the preparation and expenditure of the budget, he or she has great powers which can be used to reach into agencies that might otherwise be totally independent. For example, he or she can use this power to influence policies within agencies otherwise controlled by an elective board (e.g., parks in many cities) or by the bureaucracy (e.g., public health).

Despite the vast legal powers they often possess, the mayors of large cities:[2]

> frequently must mediate between the claims of contending groups, no one of which is dominant in the community. In such instances their role as decision-makers assumes greater importance. Holding the balance of power, they occupy a strategic position of influence which they can exploit to further their total program and objectives. The mayors of large cities, particularly, enjoy such opportunities. It would be grossly misleading, however, to assume that men who have reputations as strong mayors, such as Daley in Chicago, Lee in New Haven or Tucker in St. Louis, rule by fiat or by arbitrary exercise in their official prerogatives.

Robert Dahl made a similar observation relative to New Haven. He found that the mayor "was not the peak of a pyramid but rather at the center of intersecting circles. He rarely commanded. He negotiated, cajoled, exhorted, beguiled, charmed, pressed, appealed, reasoned, promised, insisted, demanded, even threatened, but he most needed support from other leaders who simply could not be commanded. Because the mayor could not command, he had to bargain."[3]

Law Enforcement Most city charters impose upon the mayor the executive function of seeing to it that laws and ordinances are enforced and that peace and order are maintained. Actual power to do this is not always granted. It is traditional, however, to give the mayor control over the police department. Even when the mayor has no other exclusive power of appointment, he or she is usually given the right to hire and dismiss the police chief or commissioner. Sometimes, however, the mayor is given the responsibility for enforcement of laws and ordinances but is deprived of any control over the law-enforcement agency. St. Louis and Kansas City have police heads appointed by the state. A few cities elect the police chiefs; in some they are chosen by the council; and in others, by a semi-independent police board.

Appointments For effective control over administration and to coordinate its activities, the mayor must have the powers both of appointment and of remov-

[2] John C. Bollens and Henry J. Schmandt, *The Metropolis,* 3d ed., Harper & Row, Publishers, Incorporated, New York, 1975.

[3] Robert A. Dahl, *Who Governs?* Yale University Press, New Haven, Conn., 1961, p. 204.

al. Weak-mayor cities are likely to have several elective administrative officers and others selected by the council. In a strong-mayor city, these officers are appointed by the mayor. In some cities, such as New York and Detroit, the mayor's powers extend to virtually all the department heads in the administrative branch and he need not consult the council or anyone else in making appointments. He is in full charge of administration. He may appoint the heads of the major subdivisions within the departments, or this power may go to the department heads. In actual practice, it does not make much difference which method is used, for a serious conflict between mayor and department head over any matter would mean the resignation or dismissal of the recalcitrant department head.

In many cities, the mayor must have the approval of the council in making appointments. This is the more common pattern and is in keeping with the system of checks and balances upon which the mayor-council plan is based. It is in accord with American traditions, but it confuses responsibility for administration; the public cannot directly fix the blame, since several persons have a hand in each appointment. In addition, it provides a gratuitous system of patronage to council members. The mayor must, in practice, consult the council before making appointments, and as in the case of the President in relation to the United States Senate, many or perhaps most of the appointments become patronage items for council members. Council members are not elected in order to make appointments, of course, and placating their patronage demands is not likely to provide an effective system for procuring able administrators in city government. The mayor, clearly answerable for administration, will more probably select persons of ability. He or she is likely to combine patronage and competence considerations in making choices; council members will probably seek only patronage. There is no pressure upon them to do otherwise.

Removals In the strong-mayor city, the chief executives can remove any member of their administration in whom they have lost confidence. In New York and Detroit, the mayors can remove almost all appointees at pleasure, even those who are nominally appointed for a specific term of years.

Because of the frontiersman's distrust of government, however, it is more common to find restraints on the removal power. Unlike the President of the United States, who commonly must have the approval of the Senate in order to make appointments but may remove all except members of the independent regulatory establishments at pleasure, the mayor often must have the council's approval for both appointments and removals. This pattern is found, for example, in Los Angeles. It is subject to the same criticism as is approval for appointment. The mayor cannot control the acts of those nominally subordinate to him where this system exists.

It is also common to restrict the mayor's removal power by providing that he or she may make removals only "for cause." This means, usually, removal only after notice and hearing, and the action of the mayor is in such cases normally subject to review by the courts. The mayor's status is lowered if appointees may defy him or her or if the mayor is forced into a court fight over a dismissal. If a mayor loses such a fight, morale problems are especially likely to be serious. In practice, however, the notice-and-hearing requirement may not seriously impair the removal power of the mayor, although it does discourage hasty decision making.

In many cities, department heads are civil service employees. Despite this, the mayor usually has the right to choose department heads and to remove them if he or she thinks they are not doing a good job. In the event of the removal of a department head who has civil service tenure, the employee is reduced in status and given other assignments but is not dismissed from the service.

Ceremonial Functions

In every city, beauty queens must be crowned, conventions greeted, presidents introduced, parks dedicated, cornerstones laid, baseball seasons opened, parades led, and charity drives launched. The mayor is expected to do all these things. In fact, it is partly because he or she must do them that the office of mayor is retained under the commission and council-manager forms. The mayor is the symbol for the whole city.

Probably the typical mayor enjoys the attention on these occasions. He or she is surely aware of the free publicity. In smaller cities, this duty of the mayor is not time-comsuming, as it is in larger cities. In the very largest cities, the ceremonial function becomes a real burden taking up valuable time that could be spent upon the pressing problems of administration or policy making. It is partly for this reason that a deputy mayor is appointed in New York.

Whatever the size of the municipality, Americans are always likely to "try to get the mayor to be there" whenever a committee plans some function, modest or mammoth. The mayor interested in his or her political future will try to be on hand.

Duties as a Lobbyist

Because cities are largely at the mercy of the state legislatures, city officials necessarily follow closely the course of proposed legislation affecting them. The cities are collectively protected in most states by the lobbying activities of the state league of municipalities, just as their interests on the national level are looked after by the American League of Cities and the United States Conference of Mayors. Large cities may have paid lobbyists at the state capital and in Washington.

At times, when legislation of particular importance to a certain city or group of cities is being considered, their mayors may be called to the state capital by the secretary of the league of municipalities so they may use the prestige of their offices in an attempt to protect the interests of their cities. Political skill is especially important at such times.

Judicial Powers

In early America, the mayor exercised minor *judicial* powers as well as having a seat in the *legislative* body and serving as chief *executive*. For example, a provision of 1851 special act charter of Davenport, Iowa, provided that the mayor "shall by virtue of his office be a justice of the peace, and as such shall be a conservator of the peace."

Some cities still have a "mayor's court," and legally the mayor of New York is such a judge, but in practice the use of this power is disappearing. Also, because the mayor is in a position analogous to that of the governor and the President, he may have power to grant pardons for violations of city ordinances (but not of state or national law). The exercise of this power is today comparatively rare.

THE OFFICE OF MAYOR

Selection of the Mayor

The way in which the mayor is chosen varies a good deal according to the form of government. (See Table 8-3.) In all but a few mayor-council cities, the mayor is elected directly by the voters. He or she is chosen in this fashion in about 78 percent of the commission-plan cities but in only one-half of the council-manager cities.[4] In such large municipalities as Kansas City, Dallas, and San Diego, however, he is elected directly.

The public is accustomed to electing the mayor and probably feels more comfortable with a charter that gives it that privilege. The popular election of the mayor tends to evaluate him in public prestige and to provide him with high status, which he finds useful if he seeks to be a legislative leader.

A study comparing recruitment patterns for mayors of Nashville, New Haven, and Chicago concluded that, reflecting national trends, the mayor's office was increasingly held by those with a good deal of formal education and by professional politicians rather than amateurs. The office was, however, found

[4] Data on the methods of selection of mayors are available in the current issue of the *Municipal Year Book,* International City Management Association, Chicago.

TABLE 8-3. Method of Selection of Mayors in Cities over 5,000 Population, by Form of Government

Form of Government	Percent Directly Elected	Percent Selected by Council	Highest Number Votes in Council Election
Mayor-council	97	3	0.1
Commission	78	21	1
Council-manager	50	49	1
All cities over 5,000	75	24	1

Source: Municipal Year Book, 1968, International City Management Association, Chicago, 1968, p. 55.

relatively unattractive by local social and economic elites and regarded as less prestigeful than state or national office.[5]

The mayor may also be selected by council. This is the method used in slightly less than half of the council-manager cities and in many commission cities. But it is used in only 3 percent of the mayor-council cities of over 5,000 population. These appear to be chiefly in places in which the government has evolved from the village or township structure.

In a few cities, the person who receives the highest number of votes for council becomes mayor. This is uncommon but can be found, for example, in Hartford and Kalamazoo, both manager cities, and in a very few commission cities. A few mayor-council cities also make the person with the highest number of votes for council the mayor. This is true, however, only where the structure has grown from the old village type of government, based upon English traditions and without a clear separation of powers.

Those Who Serve

Throughout American history, mayors have typically been persons well respected in the community, often slightly older and of slightly higher social status than the average council member, but seldom from the richest or most prestigeful residents. (In its history as a city, Boston has had only three mayors—two Quincys and one Eliot—drawn from the Brahmin aristocracy, for example.) Some working-class people have become mayors, especially during the high point of know-nothingism in the 1850s, but some make their way to the office today—Mayor Frank L. Rizzo of Philadelphia and Mayor Thomas Bradley of Los Angeles, both former policemen, for example.

Beginning in the late 1960s, a number of large cities have elected black mayors: Atlanta, Cleveland, Detroit, Gary, Los Angeles, and Newark, for example. Hundreds of smaller cities, especially in the South, also have black mayors. So do some Northern suburbs.[6] With the increasing political demands of women in the 1970s, female mayors were elected in large numbers of suburbs and also in some middle-sized cities. The first woman mayor appears to have been Bertha J. Landis of Seattle, who served in the mid-1920s. In the 1970s, Davenport, Iowa (pop.: 98,469), Hartford, Conn. (pop.: 158,017), Okalhoma City (pop.: 367,856), and San Jose (pop.: 445,779), all had women mayors, as did many other slightly smaller cities. Up to the present, women have always been more likely to become mayors in council-manager cities than under other forms.

With the lowering of the voting age to eighteen, a few teen-agers became mayors. A small town in Iowa first elected an eighteen-year-old college student. Some other smaller places followed. More commonly, some persons in their twenties became mayors; the largest city with one was perhaps Madison, Wisconsin, in the mid-1970s. There a "radical activist" of the 1960's campus scene was

[5] Mayer N. Zald and Thomas A. Anderson, "Secular Trends and Historical Contingencies in the Recruitment of Mayors," *Urban Affairs Quarterly,* 3:53–68, June, 1968.

[6] See Edward Greer, "The New Mayors: Black Power in the Big Cities," *Nation,* 219:525–529, Nov. 23, 1974; James E. Conyers and Walter L. Wallace, *Black Elected Officials,* Russell Sage Foundation, New York, 1976.

elected—and he promptly lost the support of many who had voted for him while picking up backing from former opponents as he faced the realities of the differences between mere dissent and the requirements of governing.

Salary

The pay of the mayor varies according to both the size of the city and the structure of its government. In general, the salary varies directly with the size of the city, as might be expected. Small cities are likely to pay only a token salary, something less than $1,000 a year. New York, at the opposite extreme, pays $45,000.

In a commission-plan city, the mayor usually receives the same pay as the other commissioners, or a few hundred dollars additional. There are some exceptions where the mayor may receive quite an appreciable amount more. In manager cities, the same general rule applies.

It is not uncommon for the mayor to be paid less than some of the subordinates. The city engineer, the health officer, the attorney, and especially the superintendent of schools are likely to be paid more than the mayor, except in the very largest cities.

The average length of service of a mayor is approximately four years, and in running for and accepting the office there is a grave risk of damaging one's personal reputation. Clearly, persons with administrative and leadership ability can make more money, with a longer professional life, in private endeavor. Yet few arguments presented to the voters are greeted more coldly than those suggesting a higher salary for the mayor.

Term of Office

The Jacksonians insisted upon terms of not over two years, for they believed in keeping government "close to the people." The traditional term of office in New England was one year—from one town meeting until the next.

The term of office of the American mayor today depends to some extent upon the type of city-government structure in the particular city. The two-year term was still dominant in mayor-council cities in 1971, especially in those of the weak-mayor type and in cities under 5,000 population. Most council-manager cities had two-year terms, too. Commission-governed cities, on the other hand, were likely to have four-year terms.

Terms of less than four years allow the mayor little time to establish a record or to devote to the job. With a two-year term, campaign for reelection begins almost as soon as the results of the first campaign are in. Some cities cling to the cynical rule prohibiting the mayor from succeeding himself or herself. During the palmy days of the Republican machine in Philadelphia (until 1951), the charter of that city had such a rule. However, it did not appear to weaken the machine in the least.

Removals

The mayor who is incompetent, callous, or unrepresentative of the wants of the dominant public may be removed by allowing his or her term to expire or by securing defeat at the next election. There are times, however, when the public may wish to terminate the authority of a chief executive before his or her regular term expires. This is particularly true when he or she is thought to be guilty of what the lawyers call non-, mis-, or malfeasance in office. That is to say, if he or she fails to perform duties, or does them in an unlawful manner, or does illegal things under the mantle of office. There are several remedies at law in such cases.

First of all, there is the *recall.* As has already been noted, it is unlikely, under this device, that the case will be decided on its merits.[7] But several other (and incidentally older) remedies are available.

In most cities, the mayor may be removed by action of the council—an ancient common-law power. Most charters require a vote of something more than a simple majority to effect a removal, however. It is also possible for the mayor to be removed by a court order for certain causes as prescribed by law. In Michigan, New York, North Dakota, and Ohio, the mayor may be removed by the governor. All three of these removal techniques are "for cause" only. The courts have regularly held this to mean that there must be a presentation of specific charges, due notice to the official whose removal is sought, and a hearing, usually public. It also means that the official may appeal to the courts if he or she feels that the procedural safeguards to which he or she is entitled have not been followed.

Vacancies

If a mayor dies, resigns, or is removed from office, the law or charter provides for an immediate replacement. It is quite important that there always be someone to serve as mayor. Since the mayor leaves the city from time to time for a vacation, a conference, or a convention, it is also necessary for someone to act in the temporary absence.

The succession may pass to the presiding officer of the council or to some administrative officer, most commonly the controller. In some cities, if the office is vacated, the council is allowed to choose the new mayor, not necessarily from its own membership. If the next election is some time off, say more than six months or a year, the law may provide for an acting mayor and a special election to choose a person to serve out the term.

Legal Qualifications

Virtually every city has charter provisions requiring the mayor to be a United States citizen, to be of a certain minimum age, and to have lived in the city for a certain minimum number of years. It might be required, for example, that the mayor must be at least thirty years old and have been a city resident for three years. These rules are probably largely in imitation of the requirements in the United States Constitution for the presidency. They are of little practical meaning—even the citizenship requirement—for no alien could be elected to a mayoralty position in any American city today.

[7] See above, pp. 120–121.

THE CITY MANAGER

City managers are persons of importance in most cities where the office exists. They are also persons of great power. But the power they possess is, in most cases, used in a different manner and toward different ends than that of the old-fashioned machine leader.

Qualifications of the Manager

It is a basic part of the theory of council-manager government that the entire administration of the city be professionalized. Managers are supposed to be trained to use the tools of administration and, especially in smaller cities, to possess a technical skill, such as engineering, as well. The manager needs to be a diplomat, for his or her job is dependent upon an ability to get along with the council. The manager is supposed to be a politicain of a special sort, too, for the job calls for giving advice on matters of public policy without becoming ensnared in the political process when these problems become campaign issues. Are managers actually able to do all these things? What sort of people are they?

According to one study, the typical manager was in his early forties, had a college degree in one of the social sciences, and served in a city of under 10,000 located within a metropolitan area.[8] In the years after World War II, the manager plan had become most popular in small, suburban communities, but only in a statistical sense. It had also been growing in popularity in middle-sized and large cities. In the mid-1970s, 76 percent of all managers were in municipalities of under 25,000 population, and 27 percent in communities of under 5,000.[9]

In the early days of the plan, managers were most often engineers, and in smaller cities this profession is still preferred, the manager also serving as the city engineer. The trend in medium- and larger-sized cities is away from hiring engineers and persons trained in business administration as managers. More and more universities are offering special training in public administration designed to prepare students for the city-manager profession. After graduation, these trainees advance through the administrative hierarchy of city governments until they become managers, many of them later moving on to larger cities with higher pay and greater prestige. This training provides the future manager with more of a background in the social and economic character of the city than was formerly the case.

Only 7 percent of the managers appointed in 1965 came from nongovernmental jobs; 60 percent had been employed in other manager cities—as the manager, as the manager's administrative assistant, or as an intern. Managers are thus receiving better on-the-job training today. In 1939, only 23 percent of those hired came from administrative positions in other cities.

The profession of manager appears to carry enough salary and prestige to

[8] Davis S. Arnold, "A Profile of City Managers," *Public Management,* 46:56–60, March, 1964.

[9] David A. Booth, "Council-Manager Government in Small Cities," *Public Management,* 55:7–9, November, 1973; Werner E. Mills and Harry R. Davis, *Small City Government,* Random House, Inc., New York, 1962.

make it a sufficiently worthwhile occupation for many to spend a lifetime in it. In 1964, only 6.4 percent of the managers left the field, a number which included those who died and retired.[10]

Selection and Tenure of the Manager

Perhaps the most important task faced by a council is the selection of the manager. How does the council go about doing this? Council members, encountering the problem relatively seldom, may not know how to approach it. They may know that there are qualified persons about the country who might be interested in the position, but they may not know their names or how to go about finding them. The International City Management Association has published a helpful pamphlet for cities, *The Selection of a City Manager* (revised, 1965). On request, the Washington headquarters of the Association often assists cities in securing qualified applicants and publishes notices of available openings. Similar assistance may also be secured from the state leagues of cities and departments of political science in nearby universities.

The council may consider one of the city's department heads for promotion to manager. Leading managers whose names and reputations are known to the council members will probably be asked to offer names of possible candidates. From such a list the council can then proceed to invite interested persons to apply. (Some unsolicited applications will be received.) The council may next reduce further the size of the list and then invite those still being considered to appear, if possible for personal interviews, before finally choosing the person to whom the job is to be offered. The process is thus similar to the selection of other *professional* staff members in government. The procedures described here are favored by the managers' professional organization, for they tend to discourage the selection of a nonprofessional.

The manager is normally selected by the council by majority vote and is dismissable by the council at any time by the same method. For the plan to work according to the model, it is essential that the council be allowed to remove the manager at any time and for any reason that the council majority thinks sufficient. Otherwise, the administration of the city becomes autonomous and irresponsible, uncontrolled by the machinery of democracy. Since ultimate responsibility for all that takes place in city government rests with the council, this body is assigned the job of overseeing the manager's activities.

In some cities, a practice has developed whereby each new council majority chooses its own manager, but this is not the general rule. The manager is supposed to be a professional administrator. If this is how he or she is perceived by council members, there is no reason why he or she should not be continued in the job despite transient council majorities. It is significant to note that the average tenure of a manager in a city today is about seven years and that it would be longer except for the shortage of managers, which has encouraged their promotion to higher-paying jobs.

[10] See the *Municipal Year Book, 1966,* International City Management Association, 1966, p. 508.

In Florida, a study found that the tenure of managers was highest in cities where politics was low keyed, with little competition for office and few policy conflicts. In cities with high conflict levels, the manager often came to be identified with a particular faction, as a result of his position as a community leader. If the faction with which he had been identified lost, he might find himself out of a job. In such cities, council members also tended to protect themselves by seeking to have major policies identified with the manager rather than with themselves. The manager, therefore, was sometimes the victim of scapegoating if the policies proved unpopular.[11]

Tenure varies considerably from one community to another. In the Florida cities studied, average tenure was only slightly more than three years,[12] about one-half that in Illinois.[13] Most commonly, terminations are given to managers in their first two years on a job, to those with relatively less experience and education,[14] and to managers in cities with declining or slowly growing populations.[15]

A few charters permit the removal of the manager through the use of the recall. This is not in keeping with the model, because it allows the council to shirk its responsibility for the manager and because it almost of necessity embroils the manager in campaigning: He or she becomes something of an appointive mayor instead of a manager and must ride the political waves to prevent removal. Political, rather than professional, motivations become, of necessity, paramount.

The Jacksonian influence dies slowly in American politics, and it is still to be found affecting the hand that writes the council-manager charter. The extraordinary majority, such as two-thirds or three-fourths of the council, sometimes appears in the rules governing the removal of the manager. Charters also may permit dismissal only "for cause." Such a rule has the effect of putting final discretion in the hands of the courts rather than the council. Some charters require advance notice of one or more months to the manager who is to be removed. This creates lameduck managers and a stalemated government.

The model calls for the council to have full power over hiring and dismissing the manager. No argument for limiting the powers of the council can circumvent the fact that the manager plan can work effectively only if a majority of the council members have confidence in the manager.

Place of Residence Most council-manager charters logically provide that the manager need not be a resident of the city at the time of appointment, for the council is looking, not for a deserving local politician, but for a professionally competent administrator. At one time, it was quite common to hire a person from outside the city. Until 1929, about one-half of the managers hired were nonresi-

[11] Gladys M. Kammerer and John M. DeGrove, *Florida City Managers: Profile and Tenure,* Public Administration Clearing Service, University of Florida, Gainesville, Fla., 1961, pp. 34–35.

[12] *Ibid.*

[13] Charles A. Willis and Thomas Page, "Tenure and Turnover in Illinois Managers," *Illinois Government,* 12:3, October, 1961.

[14] Edwin O. Stene, "Short-Term Managers," *Public Management,* 43:146–152, July, 1961.

[15] Edwin O. Stene, *The City Manager: Professional Training and Tenure,* Governmental Research Center, University of Kansas, Lawrence, Kans., 1966, p. 34.

dents. With the coming of the Great Depression there was a reversal of this trend, and in 1933, only 17 percent of those appointed came from outside the city. This was probably the result of two considerations: (1) a desire of local politicians to keep scarce jobs "at home" and (2) the possibility of hiring local persons at a lower salary.

During and after World War II, high employment, combined with a rapid expansion in the number of manager cities, resulted in a definite shortage of qualified managers. Cities turned to other cities in order to get chief administrators. The number of appointments from outside the city accordingly rose to all-time highs. In 1965, two-thirds of new managers hired were from outside the city. These figures probably also reflect a growing emphasis upon securing trained and experienced persons, persons who may not be available locally. Furthermore, the percentage of nonresidents hired as the first manager of a city adopting this form has always been high, and the rate of new adoptions has been unusually high in recent years.

Salaries Obviously, if managership is to become a real profession with persons willing to make a lifetime career of it, the pay opportunities must be sufficient to attract able persons. The data indicate that managership affords fairly good salaries.

Some opposition to the manager plan has been generated because salaries are thought to be *too* high. Public opinion in this country is often not sophisticated on this matter and may sometimes oppose the payment of salaries necessary to attract the talent wanted. This tendency is one of the common causes of disillusionment in the manager plan. In the postwar period of high employment and inflation plus a shortage of trained managers, many of those hired were incompetent. A city may not expect to find a manager capable of doing a satisfactory job unless sufficient salary is offered.

The Duties of the Manager

While charters vary widely and none conform in all details to the provisions of the *Model City Charter* of the National Municipal League, a manager, in the model and often in practice, has all or most of the following responsibilities:

1 Overseeing enforcement of all laws and ordinances
2 Controlling all departments, with power to appoint, supervise, and remove department heads and bureau chiefs
3 Making recommendations to the council on such matters as thought desirable
4 Keeping the council advised of the financial condition of the city and concerning future needs and trends
5 Preparing and submitting to the council the annual budget
6 Preparing and submitting to the council reports and memoranda such as are requested
7 Keeping the council, and indirectly the public, informed concerning the operations of all aspects of the city government

8 Performing such other duties as the council may legally assign

In a sentence, the manager has full responsibility to the council for the conduct of the administration of the city.

The Manager and the Council

When a city adopts the manager plan, the function of the council undergoes a considerable change, even if the city has previously operated under the strong-mayor form. The study by Stone, Price, and Stone[16] found that the council was relieved of most of its tasks of hiring department heads and subordinate employees. (See Table 8-4.) In all but a few cities, the mayor and council were relieved of the duties of supervising the employees. Because of provisions of charters and state laws, however, councils were not relieved of the great mass of minor details that have historically been handled by that body. Even though the volume of work performed by the council could not be reduced, "the point of view and the approach of the council to municipal policy was different."[17] The difference resulted from reliance upon the manager for many things that could not be furnished in the same fashion by the mayor or a council committee.

Members of the council may disagree with the manager concerning the characteristics of the managerial role. In cities that have not long had the manager plan, this disagreement may be serious, with most of the council to one degree or

[16] Harold A. Stone, Don K. Price, and Katherine H. Stone, *City Manager Government in the United States,* Public Administration Service, Chicago, 1940, chap. 8.

[17] *Ibid.,* p. 174.

TABLE 8-4. Manner of Selection of Department Heads in Florida Council-manager Cities

Selection Method	Number of Cities	Percentage
All appointed by manager, with virtually automatic council approval	58	76.3
Some appointed by the manager with virtually automatic approval; council appoints the rest	14	18.4
Check with council on who it wants; if at all qualified, manager appoints their choice	2	2.6
Council majority faction dictates appointments	1	1.3
Not reported	1	1.3
Total	76	99.9

Source: Gladys M. Kammerer and John M. DeGrove, *Florida City Managers: Profile and Tenure,* Public Administration Clearing Service, University of Florida, Gainesville, Fla., 1961, table 17.

another rejecting the manager's concept of his job.[18] In Colorado cities where the plan had been operating for a number of years, relatively few council members were found to dissent from the manager's definition of his role. But in another study, of all council-manager cities in the San Francisco Bay area, conflicting images of the manager's role seemed to be deep-seated and permanent in character.[19] (See Table 8-5.) A study of 2,082 cities in the fall of 1973 revealed many council-manager interfaces that were possible sources of role conflict.[20] Even so, the actual amount of strife generated over conflicts in role perception historically seems to have been very limited.

In most cities, the manager presents significant matters to the council for consideration. Since they are not initiated by council members, the council is normally free to consider such items on their merits, having no vested interest in them. New business coming before the council is normally first referred to the manager for a report at a future meeting. The manager, in making a report, is in

[18] John C. Buechner, *Differences in Role Perception in Colorado Council-Manager Cities,* Bureau of Governmental Research, University of Colorado, Boulder, Colo., 1965.

[19] Ronald O. Loveridge, *The City Manager in Legislative Politics,* Bobbs-Merrill Company, Indianapolis, Ind., 1971.

[20] Robert J. Huntley and Robert J. Macdonald, "Urban Managers: Organizational Preferences, Managerial Styles, and Social Policy Roles," *Municipal Year Book, 1975,* International City Management Association, Washington, 1975, pp. 149–159.

TABLE 8-5. Conflicting Images of the Manager's Role

	Percentages			
	Agree	Tend to Agree	Tend to Disagree	Disagree
A city manager should assume leadership in shaping municipal policies				
Manager responses ($n = 57$)	39	49	7	5
Councilmen responses ($n = 296$)	16	26	19	39
A city manager should act as an administrator and leave policy matters to the council				
Manager responses ($n = 58$)	7	15	57	21
Councilmen responses ($n = 298$)	69	19	11	1

Source: Derived from Ronald O. Loveridge, *The City Manager in Legislative Politics,* Bobbs-Merrill Company, Indianapolis, 1971.

a position to consider the effect of possible forms of action upon all departments of the city. (See Table 8-6.)

Most managers prefer to make their reports in writing. Of course, they are also quizzed orally by council members concerning various aspects and implications of the report at council meetings. Most managers also make recommendations for action in connection with a report.[21] Some managers present only one recommended line of action, the one they consider the professionally sound solution. Other managers present two or more possible approaches, thus affording the council opportunity to choose. The council may not always choose as the manager would prefer, but the latter knows that the council may be the best judge of what is most acceptable under prevailing local conditions.

Although the manager plays a public role of "the expert" who is available only to answer questions and to administer, in practice, managers or their subordinates are the principal sources of policy innovation in cities today. Ideas, if managers or their staffs do not think of them in the first place, are likely, in most cities, to come from interest groups, rather than from council members. Once an idea is placed upon the community agenda, the manager becomes a major leader in securing its adoption, although he or she is usually discreet concerning personal views until the council has given formal approval.

[21] See Clarence E. Ridley, *The Role of the City Manager in Policy Formulation,* International City Management Association, Chicago, 1958; Charles R. Adrian, "Leadership and Decision-making in Manager Cities: A Study of Three Communities," *Public Administration Review,* 18:208–213, Summer, 1958; B. James Kweder, *The Roles of Manager, Mayor and Councilmen in Policy Making: A Study of Twenty-one North Carolina Cities,* Institute of Government, The University of North Carolina, Chapel Hill, 1965.

TABLE 8-6. Approaches to Policy Recommendations by Florida Managers

Method of Presentation	Number of Managers	Percentage
Present alternatives with supporting facts, manager's choice	52	68.4
Present only manager's choice with supporting facts to avoid confusing council	8	10.5
Combination of the above	6	7.9
Present major alternatives with facts, no specific manager recommendation	4	5.3
Present manager's solution with little or no supporting facts	1	1.3
Other	5	6.6
Total	76	100.0

Source: Gladys M. Kammerer and John M. DeGrove, *Florida City Managers: Profile and Tenure,* Public Administration Clearing Service, University of Florida, Gainesville, Fla., 1961, table 11.

The Manager and Elections

Managers perform many functions of community leadership similar to those performed by council members or the mayor. They are often active in service clubs, charitable organizations, churches, and the like.[22] They may make public speeches in which they seek to explain a new policy which has been approved by the council (and which they may have originated). They may speak on the positive side of a proposed referendum on a bond issue (as frequently does the school superintendent who holds a parallel position with the school board), but they are prudent not to do so if the question involves partisan or factional issues.

One study of the council-manager form in Illinois has concluded:[23]

> While the initial choice of a manager to serve at the pleasure of the council may not be a political question, the question of his retention becomes political in the sense that each councilman is likely to be answerable to some organized segments of his constituency on his attitude toward the manager. Thus, much of what a city manager does has a continually measured political impact. His prominence in the city administration necessarily focuses some attention on him which is subtracted from the elective political body to which he is answerable.

Neither in the model nor in practice, however, do managers engage in direct political activities. They do not appeal to the voters over the heads of the council members, or campaign against council members who have frequently opposed their policy recommendations, or support candidates or policies for personal or factional reasons. They can fultill an almost inevitable role as policy leaders without themselves becoming a political issue, by making sure that their recommendations are always "controlled by expert knowledge and professional interest, never by selfish considerations or political friendships.[24]

Managers who do not observe this rule will eventually lose their jobs, and their reputations—and hence employability elsewhere—will likely suffer. Sometimes a manager does offer assistance to one faction in a campaign, as the Cincinnati manager did in 1953, but under those circumstances ceases to be a professional manager, becomes a politician, and will keep that post only so long as his or her faction has a majority on the council.

The Manager and Public Relations

Unlike the government of any other type of city, the city with a manager has a nonelective person serving in the position upon which chief public interest and attention is focused. Whether the manager likes it or not, to him or her falls the greatest responsiblity for "selling" the manager plan, for making citizens satisfied with their government, and, often, for popularizing policies which the council has decided to undertake. The manager and assistants meet the public daily, and the nature of these contacts has a great deal to do with the popularity of the manager, of the council members by whose leave he or she holds the job, and of city government itself.

[22] Stone, Price, and Stone, *op. cit.,* pp. 243–244.
[23] Willis and Page, *op. cit.,* p. 3.
[24] Stone, Price, and Stone, *op. cit.,* p. 244.

All managers are necessarily aware of the importance of public relations, but they are not all equally adept in handling them. The Stone, Price, and Stone study found that some managers "had the knack of speaking and acting in a way that won confidence and brought about harmonious relations; others, no matter how hard they tried, never seemed to say in the right way what they wanted to say or to do in the right way what they wanted to do. How the manager spoke, acted, and conducted himself was often more important than what he said or accomplished."[25]

Some managers, like other chief executives, have assumed that the services of the city speak for themselves and have paid little attention to municipal reports to the public, have disliked making speeches, and have sought to avoid newspaper publicity. Most of them have recognized, however, the importance of informing the public about the functions performed by city government and the manner in which they are performed.

The Manager as a Professional

The International City Management Association (ICMA) is the professional organization to which most managers belong. The Association seeks to encourage high standards. It has a code of ethics and a committee on professional conduct. There would probably be legal complications if a city attempted to require formally that the manager be a member of the ICMA, but such a rule seems unnecessary, since the council is always answerable to the voters for the manager and since it might be considered improper for a private organization to determine qualifications for a public position. State licenses are less necessary than in, say, law or medicine, since managers do not practice directly before a relatively helpless and uninformed public, but rather before a council with complete power over the professional life of the manager.

The Stone, Price, and Stone study found that:[26]

> Perhaps the strongest support for the position the city managers took in regarding themselves as professional men lay in their attitude and in their conduct. Many city managers thought of themselves as professional executives devoting themselves to a job which required technical skill and a high sense of moral obligation. Many felt that they were selected as managers because they possessed special qualifications for the position and that political and private connections played no part in their appointment. With a large majority of managers, the job was the thing. Because city managers generally live up to the ideals which they had set for themselves through the International City Managers' Association, they were quite widely recognized as professional men.

OTHER EXECUTIVE OFFICERS

Most cities elect at least one administrative officer in addition to the mayor. Some elect as many as five others. For the most part, such officers are likely to be

[25] *Ibid.*, p. 159.

[26] *Ibid.*, pp. 67–68. By permission of the Public Administration Service. On managers as professionals, see also two articles by George K. Floro: "Continuity in City-Manager Careers," *American Journal of Sociology*, 61:240–246, November, 1955; and "Types of City Managers," *Public Management*, 36:221–225, October, 1954.

the clerk (or recorder), the city attorney (or corporation counsel), and various fiscal officers. In addition, certain department heads who are nearly always appointed are important persons in the policy-making process. Of these, the treasurer, controller, auditor, and assessor are discussed in Chapter 13. The police chief, still sometimes elected, is discussed in Chapter 15, the city engineer and city planner in Chapter 14. The duties of two other officers will be mentioned here.[27]

Clerks are, in form, only the record keepers of the city. They also usually serve as secretary to the council and keep the formal minutes of its meetings. In practice, however, clerks may become much more than office managers. Indeed, they may become virtual city managers in small communities. One reason for this is that they often serve a long time in the job. The public prefers to keep the position elective, but it also regards the clerk as being essentially noncontroversial in character. Thus, in municipalities of all sizes, clerks are likely to be persons of modest ability who make the job a career. Because they gradually come to know more about the minutiae of government perhaps than any one else, they are relied upon for background details. From this responsibility, it is often a short step to giving advice when asked and then to initiating suggestions. Because the consequences of any action this advice may generate will be attributed to others—the council members, the mayor, or the manager—clerks go on their bland way toward retirement, calmly riding above the storms of controversy that confront their colleagues.

One study has indicated that, in cities of under 10,000 population, a clerk has a great deal to do with policy formulation—that he or she does do, in a great many cases, the things suggested here. The study also indicated that certain factors reduced the importance of the clerk in a policy-making role, however. A part-time clerk was generally less effective than one who was constantly on duty. Women clerks were not usually as effective as policy leaders. And clerks in council-manager cities were more likely to be restricted to ministerial (routine) duties than was the case in other cities.[28]

Cities today are not likely to elect the city attorneys. The attorneys remain, however, important policy-making officers, as they were a few generations ago when the voters expected to be allowed to select them directly. In larger cities, in strong-mayor, and in council-manager cities, the attorneys are usually selected by the chief administrative officers and report directly to them. In such cases, attorneys are influential as policy makers, but they are subject to general oversight and direction by their chiefs, and this gives them a fairly definite policy framework within which to work. In other cities, and particularly in small communities, the council may select the attorneys and rely heavily on their advice since they have a near monopoly on the legal skills that are essential for effective municipal

[27] Special districts also sometimes have elective officers, or they may have elective governing boards which appoint professional managers as chief administrators. For the example of the school superintendent in this role, see Thomas H. Eliot, "Toward an Understanding of Public School Politics," *American Political Science Review,* 53:1032–1951, December, 1959.

[28] Walter D. De Vries, "The Role of the Fourth Class Michigan City Clerk in Municipal Decision-making," Unpublished master's thesis, Michigan State University, East Lansing, Mich., 1955.

management.[29] The attorney and the clerk are the two most likely policy leaders in places of under, say, 10,000 people.

Regardless of size of community, city attorneys are important for other reasons: (1) Dillon's rule makes both council members and administrators dependent upon them for opinions as to what the city is legally authorized to do. Because they must be consulted constantly in this regard, they have great opportunities for becoming general policy advisors. (2) To a considerable extent, they decide upon enforcement levels, though they may not be permitted to do so unilaterally, especially if they are not elected directly. Attorneys have much to say about which laws are to be enforced and how sternly they are to be enforced. They do not have the great power of the elective state's attorney in this connection as a rule, but they may be able to make great changes in the original intent of city ordinances and state laws in the way in which they administer them.

The lesser executive officers of the city, whether elected or appointed, are important to citizens because, despite their low visibility level, they significantly affect policy making. Though the citizen may not know it, when the headlines proclaim "Mayor Zilch Announces New Bonding Program" or "Councilman Announces Tax-Free Parking Scheme," the persons given the credit are only acting out their roles in the play. The playwright probably will not even be mentioned in the news story. His or hers is merely one of those "unimportant routine" offices of the city.

SELECTED READINGS

Baida, Robert H.: "The City Attorney: What's Ahead?" *Public Management,* 53:4–8, August, 1971.

Blackwood, George: "Boston Politics and Boston Politicians," in Murray B. Levin, *The Alienated Voter: Politics in Boston,* Holt, Rinehart and Winston, Inc., New York, 1960. (Recent Boston mayors.)

Booth, David A. (comp.): *Council-Manager Government, 1940–1964: An Annotated Bibliography,* International City Management Association, Chicago, 1965.

Bromage, Arthur W.: *Urban Policy Making: The Council-Manager Partnership,* Public Administration Service, Chicago, 1970.

Greer, Ann L.: *The Mayor's Mandate,* Schenkman Publishing Co., Cambridge, Mass., 1974. (A case study of the role of mayor in a heterogeneous community, in this case Waukegan, Ill.)

Greer, Edward: "The New Mayors: Black Power in the Big Cities," *Nation,* 219:525–529, November 23, 1974. (Why the growing numbers of black mayors are highly restricted in what changes they can effect.)

Hadden, Jeffrey K., Louis H. Masotti, and Victor Thiessen: "The Making of the Negro Mayors, 1967," *Trans-action,* January–February, 1967, pp. 21–30.

Hamburger, Philip: "The Mayor," *The New Yorker,* Jan. 26 and Feb. 2, 1957. (A profile of Robert F. Wagner, Jr., of New York.)

[29] For a case study of an upstate New York village, see A. J. Vidich and Joseph Bensman, *Small Town in Mass Society,* Princeton University Press, Princeton, N.J., 1958, pp. 127–129. For the clerk in the town surrounding the village, pp. 144–146.

Hentoff, Nat: "The Mayor," *The New Yorker,* Oct. 7, 1967, and May 3, 1969. (Profiles of Mayor John Lindsay.)

Hoan, Daniel W.: *City Government: The Record of the Milwaukee Experiment,* Harcourt, Brace & World, Inc., New York, 1936. (The experiences of a famous mayor.)

Hollis, Melvin G.: *Reform in Detroit,* Oxford University Press, New York, 1969. (A history of the turn-of-the-century businessman-reformer, Mayor Hazen S. Pingree.)

International City Management Association: *A Suggested Code of Ethics,* International City Management Association, Chicago, 1962. (A code suggested for all municipal officials and employees.)

Johnson, Tom L.: *My Story,* B. W. Huebsch, Inc., New York, 1911. (Autobiography of a famous mayor of Cleveland.)

Kammerer, Gladys M., and others: *The Urban Political Community: Profiles in Town Politics,* Houghton Mifflin Company, Boston, 1963. (Case studies of council-manager politics in Florida.)

Kinnard, William N., Jr.: *Appointed by the Mayor,* rev. ed., The Bobbs-Merrill Company, Inc., Indianapolis, ICP no. 63, 1961. (The study of a "weak" mayor on appointments in a small Eastern city.)

Levine, Charles H.: *Racial Conflict and the American Mayor,* D. C. Heath and Company, Lexington, Mass., 1974. (A theory of the effect of racial tensions and the effectiveness of mayors. Offers three case studies.)

Loveridge, Ronald O.: *City Managers in Legislative Politics,* The Bobbs-Merrill Company, Inc., Indianapolis, Ind., 1971. (Finds that managers perceive the council's role differently from the way council members do—and vice versa.)

Lowi, Theodore J.: *At the Pleasure of the Mayor,* The Free Press of Glencoe, New York, 1964. (A study of the recruitment, performance, and powers of New York political and career bureaucrats.)

Mulrooney, Keith F. (ed.): "Symposium on the American City Manager," *Public Administration Review,* 31:6–46, January–February, 1971. (The strengths and weaknesses of the manager relative to contemporary urban social issues.)

"New York City: Is it Governable?" *Newsweek,* May 31, 1965. (An article cataloging some of the great numbers of fantastically difficult problems the mayor of New York must cope with as a policy leader.)

Reichley, James: *The Art of Government: Reform and Organization Politics in Philadelphia,* The Fund for the Republic, New York, 1959.

Ridley, Clarence E.: *The Role of the City Manager in Policy Formulation,* International City Management Association, Chicago, 1948.

Rowat, Donald C.: *The Ombudsman, Citizen's Defender,* University of Toronto Press, Toronto, 1965. (Description of existing and proposed complaint officers and arguments pro and con concerning the post.)

Ruchelman, Leonard (ed.): *Big City Mayors: The City in Urban Politics,* Indiana University Press, Bloomington, 1970. (Collection of essays by political commentators, including mayors, on problems in such cities as New York, Chicago, Boston, Cleveland, and Los Angeles.)

Sherwood, Frank P.: *A City Manager Tries to Fire His Police Chief,* The Bobbs-Merrill Company, Inc., Indianapolis, ICP no. 76, 1963. (Conflict in a Southern California city. A conflict between managerial and police values.)

Stene, Edwin O.: *The City Manager: Professional Training and Tenure,* Governmental Research Center, University of Kansas, Lawrence, Kans., 1966.

Stillman, Richard J., II: *The Modern City Manager: A 1971 Profile,* International City Management Association, Washington, 1971.

Talbot, Allan R.: *The Mayor's Game, Richard Lee of New Haven and the Politics of Change,* Praeger, New York, 1967.

Wendt, Lloyd, and Herman Kogan: *Big Bill of Chicago,* The Bobbs-Merrill Company, Inc., Indianapolis, 1953. (The story of Mayor William H. Thompson.)

Whitlock, Brand: *Forty Years of It,* Appleton-Century-Crofts, Inc., New York, 1925. (By a reform mayor of Toledo, Ohio.)

Chapter 9

The City Council

The historic functions of legislative bodies in Western civilization have been those of communication, debate, criticism, investigation, and modification. In recent centuries, the popular assemblies have also been accorded the task of declaring and thus legitimatizing the law—a function once performed by the courts.[1]

City councils, as local legislatures, have generally performed the historic role of assemblies. Under colonial frontier influence, however, American councils became somewhat more positive instruments of policy leadership. The weak-mayor–council arrangement of frontier days placed the council in center stage, and Americans became accustomed to thinking of the councilmen as community leaders and as policy innovators. With the rise of the strong-mayor and council-manager plans, however, the council retreated to its traditional, essentially passive and symbolic functions—debate, criticism, investigation, and the formal declaration of the rules through resolutions and ordinances.

Reformers of several decades ago distrusted councilmen, or the role of the ward alderman, at any rate. Aldermen, by and large, were interested in the daily,

[1] See Charles R. Adrian and Charles Press, *The American Political Process,* 2d ed., McGraw-Hill Book Company, New York, 1969, chap. 13.

short-range considerations of neighborhood constituents, in favors to beset individuals, and in jobs—but not in overall policy development or in middle-class morality. Those who wrote the modern charters of cities, therefore, concentrated power in the chief executive—the mayor or manager—where they could expect policy leadership without the beclouding influences of errand running, of patronage considerations before program contest, or of neighborhood concerns before community-wide interests. As a result, the council's role is now less that of leadership and innovation than it was a century ago.

The pattern of council functions varies with the forms of city government, however. The duties of council members vary from the situation in weak-mayor cities, where each alderman, in addition to sharing in policy-making duties, serves very often as a ward supervisor of administrative functions, to the council-manager city, where he or she usually has only policy-making duties. The type of person who serves on the council also varies considerably from place to place, but the differences are based upon the size of the city as well as the forms of government.

LEADERSHIP AND CONFLICT

Varying Functions of the Council

In cities in which council members are elected by wards, the popular assembly of the community is most likely to perform the function it did during the nineteenth century. In one study of a city of about 50,000 population, the ward aldermen controlled patronage in their wards, carefully divided up the allocation of money for street repair, and were generally much more concerned with caring for the special wants of constituents than they were with overall policy development. In a city largely untouched by reform, the councilmen from all except the middle-class wards had not finished high school. They were neither very articulate nor capable of conducting public deliberations in an effective fashion. As a result, they sought protection from outside criticism through collective action. The majority faction (made up of aldermen from the working-class wards) spoke, to a considerable extent, as a single voice. There were no outstanding policy leaders on the council. The minority could not even exploit the weaknesses of the dominant faction.[2]

Three other cities with strong managers, on the other hand, had councils consisting of persons with considerable education and business or professional experience. The members were elected at large and generally did not want to be bothered with errand running for constituents—in one city it was customary practice to refuse to do so under all conditions. In these cities, members "did not emerge as either general policy innovators or general policy leaders. The individual councilman, rather, was likely to assume leadership in connection with a specific issue or function of government. He developed pet interests or came to

[2] Oliver P. Williams and Charles R. Adrian, *Four Cities,* University of Pennsylvania Press, Philadelphia, 1963, chap. 11. For aldermanic politics in Chicago, see Martin Meyerson and E. C. Banfield, *Politics, Planning and the Public Interest,* The Free Press of Glencoe, New York, 1957.

know one area of municipal activity especially well and concentrated upon that."[3]

A larger study—of eighty-eight council-manager cities—found that "while the number of policies initiated by councilmen in any one city is not large, they usually are on issues of considerable importance." Also it was found that:[4]

> Although the prestige of the council has not diminished in council-manager cities, the character of council action has changed as the city manager and others in the administrative organization make more of the recommendations for council consideration. The council naturally depends on the manager and his staff to study the problems and recommend solutions.

Of 206 proposals introduced in the city council of Los Angeles, a weak-mayor city, in a single month of 1959, only 10 percent were initiated by the mayor or councilmen; about 40 percent were developed by members of the city's bureaucratic experts; the remaining one-half came from individuals or various interest groups.[5] The mayor or members of the council often served as leaders in guiding proposals toward adoption. Bureaucrats were of great influence because of their near-monopoly of the technical competence needed to evaluate proposals in terms of their applicability to the local administrative process and to local existing conditions.

Conflict and Consensus

In general, the larger the city, the less likely there is to be consensus. Conflict becomes a part of daily public life in the large city, and public policies that are hammered out are likely to represent uneasy compromises, not supported by a stable majority of either citizens or council members. In these cities, conflict among the citizens is normally reflected by conflict on the council—and this in turn leads to factionalism on the governing board.

Of fifty-one Los Angeles County cities in one study, 36 percent (eighteen cities) reported the existence of factions on the council. In addition, many other cities had councils which divided occasionally over a basic issue of policy. The councils split most often over zoning matters, but it was policies concerning personnel and capital improvements that were most likely to create enduring splits.[6]

Factions may be organized, or they may be made up of the majority group, which was elected through endorsement of some recruiting organization, against the unorganized minority. They may exist primarily along liberal-conservative lines, as in the Minneapolis council for a long time, or they may divide according

[3] Charles R. Adrian, "Leadership and Decision-making in Manager Cities: A Study of Three Communities," *Public Administration Review,* 18:211, Summer, 1958.

[4] Clarance E. Ridley, *The Role of the City Manager in Policy Formulation,* International City Management Association, Chicago, 1958, pp. 17, 52.

[5] Harry W. Reynolds, Jr., "The Career Public Service and Statute Lawmaking," *Western Political Quarterly,* 18:621–639, September, 1965.

[6] Robert J. Huckshorn and C. E. Young, "A Study of Voting Splits on City Councils in Los Angeles County," *Western Political Quarterly* 13:479–497, June, 1960.

to neighborhood versus more general interests, or city boosters versus low-tax advocates, or on some other basis. The dominant faction may have a strong majority or, because city councils are usually small, a majority of one. In the latter case, of course, any tendency of majority-faction members to defect on certain issues is crucial, for such a defection reverses the majority and minority situations. In one study—of a Massachusetts city of 50,000—such defections were most likely to occur when a councilman was faced with supporting the particular demands—for improved water supply, sidewalks, or street repairs—of his own constituents. The sanctions of his colleagues as a group were powerful, but not as powerful as the sounds coming from those who would, at the next election, support him—or turn him out.[7]

In contrast to the large and middle-sized cities are the small towns. In populous communities, those who disagree are expected to say so, even at the final vote on a measure, if necessary. But the picture is quite different in the village where a consensus of values reduces political disagreements to a discussion of jots and where society may expect councilmen to agree unanimously:[8]

> Within the formally constituted governing agency of the village, the village board, politics is conducted on the principle of unanimity of decision. In two years of observation of village board meetings in Springdale, all decisions brought to a vote were passed unanimously. The dissent, disagreement and factionalism which exist in the community are not expressed at board meetings. Through a process of consultation prior to an official meeting and by extended discussion involving the entire group during the meeting itself, a point is reached when it seems reasonable to assume that everyone will go along with the proposed action. Only then, as a final parry, will someone suggest that a motion be made to propose the action. After a short period of silence which provides a last opportunity for futher discussion prior to the motion, the motion is made. Whereupon it is assumed that the motion is passed, or, if brought to a vote, as occasionally happens, it passes unanimously.

THE PEOPLE WHO SIT ON COUNCILS

Council Types

Council members have many impressions of their own role. Some of them are frankly concerned with respresenting a particular interest, perhaps blacks or realtors. Others want to create a "city beautiful." Still others regard themselves as caretakers, guardians of the taxpayers' pocketbooks. Most commonly—according to one study—councilmen hold one of two self-perceptions:[9]

> Some drew an analogy between the functions of the councilman and the member of the corporation board of directors. Others viewed themselves as a vehicle through which the wishes of the public could be translated into public action.

[7] J. Leiper Freeman, "A Case Study of the Legislative Process in Municipal Government," in John C. Wahike and Heinz Eulau, *Legislative Behavior,* The Free Press of Glencoe, New York, 1959, pp. 228–237.

[8] A. J. Vidich and Joseph Bensman, *Small Town in Mass Society,* Princeton University Press, Princeton, N.J., 1958, p. 110.

[9] Williams and Adrian, *op. cit.,* chap. 11.

The first view implies that the public interest is both ascertainable and indivisible. The good of the city, like the good of the corporation, must be stated in all-encompassing terms. This requires the councilman to view himself not as a delegate, but as a person possessing a mandate to use his own judgment in solving the problems presented to him. This judgment is shaped not only by his personal values, but by the exchange of views on the council. Thus the councilman is a participant in dialogue which "serves the interests of all the people."

The second view asserts instead that the job of the legislator is to do what the people, both individually and collectively, want. The councilman is a public servant who should entertain the requests and grievances of citizens and attempt to accommodate their desires, if it is possible within the framework of the law. The public interest is articulated by the adjustment of individual claims expressed through the representatives. Each councilman is an advocate of what he believes to be his constituents' desires.

The City Hall Club

Because councils are generally small—the national average size is six members—council members are not merely the impersonal spokesmen for their consciences or their constituencies. They are also members of a small group. The council is a club which tends to band together against the outsiders. It also has certain rules concerning what a member can say about another member without being ostracized. The intimate knowledge that members gain of one another's idiosyncrasies modifies their behavior.

As one study has noted:[10]

> Once elected to the council, the legislator became part of an organization in which members had different roles to play and the different degrees of prestige, participation, and authority he enjoyed depended in considerable measure upon the committee posts assigned him. As in most other legislative bodies in the United States, the criterion of seniority was a traditional basis . . . for determining committee assignments.

The Members

In the vast majority of American cities, typical council members are local business persons, well respected in the community, active in civic organizations, and often college graduates. They run for the council because of the prestige and power the position affords.[11] They may consider the fact that the prominence of the position will help their business, but often they are merely acting out of sense of community responsibility. They are not likely to be among the top business people in their earnings and standing, but generally they are prosperous. They are usually above average in intelligence, but it is not necessary for the council to consist of a group of intellectual giants or the leading persons of the community.

Most council members do not expect to move on to other political offices and do not consider themselves "politicians." The great majority of them are, by

[10] Freeman, *op. cit.*, p. 231.

[11] For a discussion of why council members run in nonpartisan Toledo, see Jean L. Stinchcombe, *Reform and Reaction, City Politics in Toledo,* Wadsworth, Belmont, Calif., 1968, pp. 79–83.

self-perception, strictly amateurs. Two-thirds of the councilmen in a Kansas study had never held any other position in government or in their political party. They were in overwhelming agreement that what they most disliked about the job was the public relations (campaigning) aspect.[12] In the San Francisco Bay area, 71 percent of the councilmen had no political ambitions beyond their present position, and 62 percent of them said they would give up their council seats rather than make great personal sacrifices if their regular jobs demanded that they do so.[13]

The council members of Los Angeles County in 1957 were, on the average, forty-nine years old; they ranged from twenty-five to seventy-six. Only 18 of 283 (6.7 percent) were women. In an area of rapid population movement, 39 percent had served two years or less. Communities with greater population stability probably have much less turnover.[14]

Outside of the very largest cities, the pay for council positions is very nominal, and the job is thought of as being a community service. An exception to this is to be found in commission-goverened cities, where the council (commission) is supposed to be made up, not simply of representative citizens of the community, but specifically of persons with executive or engineering experience. Relatively low salaries, however, have tended to attract ordinary office seekers instead. Topeka, for example, once had a commission made up of a barber, a house mover, and a cub reporter—hardly logical occupations for training in public administration.

In general, the smaller the city, the more likely it will be that council members are from among the top elite of the community. As cities increase in size, the social status of council members, in general, tends to decrease. In the largest cities, the council members may well devote full time to work at the city hall and may have run for the office partly because of the salary involved. Although venal and corrupt council members were once commonly found in these large cities, they are now a rarity. The greatest sin of the council members of the metropolis today is likely to be their allegiance to particular interest groups—a real estate board, a labor union, a group of builders, liquor dealers, downtown merchants. They are likely to view their function as that of protecting these particular groups, although they invariably claim to act "for all the people."[15]

[12] R. L. Stauber and Mary Kline, "A Profile of City Commissioners in Kansas," *Your Government,* Apr. 15, 1965. Similar findings were reported for a three-member Southern city, in Robert T. Daland, *Dixie City: A Portrait of Political Leadership,* Bureau of Public Administration, University of Alabama, University, Ala., 1956; and in John C. Buechner, *Differences in Role Perceptions in Colorado Council-Manager Cities,* Bureau of Governmental Research, University of Colorado, Boulder, Colo., 1965, pp. 23–29.

[13] Kenneth Prewitt, "Career Patterns of Local Elected Officials," a paper read at the annual meeting of the American Political Science Association, Chicago, September, 1964. See also Kenneth Prewitt and William Nowlin, "Political Ambitions and the Behavior of Incumbent Politicians," *Western Political Quarterly,* 22:298–308, June, 1969.

[14] Huckshorn and Young, *op. cit.*

[15] The old-time ward alderman was a little mayor in his own bailiwick and was sometimes, for example in Chicago, quite independent of the party organization. For brief sketches of colorful Chicago aldermen such as "Bathhouse" John Coughlin, "Hinky Dink Mike" Kenna, and "Foxy Ed"

The difference between the council in a middle-sized and a large city can be demonstrated by contrasting Davenport with Detroit.

Davenport, Iowa (1970 population: 98,469), might be called a not untypical middle-sized Middle Western city. It has a mayor-council form of government tending toward the weak category. Councilmen receive a $900 annual salary. In 1953, fifteen candidates ran for the eight positions on the council. Among these were four insurance salesmen and three real estate dealers or agents. There was one retired minister and one career woman. The remaining candidates were small business persons or white-collar workers, including a barber, a bookkeeper, a filling-station operator, a baker, a retired grocer, and a tax consultant. It is likely that in a middle-sized city with the council-manager plan and at-large elections, the candidates would have been drawn more from professional and executive categories.

Detroit (1970 population: 1,492,914) has a strong-mayor–council form of government. The council is elected at large and members receive a salary of $17,500 a year. In 1954, the council consisted of four persons who could best be called professional politicians, three lawyers, an automobile saleswoman, and a retired baseball player. Because a council position is ostensibly a full-time job and because long tenure is typical, it is not easy to distinguish clearly between professional and amateur politicians in its membership.

Minority Groups

In small cities, minority-group representation is not likely to be a major problem. In larger cities, the number of minority-group representatives on the city council tends to vary according to whether or not the council is elected at large. Where the council is fairly large and elected by wards, the ethnic groups that include political-activity patterns as part of their subculture tend to dominate; but in the case of a small council elected at large, the groups that are usually perceived of as "minorities" tend to be excluded.

Other factors are involved, too. Where political parties play a prominent part in local elections, minority-group representation is likely to be greater, since parties have historically sought the support of these groups in large cities. In cities with nonpartisan elections and a political process dominated by the business community, minority groups are usually quite badly underrepresented on city councils. The only exception to this seems to be in the case of the Irish, an ethnic group that has made political participation part of its way of life. Other minority groups appear to be too poorly organized or too little interested in local politics to be effective, or at least proportionately effective, in the larger cities.

No black or Jew was elected to the Los Angeles council between the time of the adoption of the present charter (1925) and 1953. Blacks later, however, were

Cullerton, see Charles E. Merriam, *Chicago: A More Intimate View of Urban Politics,* The Macmillan Company, New York, 1929, pp. 223–225. Lloyd Wendt and Herman Kogan, *Lords of the Levee,* The Bobbs-Merrill Company, Inc., Indianapolis, 1943, is the biography of Coughlin and Kenna, who ran the "levee"—Chicago's First Ward. A more recent ward alderman, Mathias J. ("Paddy") Bauler, is portrayed in A. J. Liebling, *Chicago: The Second City,* Alfred A. Knopf, Inc., New York, 1952, pp. 116–125.

regularly elected to the council. Only one person of Italian descent had served, and Protestants had dominated the council in a city in which a majority of the inhabitants were, and still are, Catholic. The same pattern existed in Detroit between 1919 and 1953. In the latter city, the large Polish ethnic group has also been greatly underrepresented, though in the 1960s and after, blacks were frequently elected. Blacks, lacking a cultural tradition of political participation and hence often poorly organized politically, did not become effective in local politics until the late 1950s. Even after that their influence was disproportionately less than their proportion of the population, except in the largest cities. Oscar Stanton DePriest (1871–1951) was the first black to serve on the Chicago city council, beginning in 1915. Because that city elects its council members by wards, the "Black Belt" is assured of some representation.[16] Blacks are always represented on the New York council today.

In the South, the increasing enfranchisement of blacks since about 1944 has taken place largely in the cities, with the result that black political influence is felt there too. Blacks have long been influential in San Antonio politics in the Southwest. In 1947, a black alderman was elected in one ward of Winston-Salem, defeating a white opponent. The nine-member at-large council that was elected in Richmond in 1948, after that city first adopted the manager plan, included a black as one of its members.[17] Blacks are today commonly elected to city councils in the South and elsewhere. When elections are held at large or mostly at large, blacks still are often underrepresented. In 1974, the state having the largest number of black officials was Michigan, with 194. Perhaps more significant was the fact that Mississippi, with 191, was a close second.

Women on the Council

Although in a definite minority, it is quite common to find women serving on school boards throughout the nation. They also often serve on park boards, library boards, and other special-purpose bodies. Their numbers on councils have been smaller, however, although some cities have a tradition of always having at least one woman on the city council. Peoria and Los Angeles did not elect a woman to the council until 1953. In Milwaukee, the first woman was elected in 1956. Portland, Oregon, elected a woman mayor-commissioner in 1948, but this was rare at that time. The occasional "skirt slates" that appear in small-city clean-up campaigns are reported in the newspapers throughout the land for the very reason that they are unusual. The pattern is changing and in cities of all sizes it is now common to find female membership on the council.

College Students on the Council

With the adoption of the constitutional amendment lowering the voting age to eighteen, students began to be active in the local politics of college communities. In East Lansing, Michigan, no student survived the 1971 primary election, partly

[16] On black councilmen in Chicago, see Martin Meyerson and Edward C. Banfield, *Politics, Planning and the Public Interest,* The Free Press of Glencoe, New York, 1957.

[17] Maurice R. Davie, *Negroes in American Society,* McGraw-Hill Book Company, New York, 1949, pp. 274–282.

because of lack of organization so soon after the amendment went into effect and partly because it was held in August. In Madison, Wisconsin, students have served on the city council for a number of years, while in Berkeley, California, some students, in coalition with nonstudent radicals and "street people," came within one seat of controlling the council in 1971, though their representation was less by 1975. The outlook is for increased student participation and the election of young people endorsed by them, but this is not likely to have much effect upon many city governments. College towns where a percentage of the electorate is made up of collegians are probably exceptions. If students should take a majority of seats on a council, they will come under close scrutiny by legislators, who hold almost complete control over the powers of municipalities.

Qualifications

As in the case of the mayor, the city charter commonly provides for certain minimum qualifications in age, residence, and citizenship. Other requirements may include required residence in the ward from which elected or disqualification of persons holding contracts with the city.

Most observers believe that the quality of council members has improved in the last fifty years. There are no measurements for this, of course, and the degree to which it may be attributed to an improvement in the forms of government, to a decrease in the size of the council, to a change from ward to at-large elections and from partisan to nonpartisan elections, or to other causes is not known.

THE STRUCTURE OF THE COUNCIL

Salary

In the British tradition, council salaries are deliberately fixed at a low rate in most small and medium-sized cities to discourage candidates who are interested in the salary and to make the job one in which the prestige and honor of it are the decisive elements. For this reason, membership on school and park boards and some others, including city councils, carries no salary at all in many communities.

In cities of more than about 50,000, the task of being a council member requires a good deal of time, even under the manager plan, and those who serve are required to make a considerable sacrifice. High salaries for council members in these cities often attract candidates who would make a profession of officeholding.

Salaries tend to be highest in commission-plan cities, for here the council members are also being paid as administrative heads of departments. Council-manager cities tend to have the lowest salaries, since under this form the council is a part-time body even in large cities and is restricted to legislative functions alone.[18]

[18] Council salaries are no longer reported in the current issue of the *Municipal Year Book,* International City Management Association, Washington.

Term of Office

Terms of council members range from one year to six years. One-year terms are found in cities with the town-meeting form. The six-year term is found mostly in a few commission cities, but a very few manager cities also use it.

In recent years, the four-year term has become the most common in American cities. In general, the larger the city, the more likely it is to have a four-year term. In about 35 percent of the cities, the terms of all council members expire at the same time. The larger the city, the more likely this is to be true. Overlapping, or staggered, terms are most likely to be found in council-manager cities, where the emphasis has traditionally been upon imitating the business corporation and in playing down the "errand runner" aspects of city government. Some argue that staggered terms provide desirable continuity in a council, but this is achieved in any case by the American practice of giving long tenure in office to council members.

In 20 percent of the cities of over 25,000 population, council elections are held simultaneously with school or other local elections; in 14 percent, with state or national elections; and in 66 percent, independently. Seventy-one percent of the nonpartisan, but only fifty-one percent of the partisan, cities hold independent elections.[19]

Size of Council

Councils range in size from two members in several cities to Chicago's fifty. In the case of the former, the mayor practically becomes a councilman, in order to break any tie. In an earlier day, councils sometimes ranged in size to above 200 members. Something of a dilemma is encountered in trying to determine the most effective size for a council. A large council is cumbersome and tends to obscure the legislative process by working through committees. A small council is sometimes said to lack representativeness and raises some questions concerning the function of criticism. A small council becomes involved in personal relationships that make it difficult for members to criticize other members freely. Some reformers have held, however, that the small council has not been proved bad, while the large one has. In any case, the trend in recent years has been toward smaller councils.

Very roughly speaking, the size of the council increases as the size of the city increases. A more important variable, however, is to be found in the type of structural form. In commission cities, the size of the commission tends to remain the same regardless of the size of the city. The commission is made up of five members in a preponderant number of cases. Council-manager cities tend to increase from five to nine members as the size of the city increases, but there are many exceptions to this. In the case of mayor-council cities, it is not possible to find very much of a relationship between size of city and size of council.

[19] Eugene C. Lee, "City Elections: A Statistical Profile," *Municipal Year Book, 1963,* International City Managers' Association, Chicago, 1963, pp. 74–84.

Unicameralism

At the turn of the century, about one-third of the cities of over 25,000 population had bicameral (two-house) councils. The figure had once been higher, but never included one-half of the cities. From the days of the reform movement of that period until the present, the number of these imitations of Congress and the state legislatures has diminished. No logical basis can be found for a two-house municipal council, and only one community still is known to use it (Everett, Massachusetts).

The city of New York has a council elected by wards and a board of estimate with an ex officio membership. The board consists of the mayor, the controller, the president of the council, and the president of each of the five boroughs. However, a system of weighting the votes of each of these elective officers gives control to the first three. The board had the power to make up the New York budget before 1933. Since that time, the board has the budgets of the city submitted to it first. It holds hearings and may alter the budgets in any way it sees fit. After it has passed them, they are sent to the council, which has powers only to reduce or delete. The council "has no important power in adopting local laws which the Board does not share on equal terms; the Board is, in effect, the upper chamber in a bicameral city legislature."[20]

Election by Wards

There is a strong tendency today to elect members of the council at large, except in cities of over 500,000.[21] Well over one-half of the cities of more than 5,000 population now elect at large, and a much greater percentage of the smaller cities do so. (See Table 9-1.) Again, the pattern that prevails depends to a large extent upon the structural form. Nearly all commission cities, for example, elect their members at large, since each member of the commission is a department head and almost necessarily is chosen by all the voters. The towns of New England usually elect at large, since most of these places are quite small and all of them grew out of a rural tradition. The manager plan strongly leans toward election at large. Weak-mayor cities tend to use a ward system, which they have inherited from the nineteenth century. A few cities nominate by wards and elect at large in an attempt to secure better geographical distribution without complete parochialism on the council.

Cities that elect by wards face apportionment problems. Once the United States Supreme Court had decided, in the *Reynolds* case, that state legislatures must be apportioned as strictly as possible according to population and that when legislatures determine the boundaries of Congressional districts, they must make certain that these districts are, "as nearly as practical," equal in size, it was generally believed that the Court would also soon require local governing bodies, including city councils, to follow the same general rule, and this did prove to be

[20] Wallace S. Sayre and Herbert Kaufman, *Governing New York City,* Russell Sage Foundation, New York, 1960, p. 627.

[21] See, however, George E. Berkley, "Flaws in At-Large Voting," *National Civic Review,* 55:370–373, May, 1966.

TABLE 9-1. Method of Electing Members of Council in All Municipalities of over 5,000 (in percent)

Type of City Government	Elected at Large	Elected by Wards	Elected by Combination*
Mayor-council	44	32	21
Commission	85	12	80
Council-manager	70	20	8
Town meeting	88	6	2
Representative town meeting	78	17	4
All over 500,00C	35	20	23
All over 5,000	59	25	14

*"Elected by combination" refers to the election of some councilmen by wards and others at large within the same city.
Source: Municipal Year Book, 1968, International City Management Association, Chicago, 1968, p. 59.

the case. A number of cities promptly proceeded to amend their charters to comply with the Supreme Court position; others were brought into state and federal courts in cases urging that city charters and state statutes not providing for substantially equal representation be declared unconstitutional. But most of the municipalities in the United States are not directly affected by this problem, for they elect their council members at large.

The great size of cities such as New York and Chicago seems to suggest the use of ward representation. It is argued that election by wards provides a short ballot and gives representation on the council to the various ethnic, racial, and economic areas of the city. On the other hand, aldermen selected from small wards tend to become errand runners. They are unable safely to consider the needs of the whole city lest they be told by their constituents that they were sent to the city hall to protect the interests of their own ward. Attempts at "statesmanship" only produce candidates who say, "If Torkelson can't look after this ward and its interests, I can." Furthermore, city populations are constantly shifting—in general toward the periphery. This means that a ward system, especially one written into the charter, eventually becomes gerrymandered. The slums and the periphery become underrepresented, at least temporarily, to the profit of the intermediate areas.

Minority groups sometimes make strong arguments for ward election on the ground that this is the only way for them to get a voice on the council. Black groups have felt especially strongly about this though as their populations approach 50 percent of the city, they see more advantages in at-large elections. In the past, in many cities, it has not been difficult for white politicians to gerrymander ward boundaries to keep blacks off the council. Los Angeles and Detroit each have large black populations. Detroit elects all at large. Los Angeles elects by ward. Until the mid-1950s, neither city elected a black to the council.

Election at large lengthens the ballot, forces the establishment of a council so small that it may not be representative in a large city, and gives the election to the candidates who can find financial backers able to pay the expense of a city-wide campaign. Council members can be more aloof to popular demands or to those of organized interest groups when elected at large (and especially when operating under the professional values orientation of the council-manager plan).[22]

Because large and medium-sized cities encounter a dilemma in seeking to choose between ward and at-large elections, compromises are common. Houston elects three members at large and five by wards. Buffalo chooses nine council members by wards for two-year terms and six at large for four-year staggered terms. Nearly one-fourth of the mayor-council cities use some sort of combination of the two devices.

Type of Ballot

Almost two-thirds of the city councils in the United States in places of over 5,000 population are elected on a ballot without party designation. (See Table 9-2.) The nonpartisan ballot is found most commonly in manager cities, since both nonpartisanship and the manager plan grew out of the reform movement. Because the representative town meeting is a recent development in New England, it, too, is usually nonpartisan. The commission plan, also a product of the early reform-movement years, is predominantly nonpartisan, but to a lesser extent. Its popularity declined before it received the full impact of the nonpartisan movement.

This leaves only the mayor-council city and the traditional New England

[22] Betty H. Zisk and others, "City Councilmen and the Group Struggle," *Journal of Politics,* 27:618–626, August, 1965.

TABLE 9-2. Type of Ballot, Members of Council, in All Municipalities of over 5,000 (in percent)

Type of City Government	Partisan	Nonpartisan
Mayor-council	51	49
Commission	31	69
Council-manager	18	82
Town meeting	44	56
Representative town meeting	39	61
All over 5,000	35	65

Source: Municipal Year Book, 1968, International City Management Association, Chicago, 1968, p. 58.

town as the centers of partisan municipal activity, but even here only one-half or less have partisan ballots. City and town governments that have not been reconstructed tend to retain the partisan ballot, and some cities are required by state law to use it.

Large cities might be said to tend to use the partisan ballot for the council, but such a statement would have to be made with caution. Two cities of over 1 million people, Los Angeles and Detroit, use nonpartisan ballots. Chicago has nonpartisan elections, but this is true only in a formal sense. All offices other than those of the aldermen are on a partisan ballot. All the aldermen are elected in single-member wards. This makes it so easy for the parties to give direct support to an aldermanic candidate and to have this support made known to the voters that Chicago does not fit into the pattern of most cities with a nonpartisan ballot.[23]

ORGANIZATION AND PROCEDURE

The Presiding Officer

The mayor may preside over the council, or a member of the council may serve as its presiding officer. In the latter case, the presiding officer may be selected either by direct popular vote, by the council members from among their own membership, or by making the person who receives the highest number of votes for council the president. When presidents are elected separately for that specific office, as is the case in several cities, including the city of New York, they are sometimes not formally a member of the council and often cannot vote except in case of a tie. The function of the presiding officer is in keeping with the usual powers and duties assigned to this officer in American legislative bodies. The council may also select other officers, including a secretary or clerk, although the city clerk usually serves in this capacity.

Committees

Because city governments tend to imitate those of the state and nation, the use of committees for the preliminary work on ordinances was customary in the nineteenth century. Even today almost all city councils make some use of committees. Reformers have generally frowned on this device, since it obscures the nature of the work of the council, confuses responsibility to the public, and allows a majority of a committee (a minority of the council) frequently to determine policy by minority rule. Standing committees also tend to take over administrative functions and for this reason are opposed by advocates of the reform-movement principles.

Standing committees are generally used in mayor-council governments, particularly of the weak-mayor type, but they are less common in council-manager governments. In manager cities, the council as a whole looks to the manager to do the preliminary work on ordinances, making committees less necessary. Be-

[23] The effect of nonpartisanship upon the political process is discussed in Chap. 5.

cause such committees tend to become involved with routine administration, they are especially disapproved of by experts on the manager form. Special committees are frequently utilized, however.

In those cities making extensive use of committees, the system works largely in the same manner as does the committee system of Congress or the state legislatures: The council as a whole becomes chiefly a ratifying body for the actions of the committees. Even if the council has authority to override a committee recommendation or relieve the committee of further consideration of a bill, these things are not likely to happen, since each council member—like each member of Congress—will tacitly agree to allow other council members to be supreme in their committee areas if they will extend the same privilege in return.[24]

Some cities with small councils make frequent use of the committee of the whole, which is not a committee at all but simply a convenient method for considering legislation in an informal atmosphere. Other cities hold an informal executive "conference session" before each meeting. If the city has a manager, he or she will probably attend. These sessions may be used to decide in advance the manner in which each item on the agenda will be disposed of. The formal session then becomes a hollow ritual, having given way to an informal, extralegal committee. This device is criticized as creating a "hidden government." Secret council sessions are an issue in many cities from time to time, and Akron banned secret meetings of all city boards and commissions in 1954, indicating that the problem is not confined to the council alone. Many states have banned secret meetings of public bodies.

Meetings

The frequency of council meetings depends upon the size of the city, local custom, and the complexity of current issues in the community. In cities with part-time lay councils, meetings are likely to be at night. In small towns the meetings may be only once a month. In the largest cities the council members will probably meet almost daily in committee or committee-of-the-whole sessions, with one formal meeting each week, perhaps at night, in order to allow interested citizens to attend.

POWERS OF THE COUNCIL

The functions, and hence powers, of the council are basically the same in mayor-council and council-manager cities. In places operating under the commission plan, the council is also the multiple-executive administrative body. For purposes of this section, this special function of the commission will be ignored.

Determination of Public Policy

The most important task of the council, of course, is to pass ordinances and resolutions formally establishing public policy for the community. The council passes on public improvements and exercises such portions of the state police

[24] A description of a large, machine-controlled council working through committees is given in Merriam, *op. cit.* See also Arthur W. Bromage, *Councilmen at Work,* George Wahr Publishing Co., Ann Arbor, 1954.

power to regulate and control the health, safety, and morals of the community as it is authorized to do. City plans are passed upon by the council, as well as modifications of the land-use control ordinances. The council makes policy for the municipally owned utilities and exercises control over those that are privately owned to the extent allowed by state law. A study of ninety cities in the San Francisco Bay region emphasizes the importance of the councilmen's own perceptions, orientations, and images of the future when faced with similar problems.[25]

Taxation and Appropriation

While the current trend is toward executive preparation of the budget, the council must still vote the funds. Changes in the city tax structure are also made by the council, subject to the rules of the charter. The council also buys and sells city property. In most cities, the council has the power to pass upon all contracts, or at least upon the large ones. This is really an administrative function, but the power traditionally belongs to the council. Its action of approval or disapproval is a symbolic act on behalf of the citizenry.

Supervision of Administration

In a manager city, the administration is directly answerable to the council through the manager. In other forms of government, the council has an obligation to check upon the activities of the administration. It does this by receiving auditor's reports, by appointing investigating committees, by requiring testimony or reports from department heads and others, and by reviewing the activities of the various departments at budget hearings. Depending on the provisions of the charter, the council may be able to shuffle functions and bureaus to suit itself and to establish many rules of procudure of the departments.

In weak-mayor cities of the past and present, and especially where aldermen represent wards, the council has carried its oversight of administration to great extremes. Each committee of the council may engage in constant and detailed oversight of the department heads, creating problems of morale and confusion as to who is boss. Council members may tend to supervise functions operating within their wards, concerning themselves with details essentially administrative in character.[26]

Other Powers

The council in many cities serves as the city board of equalization or review, hearing appeals from taxpayers on their property assessments. The council often has the power to pass on the appointments of the mayor, and in many cities it makes a goodly number of appointments of its own. In addition, it has the power to remove the mayor and other officials under certain conditions. Many other minor functions are assigned to the council. Their nature varies considerably from one city to another.

[25] Heinz Eulau and Robert Eyestone, "Policy Maps of City Councils and Policy Outcomes: A Developmental Analysis," *American Political Science Review,* 57:124–143, March, 1968.

[26] Arthur W. Bromage, "Mayors, Councilmen, and Citizens," *Governmental Affairs Bulletin,* Bureau of Governmental Research, University of Colorado, Boulder, Colo., June, 1966.

PRACTICAL PROBLEMS FACING THE COUNCIL

Certain problems confront the council in any city of any size: metropolis, suburb, county seat, or small town. M. Nelson McGeary, a political scientist, while serving as president of the State College, Pennsylvania, Borough Council, made most of the observations summarized in the following section.

Difficulties in Determining Public Opinion

The council member always has difficulty in determining the prevailing views of the public. This is the case in cities of all sizes, not just in the large ones. McGeary, for example, found that it was very true in his modest-sized borough of about 9,500. A few people are always vociferous. The great majority are silent most of the time. Because this is so, council members quickly learn (or should quickly learn) that they cannot determine public opinion simply by counting the pros and cons expressed by office visitors or in letters to them or to the editor. (Letters to the editor in the local newspaper may have actually been written by the editor.) Council members also soon learn that they will hear from constituents more quickly if they disapprove of one of their acts than if they approve.

McGeary found that even when persons express themselves, they may not state their true opinion. He writes of one case in which a man wrote a lengthy letter to the local newspaper on some current issue. When the councilman said he was glad to know where the citizen stood, the letter writer astounded everyone by explaining that his comments in the newspaper did not express his "real feelings."[27]

Although the importance of interest groups in the political process is generally well accepted by political scientists and by members of state legislatures and Congress, organized interest groups appear to be much less active and influential at the municipal level. They are not important in some cities even as a communications apparatus. Interviews with 112 councilmen from twenty-two cities in the San Francisco Bay area revealed that:[28]

> Most councilmen do not view interest group activities as indispensable to the political system. About three-quarters of our respondents are either neutral or negative toward such groups. They do not encourage group approaches, and they do not turn to such groups for help. It appears that the "group struggle" in local political systems (at least in these twenty-two cities) takes place largely in a one-way street upon which relatively little traffic is noticed or invited by those who dwell at the upper end.

Difficulties in Adjusting to Criticism

Citizens are accustomed to the elaborate ritual of criticism by circumlocution found in everyday life. If they are elected to the local council, they find that their actions now become subjected to a different, more open, more straightforward, and more vigorous criticism. Some of it is informed and responsible. Some of it is uninformed and irresponsible. Council members must learn to hide their feelings

[27] M. Nelson McGeary, "The Councilman Learns His Job," *National Municipal Review* (now *National Civic Review*), 43:284–287, June, 1954.

[28] Betty H. Zisk, *op. cit.,* pp. 618–646.

and to accept these comments without undue sensitivity. But they must not become so immune as to ignore the warning flags of changing public opinion, at least not if they want to be reelected.

Difficulties in Learning to Trust Expert Advisers

The council member is usually a lay citizen serving only part time at the job. Even in fairly small cities, and especially in large ones, he or she must learn to trust the advice given by specialists and to rely upon this in making public policy decisions. If the shade-tree expert says that extensive trimming will help preserve the trees, the council member must overcome a preference for trimming the budget and instead vote the money for the trees—if any is available. Of course, the council members cannot simply accept the advice of experts, enact it into an ordinance, and go home. It is not that simple. McGeary points to difficulties that the council member must face when (1) the experts present, as they often do, original estimates of the costs of large projects that are unrealistically low; and (2) the experts disagree among themselves as to the best solution to a problem. Many a councilman has voted for a sewage-disposal plant only to discover later that it cost 50 percent more than the original estimates. Not only may disagreeing experts keep council members awake nights, but so may differences between prevailing grass-roots opinion and expert opinion, for these often differ. No council member can simply accept the word of a civil engineer as to how and where to build a sewage-treatment plant or what its capacity should be. As the neophyte council member will quickly learn, dozens of butchers, bakers, and housewives consider themselves lay experts on all types of engineering and other technologically complex problems.

Difficulties of Informing the Public

Council members must let the people know what they are doing and why they are doing it. Communication with a preoccupied and often apathetic public is difficult.

Difficulties in Making the Right Decision at the Right Time

An inexperienced or impetuous council member is sometimes guilty of making a decision too rapidly for it to represent informed behavior. All the arguments pro and con may not appear in the first few discussions of an issue. Facts that arise later may make the council members who have already committed themselves look ridiculous. Of course, the person who will not make up his or her mind, or who always follows the lead of someone else, is of limited value, but "a councilman seems to command respect, and may save himself considerable embarrassment if he takes a definite position only after the facts are in."[29]

Concluding Statement

McGeary has summarized his experiences by saying that "serving on the council is a headache. But democracy is based on the supposition that some citizens will

[29] McGeary, *op. cit.,* p. 287.

be willing to endure headaches. Actually the travail is not unbearable. And sometimes, for brief periods, it is forgotten—believe it or not—in the knowledge that some little service is being offered."[30]

SELECTED READINGS

Barber, James D.: *Power in Committees,* Rand McNally & Company, Chicago, 1966. (Examines the Connecticut town boards of finance and their decision-making procedures in a laboratory setting.)

Blair, Louis H., and Robert E. Winnie: *The Forgotten Men of Government: Local Legislators,* The Urban Institute, Washington, 1972.

Bromage, Arthur W.: *Councilmen at Work,* George Wahr Publishing Company, Ann Arbor, Mich., 1954. (By a political scientist who served on a council.)

Conyers, James E., and Walter L. Wallace, *Black Elected Officials: A Study of Black Americans Holding Governmental Office,* Russell Sage Foundation, New York, 1976. (A nationwide profile.)

Downes, Bryan T.: "Issue Conflict, Factionalism, and Consensus in Suburban City Councils," *Urban Affairs Quarterly,* 4:477–497, June, 1969.

Eulau, Heinz, and Robert Eyestone: "Policy Maps of City Councils and Policy Outcomes. A Developmental Analysis," *American Political Science Review,* 57:124–143, March, 1968.

Huckshorn, Robert J., and C. E. Young: "A Study of Voting Splits on City Councils in Los Angeles County," *Western Political Quarterly,* 13:479–497, June, 1960. (A study of council factions and coalitions.)

Prewitt, Kenneth: *The Recruitment of Political Leaders: A Study of Citizen-Politicians,* The Bobbs-Merrill Company, Inc., Indianapolis, 1970. (Council members in the San Francisco Bay area.)

Sayre, Wallace S., and Herbert Kaufman: *Governing New York City,* Russell Sage Foundation, New York, 1960. (Contains information and bibliography on New York City Council.)

Stinchcombe, Jean L.: *Reform and Reaction—City Politics in Toledo,* Wadsworth, Belmont, Calif., 1968.

Vidich, A. J., and Joseph Bensman: *Small Town in Mass Society,* Princeton University Press, Princeton, N.J., 1958. (The council of an upstate New York village.)

Weaver, Leon H.: "Representation of Minorities in At-large Elections in City and Village Governments under Michigan Law," *Journal of Urban Law,* 49:131–161, August, 1971. (Various structural features that can help provide minority representation in at-large situations.)

Wendt, Lloyd, and Herman Kogan: *Lords of the Levee,* The Bobbs-Merrill Company, Inc., Indianapolis, Ind., 1943. (Concerning the aldermen from Chicago's first ward, the "levee.")

Williams, Oliver P., and Charles R. Adrian: *Four Cities,* University of Pennsylvania Press, Philadelphia, 1963, chap. 11. (Social backgrounds of council members in four middle-sized cities.)

Zisk, Betty H., Heinz Eulau, and Kenneth Prewitt: "City Councilmen and the Group Struggle," *Journal of Politics,* 27:618–646, August, 1965. (Part of a study of council members in the San Francisco Bay area.)

[30] *Ibid.*

E

The Relationships among Governments

Chapter 10

Decisions for Metropolitan Areas

Nowhere in the United States today does the sociological and economic metropolitan area coincide with a single governmental unit that includes the entire area. From the time of the Great Depression to the present, local business leaders, reformers, and many students of politics have advocated bringing the sprawl of urban settlement under one government, just as it was in the Great Cities of the nineteenth century.

Why is a change advocated by students of "metropology"? Victor Jones, a leading authority, has put it this way:[1]

> A metropolitan government is desirable (1) when coordination of a function over the whole area is essential to effective service or control in any part of the area; (2) when it is desired to apply the ability to pay theory of taxation to the area as a whole, instead of allowing each part to support its own activities at whatever level its own economic base will allow; (3) when services can be supplied more efficiently through large-scale operations; and (4) when it is necessary in order to assure citizens a voice in decisions that affect them at their places of work and recreation as well as at their places of residence.

Some question the assumption that a single metropolitan government is de-

[1] Victor Jones, "Local Government Organization in Metropolitan Areas," in Coleman Woodbury (ed.), *The Future of Cities and Urban Redevelopment,* The University of Chicago Press, Chicago, 1953, part IV, p. 508.

sirable or that it will have much effect in meeting the pressing problems of the core city.[2] By diluting the votes of blacks and the poor of the core city with votes of middle-class suburbanites, the salutory effects of election of black mayors and council members will be lost and blacks' view of governmental legitimacy reduced. At least one person argues that improvement is more likely to occur as the result of a bargaining process among units with infusion of funds and some direction from state and national levels, than in centralization of all services under one metropolitan government.

Numerous proposals have been made over the years for reorganizing governments of metropolitan areas. There is no current trend toward the adoption of a particular governmental arrangement, nor has anyone been able to devise a plan that would be both practical and successful. Some isolated exceptions are to be found, however, some makeshift and temporary devices have been put to use in various places, and the past efforts are worth studying, in any case, if only that the reasons for their lack of success may be seen.

PROPOSALS FOR METROPOLITAN-AREA GOVERNMENT

Annexation

Superficially, the most obvious method of keeping the sociological and legal cities identical would seem to be for the core city to annex fringe areas as they become urbanized. Formerly this method was widely used to expand the city's legal boundaries to keep pace with the actual urban growth, but it has become increasingly unsatisfactory, because noncity residents are no longer concentrated along city boundaries but are widely dispersed. Although annexations have increased in both number and importance in the last two decades, they seldom succeed in equating the political with the sociological city. Milwaukee, as a not untypical example, has annexed a good deal of territory over the years, but it does not have metropolitan-wide government. The reason for this is that the laws in nearly all states provide that outlying areas may be annexed only after a referendum has been held and the annexation is approved by the voters of the outlying area as well as those of the core city. Only in a few states, notably in Texas and Virginia, is the core city relatively free to expand its boundaries as the surrounding unincorporated area becomes urbanized.[3]

Annexation is usually unpopular in the fringe areas. This is a reflection both of local pride and of the persistent belief that taxes will be higher within the core city, as well as of various other values of suburbanites discussed in Chapter 2.[4]

[2] Robert L. Bish and Vincent Ostrom, *Understanding Urban Government, Metropolitan Reform Reconsidered,* American Enterprise Institute for Public Policy Research, Washington, 1973. See also Robert L. Bish, *The Political Economy of Metropolitan Areas,* Markham, Chicago, 1972.

[3] For a discussion of recent trends from which facts in this section are taken, see *Municipal Year Book, 1975,* International City Management Association, Washington, 1975, pp. 23–29. See also Bureau of the Census, *1972 Boundary and Annexation Survey,* Washington, 1973.

[4] Charles Press, "Attitudes toward Annexation in a Small City Area," *Western Political Quarterly,* 16:271–278, June, 1963; and Charles Press, "Efficiency and Economy Arguments for Metropolitan Reorganization," *Public Opinion Quarterly,* 28:584–594, Winter, 1964.

After 1890, few large annexations took place in the United States until after World War II, when there were several, especially in Texas. Most recent annexations have been of only a few acres. However, in the decade of the 1950s, more than 6 million persons were annexed to core cities and the amount of annexation activity appears to have increased in the 1960s and declined somewhat in the early 1970s.

These facts stand out in the pattern of recent annexations: Cities in the 20,000 to 250,000 range are more likely to annex territory than either smaller or larger cities. The very largest core cities have practically ceased annexing. The number of large annexations is fewer than in the 1960s, and the resident population in annexed areas is less. Annexation is more likely to occur in the newer cities and in the South and Southwest. Cities of the Northeast have almost ceased annexing.

Technically the annexation of an incorporated area, that is, one city by another, is a merger. Such mergers are very rare, and when they occur, they are not of a large core city and smaller suburb but generally of two cities of similar size.

Easily the most important factors encouraging fringe areas to want to become annexed are sewerage and water-supply services and high schools. All other services furnished by cities are of far less interest. Sewerage—and especially sewage-disposal—facilities are very expensive and inefficient if used only by small units of government. An adequate *source* of water supply is often a serious problem, too. Building a high school is also expensive; but in some states, school districts can consolidate without political annexation of the outlying area to the city.

An early study indicated that officials in cities annexing territory felt, in more than four-fifths of the cases, that the new areas in the years immediately ahead would not pay as much in taxes as the city would spend on them. About the same proportion believed, however, that in the long run the areas would pay for themselves.[5]

Most state laws on annexation are unsuitable as a means for securing a single metropolitan government. The requirement of obtaining permission from all areas concerned, combined with the fact that suburban dwellers are likely to take a short view, heavily overlaid with concerns about access, representativeness, and the maintenance of life-styles (all carefully cultivated by fringe-area officeholders protecting their own jobs) help make this approach a slow-moving one. It is significant that the large annexations usually take place where state laws do not require the direct approval of fringe dwellers.

One study found that among the factors associated with successful annexation was the form of government of the core city. Council-manager cities were more successful in annexation than were other types of cities. Another important

[5] John C. Bollens, "Metropolitan and Fringe Area Developments in 1952," *Municipal Year Book, 1953,* International City Management Association, Chicago, 1953, pp. 33–48.

factor was related to the socioeconomic character of the core city. Those with a large number of persons of the middle class were generally more successful, probably because of the greater compatibility of life-styles between suburbanites and core-city dwellers. Newer cities were also more likely to be able to annex territories than were older ones, for the latter seemed to have well-established political styles and traditions creating an inertia that was not easily overcome. This study concluded that "annexation is a likely integrative device in younger urbanized areas and those in which social differentials between city and suburb have not crystallized. . . . On the other hand, in older urbanized areas and in urbanized areas where the suburbs have become socially differentiated from the central city, integrative demands will have to be met through devices other than annexation."[6]

Annexation without Elections

Texas, California, and Virginia lead in annexations in the postwar period. Texas and Missouri allow annexation of unincorporated territory by amendment of home rule charters without a popular vote. Texas also permits annexation simply by an ordinance of the core city, if the home rule charter so provides.[7]

Virginia has an unusual annexation procedure whose origins are hidden in colonial obscurity. In that state, whenever a fringe area begins to urbanize, the core city seeks control over the outlying land through a judicial proceeding before a three-judge court. The city is permitted to present the rational case for annexation, and the court is obligated to decide the question on the basis of its interpretation of the interests of the entire community—not on the basis of pecuniary interests of the suburban or city taxpayers. Under these circumstances, the city usually wins its case. Limited possibilities for judicial annexation of suburban areas by core cities also exist in five other states.[8]

Jones, while viewing the Virginia method as more productive than that in nearly all other states, has suggested that annexation questions might best be handled by a state administrative body on the order of the postwar Local Government Boundary Commission in England.[9] It is not easy for a court to settle annexation questions on facts alone or to separate facts from values and interests. These distinctions need not be made by an administrative body, which could also more easily reflect changes in public policy, could initiate action rather than wait for cases to come before it, and could settle problems on bases other than those proposed by the parties at issue.

A definite if slow trend away from the referendum as a necessary part of the annexation procedure has been noted in recent years. In 1959, the Minnesota

[6] Thomas R. Dye, "Urban Political Integration," *Midwest Journal of Political Science,* 8:430–446, November, 1964.

[7] Stuart A. MacCorkle, *Municipal Annexation in Texas,* Institute of Public Affairs, University of Texas, Austin, Tex., 1965.

[8] Victor Jones gives details, *op. cit.,* part IV, pp. 564–566. The Virginia plan is evaluated in Chester W. Bain, *Annexation in Virginia: The Use of Judicial Process for Readjusting City-County Boundaries,* University Press of Virginia, Charlottesville, Va., 1966.

[9] *Ibid.,* pp. 568–572.

legislature established a Municipal Commission. It was given authority to hear petitions for incorporation, detachment, and annexation of land within the state. On the basis of certain criteria, the commission was authorized to decide, after hearing, on questions of proposed incorporation of villages or cities within the three most populous counties of the state. In the other counties of the state, the county governing board was authorized to decide the same questions, using the same criteria. A similar law, also designed to provide more rational and systematic procedure for incorporation and annexation, was adopted in Wisconsin that same year and later in New Mexico and Michigan.

In 1963, the California legislature provided for a Local Agencies Formation and Annexation Commission for each county. The purpose of this legislation was not only to require some kind of systematic study of proposals to create additional special districts in the state (at the time, California had 1,962) but also to provide a more rational approach to incorporation and annexation. The commission consists of two county officers, appointed by the board of supervisors, and two city council members, appointed by all the mayors of the county meeting as a selection committee. These four persons choose a fifth member. On the basis of criteria prescribed in the statute, they decide whether or not to permit the creation of a new special district, the incorporation of a new city, or the annexation of territory to an existing city or special district.

It seems unlikely that annexation to the core city or merger of two or more cities will be the approach used in the forseeable future for achieving metropolitan-wide government. The new patterns for annexation and incorporation are designed to provide more rational local government boundaries, not to make metropolitan-area governments easier to secure.[10]

Special Districts

If annexation becomes impossible, the next approach that might suggest itself would be to take those functions in which a particularly evident need for metropolitan-wide administration is seen and create one or more special districts to administer them. Hence, covering all or part of a metropolitan area, there might be park, sewerage, water, parking, airport, planning, or other districts. On this beginning, some hope of a metropolitan government might develop.

"Special districts," one observer has noted, "are the least known and least understood units of government in the United States. Yet, paradoxically, there are . . . more special-district governments in the nation than all other units of governments combined."[11] (This includes school districts in the special-district category.)

A special district is an organized unit of government, having substantial autonomy from other governments, its own taxing and—usually—its own bonding authority.[12] In particular, since it has its own fiscal authority and a governing

[10] See Kenneth G. Bueche, *Incorporation Laws: One Aspect of the Urban Problem,* Bureau of Governmental Research, University of Colorado, Boulder, Colo., 1963.

[11] W. G. Thrombley, "Texas Special Districts," *Public Affairs Comment,* 4:1, March, 1958.

[12] U.S. Bureau of the Census, *Governments in the United States,* 1957, p. 9. These reports are issued every five years.

body, it exists as a separate unit of government performing some public service. Districts exist for such varied purposes as recreation, sewage disposal, airports, planning, parking, and mosquito abatement. They may have boundaries coterminous with other units of government, such as cities or counties, or they may overlap other units. They exist in both rural and urban areas and are to be found in every state in the Union, though one-half of the national total, excluding schools, are located in ten states: California, Illinois, Kansas, Missouri, Nebraska, New York, Oregon, Pennsylvania, Texas, and Washington.

Growth of Special Districts

The general trend of special districts has been one of an increase in numbers since the end of World War II. This is true even though the most common form of special district, the school district, *decreased* by 53 percent between 1942 and 1957. Even between 1967 and 1972 the reduction was continuing, but at a slower pace (27 percent). This countertrend was the result of special factors, however, and nonschool special districts increased by 74 percent over the same period. By 1972, there were almost eight times as many nonschool special districts as there were counties. The total of such special districts exceeded the total of municipalities in the nation. These same districts had twice as much debt as counties and one-half as much as the state governments. Despite all the vast amount of school construction that took place in the postwar years, special districts other than for schools have debts nearly the size of those for schools—a reflection of the fact that the functions generally assigned to special districts are of high-cost, capital-outlay type.

Most nonschool special districts are in rural areas, particularly those for fire protection, soil conservation, and drainage, which together make up about one-half the total districts. But quite a few are in urban areas, especially fringe areas, as are many cemetery districts and most housing authorities. These five types taken together make up about two-thirds of the number of special districts.

Ad hoc districts may be governed by a body appointed by the state; one appointed by officials from the local governments overlaid by the district, with members being either appointed especially for the position or in ex officio capacities; one appointed by a judge; or, sometimes, one elected by the voters of the area. The variety is almost endless, but since the last possibility is not the usual one, special-purpose districts ordinarily do not come within the direct oversight of the voting public.

Reasons for Current Trend

The need for an area-wide approach to problems exists in rural areas (as in the case of drains that cross township and county lines) and in urban areas. Problems requiring such an approach have especially increased as urban populations have increased. Other solutions failing or seeming to be politically impossible, the special district has been turned to. It has been very popular in many rapidly urbanizing states and has, as in California, served as a substitute for incorporation or for a fringe government of less area than the county.

Often districts are the only means by which essential services can be supplied in a metropolitan area. The pattern of use for the special district is a strange one, however, seeming to depend upon local customs and perhaps upon the accident of the gradual accumulation of rigid constitutional and statutory restrictions controlling general governments and discouraging the use of the existing units for newer services. For example, one might expect special districts to be used especially in states not having townships, but six of the ten states with the most special districts also have townships in all or part of the state. Special districts are very popular in the West, where they are especially used for the procurement, distribution, and allocation of scarce water supplies. But they are found in every part of the land.

In both rural and metropolitan areas, the number or complexity of arrangements of governmental units does not appear to be based on observable need. (See Table 10-1.) The number of special districts exclusive of school districts varied from 15 in Hawaii to 2,407 in Illinois. Of the nonschool special districts, about a third were located in five urban states: California, Illinois, New York, Pennsylvania, and Washington; yet the highly urbanized states of Connecticut, Massachusetts, Michigan, and Ohio had relatively few such districts.[13]

There are several reasons for the trend toward special districts. Citizens learn that their state or other states authorize districts to perform certain services. The approach usually has strong appeal. Citizens do not resist it as they do attempts at governmental consolidation, since they expect that it will be less expensive and that it will preserve the independence of their local government. Interest groups that may want services performed by government (amateur pilots wanting an airport, physicians wanting a hospital), together with the professional administrators of particular functions, characteristically want their special problems handled in a special way by a special organization.[14] School administrators have long

[13] U.S. Bureau of the Census, *1972 Census of Governments.*
[14] As Victor Jones has pointed out, *op. cit.,* pp. 527–528.

TABLE 10-1. Units of Government, 1952-1972

Governments	1952	1972	Percent Change
United States	1	1	
States	48	50	4.2
Counties	3,052	3,044	−2.6
Municipalities	16,807	18,517	10.2
Townships and towns	17,202	16,991	−1.2
School districts	67,355	15,781	−76.6
Special districts	12,340	23,885	93.6

Source: U.S. Bureau of the Census, *1972 Census of Governments.*

ago convinced the American public that they should be independent of the rest of local government, and the school district is both the most common and the best-known special district. Others have followed the lead of the educators and the interest groups supporting them. The special district has also had great appeal to the wistful who would take their pet governmental function "out of politics."

Pros and Cons of Districts

The advantages of special districts are said to be several. Special districts make possible the provision of governmental services when and where they are most needed and limit the financial burden to residents most directly benefited, while at the same time they skip lightly over the myriad local-government boundaries which otherwise stand in the way of making these services available. Other units of government frequently cannot or will not supply these services. Consolidating local units is often politically unfeasible. By leaving the political status quo undisturbed, the social need is met with a minimum of resistance; political loyalties are not disturbed; jobs are not threatened; property-tax payers need have little fear of being assessed for someone else's benefit. Usually, the debts and costs of special districts do not count in determining debt and tax limits of regular local governments, and the bonds of such districts are sometimes more easily marketed than are those of other local governments.

Disadvantages of special districts, it is argued, include the fact that the behind-the-scenes way in which they generally operate helps to make them especially profitable for lawyers, engineers, bankers, bonding houses, and sellers of equipment, services, and real estate. They are often disigned to meet short-range needs and not only do not consider more permanent approaches but, by taking the urgency out of the situation for at least a considerable portion of a community, serve to forestall efforts toward long-range, rational governmental organization.[15]

Special districts have often done very good jobs in construction and engineering and sometimes in management. They do not necessarily eliminate political patronage, however, do not guarantee professional administration of functions, and do not remove from the arena of politics governmental functions that involve issues of policy. Special districts often result in increased costs of local government because of duplication of personnel, inefficient utilization of equipment, and inability to save through centralized purchasing and other centralized housekeeping activities. They do not balance the various needs for services of a community, do not recognize the interdependence of various functions, and are not usually provided with a method for coordinating their activities and budgets with those of the other governments in the area in which they exist. If the governing board is elective, the ballot is made longer and voters are asked to fill offices in which they have little interest or competence to choose. If the governing

[15] *Ibid.*

board is indirectly chosen, as is usually the case, there is not real responsibility to the public for the function performed. Victor Jones has concluded:[16]

> A corporate form of metropolitan government in which the selection of the authority or district commission members is once or more removed from the electoral controls may give us efficient and effective government but it cannot give us good government. It is not necessary, nor is it desirable, for all policy-making officials to be directly elected by popular vote. They should, however, be subject to the budgetary control of popularly elected legislators and their policies should be subject to debate and discussion.
>
> Of course, any legislative body, whether it have jurisdiction over the matter or not, may debate anything it wishes. The object, however, is not futile and irresponsible talk. Our uneasiness should not be allayed by saying that the ordinary municipal governments are frequently corrupt, irresponsible, ineffective, and inefficient. Our job is to make them responsible and efficient. This cannot be done by slicing off the most important functions of local government and handing them over to one or several autonomous bodies.

Multipurpose Special Districts

Most *ad hoc* districts serve a single purpose, such as the Sanitary District of Chicago, which handles sewerage for over 95 percent of Cook County's population,[17] the Metropolitan Airports Commission of Minneapolis—St. Paul, and the Metropolitan Water District of Southern California, which brings water some 300 miles from the Colorado River to serve many communities in the Los Angeles area. There are some multipurpose districts in use and some states authorize them where they do not exist. Perhaps the best known is the Port of New York Authority, which handles many aspects of water, highway, and air transportation. It is, however, a joint agent of the states of New York and New Jersey rather than a unit of local government.[18]

Some observers of local government have supported the use of single-purpose special districts partly on the assumption that they will lead to general-purpose districts for metropolitan government. Such expansion has usually not occurred, however. It has not happened in the Boston, Chicago, Los Angeles, Minneapolis, and Detroit areas. Jones illustrates this failure by pointing to the history of the Massachusetts Metropolitan District Commission. This district is controlled by a commission appointed by the Governor of Massachusetts and is not in any way directly responsible to the local community. It was created in 1919 by the consolidation of three districts which furnished sewerage, water, and park services. In 1923, regional planning was added to its functions (but this has

[16] Jones, *op. cit.*, pp. 585–586. By permission of the University of Chicago Press.

[17] Unifunctional districts normally carry on incidental functions. The Chicago district produces electric power and fertilizer, and its channels are used for navigation. Illinois Legislative Council, *Chicago Sanitary District*, State of Illinois, Springfield, Ill., 1953, pp. 22–27; Ward Walker, *The Story of the Metropolitan Sanitary District of Greater Chicago*, Metropolitan Sanitary District, Chicago, 1956.

[18] The Port of New York Authority has been admired by reformers. For a frank and detailed description of its leading spirit, see Robert A. Caro, *The Power Broker, Robert Moses and the Fall of New York*, Alfred A. Knopf, Inc., New York, 1974.

since been transferred to the state), and in 1952 refuse disposal was added. In 1929, however, a separate Boston Metropolitan District was created for rapid transit, and in 1947 a Metropolitan Transit Authority was established to take over the previously privately operated elevated railway system.[19] There appears to be no trend toward making supergovernments out of the special districts.

City-County Consolidation

Until recent years, reformers have felt that consolidating the city with the metropolitan county was a desirability second only to annexation and a truer and more permanent solution than the use of the special district. This plan (there are dozens of possible variations of it) calls for an integration of the functions of the core city with the county. The county retains a partial identity, and incorporated municipalities remain independent for local purposes. City and county police, attorneys, clerks, treasurers, and health, welfare, and other departments can be combined to save the core-city taxpayers from paying for county services that they do not use and that in any event duplicate those they are already paying the city to do. Since this plan permits municipalities to retain autonomy for certain "local" purposes, it could also be viewed as metropolitan "federation."

There have been twenty-two city-county mergers through 1975. Nine occurred between 1947 and 1968, thirteen more between 1969 and 1975. The pattern is, as one would anticipate, occurring in smaller metropolitan areas. Less explainable is its popularity in Southern cities and the fact that eight of these mergers involved state capitals. Among the most discussed mergers of the last two decades are those that involved the combination of Baton Rouge with East Baton Rouge Parish (*parish* is the Louisiana term for *county*), in 1947; Miami with Dade County, Florida, in 1957; Nashville with Davidson County, Tennessee, in 1962; Jacksonville with Duval County, in 1967; and Indianapolis with Marion County, in 1970. Other more recent mergers include those in Lexington, Kentucky; Columbus, Ohio; Las Vegas, New Mexico; and Juneau, Alaska.

All such attempts have been difficult politically and complicated legally. Often they require statewide approval on a constitutional amendment referendum, or legislative approval, or a majority vote on a referendum in the core city and in the portions of the county outside. Thus, the Davidson County proposal had to "run the gamut of a dress rehearsal in 1958, a reprise that involved the two local legislative bodies, the state legislature, an advisory vote by the electorate, and the drafting of a new proposal, a bitter campaign, and the adoptions of the charter at the polls," and still was faced with judicial challenges in the lower courts and the state supreme court.[20]

In Baton Rouge, one of the chronic obstacles to approval was overcome by setting up three taxing districts so that taxes were paid at one rate in urban areas, at another in rural portions of the parish where fewer services were provided or needed, and at a third, the lowest, in some industrial areas where no services were

[19] Jones, *op. cit.*, pp. 582–583.

[20] David A. Booth, *Metropolitics: The Nashville Consolidation,* Institute for Community Development, Michigan State University, East Lansing, Mich., 1963, p. 88.

provided. Nashville and Jacksonville also have urban and general-service districts with different tax rates. Representation, another difficult knot to untie before consolidation can be consummated, was solved by adding two persons elected from the portions of the parish outside of Baton Rouge to the city council whenever that body sits as the parish council.

Three attempts, beginning in 1945, were made to consolidate the city and county in the Miami area in one way or another, but all failed. A fourth effort succeeded. A Metropolitan Miami Municipal Board was created in 1953 by the Miami City Council in cooperation with suburban municipalities which joined in after several months of negotiations. Many of the suburbs apparently were fearful of being excluded from a general metropolitan plan. A number of pressures had brought on the consolidation. They included especially those from the local daily newspapers and business leaders interested in efficiency and economy. Their activities were given indirect support by the long history of governments in the area with reputations for ineffectiveness and corruption.

The newly established board drafted a plan for a metropolitan government, with the help of the Public Administration Service of Chicago, which was strongly influenced by traditional efficiency and economy values. After the board had made its recommendations, it discussed them with the Dade County delegation to the Florida legislature in 1955. During the next year, the legislature approved the holding of a referendum on the proposal and created a Metropolitan Charter Board. In November, 1956, an amendment to the constitution was approved, and the following May, the Metro Charter was adopted. It was highly controversial from the beginning. Most municipal officials and employees in the area saw it as a threat; some suburban citizens were concerned lest they would lose access to decision makers; but residents of areas with high assessed valuations saw the plan as a device for spreading their taxes over a larger area. About a dozen efforts were made in the years following adoption to force abandonment of the plan.

The board to govern the metropolitan area was made up of five members nominated from each of the county commission districts but elected at large, one nominated and elected from each of the five districts, and one member from each city of 60,000 population or more. The county manager was to be appointed by the governing board and removable by it. Provision was made for a rather orthodox council-manager plan. The major problems in Dade County have centered around the question of the allocation of authority over various functions of government. Most of the major functions have been assigned to the metropolitan government, but with local units having some powers over what have been identified as local aspects, and with the metropolitan government setting minimum standards of performance. In cases where local units do not meet the minimum standards, the metropolitan government is authorized to assume responsibility for that function.

Metropolitan Davidson County has a mayor plus a metropolitan council consisting of thirty-five members elected by districts and five elected at large. A number of traditional county offices remain popularly elective, but boards and heads of agencies that perform essentially municipal functions are appointed by the mayor, subject to council approval. The metropolitan government can perform all functions authorized by Tennessee law for either cities or counties.[21] It is divided into urban-services and general-services districts to avoid the problem of taxing property owners for services they do not yet receive or, perhaps, even need.

Adoption of plans for metropolitan government is often dependent upon the attitudes of persons with a middle-class ideology. Support in the Nashville area came principally from persons who had a relatively high level of knowledge concerning political issues in the metropolitan area and was correlated directly with level of education. Persons who were dissatisfied with existing municipal services (especially sewers and sewage disposal) were also more likely to be in favor of metropolitan government, as were those who did not anticipate that metropolitan government might be associated with higher taxes.[22]

Not only is city-county consolidation difficult politically, but it does not guarantee that the city-county will have sufficient powers to meet all metropolitan problems, and it causes even greater political difficulties if the metropolitan area expands beyond the county limits. Despite the successful development in the Baton Rouge area, this approach to metropolitan government is not likely to bear fruit in many areas of the nation.

City-County Separation

Core-city dwellers, watching the county snowplows at work in the unincorporated reaches of suburbia and remembering that the core city bears most of the cost of county government while securing few services from it, are likely to be intrigued with the idea of separating the city from the rest of the county. This plan is not far different from the preceding one, except that instead of integrating the offices and leaving the county boundaries as they are, separation would create a city-county of the core city and create a new county of the outlying areas.

San Francisco, Baltimore, St. Louis, Denver, Philadelphia, Honolulu, and all cities of over 10,000 in Virginia are separate city-counties. Except in Virginia, there have been no separations in nearly half a century. The plan encounters much the same problems as does city-county consolidation and is no more practical politically. Outlying sections of the county desire to control the county government, as they would under separation, but they also wish to retain the benefits of county services paid for mostly by core-city taxpayers. Furthermore, this is not really an approach to metropolitan government at all, since it traps the city within its own walls (except in Virginia) and, instead of treating metropolitan problems on an area-wide basis, it serves as a kind of parochialism, with the core city retreating to its own enclosure.

Metropolitan Federation

Strong arguments, based upon efficiency, economy, and equity call for functions of government to be integrated throughout the metropolitan area. At the same

[21] Beverly Briley, "The Davidson County Story," *The County Officer,* September, 1962, pp. 406–407.

[22] Brett W. Hawkins, "Public Opinion and Metropolitan Reorganization in Nashville," *Journal of Politics,* 28:408–418, May, 1966.

time, many citizens prefer keeping government as close to the people as possible and find a psychological value in retaining the community spirit of the smaller suburb as against the impersonality of the core city. Because of the dilemma thus created, some specialists have suggested that a federal plan of government be applied to the metropolitan area with two tiers of government: one area-wide to perform functions fitting into that classification, and another for the local community to handle functions of a more parochial interest. It is sometimes suggested, for example, that such things as sewage disposal, water supply, police protection, and planning should be area-wide, while perhaps garbage collection and local street maintenance would be appropriate for the lower-tier government. This plan has been used in London, England, and Toronto, Ontario. Perhaps half a dozen American communities have considered it, but all such proposals have been defeated.

The Municipality of Metropolitan Toronto The first example of the federal plan of urban government on the North American continent was established by unilateral action of the Ontario Legislature in 1953. Without a referendum vote in the areas affected, but after extensive public hearings, the Legislature created a federal plan with a metropolitan government over the thirteen municipalities of the Toronto area. In addition, the area was disconnected from the county which had had control over it and county functions were assigned to the metropolitan government.

The action established a supergovernment six times the area of Toronto proper. The metropolitan council of twenty-five consists of the twelve suburban mayors of the cities, or reeves (supervisors) of the townships, plus twelve representatives from Toronto proper. The chairman is appointed by the provincial government. The Toronto members are the mayor, two of the four elective members of the board of control, and one of the two aldermen from each of the nine city wards.

The assignment of powers to the metropolitan government and to local units is somewhat arbitrary. The metropolis controls assessments, water supply and distribution, sewerage and sewage treatment, main highways, public transportation, administration of justice, some welfare functions, land-use planning, and supervision of local zoning. It also has concurrent powers with the local municipalities on public housing and redevelopment and parks and recreation. Other powers are left to the local units, including some that are often thought of as being metropolitan-wide in scope: fire protection, libraries, public health, building codes, and direct public relief. No provision is made in the enabling act for a later redistribution of functions. In 1967, the municipalities were reduced in number from thirteen to six and the council membership increased from twenty-four to thirty-three. Twelve seats were given to Toronto. Toronto officials were displeased, but suburbanites favored the proposal, which permitted them to continue to control when they vote as a bloc. It shifted power in planning, transportation, waste disposal, and especially welfare to the metro level, and reduced school districts to six and made them coterminous with city boundaries.

The Municipality of Metropolitan Toronto represents a major step toward an integrated approach to metropolitan government. There are some apparent weaknesses in the model established at Toronto, however. The dual responsibility of the metropolitan council to the voters is confusing. All but two of the council members must be elected annually, an approach that does not seem likely to encourage long-range planning. Furthermore, the representation is inequitable when measured by a population standard.

The Municipality, as it has been established, does not include all of the metropolitan area. Some duplication of personnel and equipment still exists because the metropolitan government and the municipalities have concurrent jurisdiction over most functions of government.

Among the criticized features of the plan is a tight land-use control which has driven up prices of land and discouraged urban sprawl. The plan not only encourages core-city building but, by encouraging greater population densities, reduces costs of providing municipal services, such as water, sewage, and streets. A Detroit journalist reports that a model home selling in the United States for $48,990 costs $105,000 in Metropolitan Toronto.[23]

Impressed with the success of Metropolitan Toronto, the legislature of the province of Ontario began in 1969 the creation of ten or more regional district governments for cities and even semirural areas. The plan, when completed, is to include all of what is known as the province's industrial Golden Horseshoe in metropolitan governments. Regional districts have also been created in Quebec and British Columbia, though both provinces permit local residents to vote on whether they wish their units to join the regional government. In Manitoba, Winnipeg was formed as a metropolitan government in 1960 with eighteen municipal units and a large green-belt area. Ten years later, the two-tier system was abandoned and one corporation was formed with fifty council members.[24]

Whether American metropolitan areas will follow the lines established by the Ontario Legislature seems unlikely, for American state legislatures are not likely to use direct and drastic action. Critics are likely to emphasize what appears to be a movement from federation to unitary government in Winnipeg and to some extent in Toronto.

The County as a Metropolitan Unit Because about two-thirds of the standard metropolitan areas are located in single counties, it is sometimes suggested that the already-existing county governments might be used as a basis for forming supergovernments. There are, however, several disadvantages to such an approach. In the first place, the county may be a poor profile of the metropolitan area. The core city may be tucked off in a corner of the county that is otherwise rural, or the metropolitan area may extend over several counties. Second, in most states, there are many legal obstacles to the county acting as a municipality. Third, the traditional structure of county government, under either the supervisor

[23] Carl Konzelman, "Toronto Home Costs Zoom," *Detroit News,* October 3, 1974, p. 13A.

[24] Terry Shevciw, "Canadian Experience with Metropolitan Government," and Jack Willis, "Metropolitan Winnipeg," *Municipal Year Book, 1973,* International City Management Association, Washington, 1973, pp. 77–78.

or commissioner system, is unsatisfactoy for urban government, especially because of the absence of a chief executive officer.

A very few urban counties have been given governmental structures that enable them to act as supergovernments. One example is Los Angeles County, which has a chief administrative officer and furnishes many urban services to unincorporated areas as well as, by contract, to incorporated municipalities. Of the thirty-one cities incorporated in Los Angeles County between 1955 and 1965, twenty-nine contracted with the county to provide all their services. In 1976, the county had some 40,000 employees and many other counties in California and elsewhere were modelling themselves upon it. Despite this, the unrepresentative and archaic structure of its government continued to be sharply criticized.[25] Westchester County in New York has, in effect, the strong-mayor plan of government with an elective chief executive. Several counties have the council-manager form. Many urban counties have a chief administrative officer, hired by the governing board and similar in function to the mayor and CAO plan in cities.[26] But even with this, the structure is often inadequate for modern purposes.

Because of the various factors militating against the use of the county as an "upper-tier" unit of government, the trend has been toward functional consolidation. Either a single function at a time is turned over to the county, or *ad hoc* arrangements are made for a function to be operated jointly by the county and the core city. This trend in metropolitan areas is perhaps supported by the fact that many officals of large cities, unlike their counterparts in smaller communities, find acceptable such transfers of power.[27] Functional consolidation in Rochester-Monroe County, New York, includes nineteen services, such as health, corrections, and airports, consolidated so that either the city or county is the sole provider of the service.

An increasing number of city-county hospitals are being established. City-county health units are becoming more common, as are joint traffic commissions. Many core cities combine with the county to build a city-county building, or to operate library, animal shelter, and police technical services. Planning, zoning, parks, welfare, and correction are among the other functions being turned over to counties or being jointly administered with counties.

The movement toward a greater use of the county has, however, been slow and piecemeal.

ALTERNATIVES TO "METRO"

Extraterritorial Jurisdiction

Under certain conditions, a city may own and control land outside of its own boundaries. It may do this either under its governmental powers, if state law permits, or by owning land in the same manner as a private corporation, in which case its powers are limited to those of the ordinary property owner.

[25] Public Commission on County Government, *Report,* County of Los Angeles, 1976.

[26] For more on counties, see Charles R. Adrian, *State and Local Governments,* 4th ed., McGraw-Hill Book Company, New York, 1976.

[27] Edward W. Weidner, *Intergovernmental Relations as Seen by Public Officials,* The University of Minnesota Press, Minneapolis, 1960, pp. 110–113.

About thirty states authorize some municipal control over the subdivision of land outside of the city limits.[28] The areas of jurisdiction vary from 1 to 5 miles. This type of control sometimes enables the core city to require the building up of land within the city before further plots are offered for sale on the periphery. Usually, however, it helps to prevent the uncontrolled growth of suburban slums by requiring suitable standards for new subdivisions. Many heavily urban states, including Massachusetts, Michigan, Missouri, New Jersey, and New York, have no such control.

Extraterritorial powers are sometimes given a city for such functions as controlling roadhouses; securing a water supply; abatement of nuisances; providing for parks (this need is often ignored until the city is built up and no land within the city limits is left); dumps, stone quarries, airports, or hospitals for contagious cases; and many other activities. Many California cities have summer camps and recreational centers in the mountains and elsewhere outside their corporate limits.

The suburbs often resent extraterritorial powers of the core city. Airports may be unpopular in one's neighborhood; yet they are necessary, and the core city rarely has space for them. A careless suburb cannot expect to be left alone if it allows a health menace to exist along the boundary between itself and the core city. If the core city constructs a park in the suburbs, there will be resentment over the city folk coming in droves into the area each Sunday. Yet the suburbanites swarm into the core city each workday. Somehow, the suburbanite is not likely to feel that the one counterbalances the other. Clearly, the dispute over extraterritorial powers is a reflection of uncoordinated independent municipalities in the metropolitan area.

Voluntary Cooperation

The lack of an overall government in the metropolitan area can be compensated for, to a degree, through the use of informal or contractual agreements between one or more cities in the area. Agreements may be made by one suburb with other suburbs, or by a suburb with the core city. These may be formally established but may also be quite informal.

It is becoming increasingly common for such intergovernmental arrangements to be made for the disposal of sewage, garbage, and rubbish; to share police radio networks; or to have the core-city police radio supply the suburban departments. Formal agreements or informal understandings concerning emergency standby assistance in the case of unusual police or fire problems are also common. A large number of core cities sell water to the suburbs on a contractual basis, either directly to the suburbanite, or to the suburb itself at a master meter. Many cities have understandings of an informal type concerning traffic-flow patterns, including such necessities as the establishment of one-way streets through two or more communities. Thousands of other cooperative arrangements have been worked out in various parts of the nation.

Voluntary agreements are edged with a coloration of the haphazard. They represent an unsystematic approach, but they ease some of the strains encoun-

[28] Russell W. Maddox, Jr., *Extraterritorial Powers of Municipalities in the United States,* The College Press, Corvallis, Oregon, 1955.

tered in furnishing services to urbanites. But the evidence is that they discourage the desire for metropolitan government.[29]

Councils of Governments

In the 1960s, a major trend toward intergovernmental cooperation was taken in the form of councils of governments in metropolitan areas. Ninety-one such agencies existed in 1969. Examples included the Association of Bay Area Governments (ABAG), established in the San Francisco area in 1961 as part of an effort to prevent metropolitan problems from being assumed by the state government. In concept, it is a confederation, with favorable decisions depending upon a concurrent majority of both city and county representatives. The general assembly meets at least twice a year, with the presidency alternating between city and county representatives, and with representation based upon membership rather than population of the various governmental units in the area.

A council of governments (COG) is usually formed as a result of activities by local officials or existing organizations that believe there is a need for an overall stimulus, usually one leading to a fear of state- or national-government control of decisions. Councils of governments usually seek to improve communications with local units, prevent domination by a single governmental unit, and improve overall planning for the future in the metropolitan area.

The Twin Cities Metropolitan Council

In 1967, the Minnesota Legislature established a council to coordinate plans in the Twin Cities metropolitan area. Members were appointed by the governor from fourteen districts into which the area was divided. The council was to act as a clearinghouse of area information but was also given the power to veto plans of any other unit which would affect regional planning. The veto could be appealed to the legislature itself. It first worked on a watershed plan and has developed coordination among plans of differing units, besides presenting regional plans of its own. In 1971, it backed a unique tax plan in the Minnesota Legislature which provides that 60 percent of any new or improved tax base will be held by the municipality concerned, but the other 40 percent will be pooled and the pool divided among all other municipalities of the area on a population basis. In 1974, it began work on controlled growth plans. A move was also launched to make the representatives on the council elective, which would in effect make it a metropolitan government of sorts. Thus far the council differs from other regional-planning organizations in that it was imposed by the state rather than being voluntary, and its representation is not decided upon by area residents or local units of government, but by the governor.[30]

[29] Vincent Morando, "Inter-local Cooperation in a Metropolitan Area: Detroit," *Urban Affairs Quarterly*, 4:185–200, December, 1968.

[30] For discussion by students or officials closely associated with the Twin Cities Metropolitan Council, Unigov-Indianapolis, and other Metropolitan governmental experiments, see Kent Mathewson (ed.), *The Regionalist Papers*, The Metropolitan Fund, Detroit, 1974.

METROPOLITICS

A vast literature has been accumulated on metropolitan areas and the difficulties of supplying urban services to them. Well over 100 surveys have been conducted. Yet, despite the reams of paper devoted to the subject, most of the proposed solutions have been based upon a priori reasoning rather than empirical data; few studies have been made concerning the climate of opinion existing in metropolitan areas or of the limits of tolerance within which proposed approaches might be feasible; little work has been done concerning the levels of awareness which metropolitan residents have of their community and its problems; no rank order of values has been worked out; few studies have been made as to why integration proposals fail.

Perspectives on the Metropolis

Interpretations of metropolitan-area politics depend in part upon one's perspective of the metropolitan area. Several perspectives have been, or might be, used in interpreting the aspect of American politics:

1 The traditional, reform-movement emphasis was upon a search for *solutions,* with an emphasis upon efficiency and economy goals rather than upon problems of securing access and representation. The emphasis was on structural reform, with the implicit assumption that, given metropolitan-wide formal institutions, metropolitan areas would be well governed. These reformers generally assumed that other citizens in the area were as well informed as they, or at least adequately well informed to react favorably to their arguments. Because they themselves had no problems of access and representation—being overwhelmingly upper middle class—they failed to observe this central problem.[31]

2 The metropolitan area may be viewed as a problem in diplomacy. That is, decision making in the metropolitan area may be seen as resembling that of the diplomatic community more than that of the political. When it is, relative size of communities, although a factor, is not so important as that of securing unanimity in decisions, as is required for agreement in diplomatic negotiations. Viewing the area as a diplomatic problem also permits us to analyze it in terms of alliances of various groups. These alliances are not always so simple as one of the core city against the suburbs. They may involve groups of suburbs against other groups, or alliances may be formed on the basis of particular functions, rather than for all purposes of negotiation.[32]

3 The metropolitan area may be viewed as a market for services. In this sense, it can be analyzed in economic terms.[33] In large metropolitan areas, many, or at least several, suppliers of services may exist. For example, the core city, plus the county government, plus some of the larger suburbs may all compete for

[31] See one of the very first such studies that makes this point, Paul Studenski, *Government of Metropolitan Areas,* National Municipal League, New York, 1930.

[32] Matthew Holden, Jr., "The Governance of the Metropolis as a Problem in Diplomacy," *Journal of Politics,* 26:627–647, August, 1964.

[33] Vincent Ostrom and others, "The Organization of Government in Metropolitan Areas," *American Political Science Review,* 55:831–842, December, 1961; Thomas R. Dye, "Metropolitan Integration by Bargaining among Sub-areas," *American Behavioral Scientist,* 5:11, May, 1962.

customers among suburbs for the distribution of water, or for sewage disposal, or for some other function. Cooperative arrangements involving buying from the lowest bidder are possible where both the purveyor and the consumer of services feel that they gain through the transaction—the fundamental requirement for an exchange in economic theory. The concept of the market also applies to the fact that residents of the area appear to choose their place of residence in terms of the amenities they desire and can afford.

4 The dozens, sometimes hundreds, of governmental units in a metropolitan area make it especially appropriate to view the metropolitan area as a part of the system of cooperative federalism. Shared decision making involves not only the traditional three levels of government, but a great amount of interlocal cooperation. To the extent that this is the case, the emphasis in cooperative federalism upon shared values and goals by professional administrators in various areas of government is especially appropriate. If the theory of cooperative federalism is reasonably satisfactory as an explanation of how decisions are made relative to American domestic policy today, the implication is that metropolitan areas will be able to operate satisfactorily (though certainly not ideally) through the use of negotiation and shared decision making and financing.

5 The metropolitan area may be viewed as a complex of local governments which, if combined into a single unit, would no longer be a local government, but which through county and state governments might be able to provide those services that strictly local governments cannot provide by themselves. Although one-third of the metropolitan areas cover more than one county—and these are generally the largest such areas—the other two-thirds may increasingly find the county a useful unit of metropolitan government. In these areas, as well as in those that cover more than a single county, the state is likely to provide metropolitan-wide services in future years. Reapportionment is especially likely to encourage the use of the state as an instrument for meeting metropolitan problems. In such fields as air and water pollution, highway systems, health services, welfare services, urban renewal, and area-wide planning, the state is particularly likely to be able to serve as a metropolitan unit of government.[34]

6 The metropolitan area can also be viewed as a set of competing and sometimes conflicting ideologies. Perhaps this view has been least investigated, but we may in the future find research relative to it important in developing public policy in metropolitan areas, where some residents are committed to the urban industrial liberalism of organized labor, others are representative of the middle-class-oriented ideology of the organization person typically found in the suburbs, and a small but sometimes politically important minority remains committed to the small-town ideology of the nineteenth century.[35]

The Failure of Integration

The value patterns of those who support plans for metropolitan supergovernments are not dominant in most communities, and the leaders of integration movements characteristically do not give adequate consideration to other values.

[34] Charles R. Adrian, "Public Attitudes and Metropolitan Decision Making," in Russell W. Maddox, Jr. (ed.), *Issues in State and Local Government,* D. Van Nostrand Company, Inc., Princeton, N.J., 1965, pp. 311–321.

[35] Charles R. Adrian and Charles Press, *The American Political Process,* McGraw-Hill Book Company, New York, 2d ed., 1969, chap. 7; also *American Politics Reappraised,* McGraw-Hill Book Company, New York, 1974, chaps. 2–4.

The result is that proposals for reorganization or metropolitan governments are rarely implemented.

Upper-income business and professional people tend to favor metropolitan government for a number of reasons. Some are concerned lest, as a result of the middle-class exodus to the suburbs, the political control of the core city be lost to low-income groups with little education. Some believe that governmental consolidation will reduce costs through economies of scale. Low-income groups tend to oppose metropolitan government for a number of reasons. Blacks fear that such a government will weaken their political power, since blacks are concentrated in the core city of the metropolitan area. Labor leaders sometimes oppose consolidation because business leaders favor it, and they assume it must therefore be to the advantage of the business leaders. Labor leaders or working-class people sometimes also oppose metropolitan plans because they include proposals for a short ballot and professional leadership. That is, they fear a loss of access and representation. Some low-income persons fear that metropolitan government would be more expensive to them, that it would result in more rapid tax increases than would otherwise be the case. The question of whether or not to have metropolitan government is not, therefore, simply a question of efficiency and economy, as the reformers of a generation ago believed, but is a political question closely related to costs and to perceived abilities to influence policy making.[36]

Suburban officeholders and the entrenched bureaucracy of the area will almost always oppose metropolitan government, and reformers seldom pay enough attention to their values and interests or show any imagination in compromising with them. The fail to recognize that *representativeness* of government and *access* to the decision makers are likely to be more important considerations for the typical citizen than are questions of efficiency and economy. Rarely does a metropolitan-area study even mention these two psychologically important factors, to say nothing of adequately providing for them.

Black voters, in particular, have been suspicious of proposals for metropolitan-wide government. In Cleveland, on ten issues submitted to referendum between 1933 and 1959, the level of support for metropolitan government steadily declined, but it declined much more rapidly among black voters than it did among whites. The percentage of positive vote among blacks declined from 79 percent in 1933 to 29 percent in 1959, while the vote in predominantly white wards declined from 69 percent to 46 percent.[37]

Reformers tend to forget that the symbols—efficiency, a bigger and better Zilchville, and the like—that they respond to with enthusiams ring no bells for *hoi polloi.* It is the latter, of course, which dominates the decision when a proposal is put to a popular referendum. Ordinary citizens are characteristically apathetic. If water flows from the tap and the toilet flushes today, they are not likely to ask whether it will do so tomorrow.

Yet, votes against metropolitan government are not necessarily votes in favor of the status quo. They may be votes in favor of gradual or incremental

[36] See Richard A. Watson and John H. Romani, "Metropolitan Government for Metropolitan Cleveland," *Midwest Journal of Political Science,* 5:365–390, November, 1961.

[37] *Ibid.,* table 2.

change rather than revolutionary change.[38]

Communicating a concept of future needs on a realistic basis is seldom done by groups organized to support metropolitan governmental reorganization. Furthermore, the reformers tend to put their arguments on a theoretical plane, discussing efficiency ("We have sixteen different fire departments in the metropolitan area!") without translating it into concrete terms as it affects the ordinary citizen. Examples are often not made meaningful. It makes little impression on suburbanites to be told that their police force is amateurish and inferior if, in practice, their community has little crime and the state police take care of the arterial highway traffic.

Concluding Statement

Each structural plan so far tried for the government of metropolitan areas in most cases either is basically unacceptable to groups politically powerful enough to block adoption or has proved to be ineffective as a method for dealing with perceived problems. Any proposal that does not meet the requirement of responsiveness to the general public must be dismissed—as it will be by the electorate—as lacking accord with our basic concepts of democratic theory.

Referring back to the Aristotelian mode of analysis, Norton Long has noted that "the search for metropolitan government is the search for a potential metropolitan governing class, the institutions through which it can function and a set of ideal goals which it can embody and which will render its leadership legitimate in the eyes of the people."[39] Here we find the reasons for slow progress in metropolitan-area government. The institutions for such government have not evolved because there is no consensus on goals and no acceptable governing group. The proposals put forth by self-appointed community leaders diverge so widely from the wants of a great portion of the citizenry that these volunteers for a leadership class are not accepted as legitimate representatives. Their offerings are rejected when the voters are polled, and no trend toward consensus on the three Aristotelian components can be discerned.

SELECTED READINGS

Adrian, Charles R.: "Metropology: Folklore and Field Research," *Public Administration Review,* 21:148–157, Summer, 1961. (A criticism of conventional metropolitan-area studies.)

Bain, Chester W.: *Annexation in Virginia: The Use of Judicial Process for Readjusting City-County Boundaries,* University Press of Virginia, Charlottesville, Va., 1966. (The oldest nonreferendum system.)

Banfield, Edward C., and Morton Grodzins: *Government and Housing in Metropolitan*

[38] Robert Warren, "Political Form and Metropolitan Reform," *Public Administration Review,* 24:180–187, September, 1964.

[39] Norton E. Long, "Recent Theories and Problems of Local Government," in Carl J. Friedrich and Seymour E. Harris (eds.), *Public Policy,* Graduate School of Public Administration, Harvard University, Cambridge, Mass., 1958, pp. 285–295. Quote is from p. 295. Reprinted in Norton E. Long, *The Polity,* Rand McNally & Company, Chicago, 1962.

Areas, McGraw-Hill Book Company, New York, 1958.

Berry, Brian J. L.: *The Human Consequences of Urbanization,* St. Martin's Press, New York, 1973. (Sets up a scale of governmental control of land-use systems from little to maximum control and describes systems conforming most nearly to type.)

Bish, Robert L.: *The Public Economy of Metropolitan Areas,* Markham, Chicago, 1971. (Argues that competition and cooperation among urban units in a metropolitan area leads to desirable outcomes.)

Bish, Robert L., and Vincent Ostrom: *Understanding Urban Government,* American Enterprise Institute for Public Policy Research, Washington, 1973. (Attacks metropolitan-reform assumptions.)

Bollens, John C.: *Special District Governments in the United States,* University of California Press, Berkeley, Calif., 1957.

——: *The States and the Metropolitan Problem,* Public Administration Service, Chicago, 1956.

—— and Henry J. Schmandt: *The Metropolis,* Harper & Row, Publishers, Incorporated, New York, 3d ed., 1975. (A summary of studies on metropolitan politics, ecology, and economics. Includes a fine bibliography.)

Booth, David A.: *Metropolitics: The Nashville Consolidation,* Institute for Community Development, Michigan State University, East Lansing, Mich., 1963.

Caro, Robert A.: *The Power Broker, Robert Moses and the Fall of New York,* Alfred A. Knopf, Inc., New York, 1974. (A frank account of an administrative buccaneer.)

Committee for Economic Development: *Reshaping Government in Metropolitan Areas,* Committee for Economic Development, New York, 1970. (Classic reform statement in pamphlet form.)

Downs, Anthony: *Urban Problems and Prospects,* Markham, Chicago, 1970. (Essays on a variety of urban problems.)

Duncan, Beverly, and Stanley Lieberson: *Metropolis and Region in Transition,* Sage Publications, Inc., Beverly Hills, Calif., 1970. (The evolution of some major urban centers.)

Elazar, Daniel J.: *Cities of the Prairie: The Metropolitan Frontier and American Politics,* Basic Books, Inc., New York, 1970. (Patterns of change in ten middle-sized midwestern metropolitan areas.)

Eldredge, H. Wentworth (ed.): *Taming Megalopolis,* Anchor Books, Doubleday & Company, Inc., Garden City, N.Y., 1967. (Two volumes of essays by experts from many fields—generally pro metropolitan reform.)

Friesma, H. Paul: "The Metropolis and the Maze of Local Government," *Urban Affairs Quarterly,* 2:68–90, December, 1966. (A criticism of the assumptions made in recent metropolitan research.)

Friesma, H. Paul: *Metropolitan Political Structure: Intergovernmental Relations and Political Integration in the Quad Cities,* University of Iowa Press, Iowa City, 1971. (A study of Davenport, Iowa, and three cities across the Mississippi River in Illinois.)

Greer, Scott: *Metropolitics: A Study of Political Culture,* John Wiley & Sons, Inc., New York, 1963. (The politics of reform in Cleveland, Miami, and St. Louis.)

Hanson, Royce, and others: *Reform as Reorganization,* Johns Hopkins University Press, Baltimore, 1974. (Five essays that examine the impact of metropolitan reform from different perspectives.)

Havard, William C., and Floyd C. Corty: *Rural-Urban Consolidation: The Merger of Governments in the Baton Rouge Area,* Louisiana State University Press, Baton Rouge, La., 1964.

Hawkins, Brett W.: *Nashville Metro: The Politics of City-County Consolidation,* Vanderbilt

University Press, Nashville, Tenn., 1966. (Study of the Nashville-Davidson County consolidation of 1962, which Hawkins sees as stemming from unique local political conditions.)

Hawley, Amos H., and Basil G. Zimmer: *The Metropolitan Community,* Sage Publications, Inc., Beverly Hills, Calif., 1969. (Explores attitudes of citizens and officials of both core cities and suburbs.)

Hayes, Forbes B.: *Community Leadership,* Columbia University Press, New York, 1965. (A study of one of the oldest private metropolitan-area research organizations, the New York Regional Plan Association.)

Hein, C. J., and others: *Regional Governmental Arrangements in Metropolitan Areas,* Institute for Community Studies, Kansas City, 1973. (Nine case studies.)

Jones, Victor: "Local Government Organization in Metropolitan Areas," in Coleman Woodbury (ed.), *The Future of Cities and Urban Redevelopment,* The University of Chicago Press, Chicago, 1953. (The best historical study of metropolitan organization.)

Kaplan, Harold: *Urban Political Systems: A Functional Analysis of Metropolitan Toronto,* Columbia University Press, New York, 1967.

Martin, Richard: *Consolidation: Jacksonville-Duval County, the Dynamics of Political Reform,* Crawford, Jacksonville, Fla., 1968. (A journalistic account.)

Martin, Roscoe C.: *Metropolis in Transition,* Housing and Home Finance Agency, Washington, 1963. (A study of efforts to achieve metropolitan-wide government. Has good bibliography.)

Mathewson, Kent (ed.): *The Regionalist Papers,* The Metropolitan Fund, Detroit, 1974. (A particularly good series by persons familiar with the operation of various metropolitan governmental innovations.)

Metropolitan Communities: A Bibliography with Special Emphasis Upon Government and Politics, Public Administration Service, Chicago, 4 vols., 1956–1969.

Miller, Delbert C.: *Leadership and Power in the Bos-Wash Megalopolis,* Wiley-Interscience, New York, 1975. (Influence of networks of leaders and institutions along the East Coast.)

Neiman, Max: *Metropology: Toward a More Constructive Research Agenda,* Sage Professional Papers in American Politics, ser. no. 04–024, Sage Publications, Beverly Hills, Calif., 1975. (Just as Adrian, in the cite above, called for a second generation of metropolitan researchers, Neiman here calls for a third.)

Ostrom, Elinor, and others: "Do We Really Want to Consolidate Urban Police Forces? A Reappraisal of Some Old Assertations," *Public Administration Review,* 33:423–432, September, 1973. (In the Indianapolis metropolitan area the usual assumptions about the advantages of a metropolitan police force are not borne out.)

Reining, Henry, Jr. (ed.): "Governing Megacentropolis," *Public Administration Review,* 30:473–520, September–October, 1970. (Six articles on problems of govering the metropolis.)

Schmandt, Henry J., and William H. Standing: *The Milwaukee Metropolitan Study Commission,* Indiana University Press, Bloomington, Ind., 1965.

——, Paul G. Steinbricker, and George D. Wendel: *Metropolitan Reform in St. Louis: A Case Study,* Holt, Rinehart and Winston, Inc., New York, 1961.

Simon, Herbert: *Fiscal Aspects of Metropolitan Consolidation,* Bureau of Public Administration, University of California, Berkeley, Calif., 1943. (A classic study, still valuable. Shows that with metropolitan-wide government, consolidation would result in higher taxes if services were made uniform.)

Smallwood, Frank: *Metro Toronto: A Decade Later,* Bureau of Municipal Research, Toronto, 1963.

Smith, Robert G.: *Public Authorities, Special Districts and Local Government,* National Association of Counties Research Foundation, Washington, 1964. (A study covering five states.)

Social Science Panel on the Significance of Community in the Metropolitan Environment of the Advisory Committee to the Department of Housing and Urban Development Assembly of Behavioral and Social Sciences, National Research Council: *Toward an Understanding of Metropolitan America,* Canfield Press, San Francisco, 1974. (Good, concise discussion, with excellent bibliography.)

Sofen, Edward: *The Miami Metropolitan Experiment,* Indiana University Press, Bloomington, Ind., 1963.

Steiner, Gilbert Y.: *Metropolitan Government and the Real World: The Case of Chicago,* Center for Research in Urban Government, Loyola University, Chicago, 1966. (A sharply critical evaluation of a metropolitan-government proposal for Chicago.)

U.S. Advisory Commission on Intergovernmental Relations: *Reports,* continuing from 1960. See especially *Regional Goverance: Promise and Performance,* U.S. Government Printing Office, Washington, 1973.

Wenum, John D.: *Annexation as a Technique for Metropolitan Growth: The Case of Phoenix, Arizona,* Institute of Public Administration, Arizona State University, Tempe, 1970. (A case study.)

Whyte, W. H., Jr., and others: *The Exploding Metropolis,* Doubleday & Company, Inc., Garden City, N.Y., 1958.

——: *The Last Landscape,* Anchor Books, Doubleday & Company, Inc., Garden City, N.Y., 1968. (Discusses the politics of open space.)

Willbern, York: *The Withering Away of the City,* University of Alabama Press, University, Ala., 1964.

Williams, Oliver P.: *Metropolitan Political Analysis,* The Free Press, New York, 1971. (Explains the metropolis using "locational" theory.)

——, and others: *Suburban Differences and Metropolitan Policies,* University of Pennsylvania Press, Philadelphia, 1965.

Wilson, James Q. (ed.): *The Metropolitan Enigma,* Anchor Books, Doubleday and Company, Inc., Garden City, N.Y., 1968. (Essays mainly by Harvard faculty, focusing on urban breakdown within a variety of service areas.)

Wood, Robert C: *1400 Governments,* Harvard University Press, Cambridge, Mass., 1961. (The New York metropolitan area.)

——: *Suburbia: Its People and Their Politics,* Houghton Mifflin Company, Boston, 1959.

Chapter 11

Cities in the Federal System

Until about 1930, local functions were planned, administered, and largely financed in most states by local governments themselves. Cities, within the powers granted by states, did much as they pleased. The pattern then began to change, with both states and national government beginning to show more concern about how these functions were carried out. What began as a tendency with the New Deal became a dominant trend in the 1960s; a change of the balance in the federal system that began as one of degrees, in time became a change in kind; a new kind of federalism emerged. America's federal system shifted the balance of responsibilities among levels of government; states took a primary interest in how local functions should be financed and administered; the federal government became an important partner in the planning and financing of many urban functions and exercised a growing influence on how cities would administer them.

Precise turning points are difficult to identify. The federal breakthrough may have come during the New Deal of the 1930s or with the passage of federal aid to education, as advocated by President Kennedy, hopefully to upgrade opportunity for the disadvantaged. Certainly the dam had broken after the 1964 election, with the outpouring of federal funds to urban areas as the heart of the Great Society program of President Johnson similarly redistributive in purpose. These federal funds included urban-renewal grants, housing programs, various Office of Economic Opportunity ("antipoverty") programs, Model Cities grants, and others which are described in introductory American government textbooks. By 1966, partly to centralize many of these new federal contacts with urban governments, a cabinet post of Secretary of Housing and Urban Development (HUD) was created.

State influence in local governmental administration came less suddenly and more on a function-by-function basis, as various departments such as health, education, highways, and others began to discern a state purpose in the way local services were performed. If there was a turning point, it also came in the early 1960s when the United States Supreme Court ruled that state legislatures must be apportioned in both houses on a population standard.[1] Not only was representation from urban areas sharply increased in many states, but legislatures became more receptive to discussing the problems troubling modern society in urban areas.

The significant fact of the new federal balance is that cities can no longer do much as they please. The national and state governments have recognized that they have a responsibility and purposes of their own in respect to the quality of life that their citizens experience locally. This responsibility is only dimly spelled out. As yet, there is no clearly stated, consistent national urban policy. There is only a general belief that there should be one and that it should push in the direction of equalizing opportunities for all American citizens. At the state level, policies continue to be made by function and the search there is also for a pattern for overall coordination.

In the Nixon administration, federal aid to cities declined in relative terms, but dependence upon it may have increased. And while aid was reduced, federal policies, especially in conditions to grants, "affirmative action" requirements, and planning preconditions, did not decline. Local officials complained of more red tape for few dollars.

THE NEW FEDERALISM

Until relatively recently, doubt existed about whether the federal government could constitutionally even be concerned with urban functions, traditionally regarded as state or local, except perhaps to give occasional supplemental aid in emergencies. By the end of the 1960s, if not before, the last of these doubts had evaporated. One scholar has argued that the legal pattern that emerged was not one in which each level of government has functional responsibilities of its own, or even one of cooperative federalism. The new pattern, realistically and legally as well, is one of permissive federalism.[2] State and local governments handle those functions that the federal government permits them to. Supreme Court interpretations of the Constitution ever since the 1930s allow the national govern-

[1] *Baker v. Carr,* 369 U.S. 186 (1962). See Charles R. Adrian, *State and Local Governments,* 4th ed., McGraw-Hill Book Company, New York, 1976.

[2] Michael D. Reagan, *The New Federalism,* Oxford University Press, New York, 1972.

ment to achieve its own goals in urban areas, with or without the aid of state or local governments.

A national takeover of urban functions has not of course occurred, nor is it likely to. If the states and cities lack the legal power to prevent it, they certainly do not lack the political power to preserve their own influence. They are still very much important elements of the system of planning, administering, and financing urban services. The increase of federal involvement in this process, however, has been great in recent years, as is indicated in a study by the Advisory Commission on Intergovernmental Relations. It isolated ninety-five areas of state or local activity for which federal grants were available in 1968. Seventy percent of these came into being after World War II, no less than forty-one percent in the five years, 1961–1965. These ninety-five activity areas provided 379 separate grant offerings. Of these, 219 or 58 percent had been added between 1963 and 1966. The rise in federal expenditures for such state and local activities tripled in the decade of the 1960s, rising from $8 to $25 billion. As a percentage of all federal expenditures, such state and local funding rose from 8 to 13 percent.[3]

The pattern of federal contacts also became more experimental. At the beginning of the New Deal in 1933, federal-government agencies had made some direct approaches to city governments, but they were uncommon. In the 1960s, such bypassing of state governments increased, and, indeed, a number of programs were instituted with federal grants going directly to *ad hoc* private groups or to newly formed local agencies, largely separate from the formal city governmental structure. Thus even the elected local governments felt bypassed.

During the Nixon years, an attempt was made to discourage this kind of direct relationship. (Congress had tried to do that same thing immediately after World War II.) Local officials had particularly objected to programs of the "War on Poverty's" Office of Economic Opportunity (OEO) and Model Cities, as had President Nixon and many who had voted for him, and these were phased out or transformed to bring them more under local governmental control. Secondly, grants went to local governments: "revenue sharing" was introduced as a substitute for a number of previous programs. Block grants, such as the Housing and Community Development grants of 1974, were substituted for some special-project grants. Both of these moves had the effect of channelling federal funds directly to locally elected officials rather than to private agencies or specially created administrative units. Finally, the Council of State Governments and other groups lobbied with partial success in Congress to have federal funds continued to be channelled through the states as they had been between 1946 and the beginning of the "War on Poverty," with states in certain respects holding the right of veto over local governments. A number of changes were made in this direction.

Between 1967 and 1972, federal expenditures on state and local functions increased by 82 percent. Yet the major part of financing still came from state and

[3] These figures are summarized and discussed in James L. Sundquist and David W. Davis, *Making Federalism Work,* The Brookings Institution, Washington, 1969, pp. 1–2.

local sources: of the $189.7 billion raised for urban functions, 44.4 percent was raised by states, 39.0 percent by local governments, and only 16.6 percent by the national government.[4] Thus the new federalism continues to evolve. The heady, if rather naive, feeling that all urban problems could be quickly solved if only the federal government poured money into core cities has subsided. The new pattern is more tentative; it is one of the national government providing some loose guidelines and encouraging state and local governments to define the problems and justify to the federal bureaucrats how they think the funds might best be spent.[5]

STATE RELATIONS WITH CITIES

What has been happening to the relative balance between the states and their subdivisions? The picture is quite clear: The states have expanded their role in society at a greater rate than have local governments. Local governments have come to depend more and more upon the states for financial assistance, and the states have generally seemed to prefer to give this assistance through grants-in-aid or shared taxes rather than through expanding the tax base of local government. Furthermore, certain functions that were once principally the responsibility of some local unit of government have been or are being transferred to the states or are now shared by state and local governments. Thus, the states are financing (with the federal government) most of the cost of public welfare, once exclusively a private or local function. Furthermore, increasing highway mileage is being turned over to the states from counties and cities, and the states are rapidly expanding their contributions to primary and secondary education, once financed entirely out of local property taxes paid to the local school district. Finally, state supervision of local functions has become more detailed and regularized.

Functional Relationships, the Typical Pattern

When the rural areas dominated state legislatures, the political conflict between them and those who governed the large cities sometimes took the form of legislative acts that, in effect, attempted to run city government. The tendency in recent years has been to turn supervisory functions over to the administrative rather than to the legislative branch of state government. Local professional technicians feel more at ease and have less of a feeling that they will be exploited when they deal with state professionals rather than with the politicians of the state legislature.[6] A smoother, more confident relationship is the result. The community is likely to gain, too, for the *motivation* of the professional administrator is different

[4] U.S. Bureau of the Census, *1972 Census of Governments.*

[5] For a critical view of this pattern, see Theodore Lowi, *The End of Liberalism: Ideology, Policy and the Crisis of Public Authority,* W. W. Norton & Company, Inc., New York, 1969. For that of solving core-city problems merely by spending enough federal funds, see Norton E. Long, *The Unwalled City,* Basic Books, Inc., New York, 1972.

[6] Edward W. Weidner, *Intergovernmental Relations As Seen by Public Officials,* The University of Minnesota Press, Minneapolis, 1950.

from that of the politician, and this is likely to have an important effect upon the eventual handling of local problems. Professional administrators have their reputations at stake in everything they do, and their success is measured in terms of acceptance of their work by their professional peers, not only within the state, but also within the professional organizations to which they belong.

Administrative contacts between the city and the state are characteristically on a *functional* basis. That is, members of the state department of education oversee the activities of the local school district; the state department of health watches the activities of the local department of health; and so on. Because city-state relations have experienced a gradual unplanned growth on a piecemeal, function-by-function basis and because there have been few systematic overhauls of municipal governments in this country of the type that have taken place in England, functional supervision is often uncoordinated and subject to duplications and omissions. Nevertheless, it is still the common method of state supervision of urban activities.

Areas of Supervision

What local government functions are subject to state oversight today? Most of them, might be a brief answer. In particular, the state is especially watchful of municipal activities that involve (1) the expenditure of state grants-in-aid (e.g., in education, the building of expressways within cities); (2) those areas of national grants-in-aid which are administered through the states, but under conditions requiring state supervision of the expenditures (e.g., the building of airports in some states); and (3) those activities in which the state as a whole has a particular interest (e.g., the spread of communicable diseases, law enforcement, finances). The principal areas of control are those of education, finance, health, highways, and welfare, but to these must be added airports, fire prevention, libraries, housing, personnel, planning, police administration, and even control of municipally owned public utilities, among others.

Techniques of Supervision

From all that has been said in this book and elsewhere about the tendency for the state to become involved in policies affecting local areas, it might be assumed that activities are controlled by heavy-handed bureaucrats from the state capital, armed with court decrees and administrative orders. Although these devices do play a part, it has been the practice of most of the state agencies to try persuasion, education, and other noncoercive techniques wherever possible. The big stick is brought into play principally whenever the state overseers find evidence of incompetence, irresponsibility, or corruption.

State agencies exercising supervision usually start by requiring *reports* from local communities. This serves the purpose of warning the state when and where trouble spots begin to appear, and it tends to channel local activity, since the reporting officials, knowing that they will be judged by their professional peers, will want to "look good." The state agency can furnish *advice and information.* This is especially important for the smaller communities, where amateurs may be floundering about seeking to do an adequate job with little experience or where overworked professionals may not have time to keep up with the latest techniques in their fields. The smaller cities and villages have technicians who are likely to recognize the genuine need for advice and seek it. To simplify requests for such help, Tennessee and Maryland have established a clearinghouse for information—a Municipal Technical Advisory Service—in connection with the state university, and some other states have municipal research bureaus, some of them connected with a state school.

One step beyond advice is *technical aid.* State agencies, with (perhaps) a relatively larger budget and with more specialized equipment and personnel, are particularly in a position to aid the local amateur or semiprofessional. How effective can the chief of police in a village of 1,500 people be against the professional criminal? And how much experience or scientific equipment can be put to use in the rare event of a murder in his town? And how much does the overworked local general practitioner know about public health, even though he or she may bear the title of health officer? How much special equipment are the citizens of the town willing to afford when it is needed? State agencies in these and in dozens of other circumstances and activities stand ready to offer technical information, advice, and equipment.

Other approaches failing, the state may also make use of its *coercive power.* Among other things, its agencies can *grant or withhold permits* for certain things (e.g., to dump raw sewage into a stream under prescribed conditions) or *issue orders* (e.g., to build a sewage-treatment plant); or *issue rules and regulations* which are technically called ordinances (e.g., to prescribe the technical standards for water-supply purification); or *withhold grants-in-aid* if standards prescribed by state, or sometimes federal, law are not complied with; or *review decisions* of local agencies (e.g., the power of the state tax-equalization board to review the determination of local boards and perhaps to order reassessment in extreme situations); or require *prior permission* from a state agency (e.g., the power of some state health departments to pass on the qualifications of local health-officer nominees); or *appoint certain local officials or remove them* (e.g., the local police chief). It is even possible in most states, as a last resort, to apply *substitute administration.* That is to say, in extreme cases the state may suspend local self-government altogether for some or all functions and allow state officials to govern instead. This is particularly true in the fields of finance, public health, and education.

The Special Problem of Large Cities

The relationship between the state and the large-city technical specialist may sometimes become strained when the city functionary believes he or she is more competent than is his or her nominal supervisor on the state level. Is the manager of a large-city airport able to get along without advice from the state airports commissioner? He is likely to think so. Is the city superintendent of schools who visits Washington, D.C., frequently and is on a first-name basis with federal granting officials in the Office of Education likely to be awed by the state "superiors"? It is by no means unheard of for an extended feud to color relationships between the department of a large city and the corresponding agency of the state. When this occurs, the state department may in effect write off the large-city agency and devote most of its efforts to the other urbanized areas of the state.[7]

Coordination of Functional Supervision

With the growing involvement of both state and federal levels of government in urban programs, the need for some overall patterning of these activities has been especially felt at the state level. This is a role the states seem to be carving out for themselves in the new federalism. Between 1970 and 1975 at least fourteen states set up special commissions to take an overview of the problems and administration of services in urban areas. Most of these bodies issued a few reports over a two-year period, lobbied in the legislature and with the governor for implementation of a few proposals, and then died. However, the Illinois Municipal Problems Commission, the New Jersey County and Municipal Government Study Commission, and the Tennessee Local Government Planning Advisory Commission all were made permanent bodies. Those in Illinois and New Jersey contain legislative members from both houses, as well as urban officials. The function of these bodies will be to continue to have staff studies made on what they regard as major urban problems. Their clientele will be the legislature and the governor especially, as well as urban officials and general citizens.[8]

Departments for General Supervision

Departments of local government, such as the Ministry of Interior in France or the Ministry of Local Government in Great Britain, are not to be found in the United States. The traditions of local initiative are still strong. Only a few American states have made some move toward centralized supervision.[9]

Beginning in about 1957, and coincident with the rising demand for a federal urban-affairs department, a few state agencies dealing with a major aspect of local government were created. These newer agencies have a great variety of powers and are organized in various ways. Quite a number are legislative agencies, designed to assist the legislature in the development of local-government legislation. Some are concerned primarily with finance. Hence, California in 1959 established a local allocation division and office of planning in the Department of Finance. This agency was oriented toward the approach earlier adopted in New Jersey. In Minnesota, the Municipal Commission, established that same year, is concerned fundamentally with the question of determining local-government boundaries in metropolitan areas in a rational and systematic manner.

[7] For a discussion of this problem, see Floyd Stoner, "Implementation of Federal Education Policy: Defining the Situation in Cities and Small Towns," a paper presented at the Midwest Political Science Convention, May 1, 1975, Chicago.

[8] Vincent L. Morando and Gerald J. Miller, *Memorandum Assessing Commissions to Study Metropolitan/Local Governments,* Institute of Government, University of Georgia, Athens, 1975. The Commissions of fourteen states are described by organization and impact.

[9] Some of the cases cited will be found in Council of State Governments, *Report of the Committee on State-Local Relations,* Council of State Governments, Chicago, 1946, pp. 37–38, 48–50.

Michigan and California had similar boundary commissions, as did seven other states in the mid-1970s.[10] Some are designed principally to provide technical information and assistance to local governments and may be connected with a state university. Thus, in 1959, Maryland established a Municipal Technical Advisory Service as a part of the University of Maryland. This agency was modeled on one by the same name established a decade earlier in Tennessee. Today, much interest centers around the establishment of state planning commissions and state agencies to provide area-wide services, particularly in metropolitan areas.

Some states prescribe uniform systems of accounts for municipalities. Most states have some degree of state jurisdiction over auditing of municipal accounts. Nearly one-half of the states require municipalities to submit financial reports periodically. Many states provide budget forms for municipalities, and the state form is compulsory in many states. Nearly one-half of the states supervise municipal debt to one degree or another, often passing upon the legality of an issue before it is sold. A few states actually inquire into the "necessity" and wisdom of municipal bond issues. North Carolina and sometimes New York and Virginia handle the sale of bonds to private investors on behalf of municipalities.[11] In most cases, however, these state activities are carried on in a decentralized manner.

New Jersey, with a Division of Local Government in the State Department of Finance and Taxation, has gone the furthest toward an integrated bureau to direct state contacts with local governments. The New Jersey division has the duty of investigating on a continuous basis the programs of local government and hence has information available for the legislature that does not exist in most states. The principal action of the division has been in the fiscal area. It has power to regulate local methods of budgeting and financial procedure. It makes certain that localities provide enough funds to service their debts and can even require local levies to reduce deficits. It supervises regular audits of the cities. Annual fiscal reports must be made by the cities on state-prepared forms. The Local Government Board, which sets policies for the division, may take over control of a municipality if it falls into an "unsound financial condition," as defined by law.

Although the board has been active primarily in the field of finance, it has become a general overseer of local government to a degree. It has made investigations into conservation, public health, education, housing, planning, and metropolitan consolidation.

Indiana has centralized fiscal control under the state Board of Tax Commissioners, but this agency does not act as a local-government office otherwise. It

[10] Anthony G. White, *Local Government Boundary Commission,* Council of Planning Librarians, Monticello, Ill., 1973; John Goldbach, *Boundary Change in California: The Local Agency Formation Commissions,* Institute of Governmental Affairs, University of California, Davis, 1970.

[11] T. E. McMillan, Jr., *State Supervision of Municipal Finance,* Institute of Public Affairs, University of Texas, Austin, Tex., 1953, provides details. See also, Leonard E. Goodall, *State Regulation of Local Indebtedness,* Bureau of Government Research, Arizona State University, Temple, 1964.

has the power to review local budgets and reduce appropriations, tax levies, and bond issues. It may prohibit the issuance of bonds. The commission has a wide range of discretion under the law.

Alaska has a Department of Local Affairs. Without resorting to the use of an integrated agency for the supervision of local government, other states control some aspects of local finance. A Local Government Commission in North Carolina has wide powers in controlling local bond issues, and Iowa and New Mexico exercise more direct fiscal supervision than does the typical state.

An Office for Local Government was established in New York in 1959. The purpose of the office was to assist the governor by providing advice relative to policy affecting local governments, to act as the representative for local governments with regard to state programs, and to provide a service to municipalities through consultation and information.[12]

Substate Regions

By 1975, forty-five states had encouraged the establishment of substate regions for all or part of their area. In most cases these were voluntary units which cities or counties could join as they wished. A number were set up as councils of governments in metropolitan areas, as places where common problems could be worked out among units. Others were planning and development units used to prepare regional plans and for federal-grant applications that required them.[13]

The problem is that there are a multiplicity of such substate units. Some twenty-four different federal programs have required creation of such bodies for purposes of gaining or administering federal grants. State agencies likewise have often established their own local districts to suit their needs, so that health-department administrative-district lines are likely to differ from those of the highway or education departments. Added to this are also a number of voluntarily created local regional units, special districts created to handle a single function such as water or sewage, as well as metropolitan-area councils or other substate planning organizations. It is impossible to give a precise count of these units because the number is steadily growing. The number of COGs grew from 25 to 600 between 1962 and 1972. States created an additional 488 districts and the estimate of those spawned by federal programs is 1800.

Initially these units, especially those formed voluntarily in metropolitan areas, were regarded primarily as fact-finding clearing-houses with a staff to collect data about the urbanized unit. From this base they drifted easily toward physical planning. A number are in fact called planning and development commissions, as well as councils of governments. The early plans were generally of such physical features as sewage-disposal lines, solid-waste disposal, transportation routes, or coordination of airport construction. This led naturally to the unit being designated to prepare plans and to grant proposals for state or federal funds, and this

[12] *Office for Local Government.* State of New York, Albany, N.Y., 1964.

[13] See David Walker and Albert Richter, "Regionalism and the Counties," *The County Year Book, 1975,* National Association of Counties and The International City Management Association, Washington, 1975, pp. 14–18.

took the substate regional commissions into considering nonphysical planning as well as economic development. For example, many small cities or counties have difficulty recruiting and paying a qualified public health officer. State health departments have encouraged the creation of multicity or multicounty departments, and these logically can be tailored to the same boundaries as the planning and development units.

A third area of activity that emerged was to provide technical assistance to smaller urban units. Again, this has been especially helpful in respect to physical planning activities and in the preparation of grant applications.

Finally, states have stepped into the picture. Michigan, for example, in 1972 required the membership of all units in substate planning and development commissions and gave these bodies the responsibility for creating regional plans. Federal grants and the acquisition of some state funds then were required to meet with the approval of the regional planning units. In this way states are experimenting with methods of control that are both more generalized than the usual functional supervision by state departments and closer to the local units concerned, so that they can be varied to suit a region's special features and problems.

One difficulty faced in the organization of a single set of substate regions is that so many such organizations already exist. The first step out of this maze appears to be the designation of one set of substate districts by state government to process grants, create regional plans, and be used by all or most state agencies for their administrative supervision.

A second difficulty is that of determining representation. Often each county and even each city or township has at least one representative, with larger units being allocated additional representatives. Core cities under such a system are likely to be markedly underrepresented by population. In 1975, Flint, Michigan, brought suit challenging the right of local planning and development commissions to make policy decisions without being apportioned on a strict population basis.

A Summary Note

Current trends suggest that states are attempting to move from function-by-function supervision of the administration of urban services to some attempt at overview. Such tendencies will introduce more coordination among city services and will, as well, supplement the federal goal of partially redistributing national resources, so that all persons receive urban services that meet acceptable minimum standards of performance.

In general, technical assistance and advice and loose supervision rather than tight control are the ideals sought in this country by both state and local officials. Although state performance requirements grow, state dictation to local officials has been unusual, and state officials have applied sanctions only very reluctantly. In most cases, political expediency dictates this practice even when it is not called for by good administrative procedure, as it usually is. Local officials are powerful and well organized for political action and lobbying. The state agency that seeks to apply pressure thoughtlessly may find its appropriation reduced for enforcement purposes for the next year. The advancement of standards and techniques is being achieved, in any case, more through voluntary associations of local officials and professional technicians in the same field than through central tutelage of local officers.

All the figures indicate that an increasing financial superiority exists on the part of states in relation to their local subdivisions. They show that we can expect an increasing amount of lobbying by local government officials before state legislatures and that state governments will become more and more the political battleground for the resolution of many financial problems relative to local services.

NATIONAL ADMINISTRATIVE RELATIONS WITH CITIES

National Government Advice and Assistance to Cities

More than 100 federal-government agencies supply more than 500 services to cities in the United States. These include items as varied as the well-known cooperation between local police officers and the FBI and the thousands of technical pamphlets on every subject from adequate specifications for fire fighters' gas masks to techniques for estimating land values.[14]

The U.S. Civil Service Commission furnishes local personnel agencies with information on examination techniques and will furnish testing materials. The Bureau of Standards makes technical information available to cities concerning commodity specifications, a valuable service, since not many cities can operate adequate testing bureaus. The bureau will make performance tests on all kinds of material and equipment at cost. It also provides cities with model building, fire, plumbing, elevator, and other codes.

The Bureau of Mines and Environmental Protection Agency give technical advice on air-pollution problems. The Civil Aeronautics Administration tells city officials about the uses to which they might put airplanes or furnishes them with a model airport-zoning ordinance and may even give them a surplus federal airport. The General Services Administration sells surplus federal buildings to cities at "50 percent off."

The U.S. Public Health Service furnishes a host of things: advice on sanitation problems; technical assistance; grants for planning and loans for constructing sewage-treatment plants to overcome water pollution; advice on organizing and staffing a municipal health department; and cash grants through the state for research on heart disease.

FBI agents not only arrest law violators who have left the state, but they testify without charge as experts on handwriting, tire treads, hairs and fibers, and shoe prints. The local police can find out from them without charge the marks made by a certain typewriter or the kind of headlight glass used in a 1972 Toyota. The FBI academy trains city police officers to serve as instructors in local police academies, while the Bureau of Narcotics instructs uninformed police officers in drug identification and enforcement methods at the bureau's training school.

[14] See R. H. Blundred and D. W. Hanks, *Federal Services to Cities and Towns,* American Municipal Association, Chicago, 1950, from which the following illustrations are drawn. Some of them may have since been discontinued; others have been added.

Many other federal agencies cooperate with local officials from time to time, giving advice or assistance upon request. Local administrators can go to Housing and Urban Development for advice on problems of race relations in public housing; to the Bureau of Prisons for methods of designing, building, and operating a jail; to the Public Roads Administration for help with a parking survey; to the Bureau of Ships for help in learning how to fight a harbor fire; to the Fish and Wildlife Service for surplus bison and elk for the local zoo; and to the Curator of the Navy for a list showing the shipping weights and handling charges on obsolete warships for the city park. These are only a few of the total number of services available.

Federal Approval of Municipal Activities

The city, in its proprietary capacity, often acts as an ordinary corporation, and when it does so, it must get federal approval wherever such approval would be necessary in the case of a private corporation. When federal grants-in-aid are involved, the city must often get approval from the appropriate federal agency for governmental functions, too. For example, if a city operates a radio station, it must get a Federal Communications Commission license; if it builds a freeway with the aid of federal funds, it must have the proposed route approved by the Public Roads Administration; if it builds a bridge, it must have the plans approved by the Corps of Engineers. Municipal administrators thus have frequent and varied contacts with federal agencies.

The list of federal supervisory controls is almost endless. However, it would be wrong to conclude that the federal government makes all the rules in American society. The areas of federal control are relatively few, and it is not politically expedient for Congress or federal administrators to seek to impose many effective policy controls upon the states or their subdivisions. In fact, many—perhaps most—administrators do not even want to have coercive powers of this kind. But where they exist, federal controls are often absolutely necessary. State and local radio stations, for example, could not operate effectively without being coordinated with commercial stations. Other rules are not viewed with alarm by state and local administrators because their sense of professional standards agrees with the sense of professional standards of the federal enployees with whom they deal. They therefore see themselves as being involved in a cooperative venture to apply professional standards and do not feel coerced. This was the finding, for example, of the Michigan "Little Hoover" Commission study in 1950. Furthermore, despite the impression sometimes created, federal administrators usually try to be reasonable in administering the law and seek to work out problems jointly rather than by fiat. Still, in the event of an unresolved difference between a federal agency and the state or local government with which it is dealing, the federal requirements must be met if the state or local government wishes to qualify for federal aid.

The Federal Government and Suburbia

Among the federal programs that have had a great impact on metropolitan areas is that guaranteeing banks against loss on home loans made through the Federal Housing Administration (FHA) and, later after World War II, the Veterans'

Administration. Note that no grants to cities or states are involved in these programs. These low-interest mortgages made possible the middle- and working-class move to suburbia. Few other urban programs of the federal government have been so successful in achieving their goal or have had a greater impact on the pattern or quality of urban life.

Federal Grants-in-Aid to Cities

The most visible impact of the federal government on cities has been through grants that encourage states, cities, or other local governments to undertake certain programs. Such funds may be quite specific or very general in their requirements.

The form federal grants take determines the degree of freedom of choice of urban officials. The most restrictive grants are called "categorical aids." In these a problem is identified, for example, blindness, and money is allocated to establish specific programs to deal with that problem. A less strict form of grant is called a "project grant." The urban administrator must prepare a grant proposal which may be either funded or denied. Examples are urban renewal and some public health grants. In these, each proposal must deal with a specific problem, but some local variation may be introduced. Nevertheless the federal agency usually provides specific guidelines for such grants, and often the urban administrator finds in a visit to Washington that informal guidelines also exist as to the kind of proposals that will be most favorably received. A looser type of control is exercised through what are called "block grants." In these, a broad area of problems is designated, for example, housing and community development, and funds are allocated to every community in the nation. Local officials must devise programs that fit into the loose guidelines and when they do so, they qualify for a fund allocation. The least restrictive grant of all is that with few or no requirements on what the funds may be spent. The current example is in so-called "revenue sharing."

Under the New Deal of the 1930s, grants to state and local governments were categorical grants. The period of the 1960s, of the "Great Society," favored wider use of project grants, partly because it was believed this would result in more innovative programs. The Nixon administration, responding in part to the desire for more local freedom of choice and in part to complaints about preparing detailed applications which might later be denied, encouraged trying block ("revenue-sharing") grants.

Major Urban Grant Programs

The Department of Housing and Urban Development (HUD) at its inception announced that metropolitan-wide planning would be a principal aim to be accomplished by its grant program. It was thus continuing federal policy that, since the Housing Act of 1954, had provided for the funding of substate regional-planning organizations. The Metropolitan Development Act of 1966, the "Model Cities" program, required a statement by a state or regional-planning agency that the project did not conflict with regional plans. In the Intergovernmental Cooperation Act of 1968, funds were extended for regional planning in nonmetropolitan areas. Second, HUD has been concerned with the construction of public housing in recent years, particularly in the suburbs. It has moved from the early New-Deal plans for large-tract and high-rise development to experimenting with scattered units within communities and rent-supplement plans. Of importance in its potential impact on city life are, in addition, the programs of the Department of Transportation, established in 1967. In 1973 for the first time, part of the Federal Highway Trust Fund was allocated to mass transit. In 1974, the Urban Mass Transportation Assistance Act, signed by President Ford, provided for an \$11.8 billion program to aid mass-transit systems over a six-year period. Another agency with a major impact on the quality of urban life is the Department of Health, Education and Welfare. But most federal agencies now have some urban programs. Even the Department of Agriculture, through involvement in the food-stamp and school-lunch programs, has influence on the quality of urban life.

The agencies concerned with the social problems of large cities have been more controversial than those working on urban beauty and transportation.[15] The Office of Economic Opportunity (OEO) was established in 1964 as a unit of the Executive Office of the President. Its program has been to fight poverty. One of its most ambitious programs was Project Head Start, begun in 1965 in 2,500 urban and rural communities. The program was to prepare children for schooling and included educational stimulation, medical checkups and treatment, and an attack on dietary problems. About one-half of the antipoverty funds were dedicated to a community-action program designed to help the poor help themselves. It included literary courses for adults, birth-control clinics, legal aid, and the Head Start project. A domestic peace corps named VISTA (Volunteers in Service to America) was also established to aid economically depressed areas.

In 1974, antipoverty programs of the OEO were extended for three years. These included Head Start, Follow Through, and Community Economic Development. But funds were reduced and the community-action programs were placed in a new agency, the Community Services Administration, within the Department of Health, Education and Welfare. Earlier, Model Cities was replaced by "revenue sharing," along with housing, urban renewal, open-space parks and recreation, and water and sewage programs.

A continuing controversy concerns whether federal grants permitting great independence to urban officials and administrators reach the most serious problems of urban areas, particularly the problems of core cities. The initial experience under "revenue sharing" (the State and Local Fiscal Assistance Act of 1972) was that the core cities at best broke even; their new revenue-sharing funds barely were sufficient to replace funds lost from discontinued programs. Some cities ended up with less. Earliest reports of spending patterns showed some shift from human-aid functions to purchase of physical facilities, particularly to the

[15] See Seymour Z. Mann, *Chicago's War on Poverty,* Center for Research in Urban Government, Loyola University, Chicago, May, 1966; and Norton E. Long, "Urban Poverty and Public Policy," *Business and Government Review,* University of Missouri, July–August, 1964, pp. 31–38.

purchase of police cars and equipment. It should be noted, though, that such purchases are nonrecurring budget items, as opposed to expenditures in operating programs which, once made, tend to become an ongoing budget commitment. The proposals made under the Housing and Community Development Act of 1974 have also been criticized because of their emphasis on middle-class amenities at a time when low-income housing is in short supply.[16]

Federal-City Relations and Urban Problems

The trend, established in the 1930s, toward closer and more direct federal-city relations and increased financial aid to cities seems destined to continue and eventually to expand. This is so for several reasons: (1) federal agencies have a great potential for assisting cities because they have both specialized personnel and equipment which the cities need but cannot afford, or are unwilling to afford, and often cannot get from the state; (2) legislatures have often closed their eyes to the financial problems of the core cities, while the national government has met the call, at least to a degree—and if the national government has helped a few times when the states have failed, it is likely to be asked for help again; (3) the present level of taxes and the nature of the tax structure leave both the municipalities and the states in a position that will put them in financial distress in the event of even a moderate depression, and it is therefore likely that, in "bad times," cities will ask for increased federal government assistance.

Two continuing issues are: (1) Is it proper or desirable for the national government to deal directly with the cities, bypassing the parent state government? (2) What can or should the national government do to improve the financial condition of cities? Concerning the former, critics ask: What damage is done by direct dealing? Does the state perform a function other than to provide another desk with an "in" and "out" box? Does direct relationship encourage greater federal control of cities? Might Washington one day seize the state's children and adopt them forcibly? If the cities refuse federal aid, or the states refuse to permit them federal aid (as has happened in some cases involving urban planning, housing, and airports aid), how long must the cities wait before the states provide what their leaders consider to be adequate substitute legislation? Others maintain that coordination of programs can best be accomplished by state or perhaps substate units, closer to the problem areas than Washington, D.C.

Concerning the financial needs of cities and federal government power, there are several questions. Since federal instrumentalities are not taxable by the states, are present federal payments in lieu of taxes to cities equitable? Is the federal subsidy to cities in the form of tax exemption for income from municipal bonds a rational basis for aid? If not, what should be substituted? What tax areas should the national government stay out of and leave to the cities? What kind of grant-in-aid and what size should the national government provide for cities beyond those already provided for? How much of the fiddler's bill is the national

[16] On the tendency for American democracy to favor the middle classes over the poor, see Charles R. Adrian and Charles Press, *American Politics Reappraised,* McGraw-Hill Book Company, New York, 1974.

government willing to pay while still allowing the city governments to call the tune?

An even more important question is what the federal purpose should be in urbanized areas. Its thrust has been to a greater or lesser degree redistributive. It increasingly sees the alleviation of the desperate plight of many core-city residents as a first requirement for improving the quality of urbanized living for all Americans.

A Closing Note

In an interdependent, technological society such as America is today, the major functions of government can be performed only through the joint activity and cooperation of national, state, and local governments. It is not a question of which level is to carry on these functions but rather of how all three may effectively aid and participate. This is true in education, highways, health, welfare, housing, airports, law enforcement, and other functions. The future will see more, rather than less, cooperation among the three levels of government in the United States.

SELECTED READINGS

Advisory Commission on Intergovernmental Relations: *Regional Decision Making: New Strategies for Substate Districts,* Washington, 1973.

Anderson, William, and Edward W. Weidner (eds.): *Research in Intergovernmental Relations,* The University of Minnesota Press, Minneapolis, 1950–1960. (A series of monographs reporting on relationships in Minnesota.)

Cleaveland, Frederic N., and others: *Congress and Urban Problems,* The Brookings Institution, Washington, 1969. (Congressional response to urban problems.)

Farkas, Suzanne: *Urban Lobbying: Mayors in the Federal Area,* New York University Press, New York, 1971.

Feld, Richard D, and Carl Gragton (eds.): *The Uneasy Partnership: The Dynamics of Federal, State, and Urban Relations,* National Press Books, Palo Alto, Calif., 1973. (The impact of the federal system on urban issues.)

Graves, W. Brooke: *Intergovernmental Relations in the United States,* Legislative Reference Service, Library of Congress, 1956. (An important source book.)

Gulick, Luther H.: *The Metropolitan Problem and American Ideas,* Alfred A. Knopf, Inc., New York, 1966. (A proposal concerning federal-local relationships in light of American ideology.)

Kaplan, Marshall, and others: *The Model Cities Program,* Praeger Publishers, New York, 1970. (A study of the first year of this federally funded program in three cities.)

Long, Norton E.: *The Unwalled City, Reconstituting the Urban Community,* Basic Books, Inc., New York, 1972.

Lowi, Theodore: *The End of Liberalism: Ideology, Policy and the Crisis of Public Authority,* W. W. Norton & Company, Inc., New York, 1969.

Martin, Roscoe C.: *The Cities and the Federal System,* Atherton Press, New York, 1965. (Argues for a cooperative approach to urban problems by all levels of government.)

Moynihan, Daniel P. (ed.): *Toward a National Urban Policy,* Basic Books, Inc., New York, 1970.

Nathan, Richard P., and others: *Monitoring Revenue Sharing,* The Brookings Institution, Washington, 1975.

Oakland Task Force: *Federal Decision-making and Impact in Urban Areas,* Praeger Publishers, New York, 1970. (Study in Oakland, Calif.; shows that federal programs lose much of their effectiveness because of procedural and coordination problems.)

Reagan, Michael D.: *The New Federalism,* Oxford University Press, New York, 1972.

Riker, William H.: *Federalism: Origin, Operation, Significance,* Little, Brown and Company, Boston, 1964. (Challenges the populistic interpretation given early in this century by Charles Beard.)

Schroth, Thomas N., and others: *Congress and the Nation, 1945–1964,* Congressional Quarterly Service, Washington, 1965, chaps. 4 and 10. (Excellent summary of federal-local relationships in the last generation. See also supplements.)

Segal, Morley, and A. Lee Fritschler: "Emerging Patterns of Intergovernmental Relations," *Municipal Year Book,* International City Management Association, Washington, 1970.

Sundquist, James L., and David W. Davis: *Making Federalism Work,* The Brookings Institution, Washington, 1969. (Study of twenty-nine decentralized programs, analyzing why some worked better than others.)

Virginia's Answers to Congressional Questions on State and Federal Authority, Virginia Commission on Constitutional Government, Richmond, 1963. (The states' rights, or competitive, view of federalism.)

Wildavsky, Aaron (ed.): *American Federalism in Perspective,* Little, Brown and Company, Boston, 1967.

F

The Routine and the Money

Chapter 12

Administration

Administration is a part of the political process. The term generally applies to that process of government involved in the application of general policies to specific cases.[1] Administration takes place through the organization of persons, usually those having special skills or knowledge, into a formal working group in which persons are ordered on a hierarchical basis. This administrative structure, or bureaucracy, has its own values, goals, standards, and accepted procedures. It is held together informally through a sense of dedication to professional standards of work.

DEVELOPMENTS IN ADMINISTRATION

The Growth of Administration

To have an understanding of the great size and influence of modern public management, it is necessary to compare the functions of local government today with those of, say, two generations ago. In 1913, local governments provided

[1] See, in general, Nicholas Henry (ed.), *Public Administration and Public Affairs,* Prentice-Hall, Inc., Englewood Cliffs, N. J., 1975; Dwight Waldo, *The Study of Public Administration,* Random House, Inc., New York, 1955.

much of the education of the day through the one-room school, offering minimal programs taught by poorly trained and largely inexperienced teachers who received low pay. Roads, another major expenditure program today, were largely cared for by the local unit two generations ago. They were often unsurfaced and required little care in the preautomobile age. Most states had little to do with highways before the beginnings of the good-roads movement and the adoption of the first federal-aid Highway Act. The mentally ill received no rehabilitative treatment in those days. They were given custodial care in ramshackle asylums run by untrained persons who received patronage appointments from the city, county, or state. Some patients were housed in the local jail. Welfare was a local function provided reluctantly and at the bare subsistence level; the states kept out of the field except for some institutional care. In general, state government was distant and had few direct contacts with the ordinary citizen. Local government was more active and spent more—about 6.6 times as much as state government—but it was a thin shadow of its present-day self as a supplier of services to the citizen. The growth in the activities of state governments has been the more spectacular, but both the state and local governments have become vitally important social institutions affecting the lives of each citizen each day. Public employees perform functions vastly more complicated and technical than those handled by the public bureaucracy of their grandparents' day.

The Historical Trend

Some of the developments in administrative organization have been noted earlier in this book.[2] We have seen that the legislatures at first dominated government at both the state and local levels. As legislative bodies and city councils declined in prestige and importance during the nineteenth century, they were replaced both by the direct democracy of the initiative and referendum and by a large number of elective administrative officials. Both of these trends contributed to the development of the long ballot.

As the number of governmental functions increased, so did the number of governmental agencies. Each new function tended to be established in a separate agency, usually in order to give it protection against the competing fiscal demands of the older, better-established functions. The interest groups which secured the adoption of new programs and policies generally preferred this arrangement. The more populous cities were once highly departmentalized, though reorganizations resulting from the adoption of the strong-mayor, council-manager, or commission forms have generally decreased the number of separate municipal agencies.[3] The rising number of agencies resulted after a while in a problem of accountability. It became highly difficult for the chief executive, the council member, or the citizen to know what was being done in the agencies or who was responsible for their activities.

[2] See Chaps. 2 and 7. This account borrows from York Willbern, "Administration in State Governments," in The American Assembly, *The Forty-eight States: Their Tasks as Policy Makers and Administrators,* Graduate School of Business, Columbia University, New York, 1955, chap. 5.

[3] See Chap. 7.

Administrative Developments

The municipal-reorganization movement began in the 1890s and, to a degree, even earlier. It was concerned with both the eradication of corruption and the stopping of administrative sprawl. Administrative reorganization of states, counties, and other nonschool local units followed along at a much slower pace.

The Assumptions of the Reform Movement

Nearly all the reform efforts at the state and local levels have concentrated upon making administrative changes that have been based upon the following assumptions:[4]

1 Authority and responsibility should be concentrated in the chief executive officers by placing the heads of agencies under their authority and subject to their appointment, removal, and control. This was perhaps the most basic assumption and proved to be the most difficult to achieve. Groups wishing to dominate the governmental administration of their interests have feared, probably with justification, that executive unity would increase the executive's power at the expense of their own. In cities, the dominant groups were more unified than at the county or state levels, and they wanted what they considered businesslike efficiency. As a result, strong mayors and city managers generally were given wide (but rarely complete) administrative powers, but governors were not; and counties remained without a chief executive of any kind.

2 Related functions should be integrated into single departments, and the number of departments should be few enough to permit the executive to require direct accountability from the department head. Reformers complained that there were often many agencies performing functions in the same general field with little coordination, effective planning, or responsibility.

3 Boards and commissions might properly be used for advisory, but not for administrative, purposes. Boards sometimes serve as quasi-legislative or quasi-judicial bodies; that is, they act much as legislative or judicial bodies. This type of activity arose, for example, in the case of public service commissions which had to establish rates for public utilities, and were considered acceptable. In weak-mayor cities, these boards were and still are common devices for administration.

4 Budget control should be centralized under the direction of the chief executive with auditing under the legislative body. Some characteristics of the executive budget are discussed in Chapter 13. This administrative device has had widespread acceptance in principle and has had perhaps the greatest effect of any single development upon executive control over agencies. Budget staffs, in the larger cities at least, have become the general-management arm of the chief executive, not only reviewing the budget estimates of the agencies, but also aiding in coordinating their activities. Budget offices have become important agencies for administrative supervision, though they generally have only a limited amount of control over expenditures by the departments. They apportion funds over the fiscal year and exercise certain minor controls, but they are not usually in a legal or political position to claim sweeping jurisdiction over detailed expenditures.

[4] Arthur E. Buck, *The Reorganization of State Governments in the United States,* Columbia University Press, New York, 1938, gives a complete statement of the orthodox view.

The check-and-balance tradition has been maintained through the establishment of an independent audit—independent, that is, of the executive branch.

5 The staff services of administration should be coordinated, usually through central agencies, to serve all the operating departments. This principle has received more acceptance than the others. The reason is to be found in the fact that the centralizing of housekeeping functions has been thought to be a means of saving money without the loss of policy influence by the interest groups watching over the individual agency. As a result there has been a strong trend toward the central purchasing of materials and supplies (large-volume buying brings lower prices); the operation of central warehouses, records archives, motor pools, and mailing and telephone services; and the central maintenance of buildings and grounds. Personnel recruitment has also been centralized to a considerable degree.

6 An executive cabinet should be established as a device for the coordination of governmental agencies. Cabinet members should be appointed by the chief executive, rather than elected, so that he or she might hold them responsible for their acts.

Forces for Separatism

Many forces are at work to discourage reorganization. Some of these include the following:

Agencies prefer a maximum of autonomy. A department head feels he or she will lose status if the agency becomes merely one of many bureaus in a larger department. He or she is likely to argue, from conviction, that the agency is unique both as to function and as to the process by which it performs its service, or may claim, with interest-group representatives shouting "Amen" in the background, that the integration of the agency with another will result in a lower level of service to its clientele groups.

1 There is a strong tradition of separate responsibility to the electorate for many functions of government. Generally, the public prefers to elect an officer who has traditionally been elected, even when the functions of the officer are obscure. Many voters believe that direct election is more democratic than appointment by the chief executive. Political leaders like to have several elective offices on the ballot, since this enables them to develop a slate with widespread racial, ethnic, or geographic appeal.

2 The clean-up campaigns that follow scandals often result in recommendations that encourage separatism. The usual suggestion is that the tainted function should be separated from the rest of government, given autonomous status, and "taken out of politics."

3 Clientele and interest groups normally prefer to have the function of their special concern separated from the rest of government. This preference also encourages the use of separate or "dedicated" funds. Pilots prefer a separate airport commission to a vast parks and recreation agency or public works agency involved in a dozen different activities. Their interest groups can more easily dominate policy under the former structure, but the department head or the chief executive is more likely to do so under the latter. Citizens are often in favor of the principle of "improved administration" but opposed to specific proposals that

would alter the existing pattern of operation of governmental functions in which they have interests.

4 Professional groups prefer separate organization for the functions that they regard as being a part of their profession. These groups have "organized bodies of knowledge, generally available only to members; group standards of training and performance; codes of ethical conduct; and particularly, close group ties and associations."[5] Under these circumstances, they believe that their goals, procedures, and knowledge can best be organized to benefit their clientele groups if their function is not commingled with others. Librarians do not want libraries to be administered by the school board; penologists do not want the local jail administered by the same agency that handles social welfare.

5 The strings attached to federal grants-in-aid encourage a link between federal and state and local administrators of functions, but they discourage the association of various state and local programs into a single agency. In some cases, federal-grant conditions require the establishment of earmarked or dedicated funds, which in turn encourages separate organization. (The coming of "revenue sharing" will not change this significantly.)

6 Citizens and legislators often believe that certain special programs should be placed "above politics" and hence in a separate agency. This has been true of fair-employment-practices activities, liquor control, and education, among others.

7 Legislators are reluctant to give greater power to the chief executives. They are jealous of their glamour, political power, and policy-leadership potential. Urban chief executives have been less subjected than governors to this kind of suspicion, partly because council members in cities where the reform movement has been influential, many of them busy in business or the professions, do not want to be involved in the details of administration, and partly because of the widespread use of the council-manager plan, which keeps managers always potentially subject to control by the council, since they are not independent agents with a direct popular mandate.

8 Americans have generally been suspicious of strong administrative leaders and have been more concerned with specific functions than with the abstract principle of efficient, well-coordinated government in general. Many people believe that mayors are not usually elected on the basis of issues and that turning full administrative power over to them is as uncomfortable as signing a blank check. Managers have always been viewed with suspicion because of their great power, though this feeling is, in most cities, confined to a minority of voters.

Separatism of agencies remains the rule in state and county government because of the diversity of interests and forces involved in the political arena. In cities, the dominant groups have generally preferred integration and, with some qualifications, have been able to achieve it through the strong-mayor and council-manager plans. Groups for separatism have seldom been strong enough to prevail.

The Arguments for Integration

Persons supporting reorganization movements have used two principal arguments to support their cause: (1) Integration will produce coordinated govern-

[5] Willbern, *op. cit.*, p. 116.

mental activities; and (2) responsibility to the public will be increased. It is sometimes held that there is really not much to coordinate in government. How much coordination, it is asked, is needed between those who work in the department of streets and those who work in the department of public health? The concept of coordination, it is held, goes beyond this, however. It involves more than the bringing about of cooperation between, say, the psychiatric social workers in the public welfare department and the psychiatric social social workers in the juvenile section of the probate court. Coordination also makes possible the economies of joint housekeeping activities and of the balancing off, in the executive budget, of the relative priorities of various functions of government. The chief executive is the only feasible person available to perform the role of coordinator.

The argument on responsibility is based upon the assumption that there should be but a single legitimate source of authority, the chief executive, and that the lieutenants should receive their authority from this executive. If this is the case, authority and accountability are equal to one another. Authority cannot be exercised, in the words of the Hoover Commission, unless there is a "clear line of command from the top to the bottom and a return line of responsibility and accountability from the bottom to the top."[6]

Government, its services, and its many clientele groups are all too complicated for a simple, single line of responsibility, of course. Most of those who would reorganize government recognize this, but they argue that "a general responsibility to the general public interest may be better achieved through the main line of political responsibility . . . than through the limited, specific, hidden responsibilities involved in some of the other relationships." Government, it is held, becomes more visible, and hence more subject to public scrutiny, if there is a single chief executive to be held accountable.

The Middle Ground

Once again, things are never completely black or completely white in politics. Total integration is probably never possible, and not even the most enthusiastic reorganizer could argue that separatism is the equivalent of anarchy. As York Willbern has said:[7]

> Separatism and integration are not opposites without middle ground. Neither is ever absolute. Even with an agency that appears completely independent, the [chief executive] may have much influence simply because he has produced a majority of the popular votes, has influence with the legislature, and has public prestige and constitutional responsibilities. And even in an agency over which the [chief executive] appears to have complete control, the influence of a special clientele, of the group connections and thought habits of employees, of interested [councils], and of intergovernmental relationships all will be of incalculable importance. Agencies will be grouped all along the spectrum from nearly complete independence to nearly complete subordination to central political control.

[6] Quoted in Willbern, *op. cit.,* p. 120.

[7] *Ibid.,* p. 121. Willbern was discussing state government, but the comment applies equally to municipalities.

The precise details of agency organization differ according to such things as historical accident, the wants and needs of the clientele of a particular agency, the desires of interest groups, and the personal idiosyncrasies of transient administrators, chief executives, and legislators. Because differing points of view are often held by various interested parties, questions as to whether an agency will be headed by a board or by a single administrator, the manner in which board appointments, if any, are to be made, who is to be represented on the board, the internal structure of the agency, and other such considerations are a matter not so much of deliberate planning as of negotiation among the interested parties.[8] The politics of the organization of an agency, in other words, follows the same pattern as that by which the policies of the agency are determined.

ADMINISTRATION AND CULTURE

Administration cannot be wholly scientific or neutral. It must be related to the values of the culture in which it exists. The manner in which a social-welfare, police, or educational system is administered will depend upon cultural values of the contemporary society. There is no "one best way" to care for people on welfare, for example. The level of assistance they get, whether the needs of children or of old people are emphasized, the amount of outside income that is permitted by overlooking the precise requirements of the law, the amount of training which social workers are expected to have, the philosophy of social workers toward society, government, and, in particular, toward those at the lower end of the social scale—all these things will be condition by the culture in which the program exists.

The Administrative Process

Administration is a part of the political process, not an activity fundamentally different from it. The determination of policy in the legislative body will at the same time inevitably involve questions of the means of carrying out policy. Similarly, the execution of policy always involves modification of the policy and its selective application to actual circumstances as they arise.

It should not be assumed that the degree of specialization of equipment, training of personnel, or types of organizational structure employed in a governmental unit are irrelevant. They are important variables in determining the level and cost of services, no doubt, but the kinds of equipment used, the training expected of personnel, the organizational structure, and the level of service itself that exists in connection with a given governmental function are a result of a balancing off of public attitudes, the values of those who are involved in the decision making within the legislature, the city council, and the administrative organization, and the expectations and goals of interested pressure groups. It will probably never be possible to eliminate these political considerations and to

[8] On this point, see Robert A. Dahl and Charles E. Lindbolm, *Politics, Economics and Welfare,* Harper & Row, Publishers, Incorporated, New York, 1953.

replace them with objective criteria as to how an agency should be organized and operated.

Efficiency as a Point of View

There is no one best way to administer a program or a governmental unit. This is so because the best way to one individual may be the worst way to another. It is a matter of point of view. For example, a management consultant might be asked to inspect a city health department and make recommendations as to its proper administrative structure and processes. Because, in private business, one is expected to look for ways of reducing costs and strengthening the hand of management, the consultant may see a "one best way" to organize the agency. But these recommendations, if adopted, might not only upset established lines of communication and operation—thus threatening to damage the esprit de corps of the agency—they might also threaten to weaken the influence that an important interest group (in this case, the state or local medical society) might have over the agency. This threat would certainly result in damage-control operations on the part of the interest group. It would take its case to the council or the legislature.

Who would be right in this case—the management consultant or the medical society? Who can say? If the medical society refuses to cooperate with the agency, its whole program may founder. The medical society might claim that the proposal would discourage young people from going into the medical profession. The society might be right or it might be wrong in making the claim. It might be sincere in advancing the claim, or it might simply be seeking to retain its traditional monopolistic control over medical practice and programs. Suppose that it is right and does really mean what it says. Are the few dollars that the management consultant would save for the reorganized agency—assuming that the proposal would save money—worth more to society than the social cost of a decreased supply of medical workers?

There might well be other potential effects of the proposal by the management consultant, too. For dozens of reasons that cannot be examined in detail here, the proposal, if adopted, might have the ultimate effect of reducing the scope or effectiveness of the end program of the agency, the actual services it provides for society and its members, individually and collectively. Thus, what is said to be saving money may really be a downgrading of the program, either as an intended or as an unanticipated result. The latter may come about because of changes in training requirements or pay levels or prospects for advancement or other factors involving recruiting potential and employee morale.

This example should not be taken to mean that the concept of efficiency is meaningless or that a review of administrative structure and practice could not result in improvements. To use an exaggerated illustration, it might be found that a health department is using physicians in laboratory work that could readily be done by technicians. It is doubtful if many undesirable results would follow a reclassification of such positions. Yet one could not say this for certain without an extensive examination of the whole environment in which the circumstance is found.

ORGANIZATION

Municipal-government agencies may be organized in a great variety of ways. Some of them are headed by an elective officer. Some have a single administrator appointed by, and responsible to, the chief executive. In other cases, the administrator may be chosen by the chief executive but may be removable only by a complicated process involving perhaps the civil service commission or the courts. In a fourth category are the agencies headed by boards or commissions. (The two terms mean the same.) Board members are usually appointed for long, staggered terms, and the chief executive may find members to be irremovable for practical purposes. When a board controls, an agency may be administered in a variety of ways. The chairman of the board may also serve as the chief administrator of the agency; the board may choose an executive secretary or a director, with its own powers reserved in law or practice to board policy making; the commission may be advisory only, with the chief executive appointing the administrative head; but the most common arrangement has been for the board to divide up its work among its members, each exercising considerable autonomy. Each of these structures of the boards is likely to produce a different pattern of administration.

The Administrative Code of the City

The administrative organization of cities in the past was established in state law. Changes could be made only by the legislature. Functions assigned to a particular department could not be changed to another department by order of the mayor or council, no matter how much of an improvement in municipal services might result from the proposed change. This is still the case in some states. Even in home rule cities, administrative structure can often be changed only by the local charter-amending procedures.

Modern charters, however, do not attempt to establish a rigid departmental structure but rather authorize the council to adopt an administrative code for the city establishing a plan of organization. The council is then able to rearrange departments, bureaus, and lesser agencies as changing requirements dictate. This practice is not yet the rule, however. Often city officials must go to the state legislature with a request for authority to transfer garbage collection, for example, from the public health department to the public works department. Even in home rule cities, the public is often expected to decide by referendum such things as whether there should be a separate department of traffic engineering or whether central purchasing should be consolidated with the controller's office. Some specialists believe that many decisions on administrative organization might well be left to the chief executive, without even council action being required.

A complete administrative code or manual is useful in all except perhaps small cities not only to describe basic structure, but for another reason: It explains the responsibilities and authority of the various departments and their principal officers.

The Choice of Organization: A Problem

It is not only difficult to determine the best organizational structure, it is equally a problem to determine the allocation of functions within agencies or the best place to assign new functions. For example, in the 1970s, many local officials became interested in the establishment of programs dealing with the problems of the poor. These programs cut across traditional department lines, since they deal with housing, welfare, health, employment, and many other things. How should the program be established in order to minimize conflict with existing programs and organizational patterns? What organizational pattern would best fit the needs of the aged and be most acceptable to their interest groups? The answer is not easy to find, but there is a strong tendency to establish new programs as separate organizations. This usually best suits the interests involved and seems to give the new program its best chance for survival.

Single Agency Head As compared with other types of organization, in that where an individual serves as head of an agency and is appointed by the chief executive, the agency programs are likely to be more diversified, more related to the overall balance of needs in the annual budget, less able to avoid cuts during an economy drive, more involved in the decisions that are important to the political future of the mayor or council members, less dominated by one interest group, and more easily shaken out of bureaucratic lethargy by a chief executive who is necessarily concerned with public reactions to governmental programs.

Independent Head When the head of an agency is independent of the chief executive because he or she is elected to office, cannot easily be removed, or is a career civil servant, the agency is likely to develop a strong in-group sense against the rest of the government, professional standards are likely to be the criteria used as an important measuring stick in making decisions, and bureaucratic inertia, if it becomes very great, cannot easily be overcome because of the difficulty of exerting pressure from outside. The agency becomes largely insulated from ordinary controls, although it will usually have to seek to maintain good relations with the legislative body unless it can find some means of obtaining an independent budget. Agencies with independent heads often include parks, police, social-welfare, or public health departments, although other examples also exist.

Boards and Commissions

The use of boards and commissions became widespread after the Civil War. This marked a transition from control of departments by council committees to control by the chief executive—a transition more nearly completed in cities than in state or local units of government. It also reflected a desire to take government "out of politics." Boards were either bipartisan or, later, nonpartisan in structure, members were usually appointed for long and overlapping terms, and their removal from office was normally extremely difficult.

Librarians, educators, and other professional people strongly favor independent boards over their departments. Powerful and vociferous pressure groups often wish to take functions under their wings and protect them as infants that should not be exposed to the rigorous and competitive circumstances of the ordinary governmental agency. An attempt to make the agency autonomous almost always exists in the case of functions involving special-interest groups or special-clientele groups. Other instances of this sort of thing may be found in connection with the functions of public health, public transportation, airports, parks and recreation, art galleries, and museums.

Boards and commissions seem quite inappropriate for the direct administration of any agency, and the tendency to organize in this fashion is declining. On the other hand, a board chairman, if he or she possesses administrative skill, can sometimes serve adequately as the agency head. It is not uncommon in agencies which have boards as policy-making bodies for most of the policies ultimately adopted to be generated within the bureaucracy of the agency and to be "sold" to the commission by the administrative head. In some cases, as in public health, the board views its principal job as being that of preserving orthodoxy and preventing the administrative head, who may be a layman, from doing something the profession would not approve of.

Many boards and commissions are established by law in such a way as to require interest-group representation upon them. In other cases, it is a firmly established custom for certain groups to be included in the membership. The idea of group representation seems antithetical to the traditional American skepticism about "the interests" and "special privilege," but it is very much a basic part of our political pattern.[9]

An Evaluation of Boards Millions of hours are probably spent in the United States each year by unpaid citizens serving on advisory and policy-controlling boards at the state and local levels of government. What do they accomplish? These were the findings of a study of Pennsylvania:[10]

1 Boards "study complex problems to which the elected body cannot devote enough time."

2 They insulate the legislative body and executive from certain types of political pressures. Since the members are (usually) nonelective, they can more easily do things that are thought necessary and desirable but which, in the short run at least, might be politically unpopular.

3 They do not "take politics out of important areas" of government.

4 The effectiveness of the boards depends upon the quality of the members "and not upon the advisory commission device itself."

5 They provide, especially at the local level, a great amount of staff work which, if paid for, would be very expensive. They, in other words, serve to socialize some of the cost of government.

6 Members perceive their jobs rather narrowly, tending to avoid performing a function about which they are in doubt. That is, they do not engage in "empire building."

7 Members often feel that they are not consulted frequently enough, that their advice is too freely ignored, and that they are not informed of the disposition made of their recommendations.

8 For things requiring decisive action and, outside of the work done by boards of adjustment, civil service commissions, and planning commissions, the

[9] See Alfred de Grazia, *Public and Republic,* Alfred A. Knopf, Inc., New York, 1951.
[10] *Horizons,* 5:1, April, 1958.

professional administrative staff of a department works more "efficiently" than can boards.

9 "Citizens boards and commissions can still offer effective and useful aid to officials and the community."

The larger a city is, the more likely it is to use boards and commissions.[11] This is probably also generally true of other local units. In weak-mayor cities, they are especially likely to have formal policy-making powers that exceed mere advisory status.

The reason for the existence of advisory boards in the structure of the more populous units of government stems from the old problem of citizens having less opportunity to know their officials personally when population density is high. There is, at the same time, less opportunity to participate directly in policy making. The citizens group serves in lieu of the direct consultation between officeholder and constituent that is typical in the small suburb or the rural township. It provides a measuring stick by which public reactions to programs can be gotten and a more gentle stick it is than the one that may otherwise rap the politician's knuckles at the next election. A cross section of ideas and of opinion can be furnished to those whose political life depends upon a proper assessment of community attitudes.

Boards and commissions are extremely useful to the chief executives whether they are elective mayors or appointed managers. For one thing, boards allow groups that are interested in a function to give positive advice to the administration through their appointed members. They might otherwise carp from the sidelines or complain at public hearings. For another, the use of boards involves a number of citizens in such a manner as to give them a stake in the success of an administration. This is a device that helps develop support for other programs of the chief executive in addition to the one in which the citizen is active as a member of a board. It also provides a built-in shock absorber so that the chief executive is protected from the full force of criticism against policy in a particular field. The chief executive can point out that, after all, "it was developed by the citizens on the committee," even though it may really have been a product of the fertile minds of the municipal bureaucracy and the advisory commission may merely have given its stamp of approval. And, of course, unpaid boards provide a socially acceptable form of patronage which adds to the number of persons who become obligated to defend the administration—a situation useful to the mayor who becomes a candidate for reelection, or to the manager who might run into difficulties with the council.

CHIEF EXECUTIVES

Chief executives are important in the administrative process, not alone because they may have the power to hire and fire department heads, but also because they coordinate a variety of different programs and interests. They are the principal

[11] R. B. Richert, "How Michigan Cities Make Use of Lay Citizens in Government," *Michigan Municipal Review,* 26:33ff., February, 1953.

architects of policy, and the liaison between the agencies that provide services and the clientele groups that receive them. This role is so crucial that a portion of Chapter 8 is devoted to it.

The Chief Executive's Personal Staff

In addition to major advisers, such as the budget officer, the city attorney (if appointed by the chief executive), and the planning director, and such advisory commissions as may exist, the chief executive usually, except in small cities, chooses a staff of personal advisers and assistants. These may include an administrative assistant or two, or sometimes, especially in manager cities, an intern trainee just graduated from a university training program. In larger cities, the chief executive may have a personal, confidential secretary and a number of stenographers and office assistants.

The staff of the chief executive has the task of helping the leader keep abreast of responsibilities. Needless to say, these persons are often more closely associated with an official's success or failure in office than are the department heads.

DEPARTMENT HEADS

Beneath the chief executive but above middle management and the clerical and minor employees are the principal administrators—the agency heads or heads of a large divisions. They play a vital role in policy formulation because they are likely to know the particular governmental activity better than the chief executive and the councilmembers do. If they do not, they have easy access to those who do. They advise the chief executive, who wants ideas on a program; they testify before the legislative body or its committees, telling them what they want them to know and often demonstrating great skill at withholding information unfavorable to any other point of view.

The Agency Head as a Symbol

The agency head, like the chief executive and members of the legislative body, spends a great deal of time in symbolic activities. While matters requiring a decision pile up on the desk, he or she trudges from one meeting to another, often spending an afternoon in the mayor's or manager's office, or in an interdepartmental meeting, or as an ex officio member of some board, or at a convention of a professional group with which the agency has important relations, making a comment here and there or perhaps a platitudinous speech of welcome. These activities follow much the same pattern as do those of principal executives in large corporations.

From a rational or "efficiency" point of view, this activity may seem enormously wasteful. Yet it is most important, for at the top level, the administrator (often one who has worked to the top and knows the tasks of the lesser positions within the agency) leaves to trusted aides much of the actual work that goes out. He or she spends most of the time in molding the agency members into an effective working unit; reassuring them of their importance by expressing their values in public speeches and by awarding a pin to the clerk-steno who has just completed thirty years of service; and in seeking to maintain smooth relationships between the agency and its clientele groups, its interest-group support, the chief executive, the council, the state legislature, and potential friends and enemies of all kinds. The principal job is to understand and to communicate to others the values, loyalties, and goals of the organization.

In the process of seeking to placate their various publics, the personnel in the various departments often come into conflict with one another. They compete over budgetary matters and in seeking status in the community. Some department heads feud publicly with other department heads—with resultant damage to all government, since the citizen is likely to believe the worst that each official says about other officials.

Because the status and even the survival of a government agency may depend upon the way it is perceived by the public, large local agencies maintain their own public relations staffs. Often these may not be large—the council will generally see to that—but they are important.

ADMINISTRATION AND THE PUBLIC

Public Relations in City Government

Much of the activity of everyday administration goes along with little or no notice taken of it by average citizens. Their knowledge of the services that are available to them, or of the nature of bureaucrats or of the administrative process, is likely to be very skimpy indeed. But average citizens do not automatically come by an understanding of these things. They must be told what their government is doing, and why.

It has already been noted that the political process involves not just one monolithic "public" but a series of publics, each demanding satisfactions. Citizens are rarely unanimous in their attitudes toward public matters, If they were, government officials would have few problems in public relations. Given the nature of the political process as involving the interaction of conflicting groups, public relations must normally be directed toward one or more of the interested groups in the community. Groups may be interested in municipal government because of their physical location within the community, their businesses, their tax bills, their income, their (high or low) status positions within the community, or other reasons. Each individual belongs to several publics and can become displeased with city government in connection with any one of them. He or she can also be informed about the activities of the city by being reached as a member of any one of these publics.

Municipal departments often have peculiar publics of their own, and each of them must therefore be conscious of the importance of public relations. Departments dealing with particular professional or clientele groups are especially likely to have uniquely identifiable publics. The welfare department, for example, must please (1) welfare recipients; (2) the high-status members of the community who take an interest in welfare as an avocation; (3) taxpayers who pay the bills; (4) editors or politicians who may want to take the occasional welfare cheats and make a headline case out of them; (5) grocers and others in business who have welfare recipients as customers; (6) professional social workers, who may want the department to be established as an autonomous agency; (7) ordinary citizens who are likely to believe that people on public relief are lazy, shiftless, and of a category akin to the criminal. The manager of the local airport must cope with publics that include passengers, pilots, airline officials, and people who live near airports or proposed airports; the health department must reach an understanding with the medical profession, with the Parent-Teachers Association and other pressure groups interested in the schools, with social reformers who want expanded public health services; and so on.

Gauging Public Attitudes The public officials who would keep their publics informed through an active public relations program must first of all be acquainted with the attitudes existing the community. This is no easy task to accomplish.

How can public officials go about gauging attitudes? They may employ one of the so-called public opinion polling organizations or alternatively establish a polling unit within, say, the city complaint department. But public opinion polling is quite a technical task and therefore requires specially trained personnel. It is also too expensive for most cities to finance. It is time-consuming, and the information is therefore often not available when it is needed. Perhaps most difficult of all, poll results that are unfavorable serve as ammunition for opponents of the administration, and this discourages their use.

Officials are therefore likely to turn to older methods of measurement, most of which are of doubtful reliability. All persons in the political arena, for example, engage in informal polling by noting the views expressed by visitors and letter writers. But these views may be highly unrepresentative and are of uncertain value at all times. Advisory bodies are often used as a means of measuring the attitudes and the intensity of attitudes of the important pressure group interested in a particular activity. Letters, petitions, and resolutions from groups are expressions of group attitudes and are useful as such. Uusally they express protests rather than offer positive suggestions such as advisory bodies often make. Elections, of course, may serve as a final public opinion poll by which to measure important controversies. Municipal election campaigns, in the usual theoretical model, should be conducted primarily over important policy issues, but this is not often the case. Candidates usually prefer to deal in glittering generalities and indulge in name calling and other propaganda techniques rather than to take a stand on specific issues which may lose votes, and the citizen has not usually strongly objected to this practice.

Contacts with Citizens Every public official has an obligation to inform the public of what government is doing, what it has done, and what it plans to do. Groundwork for future plans must be especially well laid if a city is to approach its problems on the basis of long-range planning. Many voters want to know what services are available from each agency of government, what it is costing, and why it is costing what it is. On the other hand, most Americans would say that no official has a moral right to use taxpayer money in a public relations program that is simply a defense of incumbent officeholders, although this is sometimes done.

Public employees who daily meet the ordinary citizen in the course of their work are probably the most important persons in helping to determine whether a public relations program is to be successful. Many public works employees are in a position to make city government either popular or unpopular. Refuse collectors, for example, meet the public daily. If they are efficient in their work and courteous in receiving complaints or informing citizens of ordinance violations, they can create much good will. So can public works personnel in replying to "sidewalk superintendents" who want to know what is being done, why, and what the cost will be.

The police are perhaps the most important public relations people the city government has. Their uniform makes them conspicuous. Police are indoctrinated in the rules of courtesy and taught while in recruit training to be living city directories, for their responses to requests for information become in effect measurements of the efficiency of the force so far as the typical citizen is concerned. And, of course, one police officer seen in uniform in a bar or caught in some wrongdoing does untold harm. He or she may represent a tiny fraction of 1 percent of the force, but can do more damage than can be repaired by a dozen elaborate annual reports.

Firefighters have some special advantages in public relations. Fire fighting is dramatic and a public relations activity in itself. Firefighters also gain good will by rescuing rat terriers from culverts and young children from trees, and by making and repairing toys in their spare time for distribution to needy children at Christmas time. On the other hand, they must overcome the popular notion that they chop down doors, smash windows, and spill chemicals on the livingroom rug with malicious glee. Fire fighting is a good example of the value in public relations of dramatic activities. Americans are quite generous in permitting the purchase of expensive fire equipment, although they are not very much interested in fire prevention, which would make the equipment less necessary. Lectures on fire prevention are normally not dramatic.

Departments vary a good deal in the nature of their public relations problems. Some of them must work hard to satisfy their clinetele, but they do not often attract general public attention (e.g., recreation); some of them are vital but work largely in a manner that seldom attracts general public notice (e.g., public health); some perform functions that are generally approved of, but are potential public relations dynamite (e.g., urban renewal); some of them are constantly under public surveillance (especially police and public works). All of them have a good deal to do with the status position of public employees in the community and the general repute of local government.

The Complaint Officer As American cities have developed, the citizenry has grown more distant from its officialdom in terms of access, and the professional bureaucracy has become both more powerful and the more common point of contact between citizens and their government, demands for some sort of complaint machinery have increased. In the early 1950s a number of large cities established bureaus designed to hear out the citizen who felt aggrieved and to remedy any situation considered to be unfair or contrary to law. These offices were most commonly established as a part of the office of mayor, for the chief executive has traditionally had a special responsibility to protect the citizen from miscarriages of justice. Mayors, like the medieval king, have seen their job as one of providing for a proceeding in equity.

More recently, interest has centered on the establishment of an officer who would be independent, not only of the chief executive, but also of the bureaucracy and the council, one who would represent the ordinary citizen who feels not merely aggrieved but also helpless in the face of the organized power of government. This officer, whose task is similar to the public defender in relation to judicial matters and the inspector general in the military, is an American adaptation of the ombudsman, an officer found in Scandinavia and some other countries. The Swedish constitution of 1809 established the office of Justitieombudsman, a position that still exists. Literally, it means officer of justice or, perhaps by implication, of equity. It has spread to many other countries and seeks to cope with the problem of the feeling of helplessness found in ordinary citizens as they confront the impersonal, formalized procedures of bureaucratic government.[12]

City Officials and the Newspapers Nothing is more important to the reputation that city government enjoys in the community than the relationship city officials have with the local newspapers. These publications, reflecting the varied views of their editors and publishers, take many different attitudes toward local governments. Many of them are responsible in their criticism. Others believe that criticism of any sort is good for circulation building. Some of them encourage the continued existence of popular superstitions, prejudices, and misconceptions concerning the nature of government. Some of them are ably edited; others are headed by persons who run the newspaper as a profitable business, but who have no discernible social, economic, or administrative concerns.

The department head may find the reporter or editor informed, responsible, and intelligent, in which case their relationship is likely to be happy and easy. On the other hand, he or she may consider the reporter or editor to be uninformed or stupid. But, whether responsible or not, the newspaper publisher controls the most important medium of communication in the city. Newspapers are normally of special influence in the formulation of local attitudes, as distinguished from attitudes on national or international matters.

Of course, the problem may be that the newspapers are represented by able persons seeking to keep the public informed, but the council member or depart-

[12] Walter Gellhorn, *When Americans Complain,* Harvard University Press, Cambridge, Mass., 1966; Donald C. Rowat, *The Ombudsman Plan,* McClelland and Stewart, Toronto, 1973, gives a history of the development of this officer.

ment head has developed a confused notion of what the press is entitled to know. Arthur W. Bromage has pointed out to public officials that: [13]

> The only attitude appropriate to press and radio relations is one of open frankness. When a newspaper or radio representative calls, there is no use pretending that you don't know something which you actually know. If you do not wish to be quoted, you can always say so. One must keep constantly in mind that public office is not private business. The press and radio operate to convey news, and you are a source of local news.

Public Reports Outside of direct contacts between public officials and employees and the citizen, and information distributed through the press, local governments inform their publics in a variety of ways: through the use of annual reports, leaflets, radio and television programs, movies, "open house" days, and talks before clubs and groups. Cities have long been required to issue some sort of annual statement of finances for public consumption. Out of this background some cities have come to issue general annual municipal reports aimed at the citizens of the community. Often these are in traditional form—dull, formal, and understandable only to persons having some knowledge of accounting. Other cities have produced clever abbreviated annual reports, with dramatic graphs, pictures, cartoons, and other eye-catching devices that still manage to convey a great deal of information.

An increasing number of cities have adopted the practice of preparing leaflets in lieu of the more expensive report. Radio and television are used by some communities. A few have brought these media into the council chamber, but most meetings are so routine in nature that it is doubtful if they appeal to many listeners and viewers, except on very special occasions. A handful of cities have produced movies to be shown to various groups about town, and other techniques have been resorted to, both by mayors anxious to defend their actions prior to an election and by managers who want continued public support for their budget requests.

In a day of intensely competitive commercial advertising, city governments have difficulty in competing. The public has been conditioned to expect representatives of all institutions to come to the individual and explain in a clear, firm voice and simple style the wares they have to sell. Many city administrations scarcely try; those that do, find the task a challenging one.

PERSONNEL SYSTEMS

Issues of policy abound in the area of municipal employee-employer relations. Many of these are submitted from time to time directly to the voters of the city. Some of them become campaign issues. All of them relate to the effectiveness of city government.

[13] Arthur W. Bromage, *On the City Council,* George Wahr Publishing Company, Ann Arbor, Mich., 1950, p. 73. This section was borrowed from E. D. Woolpert, *Municipal Public Relations,* Public Administration Service, Chicago, 1940.

Should public employees be allowed to join regular trade unions? Should they be allowed to join any kind of union at all? Should public employees have a right to strike? What sort of job security should they have? Are public employees' salaries adequate, or are they too high? These are some of the questions that the citizen may be expected to know something about.

MODERN PERSONNEL PRACTICES

It seems likely that most urban citizens do not realize the degree of professionalization that has taken place in the municipal civil service in recent decades. In October, 1973, 7,301,000 people were employed full time in local-government service in the United States. Many of them were employed by counties and special districts (including school districts), but no fewer than 1,706,000 worked for municipalities. Most of them are performing specialized jobs that require training of one degree or another. While the number of federal employees has had a general downward trend since 1945, municipalities continue to expand their services, the total number of employees, and the total size of the payroll. The number of municipal employees increased in the decade ending in 1973, for example, by 23.5 percent.

A great many people still believe, as they believed in the mid-1930s, according to a survey, and as Andrew Jackson believed well over a century ago, that government jobs are so "simple that men of intelligence may readily qualify themselves for their performance."[14] Of course, a moment's reflection leads to the conclusion that this is no longer the case. Government now performs a great many, rather than a few, functions. In the last century or so, the performance of most of humanity's activities has become specialized and mechanized. Governmental activities are no exception. Since the turn of the century, government employment has become increasingly specialized and increasingly performed by professionally trained personnel with professional attitudes toward their work.

The public, although it still has reservations about the worth of employment by government, seems to be giving ground in recognition of the changing role of government in our society. The prestige value of public jobs has increased markedly since before the Great Depression, and this is especially true among working-class, lesser-educated persons, that is, among the persons most benefiting from the availability of governmental services and from the increased security that they provide.[15]

Civil Service and the Merit System

The term civil service refers to civilian employees of government. In practice it is often used interchangeably with merit system. The latter properly refers to a method of choosing government employees on the basis of examinations de-

[14] See Commission of Inquiry on Public Service Personnel, *Better Government Personnel,* McGraw-Hill Book Company, New York, 1935; and Andrew Jackson's first message to Congress (1829).

[15] See Morris Janowitz and Deil Wright, "The Prestige of Public Employment: 1929 and 1954," *Public Administration Review,* 16:15–21, Winter, 1954.

monstrating the technical or professional competence of the applicant. The beginnings of a municipal service based upon the merit principle appeared in 1884, but, as in the case of the states, the principle did not become widely accepted until the 1930s. The national government, through its insistence upon professional competence of administrators for some programs receiving federal grants-in-aid, prodded many cities and states along in this direction.

The Civil Service Commission

The acts establishing civil service merit systems in 1883 (federal) and 1884 (New York and Massachusetts) established a semi-independent civil service commission and began a pattern that is still typical in cities as well as higher units of government. It is common to have a three-member civil service commission appointed (usually by the mayor) for overlapping terms, not more than two of the members being of the same political party. An executive secretary is normally hired to handle the actual administration of its activities.

The commission makes rules respecting examinations, classifies positions, conducts examinations, and keeps a list of eligible appointees.[16] It establishes uniform wages, hours, and conditions of labor (so that two clerks doing about the same job, but in different departments, will receive the same pay). It makes rules on transfers and promotions. It may, especially in large cities, conduct training programs. It certifies the payrolls so as to discourage payroll padding. It may have other functions, too.

The Personnel Director

In recent years, students of public administration have often criticized the use of the civil service commission to head personnel recruitment. It is argued that the commission competes with the mayor or manager for control over city employees. The resultant conflict is considered harmful to administration and to morale. It is argued further that personnel control is inherently a function of management and hence should be handled as a part of the chief executive's office—as it is in patronage systems.

The commission system was preferred in the early days of civil service reform because the administrative branch of government was corrupt and was opposed to the merit principle. Today, however, chief executives who want to run a smooth, effective administration desire competent personnel. They dare not resort to spoilsmanship; if they tried to do so, they would in any case be detected immediately.

A trend exists, therefore, toward the establishment of a personnel department under a single head, the personnel director who is responsible to the mayor or manager. Personnel then becomes an executive function and responsibility. (Many cities use an advisory civil service commission or have the commission make policy, but with all administration of policy left to the personnel director.) This form of organization has been used most often in manager cities, where it

[16] See Thomas H. Reed, *Municipal Management,* McGraw-Hill Book Company, New York, 1941, chap. 12.

began. It is more easily accepted in such cities because managers are themselves professional careerists.[17]

The old-fashioned, independent civil service commission, usually consisting of three members selected on a bipartisan or nonpartisan basis, has been much criticized. It has encouraged hostility between the personnel agency and the chief executive. Its very existence has implied that the chief executive was standing by, ready to return city employment to a patronage status at the first opportunity. Sometimes the commissions have actually been less anxious than the chief executive to establish a true merit principle of employment. Some commissions have sought to administer their policies themselves but have been lacking in the technical qualifications that a personnel director would possess. Others, as independent agencies, have been unable to get funds in order to hire a technical staff capable of preparing and administering valid and reliable examinations—and neither the council nor the chief executive has had much incentive to go to bat for the independent commission at budget hearings.

Today many specialists believe that personnel administration needs to be a part of management, as it invariably is in private enterprise. Under the leadership of a director whose professional interest is in the improvement of personnel and the methods of selecting personnel, the chief executive is given one of the most effective tools for a successful administrative record.

The Merit System and the Culture

Many artificial safeguards have been established in the past in attempts to require use of the merit system. These have included the independent commission, elaborate rules concerning tenure and dismissal, detailed examinations, complex position-classification systems, and the like. All are inadequate protection, and many devices exist for evasion of the merit principle if that is the officeholder's desire. Yet, the professional career approach to personnel administration does work in many communities because it has become a part of the political-cultural pattern. And in England, where there are no formal safeguards at all against making every appointment a political one, the system works very well indeed. The voters would not allow it to be otherwise.

The spirit, rather than the letter, of the merit system is the important thing. Many small and middle-sized municipalities cannot afford to employ professional personnel directors and staffs. The mayor, manager, clerk, or some other official may act as personnel officer. Yet in many cities that have no organized merit system, there are no spoils, and existing policy is to get the best available person for the job. The personnel methods used in any city, incidentally, are not likely to be more modern in character than are those used in private enterprise in that community.

Position Classification

In the establishment of a merit system of civil service, the various jobs of the municipality are categorized. Position classification consists of determining the

[17] See Reed, *op. cit.*, pp. 253–256; and the *Model City Charter* of the National Municipal League.

duties and responsibilities of each individual job, whether occupied or vacant, and the assignment of that position to a class together with other positions of similar or related duties and responsibilities. Thus positions may be classified, for example, as junior clerk-typist, senior budget analyst, patrolofficer, chauffeur, or personnel director. Once the duties of each position have been described, the number and type of classes must be determined, classes given a descriptive title, and positions assigned to classes. This last activity may create a good deal of controversy. Because it is part of the supervisory duty to look after the welfare of their subordinates, a bureau chief may well engage in a controversy with the personnel agency over whether his or her best stenographer fits the job description of intermediate stenographer or senior stenographer.

Although a position-classification plan may be greeted as "bureaucratic red tape" by the general public and municipal employees alike, it performs many useful functions. Classification raises employee morale by standardizing job titles. It permits the use of a uniform pay plan so that persons doing approximately the same work receive the same pay. If salaries are standardized, classification permits the use of a system of periodic pay raises. These may be based on the employee's increased value and faithful service over a period of time or on his or her receiving additional training. Often, however, they are based almost purely on the length of employment. Since the opportunities for promotion are necessarily limited, it is important to the morale of employees that they may be advanced in pay up to a maximum limit while continuing to perform the same type of duties. Classification allows for the transfer of employees among departments on the basis of their job descriptions. It simplifies recruitment, since a single standard examination may be given for a class, even though many positions in that class are to be filled.

The Requirement of Local Residence

Except for teachers and city managers, a common rule established by state law, the city charter, or the civil service commission requires that a city employee be a resident of the city—and often for a specified length of time, such as one year, before employment. This rule is an anomaly in a contemporary personnel system. It is based upon a spoils rather than a merit concept. It is a vestige of Jacksonian thinking that government jobs should be reserved for hometown persons. A merit system assumes that employees are chosen for demonstrated competence. If that is the true criterion, it matters not where persons may live or how long they have lived there. A residence requirement sometimes works a hardship upon the city administration by requiring the employment of a mediocre person when a superior one may live a few miles away outside the city limits. This problem may be especially acute in metropolitan areas with their numerous independent suburbs. Out of necessity, cities are increasingly waiving residence requirements in recruiting persons for positions demanding technical and administrative training and experience.

The Method of Dismissal

Much controversy may appear from time to time in local newspapers over the discharge of a particular municipal employee. The public's attitude concerning these widely publicized dismissals is often one of ambivalence. Nearly everyone today works for someone else–has a supervisory supervisor. Through the process of identification, therefore, the individual is likely to have an initial reaction of sympathy for someone who is dismissed from his or her job. ("After all, the same thing might have happened to me!") But on the other hand, the lay citizen is likely to complain that—according to hearsay—no one is ever dismissed from a government job, that incompetents may be transferred, or retired, or given nothing to do, but that they are never dismissed. Some will insist that the law does not permit dismissal once the status of civil service tenure is given.

This ambivalence has its counterpart among public administrators in the conflict over the "open back door" versus the "closed back door" methods of dismissal from the service. Should supervisors have the authority to discharge an unwanted employee summarily? Or should they have to serve a notice and accord a hearing before removal, and then discharge the employees only for "cause" as described in the law? And should the decision be left to the department head, or should it be made by the civil service commission?

In the early days of merit practice, it was believed that department heads—political appointees—would dismiss employees of the "wrong" political faith if there were no safeguards, and so the back door was often closed. This was essentially a negative view of administration, of course. Today the emphasis is upon executive responsibility. This means that department heads must be given wide latitude of discretionary power in running their departments so that they may show they can produce worthwhile results. If they fail, or if they abuse the responsibility, they must be prepared to answer for it.

Yet many city charters provide that civil service employees may be discharged only for cause and give the employees the right to appeal the decision to the independent civil service commission, which may order their reinstatement. The results have not been an aid to effective administration, as a rule. Independent civil service commissions often order the employees reinstated if a majority believes that dismissal is too severe a penalty for the charges made against them. Sometimes employees engage a skillful attorney to represent them at the hearings before the commission, and their attorney succeeds in turning the hearings into a trial of the head of the department, instead of an appraisal of the charges against the employee. After such an experience, the department head may decide that it is better to put up with employees who are incompetent, lazy, and even insubordinate, rather than to go through the ordeal required to discharge them.

On the other hand, municipal civil service employees expect to be accorded reasonable protection against arbitrary dismissal or discharge for political reasons. This can be provided in one of several ways. Personnel directors are sometimes given, as one of their duties, the investigation of any cases involving suspension or discharge of employees, which will have a restraining influence on arbitrary actions by department heads. Similarly, in cities where the personnel board is advisory rather than administrative, it may be authorized to investigate dismissals and to make recommendations to the manager or the mayor, who exercises final decision. This arrangement provides safeguards against abuse, without the problems that might result if an independent review were to be undertaken by a civil service commission with power to reinstate the employee.

THE PUBLIC ATTITUDE

Community Status and Municipal Employment

The Jacksonian frontiersman taught us to be skeptical of those who would "feed at the public trough." The lesson was taught so well that Americans often still accept uncritically the notion that public employees are loafers, far less efficient than those in private employment. Some citizens believe that the nature of public employment itself makes people lazy and inefficient.

While students and practitioners of municipal government are in virtually universal agreement that this viewpoint is false, it is difficult to present conclusive evidence to that effect because there is no certain basis for comparing public and private employment. In the field of private endeavor, the test of profit exists. Cities, however, operate few services that are expected to be revenue-producing. Even when they do—such as in public transportation—the service is often one in which profit opportunities are too doubtful for most businesspersons to be interested. The effectiveness of most city services—its recreation, welfare, highways, fire fighting, and other functions—can be given only a subjective evaluation. Where one person may think the city recreation program, for example, is inefficient and a waste of the taxpayers' money, another may think it excellent. No clear standard of measurement exists, and the recreation program certainly cannot be compared in efficiency with the method by which some local manufacturer makes motorboats.

MUNICIPAL EMPLOYMENT AND ORGANIZED LABOR

At least some employees in all the largest cities in the United States are members of labor unions. The smaller the city, the less likely the employees are to be organized. The number of city employees belonging to trade unions is, however, growing. It has been especially rapid during the monetary inflation of the 1970s. Many states have passed laws giving local employees the right to form unions and spelling out the conditions of bargaining. The AFL-CIO has two unions for municipal employees, the American Federation of State, County and Municipal Employees (AFSCME) and the International Association of Fire Fighters (IAFF). In addition, many city employees, such as truck drivers, belong to their own craft unions, just as do persons in private industry plying the same trade. The United Public Workers of America (UPWA) is an independent union. Many local unions are unaffiliated. Some of them are "company unions," which are illegal under the National Labor Relations Act, but the provisions of that act do not apply to municipal corporations.

PAY SCALES AND POLITICS

Salaries in Public Employment

The lesser-skilled and unskilled employees in large cities receive pay that tends to run somewhat above the average for comparable private employment. In smaller cities, pay is likely to be no better or less than private employment, although there is considerable variation. The higher pay in larger cities probably reflects in part the generally higher cost of living in those areas. It also reflects to some extent the trend toward the organization of public employees intro trade unions and employee associations for collective bargaining and the greater power of organized labor in large-city politics generally. Whether trade unions exist or not, however, the sheer numbers of governmental employees, their families, relatives, and friends are enough to exert considerable pressure upon councils to provide pay scales at a high level.

If salaries at the lower levels tend to be fairly good, pay for top government technicians and administrators is usually below the average paid similar employees in private industry. No labor union looks after the salary needs of the city attorney or the chief engineer at the city power station. Furthermore, persons in positions like these have, because of fewer numbers, far less political influence in getting pay increases.

When the rank-and-file workers in the mass-transit or public works departments of a city ask for a raise, council members will consider the possible repercussions in the next election if they are refused. No such fears need sway the council member when it is suggested that $10,000 is an inadequate salary for the city attorney in a city of 150,000 people. Quite to the contrary, the Jacksonian tradition lends public support in opposition to an increase. Since the average citizen is making less than the present salary of the attorney, psychologically he or she is unsympathetic to arguments for an increase. Council members and other legislators can make friends by refusing a raise to chief administrators and technicians. In the years after World War II, however, there has been a trend toward paying salaries at the higher levels that are equal to those on private payrolls. Only the very top positions have not been included in this trend.

Concluding Statement

Americans expect more and more services from city government. As a result, public employees have become technical specialists, skilled in their tasks. In order to obtain such persons for the public service, the elaborate art of modern personnel administration and management has been applied to our cities. The day has passed when city employment could quite harmlessly serve as a reward for faithful political effort.

To those who work for the city, their positions are not far different from similar positions in private employment. As a result, the same problems of labor-management relations arise in the city hall and in the offices of the business corporation.

The labor union is a basic institution in American life today, and public employees usually desire to share in its benefits. There may be some areas of union interest that conflict with the merit system. A strict emphasis upon seniority, often a union goal, is not in harmony with the principle. The closed shop is not permitted in public employment, since it would require one to be a union member before employment, and this would enable the union to supplant the personnel director or commission. In general, however, city governments have learned to live with labor unions. Although the two will have occasional conflicts, they can also work together toward the common goals of a better personnel system and a more satisfied group of employees.

SELECTED READINGS

Altshuler, Alan: *The Ancker Hospital Site Controversy,* The Bobbs-Merrill Company, Inc., Indianapolis, ICP no. 32, 1964. (Problems involved in contradictory technical information reflecting different professional values—in this case medical administrators and urban planners.)

Automated Data Processing in Municipal Government, Public Administration Service, Chicago, 1966.

Earle, Chester B., and Valerie A. Earle: *The Promotion of Lem Merrill,* University of Alabama Press, University, Ala., 1953. (A case study in which a councilman sought to secure the promotion of a city employee to a department headship.)

Gordon, Diana R.: *City Limits: Barriers to Change in Urban Government,* Charterhouse, New York, 1973. (Six case studies on bureaucratic resistance to urban reform.)

Joiner, Charles A.: *Organizational Analysis: Political, Sociological, and Administrative Processes of Local Government,* Institute for Community Development, Michigan State University, East Lansing, 1964. (The application of organization theory to local political systems.)

Municipal Manpower Commission: *Governmental Manpower for Tomorrow's Cities,* McGraw-Hill Book Company, New York, 1962. (A study of future personnel needs of municipal bureaucracies.)

Nigro, Felix A. (ed.): "Collective Negotiations in the Public Service," *Public Administration Review,* 18:111–138, March–April, 1968. (A symposium on the function of labor unions in urban government.)

Stanley, David T.: *Professional Personnel for the City of New York,* The Brookings Institution, Washington, 1963. (An examination of existing conditions and problems, and recommendations.)

13

Revenues and Expenditures

Municipal expenditures have expanded enormously in the last three generations. In the period following World War II, they have increased with almost every fiscal year.

Where Does the Money Go?

In a period of rising costs and increased urban populations, the demands for local-government services have been regularly increasing. At the same time, however, revenue sources have remained relatively unchanged. The result is that local-government debt continues each year to reach all-time highs.

A sharp expansion of services and of their costs cannot be met without a considerable amount of effort. Part of the cost has been offset by a great increase in the standard of living and consequent ability to pay. But the development has also helped to incite a desperate search for new revenue sources. The property tax remains the most important local tax, but local governments have sought to broaden their tax bases, looking to sales, excise, and income taxes.

Why Taxes?

The typical citizen probably has little understanding of the relationships that exist between government revenues and expenditures. The traditional practice of politicians is one of promising to perform more services in a better fashion and a lower cost than can or will the opposition. This behavior has probably helped preserve the citizen's habit of making no association between service levels and costs. Each person, of course, has some knowledge about taxes. Homeowners understand their property tax, at least they are able to determine how much they must pay, and they are likely to know whether it is more or less than the preceding year. The sales tax is known to most people because of the general practice of adding it to the marked price of goods in making a sale. The income tax cannot escape the attention of the employed person in any jurisdiction which levies it, especially since most states do not use the withholding system but require payment in one or two installments—each of which produces anguish on the part of the citizen. (Cities levying a payroll tax do use the withholding method.) Yet the economic merits of particular taxes are unknown to typical citizens. They know little more about the services that their taxes buy (except that they may associate the property tax with schools), and they certainly do not attempt to find their way through a wonderland of double taxation, grants-in-aid, shared taxes, dedicated funds, joint financing, and service charges.

It is easy for citizens to agree with the politician or commentator who says that taxes are too high, since they have no criterion against which to measure them. They balk from time to time when major tax increases are submitted on referendum, and their reluctance to pay taxes which they do not associate with services has encouraged the extensive use in America of dedicated funds, so that a new or increased tax is pledged to a specific purpose. This helps citizens understand why it is being asked for and helps persuade them to vote for it. Thus, an additional cent on the gasoline tax is pledged for road building; extra millage on the property tax may be exclusively for a library; most of the state sales tax may be pledged for grants to aid school operations. The use of dedicated funds has long been denounced by specialists in financial administration because of the rigidity it produces in the system. It leaves less room for the executive or legislative branches to make adjustments for changing demands. But the practice undoubtedly makes new taxes or service charges more palatable to the typical citizen.

EXPENDITURE PATTERNS

New functions of government have been added, and there have been some basic changes in the pattern of municipal expenditures over the years since the beginning of the century. Among them are these:[1]

1 New functions of government have appeared and have begun to challenge the old functions for importance. Some that might be mentioned include urban redevelopment, public housing, smoke abatement, airports, and parking lots.

[1] See U. S. Bureau of the Census, *Historical Statistics on State and Local Government Finances,* 1955.

2 Old functions have been greatly expanded and changed in concept. This applies to recreation, highways, health, and welfare programs.

3 State and national governments have assumed an increasing share of the cost of local government. Intergovernmental payments increased at an average rate of 21 percent a year during the decade ending in 1968. The states have enormously expanded the number, and increased the quality, of their direct services to the public in the present century.[2]

4 The states have gradually been becoming more and more collection agencies for local governments. In the late 1960s, about two-thirds of state-government education expenditures were actually in the form of payments to local governments. The same disposition was made of about 20 percent of state highway fund expenditures and over 40 percent of state welfare expenditures. Shared taxes and grants-in-aid were also important parts of other state budget items. This pattern represents, in part, the result of legislative recognition of the need for additional revenues at the local level combined with an unwillingness to delegate adequate taxing powers to local governments. So the states collect the money and then disburse it to their local governments.

5 Local expenditures have represented an increasingly large proportion of society's earnings, as measured by the gross national product (GNP). This increase has not been enormous, but it has been significant. In the 1920s, expenditures ran around 6 percent of the GNP; by 1962, they had increased to 8 percent.

6 Increases in municipal expenditures in the last generation (since about 1945) have been greater than in any previous generation, although they have not been as great as some critics have argued. In terms of personal income, local expenditures were about 50 percent higher in the mid-1960s than they had been in 1910. In Iowa, a study concluded, the "modest but significant increases can probably be attributed most directly to the improvements in the quality and extent of services provided."[3] Probably, this is generally true.

Reasonable Expenditure Levels

The question often arises: What are reasonable expenditure levels for state and local governments? Citizens are bombarded with propaganda, much of it conflicting in nature, which tells them of the unfinished business of government in providing highways, health programs, recreation for increasing leisure time, and so forth, but also of increasing debt burdens, of the need for increased taxes if current service levels are to be maintained, and of "all-encroaching government." Citizens wonder whether a new or increased tax is fair or whether they are being taken advantage of.

The question of the citizen raises cannot easily be answered. Essentially, expenditure levels are culturally determined. In the 1920s, Americans would not permit elaborate welfare or unemployment-compensation programs, to say nothing of public housing or limited-access highways. But since the Great Depression,

[2] See William H. Anderson, *Financing Modern Government,* Houghton Mifflin Co., Boston, 1973, part 5; *Municipal Year Book, 1970,* International City Management Association, Washington, 1970, p. 226.

[3] Deil S. Wright, "A Half-century of Trends in Municipal Expenditures," *Municipal Finance,* 37:1–8, February, 1965.

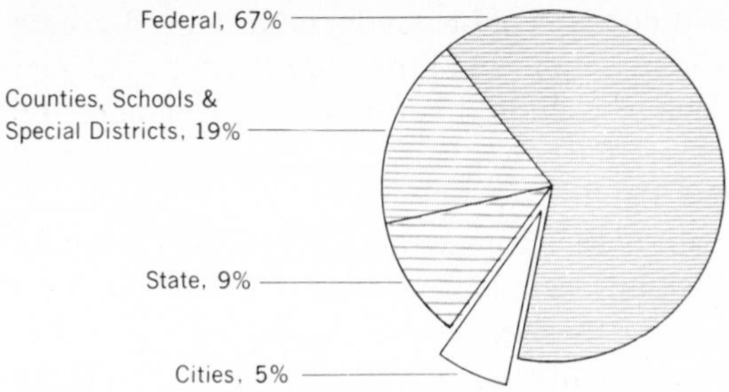

Figure 13-1 Your government dollar. (*California Taxpayers' Association.*)

they have come to expect government to provide a measure of security that is not otherwise available in an interdependent society, and they trust government further and are now willing to allow it to experiment with new programs where needs are felt to exist.

The relative ease with which money can be raised is also important in determining expenditure levels. Congress agrees more readily than a state legislature to add a new grant-in-aid program because it is relatively easy for Congress to raise the additional funds. A city or state that cannot increase services without also raising taxes or adding new taxes will be very slow to do so and will demand impressive proof before acting. (See Figure 13-1.)

The size of expenditures in any given community tends to vary, not surprisingly, with personal income levels and according to socioeconomic status characteristics, which tend to measure the same thing. The average age of community residents is a factor, however. Younger people expect more from governmental programs, perhaps in part because a younger community population tends to correlate with larger public school enrollments. Expenditures also tend to be somewhat higher in communities where the population is growing rapidly and there is an above-average rate of family formation. Rapid growth usually also requires the establishment of new municipal services and the expansion of those that already exist. Such a pattern is particularly common in new communities on the fringes of metropolitan areas.[4]

Some people—individuals or groups who want government expenditures kept to a lower portion of gross national product than do most of the people—try to keep governments from making maximum use of their taxing and spending powers. They seek to restrict spending, not so much through counterpressures upon governing bodies (though that is an important technique for them), as through the adoption of restrictive constitutional and charter provisions. Once

[4] Louis H. Masotti and Don R. Bowen, "Communities and Budgets: The Sociology of Municipal Expenditures," *Urban Affairs Quarterly*, 1:39–58, December, 1965. Similar findings are reported in Walter Isard and Robert Coughlin, *Municipal Costs and Revenues Resulting from Community Growth*, Chandler-Davis Publishing Co., Wellesley, Mass. 1957; Stanley Scott and E. L. Feder, *Factors Associated with Variations in Municipal Expenditure Levels*, Institute of Public Administration, University of California, Berkeley, Calif., 1957; and Robert C. Wood, *1400 Governments*, Harvard University Press, Cambridge, Mass., 1961.

nestled in this protective armor, restrictions cannot usually be dislodged except by an extraordinary-majority vote or a complicated procedure or both. The fact that most state constitutions have such restrictions built into them, commonly by an accumulation of amendments, makes the conservative an opponent of constitutional revision. Thus, the Citizens Public Expenditure Survey of New York opposed a 1957 proposal for a constitutional convention in that state, pointing out that "had the convention proposition been approved . . . there would have been many pressures upon the delegates to enlarge government functions and open the door to increased spending on both state and local levels."[5]

REVENUE FOR PRESENT-DAY CITIES

All taxes are ultimately derived from either of two sources: total wealth or annual income. Taxes are theoretically based upon some criterion of ability to pay, although the criteria used in various periods of history have not been the same, and a tax created in one period and logical and equitable at that time may live on into another time when its justification becomes less apparent. In some instances, payments to the government are based upon a benefit theory rather than on ability to pay, but such payments are more in the nature of service charges than taxes. The benefit theory is applied. for example, in cases of special assessments for streets, sidewalks, street lighting, and similar improvements. It is also applied in determining water and light charges and, to a degree, in motor-vehicle license fees.[6]

State Limits on Taxing and Spending

Cities have only those powers of taxation which are granted to them by the state. The only exceptions to this rule are to be found in a few home rule states, notably California and Wisconsin, where court interpretations of the constitutional home rule clause have given cities a general grant of powers to levy taxes. (Even in Wisconsin, a general act limiting municipal taxing powers in particular areas at the discretion of the legislature is valid.) States, either through the constitution or through statutes, will normally place limitations upon the taxing power of cities. The law usually states a maximum tax rate in terms of so many dollars per capita or allows an increase of only a certain small percentage over the previous year's rate or permits the city to levy a tax on only a certain percentage of the assessed value of the taxable property within the city. The last restriction is by far the most common. States also often impose conditions and regulations on the administration of municipal finances.[7]

Cities are limited in other ways, too. As a result of the famous case of

[5] *New York State Taxpayer,* 18:1, November, 1957.

[6] In general, see Anderson, *op. cit.,* part 6.

[7] Control over spending is described in T.E. McMillan, Jr. *State Supervision of Municipal Finance,* Institute of Public Affairs, University of Texas, Austin, Tex., 1953; and Leonard E. Goodall, *State Regulation of Local Indebtedness in the United States,* Bureau of Governmental Research, Arizona State University, Tempe, Ariz., 1964.

McCulloch v. Maryland (1819), federal properties within the city are not taxable. The state may exempt many other categories, such as private educational and religious properties. Beginning in the days of the Great Depression, a large number of states have adopted "homestead exemption" laws, which exclude part or even all the value of owner-occupied homes from the general property tax.

Limitations on Subjects of Taxation The subjects that may be taxed by the municipaltiy are often strictly controlled by the state. Nearly all the states determine which taxes cities may levy, for what period of time they may be levied, and under what conditions. A city that finds its property tax consistently inadequate may not, for example, decide to levy a payroll or a sales tax. The state must first authorize such a levy on a new subject.

Only a few states have been willing to permit cities to choose from a wide variety of tax sources by adopting broad enabling acts. California and Wisconsin cities have wide taxing powers as a result of judicial interpretation of constitutional home rule clauses. Pennsylvania and New York have given their cities broad taxing powers through legislation.

Limitations on Borrowing Power In addition to limitations upon taxation, the state normally also seeks to protect the public credit by limiting the borrowing powers of cities. Such a limitation may be written into the city charter or into state law or the constitution. The limit is usually expressed in terms of a percentage of the assessed value of the taxable property within the city, but it may also be a specific number of dollars, or the debt may be limited to a figure equal to the annual tax revenue of the city.[8]

These debt limits may be unrealistic and bear no necessary relationship to the wants of the city. The artificial limitations are, therefore, sometimes circumvented. Many techniques have been devised for doing this. For example, bonds issued for certain purposes, especially public utilities, may not be included under the limitation if they may theoretically be retired through revenue from the proposed project. Bonds to build a stadium, an auditorium, or a toll bridge might be paid out of revenues, and hence the courts or the legislature will sometimes exempt them from the limitation. In some states, the voters (in a few states, the property-tax payers) of a city may vote to raise the debt limit.

If either the debt or the tax limit is expressed in terms of a percentage of the assessed evaluation, the city can nearly always—and frequently does—resort to raising the assessed value of property in order to raise both the debt and tax limits. Before the Great Depression, when many states depended heavily upon the general property tax, a serious inequity resulted when large cities, encountering increasing costs, assessed property at or above full value in order to circumvent debt and tax limits. Suburbs, country towns, and rural areas might at the same time be at one-third or one-fourth of market value. Obviously, this meant that the city, with a higher evaluation criterion, would pay a much larger propor-

[8] McMillan, *op. cit.,* appendix E.

tionate share of the state tax. Few state governments today utilize the general property tax as a source of revenue, most of them leaving the field for local taxation. Large cities, however, still pay a disproportionate share of the county property tax wherever proper equalization of local assessing unit evaluations is not made. This is also sometimes a problem when rural and urban areas are combined in a school district.

Limitations on Use of Dedicated Funds The income of cities, instead of being channeled into the general fund to be used as the council sees fit, is sometimes diverted into a series of special funds, each dedicated to a particular use. This may be required by either the city charter or state law. It is common, for example, to provide that the city's portion of a state-shared gasoline tax is to be placed in a special fund for highway use only. Or 1 mill of the property-tax levy may go to the library fund, for library use only.

Some sinking funds represent money that has been set aside to pay off bonds that will become due in the future. Others are not really funds at all, merely approrpiations from the general fund, but titled "funds" in the auditor's reports.

The General Property Tax

It was stated earlier that all taxes must ultimately come from either income or total wealth. A tax must produce adequate revenue, but a long-range tax policy is often discussed in terms of equity, too. Equity is usually thought of as meaning ability to pay. In colonial America, ability to pay could best be measured in terms of property, or total wealth. Today, when most people receive a regular pay check (unlike the situation in the predominantly agricultural colonies), income is generally considered to be a better criterion.

The income tax takes into consideration the fact that not all property is equally a basis for taxes. A home, most Americans would agree, is less suitable for taxation than is a factory. A factory that is losing money is less a subject for taxation than one that is making a profit (although it might be expected to pay some taxes). The property tax makes them pay equally, the income tax does not. Saxophones, to an amateur musician, are as much a consumer good as are rutabagas, yet the former are (theoretically) taxable in many states as personal property. The income tax, in a complicated modern world, can be much more equitably administered and is less subject to evasion than is the property tax.

In colonial America, the property tax was a fairly good measure of ability to pay. There was then a much closer relationship between property owned and income received than is the case today. Despite the fact, however, that the property tax has been bitterly attacked in more recent years as being unsuitable for a modern world, and especially for urban society, it remains by far the most important source of revenue for local government. It furnished about 75 percent of all city-tax revenues in 1967. Furthermore, although reformers have often accused the general property tax of being regressive, that is, one that places a relatively greater burden on low-income persons as compared with high-income persons in terms of ability to pay, recent research indicates that when both tax burden and governmental program benefits are considered, the tax is, indeed, progressive. Higher-income persons receive relatively few services for the property taxes they pay; lower-income persons get most of the benefits.[9]

The great authority on the property tax, E. R. A. Seligman, once suggested that there is nothing the matter with the general property tax except that it is wrong in theory and does not work in practice. What are the objections to the tax?

It has already been suggested that the property tax is no longer a good measurement of ability to pay. Today, when large incomes are sometimes possible from relatively small investments, it seems inappropriate for the city to derive a major portion of its income from a tax upon homes, many of which are owned by relatively low-income persons.

Over a fifty-year period, property taxes have risen somewhat, even allowing for the changing value of the dollar. At no time in the present century have these taxes tended to decline relative to the ability to pay.[10]

The general property tax has often been poorly administered. A large proportion of property today is intangible: stocks, bonds, mortgages, and the like. These are easily hidden from the assessor. So are much jewelry and other small tangible valuables. Depreciation allowances on automobiles, furniture, and other properties far in excess of what is reasonable by market conditions are claimed by taxpayers—and are frequently allowed by assessors.

The arbitrariness of property assessment and the failure to relate it to market value is indicated in a study once conducted by the Oregon state tax commission. It found that assessments in one county ranged from 6.5 percent to 187.5 percent of the commission's figures on residential properties. Such extremes are no longer common, however.

Assessors as sometimes elected to office, even though theirs is a job requiring technical competence. Others are appointed on the basis of political considerations other than those of competence. Most assessors are honest, but many are not trained for their jobs. In the largest cities, trends toward professionalization have encouraged the development of a trained staff. Assessment in large cities is usually technically superior to the type of job done in small places.

Some attempts have been made to modify the general property tax in recent years. The withdrawal of the state from the scene has reduced or eliminated the old evils of competitive underassessment to reduce the burden of the state tax. Some states have classified property, taxing some of it at lower rates. Others have exempted intangibles or provided for the taxation of some of them at a low rate. An increasing number of them have virtually or completely exempted personal, as distinguished from real, property. The general property tax is not so inequitable or so poorly administered as it once was, but it is still not a uniformly applied tax. Furthermore, it remains an important factor in the development and mainte-

[9] Mason Gaffney, "The Property Tax Is a Progressive Tax," *Proceedings of the 64th Annual Conference, National Tax Association,* Washington, 1971, pp. 408–426.

[10] Deil S. Wright and Robert W. Marker, "A Half-century of Local Finances," *National Tax Journal,* 3:274–291, September, 1964.

nance of urban slums. This is so because improvements on property are subject to increased taxation. Many slum owners find no difficulty in charging high rents and maintaining full occupancy no matter how dilapidated the property. They, therefore, regard improvements as uneconomic. This system stands in contrast to the English, where the "rates" are levied upon the fair net income value of the property.[11]

Why Is the Property Tax Retained If there are so many objections to the general property tax, why does it remain as the core of financial support of the local government? For one thing, inertia itself helps to preserve the tax. It would seem that taxpayers generally do not support improved property tax assessments. In Wisconsin, for example, voters repeatedly turned down all referendum proposals to place assessors on a professional basis and have rejected the efforts of governing bodies to provide a reassessment of all property within some municipalities. Hence, inertia works against either elimination or modification of the tax and its administration.

A second reason is to be found in the venerable argument that any old tax is a good tax and any new tax is a bad tax. The argument, to the extent that it is accurate, is based upon the fact that society has accommodate itself to the old tax. Property values as adjusted to the property tax. When people buy homes they consider the annual tax levy as a maintenance cost, and its relative size is a factor in determining the price they are willing to pay.

A third reason is that the subjects of local-government taxation must necessarily be things that will "stay put"—and most real property (if not personal property) is not easily moved out of the city the day the assessor comes around. Sales taxes on the local level tend to drive shoppers and buyers out of the city. Taxes upon income tend to cause political complications if levied upon nonresidents and if not, tend to drive people into the suburbs. On the other hand, the real property tax does not stay perfectly put, either. High property taxes tend to drive homeowners, businesses, and industry outside the municipal limits and thus undermine the tax base.

A fourth reason for retaining the tax is that it produces a very high yield, except in severe depressions. It probably meets the test of adequacy better than does any other tax with the exception of the retail sales tax, which is collected a bit at a time and often upon the necessities of life.

Lastly, the general property tax is retained because cities need money and no one has suggested a substitute satisfactory enough to replace the yield of the tax.

The Search for Municipal Tax Variety

In looking for likely subjects of local taxation, it is necessary to consider whether or not a subject will stay in one place long enough to be taxed there and whether or not the field has already been completely preempted by the national or state

[11] See George E. Peterson and others, *Property Taxes, Housing, and the Cities,* D. C. Heath and Company, Lexington, 1973, which studies ten cities. Also Anderson, *op. cit.,* chap. 18.

government. These considerations are in addition, of course, to the requirements for a tax system seen by Adam Smith—certainty, equity, economy, and convenience.

A study of Iowa municipal taxation over a fifty-year period concluded that established programs tended to be financed by property taxes and the new programs by other means. But there was doubt as to whether the property tax could continue to finance established programs.[12]

The sales tax became popular during the Great Depression because it yielded well even in such times. It became the backbone of many state tax systems and has had limited use as a secondary tax for city governments. In 1914, St. Louis adopted a sales tax on all sales made by merchants and manufacturers. Kansas City levied a gross receipts tax in 1934. The city of New York adopted it in 1934 as a "temporary" expedient. As is the fate of most "temporary" taxes, it has become a permanent fixture in that city, varying over time from 1 to 3 percent. New Orleans, Denver, and other cities have adopted sales taxes. It has become especially popular in postwar California, where most cities have adopted such a tax ranging up to 1 percent, but with most of them at 0.5 percent. The yield from municipal sales taxes increased by 125 percent during the decade of the 1950s. In California cities and in most others, the regressive tendency of the tax has been ameliorated to a degree by exempting foods and other necessities. (A regressive tax is one the burden of which is lessened as ability to pay increases. A sales tax on necessities is considered regressive, since low-income people spend a larger percentage of their income on necessities than do high-income people.)

The income tax supplanted the tariff as the principal source of revenue for the federal government during World War I and has become increasingly important since that time. In recent years, many states have turned to this tax. Cities have, therefore, found the field largely preempted. Philadelphia, however, adopted an income tax in 1939 which has come to produce about one-fourth of the city's revenue. Many municipalities in Pennsylvania and Ohio, as well as St. Louis, Louisville, and other cities levy an income tax. The use of the municipal income tax expanded by 200 percent during the decade preceding 1960. Most city income taxes might more accurately be called "payroll taxes," for they normally do not permit any deductions, but are simply a certain percentage of the total amount of money earned by individuals, and sometimes corporations, within a city. The payroll tax has the great advantage to the core city of forcing suburbanites to help bear the cost of maintaining the city in which they earn their living and whose facilities they use daily. It is in effect regressive, however, if it allows no deductions or exemptions.[13] In many cities, moreover, the tax applies only to earned income and not income from stocks, bonds, and rents.

Organized labor has tended to oppose the payroll tax because of its regres-

[12] Deil S. Wright, "A Half-century of Trends in Municipal Property Taxes: 1910–1960." *Municipal Finance,* 37:149–155, 1965.

[13] See Robert A. Sigafoos, *The Municipal Income Tax: Its History and Problems,* Public Administration Service, Chicago, 1954.

sivity. In 1954, for example, a Cincinnati councilman who was also a CIO official resigned from the Charter party after that organization helped adopt a payroll tax in the city.

Cities secure some revenue from business taxes. These may be primarily levies to pay the cost of supervising a business directly affecting the public health, but some of them are higher levies and are designed to produce revenue beyond the cost of inspections. A city may, for example, levy a modest tax in the form of restaurant licenses, most of which must be spent upon health inspections of eating places. But other taxes may be levied upon businesses for which there exist no regulatory activities under the police power.

Public utilities often, and other businesses sometimes, are taxed upon gross earnings. One version of this tax, called an "occupational tax" (usually upon gross earned income, but excluding unearned income), is becoming widely used, especially in the South and West. Because it is difficult to determine the value of inventory and other personal property for tax purposes, experts in public finance sometimes advocate the use of such a tax on business in lieu of the personal property tax. It is often used in addition to other taxes, however.

Some cities levy a local cigarette tax. Some resort and convention cities, such as New York and Atlantic City, tax hotel-room occupancy. Mount Clemens, Michigan, another resort center, levies a tax upon every mineral bath taken within the city limits. Some tax admissions to public events. Tourists and transients are favorite objects of taxation: They cannot vote in local elections.

In a search for taxes other than on general property, cities have often followed the practice of using any subject that will yield well and will not be moved away. Equity is a secondary consideration, and taxes are added piecemeal rather than combined into a system.

Nontax Revenues

Cities receive some money annually from fines and fees. The fines are paid for violating city ordinances and state laws. The fees are charges for certain services, such as issuing marriage licenses or transferring titles of real estate.

Rather than pay for many services from general taxes, an increasing number of municipalities are levying service charges. These have traditionally been used for water supply. They are now levied in the form of charges on sewerage, garbage collection, street lighting and cleaning, snow removal, weed cutting, and others. Various formulas are used in determining these charges, but in general they are based upon the concept of payment according to benefits received.

Often service charges are levied as a means of avoiding a raise in the general tax rate. It is a means of making the tax level appear to be lower than it actually is. This can be done effectively, for example, if the sewerage charge is a flat rate or a percentage of the water bill and is added to the periodic water bill. On the other hand, service charges may serve as a means of promoting equity in local taxation. Sewerage charges, for example, may be used as a method of reaching tax-exempt property, of which there is a good deal in some cities, so that the cost of this service does not fall upon the rest of the public. Such charges are also useful where some industries contribute disporportionate amounts of sewerage to the system while others contribute nothing, and where cities are close to their tax limit (service charges are not usually counted as taxes for limitation purposes).

Some cities make a small profit from the operation of utilities. This is seldom an important source of revenue. Few transportation systems meet operating expenses today. Water departments and other utilities generally charge only enough to meet costs and to permit a reasonable allowance for depreciation and potential expansion. Sometimes, however, a surplus will be turned in to the city treasury.

Some villages and cities own and operate municipal liquor stores. These may be package stores or ordinary liquor-by-the-drink bars. Where these have been permitted by state law, they have often proved immensely profitable. Needless to say, powerful groups oppose enabling legislation for such stores.

Grants-in-Aid

Grants-in-aid are payments made by voluntary appropriation from one level of government to a lower level of government. The amount of a grant is generally independent of the yield from any particular tax or other source of income.

Specific grants are normally made with conditions attached. These conditions may require, for example, the matching of funds, the use of technically trained personnel in administering them, the maintenance of technical standards of equipment and material, or the use of the money only for certain very specific purposes.

Three principal objections are usually levied against the use of specific grants-in-aid. First, it is said that they may stimulate extravagant expenditures because the locality is spending funds which are not an immediate and obvious burden upon local taxpayers. It is said that if local officials spend money that they need not solicit from the voters, they may feel no need to spend it wisely or on necessities. Second, grants are considered a threat to local self-government and local responsibility. Since the state or national government ordinarily provides the funds only if conditions are met, they may come to supplant local government in the making of policies in these areas. The priority ranking of the grantor replaces that of the grantee, the local unit of government. It is difficult for council members to resist such temptation as an offer to pay one-half the cost of some project through a grant. The result may be, however, that an item ranked, say, fourth in the local priority moves to the top of the list and what is considered most important locally moves down to second place. The state or national agenda is thus imposed upon the community. Last, grants are held, potentially at least, to lead toward disproportionate expenditures in favor of those functions receiving grants. In other words, regardless of the merits or need of the various functions performed, some will always have a plentiful budgetary appropriation because of the grants, while others, perhaps more needy and deserving (by local-value standards), may be skimped. Grants for venereal-disease and tuberculosis control may promote these services nicely, while other functions of the health department shrivel for lack of funds.

For many years, some students of local government have advocated block grants rather than specific grants-in-aid to local governments, often calling this "revenue sharing." These are simply funds granted on simple formula with few, if any, of the strings so common for specific grants attached. In the early 1960s, Walter Heller, President John F. Kennedy's Chairman of the Council of Economic Advisors, advocated block grants to local units, but this proposal was not acted on by him and was overlooked by President Lyndon B. Johnson, who was involved in wars on poverty and in Vietnam. President Richard M. Nixon, however, advocated a plan of this type, calling it "revenue sharing." With local governments, desperately in need of additional revenues, lobbying hard for adoption, Congress passed the State and Local Fiscal Assistance Act of 1972. All general purpose local governments were made eligible for funds on a simple-formula basis that considered mainly population, but also to some extent local tax effort (an advantage to those trying hard to meet their local demands, but in effect a penalty upon any local unit that wanted to use revenue-sharing funds to reduce the local tax burden).

Proponents of revenue sharing argued mainly (with Nixon) that it would restore decision making to the local level, thus requiring greater local responsibility and pumping new life into governments "closest to the people," or (with Heller) that it could be used to bring local-spending patterns closer to the cyclic federal-government pattern by increasing grants in recessions and reducing them in boom times. Liberal opponents argued that block grants would be largely wasted by being given to comfortable small towns or to prosperous suburbs instead of to aging core cities "where the problems are"; conservative opponents argued that this would be more tax money "down the rathole," and that local units would merely spend this windfall but would not cut back on local spending or on demands for specific grants. All arguments may well have been correct to some degree.[14]

In practical terms, revenue sharing in its early years meant about $20 additional per urban resident, not a huge amount, but more than enough to encourage local-government lobbying groups to press to make the block grant permanent. This was so even though the Nixon and Ford administrations encouraged the phasing out of a number of specific grants, arguing that they had been replaced by revenue sharing. (Some cities, as a result, suffered a net loss in federal revenues.)

In 1974, the Housing and Community Development Act was adopted as a second more specialized type of block-grant program. It was designed to replace some of the "antipoverty" grants of the 1960s. This "special" revenue sharing required an application. These grants were made to local units on the basis of acceptable proposals for some type of community-development activity (broadly interpreted). Both types of block grants were favorably received by city officials

[14] See Advisory Commission on Intergovernmental Relations, *Striking a Better Balance: Federalism in 1972,* Washington, 1973; Michael D. Reagan, *The New Federalism,* Oxford University Press, New York, 1972 (opposing revenue sharing); W. W. Heller and others, *Revenue Sharing and the City,* Johns Hopkins University Press, Baltimore, 1968 (favoring the plan); and a series of studies on the effects of revenue sharing, published by The Brookings Institution, Washington, beginning in 1975.

even though they made local units still more dependent on the federal government. They seemed destined to become a permanent part of urban-government financing. In 1975, President Gerald Ford urged renewal of revenue sharing, and local-government groups lobbied hard in support.

Some early critics sharply insisted that revenue sharing had "not lived up to expectations" because citizens have not been greatly involved in local decision making and because, in the early years, very little of the funds (about 2 percent) were spent on social-service programs.[15] The law does not require public hearings before the money is spent, however, and many local officials were reluctant to use the funds for recurring costs until they knew if revenue sharing was to become a permanent feature of the federal budget.[16]

Shared Taxes

A shared tax is one imposed by one unit of government but shared with other governments according to a formula. The amount sent to each receiving unit is sometimes intended to be representative of the portion of the tax produced within the area of that unit, but shared taxes may be distributed on any basis the collector chooses. Unlike the grants-in-aid, a shared tax delivers no fixed amount; rather, receipts are entirely dependent upon the yield of the tax.[17]

Shared taxes have become increasingly popular in recent decades, and they seem to be preferred by local officals to either grants-in-aid or an enlargement of the taxing powers of local governments. Part of the reason for this is to be found in the fact that fewer strings are normally attached to shared taxes than to grants. Shared taxes also bring less criticism from local citizens than does the enactment of additional local taxes.

Taxes most often shared by the state with local units of government include those on motor fuel, motor vehicles, liquor sales, and income. Shared taxes are sometimes defended as being less in the nature of charity than the grants-in-aid, for although they are state-imposed and state-collected, they are levied upon local wealth and hence are not a largess. Because they are viewed as a local tax with the state acting as a collecting agent, local units are usually more free in using the revenue as they see fit than they are in the case of grants.

Many criticisms are made of shared taxes, however. New York State commissions in 1936 and again in 1946, discouraged the use of them.[18] These study groups pointed out that shared taxes cannot be adjusted to local needs. Some areas with little need receive more from such taxes than they can spend, while

[15] See, for example, W.W. Franz, "General Revenue Sharing: Impact on Local Decision Making," *National Civic Review,* 65:20–24, January, 1976.

[16] There is a rapidly growing literature on revenue sharing. As a start, see the reports of the National Revenue Sharing Project of The Brookings Institution, Washington. Also, David A. Caputo and others, "General Revenue Sharing," a symposium in the *Public Administration Review,* 35: 130–157, March–April, 1975.

[17] J. R. McKinley, *Local Revenue Problems and Trends,* Bureau of Public Administration, University of California, Berkeley, Calif., 1949.

[18] *Report of the New York Commission on State Aid to Municipal Subdivisions,* State of New York, Albany, N.Y., 1936; *Report of the New York State Commission on Municipal Revenues,* State of New York, Albany, N.Y., 1946.

others receive much less than their greater needs require. Grants-in-aid are better adjustable to need. Shared taxes, further, do not help to stablize local revenues. They yield well on prosperous times but tend to be withdrawn by the state during depressions, when local need for funds is most critical. Last, the manner in which shared taxes are used is less subject to control than are grants. From an ideological viewpoint, this may be argued as either an advantage or a disadvantage. But from the viewpoint of imposing standards, the state cannot be as effective through shared taxes as it can be through grants. Whatever the argument, a long look into the future will no doubt reveal the shared tax still with us.

Recent Trends

Intergovernmental financial payments exist between the federal government and the states; between the federal government and local units; between the states and their political subdivisions; and even between units of local governments. The amounts spent for each of these has been increasing in recent years, and the principal way in which most local governments have diversified their revenue sources and relieved the pressure on the property tax has been through the receipt of grants and shared taxes.[19]

Patterns vary greatly from state to state on policies for intergovernmental payments. A very low percentage of total state expenditures are for local-government aid in New England (except for Massachusetts), Montana, and South Dakota, and a high but declining percentage in Wisconsin and Colorado. Aid seems to be a function more of the balances among existing local pressures than of anything else. The national pattern does not appear to show a high correlation with any factors, whether one considers geography (except for the New England situation), rural-urban balances, or ranking by personal income as a measure of relative wealth.

Most state payments to local governments are in the areas of education, welfare, and the highways. Collectively, these make up about 85 percent of the total, though practice varies by states. Payments are also made for public safety, health, hospitals, nonhighway transportation, housing, urban redevelopment, and natural resources, among others, and some are lump-sum, or block, grants for no prescribed purpose. Intergovernmental payments are important parts of the revenues of all local units of government, and they seem destined to continue.

The Future Pattern

A conclusion on municipal taxation might hold that the general property tax will remain the backbone of the system. Several possible supplementary taxes have been considered, but none of them can replace the tax that has held the center of the stage for so long.[20]

[19] See Rowland Egger, "Nature over Art: No More Local Finance," *American Political Science Review,* 47:461–477, June, 1955; U.S. Bureau of the Census, *Historical Statistics on State and Local Government Finances,* 1955; *1967 Census of Governments,* 1969.

[20] See Frederick L. Bird, *The General Property Tax: Findings of the 1957 Census of Governments,* Public Administration Service, Chicago, 1960.

Special Assessments

Special assessments have become relatively less important since the Great Depression than they were before that time, but they are still used to a considerable extent, especially in rapidly expanding suburbs with their gross lack of services and conveniences. Special assessments are extra levies upon specific pieces of property designed to defray the costs of services or conveniences of particular value to that property.

By far the most common use of special assessments is to pay all or part of the cost of new street paving, installation of water lines, construction of off-street parking areas, and street lighting. In the last case, special assessments are most commonly levied only for ornamental lighting and not for the ordinary type. In smaller suburbs, however, and especially in unincorporated places, special-assessment districts may be created for all street lighting. Some cities defray part of the cost of developing new parks and playgrounds by special assessment.

The theory behind the special assessment is that certain neighborhood improvements installed by the city are of greater value to the nearby property owners than they are to the citizenry at large. On the other hand, they are not of exclusive interest to the nearby property owners, and the citizenry at large profit, as does perhaps the city government itself. Because of special benefit, special charges are levied. Yet it is difficult to determine a formula.

Obviously, you benefit greatly if the street in front of your home is paved. You might be expected to pay for this benefit and not enjoy this advantage at the expense of the general taxpayers of the city. Should you pay all the cost, however? Neighbors on the next street now find your street a handy shortcut when they want to reach the arterial highway. Should they pay, too? How about the Torkelsons, who are your best friends? They live miles away, but they use the street almost every day. And how about Cousin Alfreda, who comes to visit once a year? Or the department store that delivers parcels on the street? Obviously, the cost cannot be apportioned directly and precisely in relation to benefit. (Special assessments are sometimes used for arterial streets and highways, but traffic on these streets may actually depreciate the value of homes along them.)

The problem is even greater in connection with the construction of boulevards, parks, and playgrounds. A widened, beautified boulevard may generate increased traffic, noise, and dirt. Cities do not often try to determine the economic benefits or costs from such improvements. They may assess owners other than those whose property is immediately abutting, but the formula is likely to be rather arbitrary.

In trying to determine actual benefit, cities generally use a rule of thumb, assessing part of the cost to the local property owner, and having the general taxpayers of the city pay the rest. Where the city shares the cost, there seems to be no predictable basis for the percentage of the cost that it will accept. Some cities pay 25 percent of the cost; others pay 50, 80, or almost any other percentage one might name.

There is also no general agreement as to when the special assessment should be used. Cleveland, Ohio, and Alhambra, California, use it very extensively, for example. But Cranston, Rhode Island, uses it only for water lines; Albuquerque, only for new street paving; and Fall River, Massachusetts, only for sidewalks.[21]

In newly developed urban areas, the older residents are likely to feel that special assessments should be used for nearly all capital improvements and that approximately 100 percent of the cost of improvements should be paid by the benefited property owner. Older residents often contend that they have already met all the costs of their own improvements and they do not think they should be required to help pay for those of the newcomers. This type of controversy is likely to be a part of the fringe-area problem.

Four principal methods of payment for special assessments are used. One is to demand advance payments from property owners. This requires them to be prosperous or to borrow the money from a private source. The use of this method is not uncommon. Secondly, the city may make temporary loans from a revolving fund. The property owners must repay these within a relatively short length of time. Thirdly, a few cities still issue property liens to a local bank at a discount. These liens must usually be paid off in a time period of less than a year. They are lucrative for the bank but are not very satisfactory for the property owner. Lastly, and most commonly, cities issue special-assessment bonds in order to get cash to pay the contractor. The bonds, with interest charged on the unpaid portion, must then be paid off over a period of time, usually several years. This is simply another application of that popular institution, the installment plan. In Chicago, bonds must be paid in five years; in New York, in fifteen. At one time these bonds were commonly nothing but liens against property and hence could be sold to investors only if they bore a rather high rate of interest. Today, about two-thirds of the cities over 10,000 pledge the full faith and credit of the city as a guarantee that the bonds will be paid. This serves to safeguard the money of the investor and the good standing of the public credit and to make special improvements available to more property owners by reducing their interest costs.

Characteristics of Municipal Bonds Traditionally, municipal bonds were paid off by the establishment of a "sinking fund" which would, in theory, provide sufficient funds to retire the bonds when they came due. Most of the bonds of this type would be issued so that all of them would fall due at the same time. The sinking-fund method has proved to be seriously defective in several respects, particularly because: (1) The council often failed to make adequate appropriations to the fund, which must be built up regularly and systematically, or the fund was otherwise tampered with for "political" reasons; and (2) the sinking fund could come to disaster in depression times if its investments failed.

More recently, most cities have tended to favor the use of serial bonds. These bonds mature gradually, a certain percentage of them each year. The council, instead of appropriating money into a sinking fund, appropriates the

[21] *The Municipal Year Book* annually reports extensive data on special assessments.

amount for the direct retirement of part of the debt. This is the same plan that is so popular in bank loans to private individuals today: Part of the principal is paid back each month, simplifying the planning for retiring the debt.

Another development is the inclusion of a call provision in municipal bonds. This is a feature, long included in many private bond issues, whereby the bonds can be paid off at any time prior to the date of maturity, at the option of the debtor. Of course, exercising such a privilege must be offset by paying a premium—a higher price—for the bonds than would otherwise be necessary. The call provision is nevertheless likely to be profitable for a sharp drop in interest rates, or a suddenly increased income of the city might make it desirable to pay off debts ahead of maturity dates.

Types of Municipal Bonds In addition to the special-assessment bonds already mentioned above, cities commonly issue three types of bonds: general-obligation, mortgage, and revenue. General-obligation bonds are secured through a pledge that the full faith and credit of the local unit of government is available to pay them off. The community thus agrees to levy whatever tax is necessary in order to pay the interest and eventually to retire the bonds. Unless constitutional tax limits threaten to make this pledge meaningless, general-obligation bonds normally bear a relatively low rate of interest.

Mortgage bonds are normally used in connection with the purchase or construction of utilities, and they offer a mortgage on the utility as security. This type of bond has usually required a higher rate of interest than bonds of general obligation and as a result has been less popular. Sometimes mortgage bonds also involve a pledge of full faith and credit.

Revenue bonds have become increasingly popular in the years since the Great Depression. These bonds are secured by a pledge of the revenue from some self-liquidating project. Toll bridges, tunnels, and electric-light and water-supply systems may be financed in this way, Municipalities must agree to set rates high enough to pay the debt charges. Sometimes the bondholders are also given a mortgage on the utilities. Revenue bonds have several advantages for the municipality. These bonds are often not counted as part of the debt where a statutory or constitutional limitation exists. The ease with which their provisions can be enforced has made them very attractive to bond buyers.

Pay Cash or Issue Bonds?

A debate that arises in every city from time to time centers in the alternatives of paying for capital improvements by issuing bonds or by increasing taxes and paying cash. The principles of borrowing on the municipal level are far different from those on the national level. The national government itself is the principal institution for the establishment of credit-creating institutions, chiefly the banks. If the national government borrows from banks, it is borrowing credit made possible largely by its own rules. Furthermore, the internally held national debt is not passed on to other generations. The credit of the United States is psychologically intertwined with nearly all that is held worthwhile by most Americans. Its borrowing power is limited only by the faith the American people have in their government, and that faith is enormous.

Municipalities enjoy none of these advantages of the national government when it comes to borrowing. Cities cannot create credit. Municipal debt can be, and is, passed on to future generations. When it is paid off, it is not a matter of taxing Americans to pay other Americans, as is the case with the national government. The debt of Nashville is held in many parts of the nation. If it is paid off in later years, Nashvillians must pay increased taxes, the proceeds of which are then distributed throughout the nation to bondholders. The result is a lower standard of living for the people of Nashville. The public faith in any given city is also immensely less than the public faith in the United States. Municipal borrowing power is accordingly greatly limited. Except for the nontax feature, municipal bonds are treated with no more respect on the open market than are the bonds of private corporations.

When should a city borrow money? Almost everyone is agreed that it should never be in a position of having to borrow to meet current operating expenses. In the past this has happened, either because a depression has dried up the revenue sources and the city was desperate, or because local officials desired to keep taxes low as a vote-gathering technique for the next election. Borrowing to pay for permanent improvements is another matter, at least if the bonds are to be paid off before the improvement becomes obsolescent or dilapidated. Borrowing to cover a period greater than the life of the improvement is never economically sound, although city council members find that it is often politically sound to postpone payment as long as possible. Cities sometimes borrow in anticipation of receipts that are scheduled to come in later in the fiscal year. They also borrow sometimes in the face of unanticipated emergencies.

Some people have argued that municipal-bond rates are so low that cities cannot afford not to borrow; others argue that cities should not borrow at all and should use a pay-as-you-go approach. It is sometimes said that cities should always pay cash because in this way they avoid the decades of interest payments that are often involved in borrowing, payments that may total several times the original cost of the improvement. There is also no chance of default or of bankruptcy if the city pays cash. And the city is less likely to be extravagant and buy more than its taxpayers are willing to afford.

Operating a city on a strict cash basis is impossible so long as the general property tax is the basic form of revenue. A cash basis means that the expenditures of the city will vary greatly from year to year, for one does not build a municipal auditorium, a new sewer system, or an expressway every year. If expenditures vary, the tax levy will also vary, and this creates problems in the property tax. This tax tends to become capitalized, affecting the value of the property directly. A varying tax would add a great element of uncertainty to the real estate market. People also prefer to know in advance what to expect in the way of taxes.

Some municipalities attempt to reduce the need for borrowing by the use of reserve funds which may be built up in anticipation of expenditures on capital improvements. Through the use of this device, tax rates can be kept stable and yet interest need not be paid on money used for many improvements. If the municipal government can determine the normal amount of annual capital outlay, the tax rate can be set high enough to provide funds for this purpose. Often, however, cities do not plan this well, or the money on hand is used for other than capital-development purposes. Political pressures often prevent the stockpiling of funds. Bonds, then, appear to be necessary or at least the most practical approach, politically, in many communities.

Bond Prices and National-Government Policies The monetary policies of the national government are a major factor in determining the interest rates that must be paid by cities on their bonds. This is not the only factor: The credit standing of the city, the amount of existing debt, state restrictions upon taxing powers of the city, and other items are included in credit ratings. But when the United States Treasury and Federal Reserve System follow an easy-credit policy, state and local governments are encouraged to borrow; possibly they are encouraged beyond what they may later consider to have been prudent. When the federal government follows a hard-credit policy, state and local governments will find it more expensive to borrow money in order to make improvements they believe to be needed. In a time of expanding school-age populations, for example, it may be necessary to build schools regardless of the current cost of borrowing money. Federal policies are tied to political philosophies or to the business cycle; they do not consider current state and local needs and may work hardships on these units of government.

A second national-government money policy of importance to state and local governments is that of exempting the income from their bonds from taxation by the national government. A series of nineteenth-century Supreme Court decisions established the principle of intergovernmental tax immunity, according to which one government cannot tax the instrumentalities of another. This principle was, in effect, set aside by the Supreme Court around 1940, but Congress has not taxed the yield of state and local bonds because of opposition from those units of governments, from bond houses, and from holders of the bonds.

The advantage of tax exemption to the city is clear. With no taxes to be paid on interest income, the city can sell the bonds at a lower rate of interest and thus, in effect, receive a subsidy from the national government. Municipal bonds are purchased in large part by persons of high income who are seeking to avoid being placed in a still higher income tax bracket. The exemption feature thus, in effect, subsidizes individuals who least need subsidization. It is possible that this results in a greater loss in federal revenue than the amount that it saves the cities.

Some students of taxation have urged that municipal bonds be made taxable by the federal government and that the cities receive a federal grant-in-aid to replace their lost interest-rate advantage. There are many complications involved in such a proposal, however, and municipal finance officers undoubtedly prefer to keep the present system rather than to experiment with something new and unknown.[22]

A Real Urban Crisis: New York City, 1975 The city of New York has a long history of municipal fiscal problems, but its worst crisis to date occurred in 1975 when it at times did not have enough cash on hand to meet the next payroll. Mayor Abraham Beame tried unsuccessfully to get the federal government to bail the city out. President Gerald Ford refused several times to help except to amend the federal bankruptcy act to permit cities to file under it, and the city was forced to cut back on personnel and hence on services, while raising fees and fares.

The plight of the nation's largest city caused a shudder to pass through the municipal-bond market as well as all concerned urbanites who could picture their own cities moving toward the same fate. What brought about the crisis? It was the result of the culmination of a number of factors coupled with decades of bad fiscal-management habits. In the first place, the problem was made to seem worse than it is because the city of New York finances the public school system, while in most other urban places this is paid for through a special school district, and because the city also is responsible for public welfare which almost everywhere else is a charge against the county. (New York City is, in effect, a city-county.) It also operates an elaborate higher education system, rarely a municipal function elsewhere. Allowing for these extra expenses, the per capita cost of running New York in fiscal year 1974 was actually less than that of Los Angeles and not very much greater than Chicago. (The cost in New York was $401, compared with $626 in Los Angeles and $304 in Chicago. These figures are not directly comparable, however, because of different ways of calculating municipal budgets.) In terms of long-term debt, however, New York's $1,102 per capita in 1974 was 75 percent higher than that of the second most debt-ridden city, Los Angeles.

In the face of fantastically complicated service programs, the city has also had to deal with powerful trade unions in every area of urban activity, and the unions have insisted upon wage increases even while the quality of service has been declining. In other words, the taxpayers have been paying more for poorer services. And when increases were granted to the garbage collectors, say, police, fire fighters, teachers, and others demanded equivalent increases. If city officials balked, a strike would be called. A few days' accumulation of garbage (and in Manhattan it really is largely organic garbage, not just trash, for the kitchen grinder is prohibited) was usually sufficient to cause even the most miserly taxpayer to cry "Hold! Enough!" When the city found it did not have enough money to meet the new costs, it would seek state or federal aid, or would borrow the money. By 1975, all of these devices for avoiding a confrontation with the problems of spending beyond current means had become nearly exhausted, thus forcing the city government and the trade unions to turn at least part way in the direction of balanced budgets; but the short-term problem remained critical.

[22] See Lyle C. Fitch, *Taxing Municipal Bond Income,* University of California Press, Berkeley, Calif., 1950.

Whether this will represent a genuine shift in policy and outlook in New York, and hence eventually in other cities, cannot yet be known.

New York City, in many ways, was unfairly treated in the mass media and by politicians during the crisis. The city had been living beyond its income for years, true enough, but its income was restricted by a skeptical, often hostile state legislature. Although municipal wages were good, New York did not pay the highest average rates among cities of the nation in any area but sanitation. Teachers, police, and fire fighters all received more pay in several other cities. The greatest difficulty for the city (which did not, in 1975, have a higher-than-average proportion of persons on welfare) resulted from the fact that the state required the city to pay 23 percent of the nonfederal, categorical-aid welfare costs, the highest local effort in the nation. (By contrast, the large urban counties of Illinois, Massachusetts, Michigan, and Pennsylvania paid no part of this cost at all.)

President Ford and numerous members of Congress chose to use the opportunity to denounce New York City, which can easily be made to appear the perfect symbol of urban deterioration, corruption, immorality, irresponsibility, welfare loafing, rampant crime, and profligacy. Americans, traditionally suspicious of cities, found it easy to think the worst of the largest of them.

New York's problems could have been avoided by more cautious policies and less of an assumption that tomorrow's economic growth will take care of the imbalances. But the problems were real and had to be dealt with. Furthermore, they were not unique to New York or the result of spendthrift officials. The fiscal data of other large cities showed that bankruptcy could overtake almost any of them, given a combination of unfortunate circumstances.[23] As a result, the President and Congress finally decided that the potential consequences of bankruptcy were too great to risk. A plan with tough conditions was made law, and this crisis passed, though others could still lie ahead.

The plan adopted placed the city largely under federal and state authority as regards fiscal matters and limited its discretionary powers. Yet, within two months, the city was facing serious difficulties again. Although some taxes were increased, the city did nothing to reduce subsidies (primarily middle-class) it offers but probably cannot afford, particularly those of rent control, which depresses the tax base, and free tuition (plus open admissions at the City University). The city failed to pay its bondholders on the due dates.

The agreement with the federal government called for $2.3 billion in each of the following three years to be paid if the city balanced its budget by 1978 and paid back each year's loan before the next fiscal year began. Yet, the city did not move promptly to improve its notoriously poor revenue projections and after six months had made only $12 million of the $110 million cut it should have made by then. A report by an independent auditor suggested that the city might need additional permanent financing from Washington in order to repay loans from Washington—thus making it a permanent dependent of the federal government.

[23] For the background of the situation, see Congressional Budget Office, *New York City's Fiscal Problem,* Washington, 1975; and Steven R. Weisman, "How New York Became a Fiscal Junkie," *New York Times Magazine,* Aug. 17, 1975.

In 1976, bankruptcy still seemed a real possibility for New York. Perhaps its one comfort was that it was not alone. Yonkers, New York, nearly had disaster strike in 1975. Oakland, California, found itself in deep financial trouble. Many other cities seemed only a short distance behind them.

Municipal Tax Exemption for Industries

For a long time some of the states have authorized, sometimes even required, cities to exempt from property taxation for a certain number of years the manufacturing establishments of new industries in the city. The aim, obviously, is to attract industry to a city and thus provide greater wealth for the community. In some cases, tax exemption of a negative sort has been granted, too: An industry will threaten to leave the city and the state unless it is granted special tax consideration.

Beginning in 1936, the state of Mississippi went one step further with its "Balance Agriculture with Industry" program. It authorized cities to borrow money and to spend that money to buy or build industrial plants which would, in turn, be rented at a low rate to newly arrived industries. The bonds were to be retired from the rentals. Since 1951, a number of other states have adopted similar laws. These programs, like ordinary tax exemption, have been used particularly in the South in attempt to attract manufacturing. The textile industry has been most often enticed by them.

How effective has tax exemption been in attracting wealth-producing industries to a community? Studies offer some evidence to show that industries consider other factors as more important in determining sites, especially the availability of ample nonunion labor, and that cities offering special inducements gain little by such activity. In contrast, the risk is considerable, for the local tax base is undermined, and this produces serious problems in the event of a depression. When bonds have to be issued in order to build factories, a depression will find the community saddled with both the bonds and a "white elephant" factory. The Investment Bankers Association of the United States has condemned the practice for these reasons.

Tax exemptions are inequitable, too, for they are unfair to those businesses and private homeowners that do not receive exemptions. They are demoralizing to those who pay taxes faithfully. Tax exemptions assume that all in the community gain enough to warrant charging the cost to all the other taxpayers. Such is not necessarily the case, however. The system is also likely to attract unstable, fly-by-night industries that are the least likely to permanently strengthen the tax base.

Most students of taxation and of business economics condemn tax exemption or the use of public credit to attract industry. If economic conditions are favorable, if the city is well run, and if local groups such as the chamber of commerce are active, these authorities argue, there is no need to resort to inequitable and unsafe subsidies.[24]

[24] The contrary argument is given in W. E. Barksdale, "Mississippi's BAWI Program," *State Government,* 25:151–152, July, 1952.

The Politics of Industrial Recruitment

In previous generations, local government was not concerned with providing jobs in private industry for its citizens. The great business tycoons of those days possessed the image of the job giver. John D. Rockefeller, Henry Ford, and others like them were honored, in part, because they were seen as creators of work. As business became less personal and the heads of giant firms less dominating of total society, this image became blurred. Today, the role of the job giver is shared by many, but particularly by the secretary-manager of the local chamber of commerce and by the mayor or manager of the city. Effort to attract new industry is seen as a duty of the chief executive, and sometimes of the council members, too. This activity is in part ritual—it fits nicely into the image of the city as an instrument of economic growth—but it is in part in dead earnest. With American industry constantly expanding and decentralizing, many opportunities exist for cities to ensnare new plants. These differ according to the specific location of the community, of course, and the efforts made by the chief executive and the chamber of commerce representative tend to be canceled out by the almost identical efforts being made in the next town down the road, but local civic leaders are likely to feel that the effort must be made—if for no other reason than to try to keep up with the Jonesvilles.

As with other public policy matters, interests both favor and oppose city-government activity in industrial recruitment efforts. Generally speaking, local merchants and public utilities executives favor expanding the local work force because to do so offers them potentially more customers. The same interest exists for the local editor. City managers can expect their pay to vary somewhat with the size of city, so in-migration of people or annexation of new territory may be profitable to them personally.

There are opponents of expansion, too. Marginal homeowners may fear that a policy of wooing new firms will mean generous tax allowances or the extension of municipally owned utilities to new locations at less than full cost. Persons who can barely afford to own their home, and especially retired persons on relatively fixed income, are likely to see no benefit to them in the coming of another plant. They may see it as a threatened increase in the water bill and property tax. Industry already existing in the community may also oppose boosterism unless the firms that might be attracted could also become customers. If they could not, however, they are likely to be seen as competitors for the existing labor force. This means that new industry might bring pressure for higher wages. Or, especially if it is a national firm, it may bring into town a strong, active trade union. The union may represent a threat to the local balance of political as well as economic forces. Citizens, even some who may benefit financially from an increase in the local retail market size, sometimes oppose industrial expansion if it threatens to bring into the community new racial or ethnic groups or to alter substantially the existing ethnic balance.

The specific policies that a city may pursue as part of a program of boosterism vary with local conditions. Typical activities include the rezoning of land for industrial use, the extension of sewer and water lines to factory sites, efforts at annexation designed to bring potential industrial areas into the city, and a tax policy favorable to vacant land zoned industrial and to new plants. There may be a variety of other activities, too, such as a general program of beautification and of subtle or open advertising of the city as a "center of culture" and a nice place to live. (Wives of branch managers are said to sometimes have considerable influence over the precise location of plants. They are likely to reject grim, undistinguished, "uncultured" communities.)

FINANCIAL ADMINISTRATION

To most of the public, the city treasurer seems to be a very important person indeed, while the controller is an obscure bureaucrat who might do almost anything—or nothing. The auditor performs functions but hazily conceived of, but there is no doubt as to the duties of the tax collector. It is well, at this point, to examine the functions of the top fiscal administrators.

The Council

The city council formalizes basic financial policy for the city. It determines the tax rate, adopts the budget, and demands an accounting of the funds subsequently spent by the city. The budget is so much thought of as an administration document today that it is easy to overlook the fact that the council always must perform the final symbolic act of ratification on behalf of the people.

The Chief Administrator

The mayor or manager (in commission cities, the finance commissioner) acts as the chief fiscal officer of the city. Not only responsible for administration, he or she often takes the lead in determining policies both of raising and of spending money.

The Treasurer

The office held by this person is one of the oldest in local government. As a traditional office, it was one that Jacksonians insisted upon making elective. Yet, the treasurers are really glorified bookkeepers. They receive moneys according to law, the amounts of which have been determined by others. They are custodians of the city funds, although these are normally actually deposited in local banks. They must be able to account for each cent received. They pay out moneys only on orders from the controller. In none of these acts do they exercise any discretion, and they are not often called upon to advise the mayor or council on fiscal policies since, as an elected official, they are independent of them. Theirs is a ministerial office, yet one-third of the cities still do elect them.

The Tax Collector

At one time, especially in New England, an officer of this title commonly existed. Today tax collection is merely one of the jobs of the treasurer in nearly all cities. In a few places, the job is retained as a separate one from that of the treasurer, who keeps and disburses the funds.

The Controller

The controllers, or comptrollers (pronounced "controllers" in either case), or equivalent persons are obscure officers to the general public, but they are the chief fiscal assistants to the mayor or manager. They are thus the persons who perform the functions that the public often attributes to the treasurer. In about one hundred cities, the controllers are elected, but in over 96 percent of the cities in which the office exists they are appointed.

The budget is often assembled, in the name of the mayor or manager and under his or her direction, by the controller or the budget officer in the controller's office. After the budget is assembled, it is reviewed and revised by the mayor or manager, and is then submitted to the council, which usually may alter it in any way it sees fit. After the council has adopted the budget for the ensuing year, controllers assume the task of administering it. They must see to it that no department spends more than is authorized, that no department spends all its appropriation in the first quarter and is then without funds for the rest of the year, that all expenditures are legally authorized in every way, and that the departments have permission to spend before they proceed to make purchases. They must sign every payment voucher, and normally the treasurer can pay no claim against the city without the approval of the controller. They also serve constantly as the chief adviser to the mayor or manager on financial and frequently on other matters. In some cities they serve as deputy mayor.

In small cities, and often in larger ones, the functions of the controller are performed wholly or in part by the council itself. Many a council session is devoted principally to the approval of routine bills. In some cases, state law requires the council to perform this ministerial function.

The Assessor

The assessors (or board of assessors) are responsible for the valuation of property to serve as a basis for determining the general property tax. They are sometimes located within the department of finance, but often they have a separate office. And not all municipalities serve as assessing units. It was once common to elect the assessor, and about 13 percent of the municipalities in the country still do so, even though the job requires technical training.

Assessment, in theory, does not involve policy making but only the application of state and local rules to the evaluation of property. In practice, however, assessors are often important policy makers. They may have considerable latitude in deciding on the relative percentage of market value that they will assess homes as against businesses, or in rating the worth of one subdivision against another in terms of site value, or in granting favoritism to certain individuals or groups.

The assessor's office, once it has prepared the tax rolls after assessment, may send out tax bills, although this is more commonly the job of the treasurer and many tax jurisdictions do not send a bill to the taxpayer at all—it saves money not to do so. The assessor may also handle condemnation proceedings.

Boards of Tax Appeal

Because of the potential incompetence, carelessness, or arbitrariness of the assessor, machinery for appeal and review of assessments exists in every taxing jurisdiction. The board of tax appeal (it has many different names) may be a special body, or it may be the city council. In either case, its work is difficult and its members are not likely to gain many friends through the decisions that are made. The board is ordinarily subjected to great pressures from the large taxpayers of the community, and individual householders who bring in appeals are likely to present their cases in highly emotional fashion.

Beyond the local board, in theory, lie appeals to higher authority, sometimes to a county board, usually to the state tax commission, and always to the courts. But these procedures are costly, time-consuming, and, unless the local assessor is vastly incompetent, usually unavailing. Only the largest taxpayers are likely to have enough influence and find the stakes large enough to expend the effort that is required.

The Purchasing Agent

Finance departments today often contain a division of purchasing. Through it most of the city's needs for supplies, materials, and equipment are procured so that savings of large-scale purchasing may be achieved.

The Department of Finance

In some cities, all the above officers are grouped together into a department of finance headed by a director. Authorities on financial administration believe that this is a desirable organization, since it provides for direction and coordination of these several financial activities. Council-manager cities, especially smaller ones, are likely to have an integrated department of this type. But in many cities each of the finance officers is independent and may be popularly elected.

The Auditor

Auditors are the agents for the legislative branch of government. Their job is to check upon the executive branch to determine if expenditures it has made were according to appropriation and were otherwise legal. In a few cities, auditors also make recommendations to the council concerning the effectiveness of operation of the administrative agencies. Because the job is an old one, one auditor in ten is still elected, even though the position requires a knowledge of accounting. The auditor sometimes performs some of the functions described in this chapter as those of the controller.

Where auditors are not elected, they may be chosen by the council, they may be sent to the city periodically from the state auditor's office, or the council may hire a private accounting firm to do a periodic audit. Large cities are likely to have their own auditing officers, smaller cities to use private firms or be subjected to a check by the state office, or both.

The important characteristic of auditors is that they are independent of the chief executive officers. If this were not the case, the executives would simply be checking on themselves. The independent auditors, however, are likely to be free to investigate and report as they see fit. And they usually have a professional interest in doing so.

FINANCIAL PLANNING

The Executive Budget

During the enterprising years of municipal reform, "efficiency" and "economy" pressures were so great that many city councils lost part of their traditional power of control over the purse. This permitted the establishment of all or part of the executive-budget system which divided up the financial process so that the chief executive makes a recommendation for revenues and expenditures in the form of a systematic, comprehensive statement of income and outgo. The council then adopts this budget, but nearly always with an opportunity to express its own views. The executive next oversees the expenditure of the appropriations by the various departments, requiring them to spend at a rate that will not exhaust their appropriations prematurely and will keep expenditures within the requirements of the law. Finally, the council, through its auditors, checks to ascertain whether or not its instructions have been carried out and whether or not appropriate provisions of the state law have been followed by the executive. The power of the chief executive, through the budget officer, is potentially very great, both in preparing the budget itself—the document is, of course, a major policy statement, explaining how the executive would spend moneys—and in controlling its expenditure after the council votes the funds. Budget officers are, therefore, among the chief executive's top aides today. They and their budget examiners serve to advise both the executive and the council members, reviewing appropriations requests and preparing evidence in support of policy positions. They often control the conditions under which appropriations may be spent.

The trend toward centralized administration, the increasing number of functions of government, and the increasing complexity of those functions have contributed to the rapid rise in the use of the executive budget in the United States since the turn of the century. As a result of the change, responsibility—except in cities of the weak-mayor and commission types—for the innovation of taxation and appropriation proposals is placed in the hands of the executive, but with the council continuing to perform its ancient functions of criticism, review, modification, and, sometimes, rejection.

Until recent years, every budget dealt with all the minutiae that are needed to operate an office or function of government. Often the budget consisted of "line items" specifying the exact amount to be spent on a particular aspect of a function, and the funds were commonly not transferable from one line in the budget to another, even within the same department. The emphasis was upon the things to be acquired—paper clips, snow shovels, wheelbarrows—rather than upon the services to be rendered. This was necessary when public funds had to be guarded at all times against ingenious attempts at fraud. It encouraged, however, the citizen's habit of dissociating taxes from services provided. Many specialists in the field of fiscal administration have long urged that the budget should propose appropriations on a lump-sum basis. Under this plan, each agency or major subdivision would receive a single sum of money which responsible administrators would then spend as they thought best—within generally established policies of the chief executive and the legislative body. Flexibility to meet unexpected emergencies and changes in service demands would result.

Since the original Hoover Commission reports in the late 1940s, a trend has been established toward a "performance" budget. This is a method of classifying expenditures so that each agency receives a lump sum for the operation of each of its different activities: so much for snow removal, so much for purchase of new park land, so much for public welfare programs. Although the method has its weaknesses, it is designed to help make clear to both legislators and the public what funds are being used for; it makes it easier to compare past performances with future requests; and it may encourage agencies to do a better job of thinking through their needs in making requests. The budget is designed to reduce the tendency under the older budget method (appropriation by objects) to stockpile materials and accelerate the purchase of services in order to exhaust appropriations. Legislators are sometimes cool toward the performance-budget idea, feeling that it has the effect of transferring still more fiscal power to the chief executive and the bureaucracy. The most rapid adoption of the performance budget has come in council-manager cities. It is used for all or part of the budget in other cities, some as large as Los Angeles.

The Budget as Policy

The budgeting function "is a specialized way of looking at problems in decision-making."[25] It is something of a negative view in the sense that after the agencies and interest groups have made known their positions, the budget examiners, and ultimately the chief executive, must balance off the various interests against one another and against a plausible estimate of income, often reducing requests. Budget making is also positive in the sense that a public budget is a basic statement of program and policy by the chief executives. They explain in it how they would evaluate the various demands upon the public funds, give reasons for taking the stand that they do on the more controversial aspects of the program, and necessarily must stand willing to defend the explicit and implicit policies proposed in the budget. Many governments require agencies to estimate capital-outlay needs for several years—perhaps five years—in advance, thus making this part of the budget a long-range planning instrument, since capital needs cannot be considered apart from program needs. The budget, in this way, becomes to each agency a means for promoting planning.

The executive budget makes possible the coordination of the policies of various departments. Nevertheless, these opportunities are not always taken. A study of the budget process in three Illinois cities concluded that in two cities

[25] Paul Appleby, "The Role of the Budget Division," *Public Administration Review,* 17:156–158, Summer, 1957.

officials do little more than continue activities already established. However, in the third city, "budget preparation provides an occasion to challenge all current activities, to search out and identify new problems, and to suggest changes in activities to meet a re-defined set of priorities. A commitment to rationalism, furthermore, guarantees that the search for new problems and new alternatives will continue."[26]

The Parts of a Budget

A budget usually begins with a message from the chief executive which may say simply, in effect, "Here is the budget for the next fiscal year," or it may explain proposed new expenditures, tell why tax changes are requested, and otherwise explain policy positions. A brief summary of the budget for the benefit of citizens and reporters usually follows. Next comes the detailed breakdown. It may start with a statement of anticipated revenues from all taxes and other sources. This will be followed by the expenditures section, often broken down by funds: the general fund, plus a small or large number of others, such as a streets and highway fund, sometimes even a municipal-bond fund. A capital-outlay budget for new streets, buildings, and other structures will usually be presented separately from the operations budget, and the same may be true of utilities budgets, such as that of a municipal water-supply system. Provision must also often be made for governmental debt service. The budget may conclude with a statement concerning new taxes needed or the property-tax levy necessary to bring the budget into balance.

Preparing the Budget

In municipalities operating under the executive-budget plan, the document is prepared by a budget officer or controller under the chief executive. In a few cases, the budget is prepared by an independent, elected controller or an ex officio board. In weak-mayor cities, a council committee often prepares the budgets.

The process begins with the collection of estimates for the following year's needs prepared by the various agencies. In all but small cities, these are gone over by budget analysts who look for padding, inaccuracies, and inconsistencies. There may be conferences between the agencies and members of the budget division when differences arise. Such differences are likely to result from differing premises. Chief executives' own philosophy, and perhaps their evaluation of their own political strategy requirements, will affect their own view of how "needs" should be interpreted in each agency. The agency will, however, probably use different criteria in arriving at "needs." It may base these on professional concepts of standards, or upon the pet interests of the agency head, or on the pressures it feels most from its clientele groups, or upon other considerations.

When detailed estimates of the needs of each department for the coming year are available, they are set out in parallel columns with statements of the

[26] Thomas J. Anton, "Budgeting in Three Illinois Cities," *Papers of the Institute of Governmental Affairs,* University of Illinois, Urbana, Ill., 1964, p. 24.

estimated expenditures for the same items in the current year and the actual expenditures for those items in the fiscal year just completed. The budget officer next goes over the document in detail with the chief executive so that proposed changes in policy may be incorporated in the estimates.

The completely assembled budget is then ready to be sent to the council. Enclosed with it may also be the political future of the mayor, the career prospects of the young city manager, the hopes of the chief executive's critics for new ammunition in their fight, and the welfare of all the publics that reside within the boundaries of the city.

Enacting the Budget

The council has the responsibility for adopting the budget, nearly always with some, more commonly with many, modifications. It will usually hold budget hearings, either before the full body or before the tax and appropriations committees, the chairpersons of which are normally senior legislators of great power. These hearings do not often give the council members information they do not already have, but they serve to allow groups and individuals to vent their annoyances, bitterness, or frustrations. They are an important part of the democratic process. A budget hearing is more likely to be attended by representatives of interest groups, however, than by a representative cross section of the general public. Some department heads may lobby at this time to get a bigger share of the pie than was given to them in the budget division. If chief executives are weak administratively, this may be done quite openly. If they are strong, however, it must be done more subtly, for dissident department heads may risk their jobs by going over the head of the executive. Interest groups will at this time try to get favorable hearings, and those that find the legislative climate more receptive than was the executive may succeed in getting an increase in the department budgets in which they are interested. Other groups will have to fight to retain the level of funds recommended in the executive budget as legislators strive to reestablish a balance between income and outgo. Public employees may take the opportunity to try to improve their working conditions and pay, and the newspapers may use the occasion to view with alarm the ever increasing cost of government.

Usually the council is free to add, reduce, delete, or modify any part of the budget, although in some cases it may only reduce items or leave them unchanged and cannot introduce new items. In mayor-council cities, the chief executive usually has the power of the item veto and thus a final chance to preserve the integrity of the budget.

Administering the Budget

In cities with the executive budget, the head of each department must submit a work program to the chief executive (or often, in practice, to the controller) before the beginning of a new fiscal year. This program will show how much of the total appropriation for that department is desired in each month or quarter of the coming fiscal year. This is known as the "allotment system." After approval, the allotments are turned over to the accounting division of the controller's office, which will then refuse to allow any money to be spent by that department unless it is authorized by the appropriations ordinance or statute and falls within the time provided in the allotment schedule. In cases where budget administration is less well organized, no allotment system may exist, and the auditor may be the only one to check for the legality of expenditure. In small cities, the governing body may itself exercise the control function by passing directly on individual bills presented for payment.

After the moneys have been spent, the auditor checks to ascertain the legality of all expenditures and reports the findings to the council and sometimes also to the state. Even as the money is being spent throughout the year, however, the budget officer is surveying the scene for possible alterations in the next budget, for the governmental process is an unending one.

SELECTED READINGS

Buehler, Alfred G.: "Problems Presented by Proliferation of Municipal Nonproperty Taxes," Municipal Finance, 34:106–111, February, 1962. (Shows that nonproperty taxes can raise considerable revenue, but that these offer more a palliative than a cure for local revenue problems.)

Business Week, Dec. 16, 1961. (Offers a complete summary of tax benefits then offered as inducements for industrial location.)

Caputo, David A. (ed.): "Symposium on General Revenue Sharing," Public Administration Review, 35:130–157, March, 1975.

—— (ed.): "General Revenue Sharing and Federalism," Annals of the American Academy of Political and Social Science, 419, entire issue, May, 1975.

Crecine, John P. (ed.): Financing the Metropolis, Sage Publications, Inc., Beverly Hills, Calif., 1971. (Emphasizes the interaction between public and private sectors.)

Financing Government in New York City, Graduate School of Public Administration, New York University, New York, 1966. (Report to a study commission.)

Goodall, Leonard E.: State Regulation of Local Indebtedness in the United States, Bureau of Government Research, Arizona State University, Tempe, 1964.

Hillhouse, A. M.: Municipal Bonds: A Century of Experience, Municipal Finance Officers' Association, Chicago, 1936.

——, and Muriel Magelsson: Where Cities Get Their Money, Municipal Finance Officers' Association, Chicago, 1946. (Not current, but still useful.)

International City Managers' Association: Municipal Finance Administration, 6th ed., International City Management Association, Chicago, 1962.

Isard, Walter, and Robert Coughlin: Municipal Costs and Revenues Resulting from Community Growth, Chandler-Davis Publishing Co., Wellesley, Mass. 1957.

Martin, Roscoe C.: The Cities and the Federal System, Atherton Press, New York, 1965.

Moak, Lennox L.: Administration of Local Government Debt, Municipal Finance Officers' Association, Chicago, 1970.

Mosher, Frederick C., and Orville F. Poland: The Costs of American Governments, Dodd, Mead & Company, Inc., New York, 1964. (An especially valuable collection of data and analysis of revenue, spending, and indebtedness.)

Nathan, Richard P., and others: Monitoring Revenue Sharing, The Brookings Institution, Washington, 1975. (The first of six planned studies on the subject.)

Peabody, Robert L.: Seattle Seeks a Tax, The Bobbs-Merrill Company, Inc., Indianapolis,

ICP no. 49, 1959.

Scott, Stanley, and E. L. Feder: Factors Associated with Variations in Municipal Expenditure Levels, Institute of Public Administration, Univeristy of California, Berkeley, Calif., 1957.

Sigafoos, Robert A.: The Municipal Income Tax: Its History and Problems, Public Administration Service, Chicago, 1954.

Tax Foundation, Inc.: Factors Affecting Industrial Location: A Bibliography, Tax Foundation, Inc., New York, 1956.

——: Research Bibliography: Financing Municipal Government, Tax Foundation, Inc., New York, 1960.

U. S. Advisory Commission on Intergovernmental Relations: State Constitutional and Statutory Restrictions on Local Government Debt, 1961.

——: State Constitutional and Statutory Restrictions on Local Taxing Powers, 1962.

——: Tax Overlapping in the United States, 1964.

——: The Commuter and the Municipal Income Tax, 1970.

Vernon, Raymond: "The Economies and Finances of the Large Metropolis," Daedalus, 90:31–47, Winter 1961. (The revenue problems of core cities and suburbs.)

Wright, Deil S.: Trends and Variations in Local Finances, The Case of Iowa Counties, Institute of Public Affairs, the University of Iowa, Iowa City, Iowa, 1965.

Part Two

The Politics of Urban Functions and Services

In the two remaining chapters, we will shift focus to policy outputs and issues surrounding policy making in given areas of urban governmental activity. We have separated the activities, in a rough way, between those concerned with the physical design of urban areas and those concerned with human services. The two categories of course overlap and at their boundaries become indistinct.

Earlier chapters described the political environment and the machinery that makes the political process operate. What is said in them is more enduring than what follows, for the agenda of city government is transitory, subject to extreme and often unexpected changes. The issues of one year (no matter how vigorously debated) may seem very stale the next. Here we present some of the agenda items and ongoing policies of the mid-1970s.

But first we will note how the issues of the 1970s represent a tension between the desires of local residents and a broader definition of the general welfare as defined at the state and national levels.

The Urban Setting

One of the authors of this text sometimes asks his students to write short papers about an urban service problem in their hometowns or, if they wish, the city in which the university is located. One need read but a few papers to be impressed with how much the urban setting influences the definition of what is an urban service problem. Not only do the problems vary by setting, but so too do the solutions proposed and the means suggested for achieving them.

Some core-city papers are focused on the problems of street crime and the organization of police activities, and especially on discussions of why a nearby core city has one of the nation's highest murder rates. Others deal with one aspect or another of the social deterioration of core-city life resulting in part from poverty. Hanging like a great shadow over all of these discussions is the issue of racial tensions and what might be done about them. Most students, significantly, never get past describing these very human problems. Some describe programs being tried, but only a very few papers suggest hope that much will really be done to change the conditions they describe: the problems of the core city seem overwhelming.

The descriptions of urban-setting problems in small towns have a different tone. The papers center often on the amateurishness of small-town public officials. This is possibly a reflection of the feelings of sophistication of college students who have left it all behind them and who now look back on what once seemed so important as trivia. But it is also, perhaps, an uneasy feeling some students have that the problems of bigger cities are coming to their small towns which are not very well equipped to handle them: such problems as youth and drugs, the lack of recreational facilities, and the growing shabbiness and outright ugliness of Main Street. A second theme is from an older frontier tradition, descriptions of how a community cooperated to create a physical facility such as a ball field or town-meeting room or teen social center. In the larger of these cities, those that are not part of a metropolis but whose population and industry are growing, the problems of saving downtown and preventing a flight to the suburbs loom large. Such physical-design proposals as downtown malls, street-corner flowerpots, rerouting of state-highway traffic, and the use of parking lots and one-way streets are being discussed and applied. What runs through all the papers on small-town service problems is a sense that most municipal problems are not yet really so very important or so very difficult to solve, even with only semiprofessionalized personnel. Many can be solved by private rather than public efforts. Such problems are still overshadowed, in the eyes of residents, by the major social fact of small-city life, the rigidity of the local social-status hierarchy. What your father does is still more important than are most local political issues.

Those students who write about urban-service problems of the suburbs tend to be obsessed with land-use control, particularly if the suburb is middle or upper-middle class. What does one do about the threat of a mobile-home park or an apartment complex or commercial or industrial development? The debates weight the desirability of economic development against the possible costs in terms of the quality of residential life. Highway patterns and other traffic and transportation problems, water and sewage difficulties, and even solid-waste removal are popular topics. All of these problems have a common core: they are treated for the most part as technical rather than political problems. The writers confidently believe that they can be solved by the proper application of professional expertise; thus one can have both development and the even tenor of suburban life around the charcoal grill. Only two political problems are hinted at, political in that they suggest a choice among values rather than solution by professional expertise. One is the underlying theme of the steady rise of costs and tax rates; the other is the character of the neighborhood residents. In the blue-collar suburbs the issue is how long one can look the other way given the nearness to core-city boundaries and core-city problems; in the wealthier suburbs, one finds a more muted variation of the same theme. Similar to some small towners, the suburbanites for the most part like and accept their home communities pretty much as they are.

The fourth type of setting is the very specialized one of a city with a university. Few students choose to write about its problems. Some report that they feel like transient visitors with no real stake in the community's future and so they argue that they do not wish to participate, and indeed should not do so. Others still feel home ties too strong to bother; one student wrote, "Even though I'll probably never go back there to live, I still do care about what happens to that neighborhood in my hometown." As one would anticipate, older students, especially those in married housing, identify with the problems of the university community, and so too do the political activists, especially those of a radical bent. For them the university community is a place to put their ideas to the test. Overwhelmingly for the latter, the urban problem of top priority is the cost and condition of rental housing in what they call the city's "student ghetto." A minor theme is the need to train local police in the techniques of antirape control. Also discussed frequently is the heavy traffic on the main artery that separates the university from the city shopping district, much of it nonlocal in origin and destination. Less is said about racial bias in housing than was true a few years ago.

To summarize, the setting makes a great deal of difference as to what one defines as an urban-service problem. Note also that it focuses attention on one's own satisfactions. Most students write about their own immediate interests, not abstract problems or idealistic notions of reform, but problems that directly affect the way they live their own lives. In this sense they are self-centered, showing no concern for some concept of the general welfare. A common theme given this focus is that of the quality of housing, preservation or protection of a home environment.

It is probable that city residents and city officials, if left alone, would continue to define their problems in each urban setting in a fashion to suit only the local residents, or perhaps more precisely, those local residents who are politically effective. They certainly have done so in the past. But local government is no longer left alone. The prodding continues from the state level; and since the early 1930s and especially from the 1960s, programs of the federal government have had an important impact—for good or ill.

The Federal Government and Urban Services

Federal urban programs are designed to meet a broader concern than the immediate wants of residents in a particular community setting. They are supposed to provide for the "general welfare." Three assumptions underlie a variety of these federal urban programs: (1) the key to solving many social problems is reducing the inequalities among American citizens in respect to status, wealth, and political power; (2) governmental power can be used to accomplish such a narrowing; and (3) enough expertise exists in various professional disciplines so that governmental intervention is likely to succeed. All three assumptions are based on faith, but it is a faith shared widely by Americans.

Given these assumptions, federal efforts, whether through regulation, grants, or direct provision of an urban service, attempt to redistribute to some degree wealth, social status, and political power. Such programs will inevitably conflict from time to time with the desires of residents in particular urban settings. Many will be designed to help minorities rather than a broad majority of citizens. They will be criticized and resisted on that basis.

The period of the early 1970s was one of reassessment of federal programs, not only by those who had never accepted the desirability of redistribution, but by some who challenged the means used by the federal government to accomplish it. Some examples: Daniel Seligman as early as 1958 noted that tearing down slum buildings in the core city and replacing them with high-rise large-development public housing did not solve the social problems of residents. In a memorable observation that he attributes to "a close student of New York's slums" he writes:[1]

> We thought that if we could only get our problem families out of those dreadful slums, then papa would stop taking dope, mama would stop chasing around, and Junior would stop carrying a knife. Well we've got them in a nice new apartment with modern kitchens and a recreation center. And they're the same bunch of bastards they always were.

To bear him out is the Pruitt-Igoe public housing development of St. Louis, torn down in less than twenty years after completion because it was judged to be a slum. James Coleman, an early and major proponent of bussing, concluded in 1975 that bussing was a failure because it led to increased school segregation as whites fled core cities.[2] Daniel Patrick Moynihan, reviewing citizen-participation efforts in community-action programs of the "War on Poverty," concluded they were a debacle of high hopes coupled with low performance and resulted in a lingering bitterness for all parties concerned.[3] Studies of urban renewal commonly led to the observation that many plans were not really slum-clearance projects, but a callous shuffling of the very poor of the core city, often only for the benefit of land speculators or downtown businesses. Norton Long has written feelingly against the notion that social problems could be solved simply by throwing federal money at them.[4] Perhaps the most bitter criticisms of all were from those who,

[1] Daniel Seligman, "The Enduring Slums," in The Editors of *Fortune, The Exploding Metropolis,* Anchor Books, Doubleday & Company, Inc., Garden City, N.Y., 1958, p. 16.

[2] James S. Coleman, "School Integration Distorted," July, 1975, article in *Newsday,* reprinted in Lansing *State Journal,* July 27, 1975.

[3] Daniel P. Moynihan, *Maximum Feasible Misunderstanding,* The Free Press, New York, 1970.

[4] Norton E. Long, *The Unwalled City, Reconstituting the Urban Community,* Basic Books, Inc., New York, 1972.

like him, saw the federal welfare policies as a way of pauperizing the poor into a permanent dependency, a way of preventing them from achieving dignity and self-respect.

These criticisms led to several related observations about federal programs. Daniel Patrick Moynihan brought attention to what he called the scarcity of social opportunity. Only at a few points in time, he argued, are Americans prepared for bold redistribution programs. To waste these opportunities with hit-or-miss proposals, as was done in the 1960s, is to invite frustration and disillusion both in those one tries to help and in the helpers. Projects for social reform might better be viewed with professional skepticism, much as are new cancer cures by reputable medical scientists. Recognizing the present limitations in knowledge in the social sciences, he argued, as have many others, that political practitioners need to develop performance measures in the urban-service area so that new proposals can be tested in advance and old procedures reevaluated.[5]

The first applications of such measures have led to serious questioning of some cherished professional beliefs. The Coleman report on education revealed that student achievement as measured by national test scores was more related to the quality of the student's private home life and the attitude of peers than to such matters as school expenditures on equipment, degrees held by teachers, integration of schools, or type of teaching program. A study of police services paired contiguous suburban and core-city neighborhoods with similar social characteristics but served by police forces that varied widely in professionalization. Yet the researchers found, using such performance measures as response rate and satisfaction of local residents, that the police service provided by the smaller and less professionalized suburban departments was equal to or superior to that provided by the more professionalized large-city departments.[6]

A Summary Statement

The state of urban-service performance is one of tension. The urban setting leads local officials to develop programs to try to meet the immediate practical needs of their own residents. The federal government seeks to introduce policies that would ameliorate larger social problems, mainly by redistribution of important social, economic, and political resources of the nation. These may well conflict. But the problem is broader. The assessment of both kinds of policy is only in its infant stage. Students who read this can anticipate that throughout their lives research on performance of these urban functions will accelerate and hopefully will lead to some changes in policy leading to predictable and desirable consequences, whether to meet the needs of local residents in a particular setting, or to meet the state or national definitions of the general welfare.

With the warning then that the service performance at the urban level is in flux, we begin a review of major urban services in the 1970s. We will strive for conciseness. Students are encouraged to consult further such sources as the New

[5] Moynihan, *op. cit.*

[6] Elinor Ostrom, "On the Meaning and Measurement of Output and Efficiency in the Provision of Urban Police Services," *Journal of Criminal Justice,* 1:93–112, 1973.

York Times Index or Congressional Quarterly Index for latest details on federal-grant programs or rulings of the federal courts. An especially useful source of information is the Congressional Index, published annually by the Commerce Clearing House. We can only generalize about state programs, since they vary widely, though all tend in the direction of bringing more uniformity of service procedures and standards throughout the state's urbanized areas. Where practicable, we break down each service under such major headings as problems, programs, performance measures, local organization, and state and federal programs.

Chapter 14

The Physical Design of Cities

Students of cities have always recognized that their physical design has some influence on the patterns of human relationships that occur in them. For example, quite recently those reviewing the design of public housing developments have suggested that they can be built to provide defensible space for residents and thus discourage those criminal forms of human relationship that we label mugging and rape. This is accomplished by such means as eliminating dark passageways, creating areas that have windows looking in upon them, and building elevators and stairwells that are glassed in.

While physical design may be influential in affecting behavior, it is not determining. Some societies could quite possibly inhabit the old-style housing tracts without high rape and mugging incidence. This is a fact that city reformers have in the past sometimes ignored. They have felt that in creating the "city beautiful" they would create, in turn, the "community beautiful." And of course physical structures are much easier to change into new patterns than are human behaviors.

Thus in discussing the design of communities in terms of its parks, boulevards, expressways, museums, airports, water and sewage systems, etc., we are to some degree describing the kinds of human behavior that might develop in them.

We caution the student to remember a point already made: the effect of such design is very imperfectly known. As with other public policy, performance measures of their impact on human individuals are yet to be devised.

URBAN PLANNING

A major responsibility of governments at all levels today, but especially at the community level, is to plan for the use and reuse of both land and housing. In a frontier society, these decisions rested primarily in the hands of private builders and developers and were settled in a rough-and-ready fashion as long as it was expected that low-income, unskilled immigrants and migrants would accept whatever housing was left over, and as long as raw land was readily available.

Planning deals not only with streets, utilities, and the regulation of private property but also with parks, recreation, housing, slum clearance, airports, traffic, parking, public health, and a host of other things. It deals primarily with the problem of converting long-range social goals into public policy. Using prevailing cultural values and professional criteria, it seeks to correct or minimize the effects of past mistakes and to avoid them in future development.

Planners tend to approach policy making from a different perspective from that of other community decision makers. Instead of making incremental adjustments to the margins of existing policy, they are primarily concerned with the interrelationship of all the parts of the social and physical environment, emphasizing comprehensiveness rather than particularities, and long-run rather than short-run considerations.

The Problems of Planning

In former days, planners drew up master plans for communities and then often assumed their job was done, since the community would evolve just as the design foretold. After many rude shocks, planners have come to understand that planning is an ongoing process, and one that involves political as well as technical expertise.

The political problems facing planners are many. They are usually subjected to great pressures from land developers or realtors who may regard them more as peculiar obstacles in their particular business than as guardians of broader community interests. They may be urged to seek locations for industry in order to strengthen the local tax base, but almost any sites they select will be highly controversial—each citizen wants the industrial zone as far from one's home as is physically possible.

Planners today have thus become more flexible, recognizing that a plan redistributes benefits in a community. They strive to preserve as much as possible in their plans their notions of the broad community interest, while at the same time recognizing that political forces may overwhelm the best of plans.

Planners are also beginning to recognize that planning, in addition to its stated purpose, performs various latent functions. These are often not openly stated but are nevertheless important reasons for existence and support. Just as old-time political machines existed openly to nominate and elect public officials while performing in addition such latent functions as welfare, employment, and entertainment activities, so planners perform such latent functions as serving as custodians of the community conscience and ideals, expressors of community aspirations, anxieties, and guilt feelings. Planners are community psychologists and guardians of peoples' higher aspirations as well as technicians.[1]

The activities of planners remain today a subject of much public doubt and skepticism. Planners insist that they are aware of their own humbleness in attempting to predict and plan for the future, but many citizens consider planners to be presumptious if not pretentious; and council members, faced with the realities of political pressures of the world of today often overrule their long-range plans as too "impractical" or "visionary." Governor Edmund G. Brown, Jr., of California, has indicated his (and a popular) disdain for planners, saying that no individual or group of individuals can give us a blueprint for the future. Instead, he argues, public leaders must study alternatives and use trial and error. The skepticism of many concerning the utility of planning functions is nicely expressed this way: "Good planning does not drive out the bad, nor is the reverse true. They coexist and nobody can tell which is which."[2] Planning will continue for a long time to have a credibility problem.

Local Organization

The central planning agency is almost always headed by a commission which coordinates the plans of the various municipal departments and carries on planning activities of a community-wide nature. The planning commission usually has five or seven members but may have as many as fifty. It may be entirely ex officio, consisting of designated public officials, or it may be made up of citizens serving without pay, or some combination of these two. Serving the commission is a planning-department staff composed of professionals or, in smaller cities, a planning consultant who contracts with the planning commission on a job-by-job basis.

In the early days of planning, there was considerable doubt as to whom the commission and its staff should report. Sometimes they reported to the park board or some such secondary body. Usually they reported to the city council, and still do so in many cities, especially those of the weak-mayor type. But the council seldom took the planning commission seriously, often regarding it as a dumping ground for insistent cranks, a place where they could "play with pretty pictures."[3]

When urban planning came to be viewed as a vital municipal function after World War II, the tendency developed to center its activities under the mayor or manager and to make it a staff arm of the administration. This appears to be the

[1] For more on the latent functions of planning, see Charles R. Adrian, "Metropology and the Planner," *Planning 1962,* American Society of Planning Officials, Chicago, 1962, pp. 75–81.

[2] Robert Levine, *Public Planning,* Basic Books, Inc., New York, 1972, p. 128.

[3] Thomas H. Reed, *Municipal Management,* McGraw-Hill Book Company, New York, 1941, p. 305.

dominant pattern today and planners not only work through the commission, but directly with the chief executive, to whom they have, in many communities, become major advisers and policy innovators.

Because of this trend, cities that have a resident planning staff have an advantage over cities that hire a planning consultant to visit the community occasionally, or hire the planner from a nearby larger city on an overtime basis, or receive technical assistance from a state agency. (About one-third of the cities over 10,000 population have a full-time planning director.) The resident planner, furthermore, has advantages in seeking to secure public support for the products of the staff. The nonresident consultant has much less opportunity to conduct a sales campaign on behalf of a new part of the overall plan, or a new subdivision, or zoning ordinance.

Performance Measures

Planners are only just beginning to recognize the social impact of their proposals. A promising development is to move from drawing boards to computers and, visualizing the city as a system, to attempt simulations to determine how one set of variables might react on another.

State and Federal Programs

Both the state and federal governments have been most interested in planning that involves more than one local unit. As noted earlier, some states are now encouraging and even requiring the organization of substate planning and development units. The Housing Act of 1954 provided "Section 701" funds for comprehensive planning and subsequently encouraged the creation of councils of government by requiring, from 1966 on, that Model Cities projects and a number of other projects since, must meet the approval of a regional planning body which would certify that their proposals are consistent with regional plans.

LAND-USE CONTROLS

The master plan drawn up by the planning commission is not usually enacted into law but serves as a basic guide for the legislative and administrative officials. The governing body may instead formally adopt a map that becomes the official statement of policy. The policies implied in the map or in statements of principle that sometimes accompany it are put into effect through three types of land-use controls: subdivision regulations, zoning, and building-construction codes.

State governments have been most active in strengthening such regulations for unincorporated areas and small cities. The federal interest has been expressed in court cases, already noted, that challenge certain of these practices as being designed to keep out blacks and other minorities, or low-income residents.

Subdividing

Control over subdividing—the parceling of land into lots—is basic to the implementation of a plan. Subdividing is accomplished by requiring the land developer to present a "plat," this is, a map showing some or all the following: lot sizes and shapes, utilities, topography, soil types, street sizes and patterns, and other relevant data. This plat must be in conformity with established policy and may be subject to review by the planning commission, as well as by health, highway, and other authorities before it is approved. No land can be built upon until a plat is approved, though platting may not be required in commercial, industrial, or rural nonfarm areas. With this control, planners can prevent the development of land without provision for necessary services.

Where subdivision regulations are few or nonexistent, ambitious land developers have subdivided far beyond the foreseeable needs of a community and have talked or pressured the governing body into furnishing utilities to an otherwise vacant subdivision. This, in effect, forces the taxpayers to subsidize speculation in real estate.

Zoning

The control of the height, area, and use of buildings or lots may be achieved either by zoning or by subdivision deed restrictions. The former is public policy enforceable at law, while the latter are private contractual relationships enforceable in civil action before the courts. Subdivision deed restrictions are often used to protect property values where inadequate or no zoning exists. They are not a substitute for zoning, however, for in order to enforce their provisions, a resident must bring a court action against the violator. This is expensive, time-consuming, perhaps embarrassing, and often thought not worth the bother.

Zoning has now become the standard method of ensuring the efficient use of land and of promulgating many of the provisions of the master plan. The community is normally divided up into residential, commercial, and industrial zones, and perhaps into further subcategories. Zones should not be taken too literally, however, as being belts or areas of the community. A zone may be very small—it may be a narrow strip along a street or railroad track, or it may be a single lot. The location of a single lot or of a few lots of one classification in the midst of a more preferred type—"spot zoning"—may be very profitable to an owner able to sell a lot in an area zoned for single-family homes to a filling-station or supermarket chain. But it means a loss in the total value of the community. Because this loss is socialized among many persons who individually have less incentive to exert pressure than does the single profiteer, such practices take place with considerable regularity in some communities, sometimes reducing to an absurdity the concept of zoning.

In addition to restrictions concerning use of land, the zoning ordinance will usually restrict the height of buildings in relation to the width of the street, the size of yards, and the use to which the area is put. Residential and commercial zones normally have such restrictions. Further limitations are placed on area that is usable for building. In single-family-home areas, the building line may be 20 or 30 feet back of the sidewalk, for example. And apartment buildings are no longer allowed to take up the whole of the lot with little provision for sunlight and air. A building in a residential area is today generally required to come no nearer than a specified distance to the lot line—the distance being determined by the height of the buildings in the neighborhood.

Competent planning and zoning will not in itself guarantee a "city beautiful." This is demonstrated by developments in New York skyscraper construction. After World War II, a large number of moderate-sized skyscrapers—twenty to thirty stories in height—were built. The financiers of these projects were anxious to make a maximum utilization of Manhattan's expensive land. The architects were therefore forced to plan them, not with aesthetic considerations paramount, but rather so as to fit the minimum setback requirements of the zoning ordinance. Lewis Mumford has given a fitting title to the resulting "style": wedding-cake modern. (The zoning rules regarding the height of buildings usually require a certain amount of setback as the number of stories increases. Thus, a building may use the full ground space for perhaps ten stories, after which there must be 1 foot of setback from the building line for, perhaps, 4 feet of height. This allows air and sunlight to reach the lower floors.)

The Zoning Ordinance Zoning is intended, of course, to do more than merely protect property values. It is also used to ensure the availability of adequate light, air, and accessibility to all property. It protects the public health and minimizes the number of fire hazards. The zoning ordinance—which is sometimes the only formal and legal promulgation of the efforts of the planning commission—is logically based on the city's overall plans and must, therefore, be adjusted to conform with the almost constant changes in the plans.

The zoning ordinance is sometimes primarily a mosaic of the pressures applied upon the council members. Professional planners prefer that it be drawn up by the planning staff and have the endorsement of the planning commission. If this procedure is followed, the ordinance is likely to enjoy some protection from the immediate, short-range demands of effective interests. Unless the zoning ordinance—which usually must be enacted by the council in order to have any legal validity—is coordinated with the work of the planning commission, the latter will lose its principal device for implementing its plans.

Building-Construction Codes

A community with a complete set of land-use controls will have one or more building codes. These are usually known as building, plumbing, electrical, heating, and safe-and-sanitary-housing codes. They seek to enforce the subdivision and zoning regulations and the housing standards desired in the community, by requiring permits to build or install equipment. This is coupled with inspections to determine whether or not compliance has taken place or, in the case of safe-and-sanitary-housing ordinances, is being maintained.

Building inspectors and zoning administrators can destroy the effectiveness of the zoning ordinances as well as the building code by overlooking violations or granting exceptions. They are subjected to great pressures and temptations. The physical appearance, not to say the reputation, of a community may depend upon their competence and incorruptibility. Because of inadequate codes and poor enforcement procedures, FHA regulations have, especially on the outer fringe, often given home buyers more protection than have those of the local government.

Performance Measures

The stated goal of these local regulations is to preserve communities from physical deterioration and promote the health, comfort, and safety of residents. Cases in the federal courts argue they also effectively discriminate against those of a lower social class and may mask discrimination against blacks. It should be noted, however, that one school of argument holds that these regulations in the long run have proved ineffective in preventing decay or even in fruitfully guiding development. The actual social effects of these rules is yet to be fully researched.

URBAN HOUSING POLICY

American urban housing conditions have improved along with the rise in the American standard of living in the years since the end of World War II. Owner occupancy was at an all-time high according to the census of 1970, and most homes had the basic services and amenities—electricity, radios, television sets, indoor plumbing, refrigerators, automatic washing machines—even among persons of quite modest income. Most of the figures revealed by the census exceed by far comparable statistics in other nations.

Yet many Americans remain ill-housed by prevailing standards, and much blight and many dysfunctional buildings characterize our cities.

Federal Housing Policy for the Middle Class

The ecological pattern in American cities has been one of allowing the central parts of the city to decay and become low-rent housing while higher-priced housing moves outward along the periphery. Among the most successful of all federal programs was one underwriting this process for the benefit of middle-class citizens. Under the New Deal of Franklin Roosevelt, the FHA was established to guarantee home loans. Thus the ordinary risks were removed for bankers and they could reduce interest rates. This program, supplemented by a similar one of the Veterans' Administration after World War II, in effect underwrote the mass exodus to suburbia for the middle class and a substantial part of the working class. What it left behind was the very poor and those discriminated against racially in the core city.

Traditional American housing policy has always been to let low-income people live in whatever is left over. In the days before the automobile, some exceptions to this were made, since factories were located near the downtown area and workers were dependent upon public transportation or their own legs. In cities such as New York and Chicago, therefore, tenement buildings (multistoried apartments with minimal conveniences) were constructed specifically to provide housing for these people and to provide lucrative investments for absentee owners. In cities that have done most of their growing since World War I, however, few such buildings exist, and the poor live in converted and subdivided homes and apartments abandoned by the fleeing middle class. It is in the blighted housing of core cities that many American instances of social disorganization are found. Federal-government programs have attempted to address this problem.

Public Housing

Public housing had long been constructed abroad, but prior to the election of Franklin Roosevelt, it was generally regarded as unconstitutional in this country. Beginning in 1933, some fifty projects in thirty-six cities were federally constructed and administered by the Public Works Administration (PWA). It was not, however, until the U.S. Housing Authority (now a part of HUD) was created under the Federal Housing Act of 1937 that public housing could become a new national policy.

The act was bitterly opposed, however, as have been all subsequent acts and propositions calling for public housing. Opposition has come partly from realtors, bankers, and others who profit from the private housing industry. Others have said that public housing is wrong in theory: that housing, within the concepts of our prevailing economic system, belongs properly in the realm of private and not public endeavor. A third type of opposition has come from those persons who fear that public housing projects would in one way or another damage existing property values. Finally opposition has come against the architectural high-rise form which critics argue results in impersonal semitenements that encourage alienation and crime.

The Federal Housing Act of 1937 The act of 1937 provided for quasi-public corporations known as "housing authorities" to be established wherever state laws permitted. The authorities were made up of appointed officials, serving without pay in most cities. The authorities drew up the plans for federal approval, received a loan, and constructed and operated the projects. The city had to agree to eliminate unsafe and unsanitary dwelling units equal in number to the new units to be constructed. State and local governments had to contract to furnish municipal services either free or for a small payment in lieu of taxes by the national government. This generally meant that public housing would be subsidized, not only in the process of building, but afterward, too, and by both the national and local governments.

The status of the housing authority as a separate corporation had the effect of relieving the municipality of responsibility for its debts and could be used to avoid state constitutional debt limits. The local housing units, once constructed, remained to a large degree under federal control, since questions of rent levels and eligibility to reside in the project were decided by its agency. Persons whose incomes came to exceed the established maximum were required to leave the projects.

It was not even possible to get a new housing act through Congress until 1949, despite the powerful support given public housing by three leaders of the liberal Democrats, the Southern Democrats, and the Republicans, in the Wagner-Ellender-Taft Bill. The Federal Housing Act of 1949 reaffirmed the principle that providing for housing was basically a private business matter, and it did not change the fundamentals of the 1937 act. It made adjustments, however, in order to recognize inflation and the changing concepts of a minimum standard of human living.

In 1965, the amendments to the act eliminated the requirement of 20 percent local contribution, permitted local authorities to lease units from private owners, and in the turnkey program permitted a local authority to purchase units from private builders after construction or rehabilitation had been completed.

Public housing has never functioned as the planners intended, largely because it acquired a reputation for housing only the most marginal, sub-working-class persons, largely welfare recipients. Thus, the Pruitt-Igoe project in St. Louis was completed in 1956 at a cost of $36 million. It was designed to house some 12,000 persons. But working-class persons moved out as soon as possible. By 1971, only 3,000 remained. Only 16 of the 43 buildings were still in use. The others had been totally vandalized. Demolition of the whole project followed a study-committee report.

There has been little support in Congress for much expansion of public housing, and the program continues as a modest one. Since 1970, two trends have been evident: the move away from high-rise structures for families and the move from tract development to individual structures integrated into the larger community. In addition HUD has encouraged the adoption of fair-share plans, such as was adopted voluntarily in the Dayton region. Under this proposal each city would agree to have a low-income development quota based on its proportion of the region's total population.

Yet municipally administered public housing projects appear to be a permanent fixture as a local function of government. They will probably not expand beyond the small responsibility for total housing they now have, however, for the organized opposition to them is strong. Housing of a kind that would be efficient, for rental to low-income people does not fit the American dream. As a result of this, even those who would benefit often oppose it. The problem of gaining neighborhood acceptance of such projects continues to be a serious one.

Urban Renewal

The Federal Housing Act of 1949, among other things, offered aid to communities for slum clearance and urban redevelopment. Grants could be made to local units to acquire, clear, and prepare blighted areas for the construction of new dwellings. The cleared land could then either be used for public housing projects or be resold to private builders for redevelopment.

Some slums were cleared away as a result of the 1949 act, but only ten projects were completed in the ten years that followed its adoption, and only fifty-one by 1964. New slums developed at a faster rate than existing ones were cleared and some people began to suspect urban renewal had a hand in creating them. The housing acts of 1954 and others through the 1960s emphasized urban renewal. This orientation was reinforced by the concern felt by local business leaders and realtors over the downward trend in land values in the older parts of cities.

In 1973, urban renewal was one of the programs phased out, with revenue sharing substituted in its place. It had come to be bitterly criticized by core-city residents. Many professionals viewed it as a method of renewing downtown areas while the poor and blacks were crowded further out into other communities. Especially criticized were the benefits some businesses accrued (through higher property values, or increased customers, for example), the destruction of many small businesses and urban ethnic communities, and the erection of luxury apartments on some of the cleared land.

Rent Supplements

Welfare agencies had for some time provided rent money for clients. An attempt was made to extend this practice to other low-income residents who were not necessarily on welfare. Legislation passed in the Housing and Urban Development Act of 1965 (Sections 235 and 236) provided for rent supplements for low-income families. The act would permit private developers to plan projects for low-income residents with generous federal loans and grants and, under certain conditions, would permit residents to purchase dwellings. The federal government in the Real Estate Settlement Procedures Act of 1974 established regulations for limiting closing costs and, in the Emergency Home Purchase Assistance Act, provided for the purchase by the national government of mortgages to stimulate the private-housing market.

A Closing Note

Despite a considerable amount of housing construction in the years following 1946, America seems not to be keeping pace with the increase in population. The problems posed by this became still more complicated as the rate of new family formations increased in the 1960s—the marriage rate increased a generation after the sharp increase in the birthrate beginning in the war year 1942. Because the birthrate remained high until the late 1960s, new family formations increased. The result will be a continuing increase in demand for housing at least for the next decade, followed by a slackening. Housing and urban-renewal programs demonstrate the interdependence of governments under a system of cooperative federalism. Municipalities acting alone cannot possibly provide an adequate housing policy for the nation.

The federal loan programs to aid the middle class and upper-working class have generally been regarded as an outstanding success. Those designed to aid the lower-income citizens by improving the quality of housing and thereby encouraging these citizens to help themselves have been less so.

PUBLIC WORKS AND PUBLIC UTILITIES

The Administration of Public Works

Whenever a city is large enough to be organized on a departmental basis, it will have a department of public works operating under one title or another. The department usually includes many utility and other service functions—for example, divisions in charge of street maintenance, cleaning, and lighting, of bridges, of sewers and sewage disposal, of refuse collection and disposal, and of public property. Traffic engineering is frequently in the department of public works, as are municipally owned utilities, such as electricity, gas supply, public markets, and slaughterhouses, although any of these may be established as independent departments. Public transportation, airports, and water supply are in the great majority of cases, but not always, organized as separate departments.

The Department Head

The general view of professional administrators is that the public works department should be organized with a single department head responsible to the chief executive. The once-common autonomous board has generally been abandoned. This is not true, however, in the case of public transportation, electrical energy, and water supply, where the board is still often found, even in strong-mayor and manager cities.

The director of public works (often called the city engineer, especially in smaller cities) is normally an engineer of one kind or another. In small cities, it is expected that the director will possess technical qualities. In large cities, administrative ability is imperative, while engineering ability is less important and may not be a requirement at all.

Public Utilities

Public utilities are basic services provided to virtually all members of an urban community. Public utilities are not necessarily publicly owned. Many of them are, but the majority are owned and operated by private corporations, and some by individual proprietors. A list of utilities within a municipality includes street railways, busses, telephone, telegraph, electricity, water, and gas services. Other functions that are of the nature of utilities, although not always legally considered to be such, are auditoriums, port facilities, slaughterhouses, airports, and possibly toll bridges, toll roads, sewers, and public markets.

Public utilities are businesses affected with more than a usual amount of public interest and therefore expected by the public to be subjected to more than a normal amount of governmental control. They are usually granted a monopoly within their areas of operation. This is because experience has shown that competition in these areas is impractical and uneconomical. Competitive utilities have existed in the past—a few still do—but generally they have proved to be wasteful of resources and have offered inferior and costly services to the public. A public utility normally has a right to use public property (over which to string electric wires, or to operate busses) and to exercise the state's power of eminent domain. It usually charges for services rendered on a benefits-received basis, and it is subject to the control of some type of public service commission whose legal responsibility it is to protect both the provider and the purchaser of services.

Regulation

In the nineteenth century, utilities were normally operated on the basis of a franchise which was granted to local utilities, most commonly, by the city government. A franchise is a license stipulating the conditions under which a utility may operate and the privileges it is to enjoy. The franchise usually stated the quality of service that was expected of the utility and the rates that could be charged. In practice, the utilities were often little inhibited by their franchises. Sometimes they resorted to bribery of public officials, sometimes they won judicial interpretations of ambiguous provisions of the franchise by the use of superior legal talent, and in almost no cases was there a public body that had the legal authority to hold the utility to the terms of its agreement.

One of the major areas of activity of reform forces at the turn of the present century was that of public utility regulation. The method of control that gradually evolved centers around a state public service commission (bearing various titles in various states) whose duty it is to determine rates after investigations and hearings and to supervise both the service and the management of the utilities. Most commissions prescribe uniform accounting methods; they often must approve expansion plans and the issuance of new securities; and they may sometimes even be authorized to order such expansions. Commissions are constantly at work overseeing the activities of the utilities, but there is considerable variation in the degree to which they are effective.

Franchises are still granted, but they are no longer so detailed as they were in the days before public service commissions. They are usually limited to a term of years (perhaps twenty-five), rather than made to exist in perpetuity, as was once common. The franchise usually provides for the privileges to be enjoyed by the utility; it may provide for a special tax structure for it; and it prescribes some conditions which must be met by the utility. It leaves most other controls to the public service commissions. In the worst days of nineteenth-century corruption, control over franchises was assumed by the state, where it has remained for the most part.

Municipal Ownership of Public Utilities

Certain functions are commonly owned by municipalities today. Nearly three-fourths of the cities of over 5,000 own their own water-distribution systems. Nearly all of them own their own sewerage systems, and one-half of them own sewage-treatment plants. Municipal airports and auditoriums are quite common, and large cities often own incinerators.

Electricity is in the large majority of cases in private hands, although many cities own plants and lines for distributing power to street lights and traffic signals. In some parts of the nation, especially in relatively isolated cities, municipal systems exist—over 500 of them. Of America's eighteen largest cities (those over one-half a million), only Cleveland and Los Angeles have city-owned electrical generating and distributing systems for general use. Municipal gas plants are very rare. Of these largest cities, only Philadelphia and Houston produce and distribute gas. Increasingly cities or regional bodies are taking over mass-transit systems. While all the largest cities own some utilities, except for Boston, which has them operated on a regional basis by the Massachusetts Metropolitan District Commission, one city in eight owns no utilities of any kind. Private ownership is the overwhelming rule even today for most functions handled by public utilities.

THE TRANSPORTATION SYSTEM

The automobile has been the most creative and most destructive force affecting American cities of the twentieth century. Making room for it to move through and a place to park it when it reaches its destination has meant destruction of much of the nineteenth-century city and the creation of a distinctive new pattern—one usually called urban sprawl. Old landmarks and, more importantly, whole communities of urban residents have been smashed in the process. At this point, somewhat late in the process, the automobile presents a new problem to local governors: given the huge increase in the price of oil as a pawn in international power politics, will the auto be anymore a practical means of transportation for the average American, or will it return to its role of pre-Henry Ford days, a rich man's toy?

Building a Street System

It is hard to fault the city leaders for their zeal in accommodating the city to the automobile. Everything possible was done to meet the needs of drivers, even drivers who lived in the suburbs and commuted into the core city. Trees were chopped down, streets widened, and expressways driven through old neighborhoods. Only toward the end of the massive rebuilding were questions asked about the fate of residents who were in the way. It was found that many of these who were moved were low-income persons and blacks. These groups were already hardpressed to find housing and some could not afford cars. Only then did what had been viewed as mainly an engineering problem begin to take on the aspects of a political problem.

The building of expressways revealed other problems involving political choices. What route should freeways follow? How often should there be an interchange? Freeways are enormously expensive. How should they be paid for? Would a toll road be feasible? Should they be paid for out of a rebate to the city from the state gasoline tax? Out of the general revenue fund? Out of a local tax on each automobile? Freeways damage property values along their immediate routes but enhance the values of property near interchanges and at either end of them. One of their main purposes is to shore up sagging property values in the downtown area and to maintain the dollar volume of business in downtown stores. If these establishments benefit particularly from the highway, should they be asked to pay an extra tax to compensate for this advantage?

Despite the expressways and a good deal of work in improving other streets, cities are not making progress against traffic congestion. The commonplace rectangular pattern of streets is inefficient for traffic flow; most streets are still expected to provide the impossible—to serve as rapid thoroughfares and as access routes to places of business; land is too scarce and valuable and wrecking operations too expensive to clear away many existing structures for parking or to widen existing streets; citizens refuse to use public transportation except as a matter of desperation.

It has been estimated that one-third of the buildings in downtown Boston would have to be torn down to provide adequate parking space for the patrons of the remaining structures. The larger the city, the smaller the proportion of residents using their cars to get downtown. But despite this, the larger the city, the more difficult it is to find adequate parking.

Beginning with its use in Oklahoma City in 1935, the parking meter has become an almost universal phenomenon along commercial streets in American cities. The meters are, in effect, yet another tax upon the motorist. They serve as a good source of revenue for cities. This income is used for street maintenance and traffic control in some cities and to construct off-street parking facilities in others. The meters themselves do not solve the parking problem, except perhaps to speed up the shopper and other parker and to discourage all-day parking along business-area streets.

Parking space is, economically speaking, a responsibility of the firm for whom the driver works or the store to which the driver-shopper is headed. This is recognized in the manner in which shopping malls and new suburban factories are constructed. Because the original business districts were built before the automobile was developed, such provisions have not been made there. Most cities now attempt to require all new commercial places to furnish adequate parking spaces off the street, though the practice is not universal.

A problem in many cities in procuring sufficient parking lots from private sources is found in the fact that the business is monopolized in the hands of one or a few large lot owners possessing considerable political power. There are several parking-lot corporations organized on a nationwide basis, each operating in numerous cities.

Performance Measures

Until recently, the principal performance measure applied to streets and expressways was traffic flow: how many cars could be moved along in what period of time? Only recently have traffic engineers and social scientists begun to ask questions about the human impacts. Thus far, physical impacts such as noise levels are the easiest to measure.

State and Federal Activities

Most states have earmarked portions of their gas and license taxes for street construction and repair, and a portion of these funds generally is allocated to cities on a formula basis. At first, federal funds were allocated only for highways connecting cities, but this policy changed at the end of the Great Depression.

The Federal Aid Highway Act of 1944 provided that one-fourth of federal funds for highways should be used for extensions within cities. As a result, many cities are building roads with up to 90 percent of the cost paid from federal grants-in-aid. Because this is the case, many questions of routing and technical specifications are determined, not by local considerations, but by the Federal Highway Administration and its definition of the general interest. This agency must approve the route and all technical details before federal funds are made available. In most cases, the cost of building is so great that without these funds freeways would not be built.

As part of the interstate system, all large cities have developed plans for freeways leading to the central business district and, for those who wish to bypass, belting the city along the periphery. Negotiations among the various units of government involved—core city, suburbs, county, state, and the Federal Highway Administration—are complex, delicate, and time-consuming. The technicians in the state and federal agencies are likely to dominate these discussions—though the often-dissenting views of community political figures may dominate the pages of the local newspaper—and these persons are in many ways changing the face of the nation, for a modification in the arterial traffic pattern is likely to cause a great many changes in land use. Meanwhile, back at the city hall, however, local interests urge the mayor or manager to intercede on their behalf. The engineers wish to maximize traffic flow in and around cities, and they want to prohibit later rule changes (e.g., in access privileges) that will modify the principal use of a road from a traffic to a business artery; real estate operators will try to mold the shape of the new road to fit their speculations and investments; owners of unsalable land will try to convince the decision makers that their property lies directly along what is certainly the ideal route; chamber of commerce managers will point out the significance of route choice to their campaigns to attract new industry for the community; heavily mortgaged homeowners will claim that if the expressway goes within a few blocks of their homes it will ruin the value of the property—though they may want an interchange located just beyond the sound of roaring truck exhausts; merchants along heavily traveled, free-access routes will complain that the siphoning off of the traffic onto a—to them inaccessible—freeway will threaten them with bankruptcy. With an occasional nod to overriding local demands—the kind that are powerful enough to potentially involve the intervention of a legislator or member of Congress—the professional engineers go about applying their professional values to the work of serving the most numerous interest of all, the motoring public.

In 1967, a cabinet office, the Department of Transportation, was created, and from this point on federal grants became available to pay some of the relocation costs for persons displaced by urban-freeway construction. Safeguards were introduced to encourage citizen rights of appeal before clearing and construction began. The department also became concerned about mass transit. In 1969, the first grant program was passed to permit purchase of new equipment for existing public transit systems, a defraying of some operating costs, and an underwriting of research. In a 1973 act, at President Nixon's urging, monies from the Federal Highway Fund for the first time could be devoted to mass transit if the urban center so desired to spend its share. In 1974, in the National Mass Transportation Assistance Act, the federal government made large-scale grants to cities for acquisition and operation of mass-transit systems. The program, which would operate through 1980, included incentive grants for the development of corridor corporations involving several municipalities and contained a provision that the elderly and handicapped must be admitted at half-fare during non-peak hours.

What of the Future?

The American love affair with the automobile may have its days numbered, though this is by no means certain. A number of cities are following the lead of the San Francisco Bay area and are taking a closer look at subways or other forms of mass transit, although such transit systems have encountered enormous financial, administrative, and technological difficulties. At the same time, the building of freeways continues, especially in the nations's smaller core cities.

Airports: Public Subsidy for Transportation

American governments have traditionally subsidized methods of transportation, especially when they are new. We have subsidized facilities for canalboats, railways, automobiles and trucks, ocean transportation, and, after World War I, air travel. Beginning in the 1920s, cities were authorized to construct, and usually to operate, municipal airports. Today almost all the nation's largest cities have local-owned airports. In some cases this is a county function and there are several ad hoc airport authorities to cover the metropolitan areas, while in other cities the airports are leased to private operators. But in most places the city owns and operates the facilities.

So optimistic have people been about the future of air travel that municipal airports are common even in cities of under 10,000 population. The Federal Airport Act of 1946 probably encouraged many cities to construct airports that are not self-supporting and, for a long time into the future, will not be self-supporting. The act made no allowance for aid in operation and maintenance, and these costs have proved to be a great burden for many municipalities. In 1973, the Airport Development Acceleration Act continued to provide funds and advice, but this was activity that economy-minded and ecology-minded members of Congress marked for retrenchment.

PARKS AND RECREATION

Parks

The inhabitants and public officials of cities have often been slow in providing for the benefits of spacious, beautiful, and useful parks. Parks are of great psychological value, especially to the apartment or slum dweller, to whom they may be the only available substitute for a front lawn or a backyard.

Cities such as New York and Philadelphia were allowed to mature with almost complete disregard for the need for open spaces, for grass, trees, and shrubs accessible in all neighborhoods. (Slum dwellers will not use many playgrounds and green spaces that are beyond short walking distance. Open spaces such as Central Park are of limited value to low-income persons.) Even cities that expanded at a much later date, such as Detroit, failed to plan for parks. Today a belated attempt is being made in all large cities to provide small recreational playgrounds and indoor gymnasiums and swimming pools. In most cities it is now too late to provide areas for large parks that might have been set aside twenty-five, fifty, or more years ago. As a result, quite a few cities (or ad hoc park districts) have constructed parks and beaches outside of the urban areas. This practice began in 1893 in the Boston region. Outlying parks and "reservations" must sometimes be located two hours' travel or more from the heart of the city. Where this is so, it at the least causes inconvenience and traffic hazards on weekends. To those in the lower-income groups who have no automobiles, but who most need the facilities, these areas may be quite inaccessible.

Some municipalities have sought to require provisions for a reasonable amount of park and playground area at the time of, or in advance of, subdividing. The courts have not been particularly cooperative, however, and several types of such laws and ordinances have been declared unconstitutional. Of course, some cities have planned their parks carefully, fitting them into the long-range scheme of things and not waiting for a park to be located through the accident of a donated piece of land. Quite a few American cities have fine park systems. Minneapolis's is particularly beautiful. Chicago, Boston, and other cities rate near the top, too.

Zoos

A large city often makes a zoo out of one of its parks. Zoos are sometimes operated by a board and department separate from the parks department. They are expensive to maintain but are immensely popular with children and adults alike. Zoos such as in Washington are among the finest in the world. (The heavy cost of the great San Diego Zoo is considered justified by many citizens because the zoo generates a considerable tourist trade.) All municipal institutions seem to have their opponents. Some people, for example, consider zoos to be either a waste of the taxpayers' money or a cruelty to the confined wild animals. But most people love animals and like to observe them, provided that they are given adequate and expert care and attention.

State or Federal Programs

States have become concerned about regional planning to include parks, particularly for summer recreation outside of the crowded cities and suburbs. Kensington Park on the outskirts of Detroit is part of the Huron-Clinton Park authority, financed wholly, until recently, by a regional property tax.

The federal government provides some advice for such parks, but few funds to encourage development. Symbolic of its attitude is its aid to urban zoos. It provides for the disposal of unwanted wildlife possessed by a local zoo, and that is the extent of its efforts.

Recreational Administration

Many disputes have arisen over the desirable form of organization in the field of parks and recreation. Although the typical citizen probably thinks of parks and recreation as two aspects of a single function, professionals in the field are not sure. Once it was common for the city government to have separate departments for parks and for recreation, but the postwar trend has been away from this. In many cities, the school boards also provide an organized summer recreation program.

In the past, parks and recreation departments were commonly set up under autonomous administrative boards, and it was not uncommon for them to have independent sources of income so that they existed practically as separate ad hoc units of local government, similar in status to the school boards. Parks and recreation boards were (and still are) very often made up of high-status members of the community. Professional recreation workers have generally tended to favor the independent board because of the support which it gives to the recreation program, particularly when the budget is under consideration. They also argue that such a board offers a continuity of policy not to be found when the head of the department changes at the pleasure of the chief executive.

General administrators in the field of municipal management argue, however, that the parks and recreation function is not unique in its problems of management and that it should be administered as a regular department of the city under the control of the chief executive. They contend that this activity should be financed out of the general fund rather than a separate tax levy, that its budget should be treated like those of other city departments, and that the departments should make use of the municipal staff services for purchasing, personnel, maintenance, and the like. In order to maintain organized community interest in parks and recreation, there is a tendency for a board to be retained as an advisory body and hence a watchdog, while at the same time leaving administrative control under the chief executive.

Libraries

The first library supported by taxes was established in Peterborough, New Hampshire, in 1833. Sometimes libraries are privately endowed and privately operated but are indirectly agencies of the city because they receive an annual appropriation either from the council or from a special property-tax levy. This type of library, especially common in New England and the South, is controlled by a self-perpetuating board of trustees. Other libraries are entirely public, controlled either by the school district or by the city government. They usually have autonomous control through a library board, but a few cities have a single librarian reporting directly to the chief executive.

The decentralizing tendency of cities means, in many places, that the main public library is often isolated in the center of the city from which the population is receding, often in an area with a high crime rate and frequented by transients. This poses the threat that fewer people will use the libraries. The answer seems to be in a greater use of branch libraries and bookmobiles in outlying residential areas. Such a movement has been under way for years but is now being accelerated. Connected with the problem also is the question of allowing suburbanites to use the core-city library, for which they do not pay taxes. Some cities allow free use of the library to anyone who is employed in the city regardless of where he or she may live. This is another form of subsidizing the suburbs. County libraries and ad hoc library districts are arising to supply the suburbs in many places.

Again federal and state assistance in this field has been largely advisory, with no large-scale grant programs.

Museums and Art Galleries

There are far fewer museums and art galleries in the United States than there are libraries. Most large cities operate them, however. They are usually autonomously controlled in the same fashion as are libraries, and they enjoy the protection of the "patrons of the arts" in the political process. These patrons are often well-to-do and influential persons. The National Gallery of Art Extension Service provides filmstrips and other materials at postage costs to museums and libraries. A number of large-city art museums faced with mounting costs and located in declining core-city neighborhoods have had to reduce the hours of viewing. The Detroit Institute of Arts is an example.

WATER SUPPLY

Probably no single governmental domestic policy is of more importance to the future pattern of development of the United States than is that of water. It has been said, without exaggeration, that "you could write the story of man's growth in terms of his epic concerns with water."[4] Humanity is utterly dependent upon it. It determined where people first settled as they moved into new lands. It dictates the location of most heavy industry. It controls the size to which a city, whether it be New York, Denver, or Los Angeles, may grow. It limits possible land uses. Its quality affects the state of the public health, the size of the municipal budget, and the taste of a highball. Its quantity determines whether bluegrass lawns may be watered in August, a rowboat must be kept in the garage as an escape vehicle from a flash flood, or the economy of a resort area will flourish or wither. The nature of the problems involved vary geographically and according to use. In the East, for example, the principal problems center around the distribution and quality of water; in the West, the major concern is with quantity. Some industries may be able to use raw water, whereas others need the highest quality; but much of the need is taken care of by industry itself, and governments need concern themselves only about regulation. A political issue related to water supply concerns the fluoridation of water, a practice designed to reduce dental caries. Fluoridation has been especially opposed by right-wing extremists.

Local Organizations

Many municipalities receive their water supply from wells. This is a relatively inexpensive method for small cities and villages, although the water is often very hard and, until one becomes accustomed to it, unpalatable. As core-city suburbs increase in size, their wells tend to become dry, for the table level of the ground water drops.

[4] Bernard Frank, "The Story of Water as the Story of Man," in Alfred Stefferud (ed.), *Water*, U.S. Government Printing Office, Washington, 1955.

Few of the larger cities use wells. Memphis uses them. Brooklyn once did, but for many years citizens objected that the water was salty and brackish. This led to abandonment of the privately owned wells in 1947 and the use throughout New York City of water from the Catskill and other reservoirs. In large cities, however, many wells have been sunk by business firms for air-conditioning purposes. In many cities, the table level is sinking rapidly as a result, and strict regulation of these practices has become necessary. Some cities require all water withdrawn for air-conditioning purposes to be returned to the ground. New York has had such a rule since 1933. Business firms are not likely to do this voluntarily, since it adds to the expense of the system.

Most large cities depend for their water supply upon rivers, the damming of small streams, or lakes. The problem of securing a supply of relatively unpolluted water becomes increasingly difficult as urban populations grow and the amount of industrial and human waste dumped into streams increases. Cities along the Great Lakes have until recently been able to get palatable, germ-free water with a minimum of treatment. Some cities, such as Philadelphia, which uses the Delaware River, must use a great amount of filtration and chemical treatment, for their sources are badly polluted.

Cities along the ocean, such as New York and Los Angeles, have not been able to convert sea water inexpensively and have had to bring their supplies hundreds of miles from the mountains. Congress, in 1952, first authorized the Secretary of the Interior to cooperate with the state and local governments in an effort to devise a process for making use of salt and brackish water for home and factory consumption. Some progress is being made, as in San Diego, where considerable use is made of converted seawater. The principal problems are economic rather than technological. Some growing inland cities have had to resort to desperate measures to ensure a water supply. Denver, for example, gouged a 23-mile tunnel through solid rock to reach water sources on the western slope of the Rocky Mountains.

State and Federal Programs

Because water resources do not follow state or local boundaries, intergovernmental arrangements and potential problems and conflicts abound. Water supply and the quality of water in streams is now seen as a state and federal problem and responsibility. In the past both state and federal levels have given advice and financial assistance to cities in building and expanding water systems.

SANITATION SERVICES

Sewage Treatment

Municipal and other local governments bear the primary responsibility for sewage treatment, including septic-tank installation practices, and for provision of means for carrying off rain water through storm drains and holding back floods through the construction (often with the aid of federal funds) of levees and retaining walls. All these activities cost a good deal of money. Sewerage and sewage-disposal plants are among the most expensive of municipal capital outlays, and great controversies center about the means of financing them and of holding costs to a minimum. Public forums in a city considering a new sewage-disposal plant give one the distinct impression that every taxpayer is also an expert in sanitary engineering. Storm drains, too, are matters of great concern to citizens—though usually only during wet springs. A complex cost-benefit problem is frequently involved. As a result, citizens in much of the nation feel convinced in April that a new storm-drain system in their neighborhood is necessary at any cost. By August, they have forgotten their earlier view and are now certain that larger water mains or better supply sources are needed so as to make it possible for them to preserve the color of their precious bluegrass during dry spells.

Boston, in 1823, was the first American city to install a system of sanitary sewers. Other cities followed as their populations increased. In those early days, the sewage was commonly dumped into a nearby stream or other body of water. This was in itself a scientific method of disposal. Contrary to a popular impression that the downriver town drank the raw sewage of the one above it, the chemical reaction of the oxygen in the water with the sewage would convert the organic matter into nitrates and other non-disease-bearing by-products. If a sufficient supply of water was available and cities were not too close together, this approach was reasonably safe.

Today, as a public health precaution, sewage must be treated before disposal. There are several methods of treatment, and they are all normally expensive. Because cities, and often their suburbs, may try to avoid this expense, several states have established water-pollution commissions. These commissions may, if they find that a municipality is endangering the public health or the fish and wildlife of the state, order a municipality to construct a sewage-treatment plant. The state has sometimes had to resort to its coercive power and force cities into safety precautions.

Sewage-treatment plants, like those for water treatment, are least expensive if used to full capacity and if one or a few rather than many of them exist in a metropolitan area.

In 1965, Congress passed a Water Quality Act and augmented this in 1966 with the Clean Waters Restoration Act. In 1972, Congress passed the Federal Water Pollution Control Act over President Nixon's veto. In recent years, economy moves have reduced these federal programs. Nevertheless these acts, and state actions that reinforced them, established standards for water-pollution control and provided for federal funds to communities and states participating in the program. The funds were made available for the administration of planning agencies concerned with pollution control throughout a given river basin. The planning agencies are required to show that they can develop an effective, comprehensive water quality control and abatement plan which can meet federal water quality standards.

Solid-Waste Disposal

Municipal sanitation also involves the disposal of ashes, rubbish, and garbage. These may be collected separately or in various combinations, depending upon the method of disposal. Ashes are becoming less of a municipal task. Industries normally dispose of their own, while few homes or apartments are now heated by coal. Ashes, together with street dirt, make good fill for low places and are commonly disposed of in this fashion. Sometimes they are simply dumped.

Rubbish (nonorganic trash and discards) is also used for fill, or it may be dumped. Sometimes it is incinerated. Garbage (organic waste) may be disposed of by incineration, use of the reduction process, the sanitary fill, feeding to hogs, dumping, grinding at central locations, or grinding in the home. Incineration is expensive but very effective. It is used particularly in larger cities and is becoming increasingly popular. The expensive reduction process, which is used to recover waste fats, has been tried in large cities but is passing from favor. The sanitary landfill method is used quite extensively, especially in small or medium-sized cities. A major problem in some metropolitan areas is finding areas outside of the urbanized part for this purpose. Rural areas are almost universally reluctant to have such a facility within their boundaries.

Feeding garbage to hogs has been popular, since a part of the cost of collection and disposal can thereby be recouped. It is believed, however, that the feeding of raw garbage may be a method of transmitting vesicular exanthema among hogs and cholera and trichinosis to human beings. As a result, many states now require precooking of the garbage. This additional cost is causing municipalities to switch to other disposal methods, especially to incineration.

Garbage is sometimes dumped, either into a pit to be buried or into a body of water. This is usually a temporary measure, although some small places use it as a regular disposal method.

Grinding of garbage has the effect of converting it into sewage. This is a method wherein solving the garbage problem adds to the sewage problem. Grinding at central locations is quite common and works satisfactorily if an adequate sewage-disposal plant exists. The home garbage grinder has become extremely popular and new homes throughout the nation are commonly built to include them. In some places they are causing problems by overtaxing the sewerage system or the disposal plant. The increased amount of organic matter that is thereby dumped into bodies of water may constitute a threat to fish and wildlife by removing oxygen from the water to a dangerous extent. But the grinders symbolize, to the homemaker, another step in America's material progress.

Municipalities do not necessarily collect and dispose of ashes, rubbish, or garbage themselves. In some places, the job is done by a collector holding a contract from the city. In others, the city licenses several collectors. A great many cities do the job themselves, however, through a department of public works. The sewerage system is almost always operated by the city itself, but an important policy question to be settled in connection with this activity is whether storm drains should be connected to the regular sewers or constructed separately. Engineers prefer the latter method.

The federal-government program, the Solid Waste Disposal Act, has been extended through periods of financial emergency. Its purpose is to encourage testing of innovative techniques and further research of the problems.

Air and Noise Pollution

Except for a few urban areas beset with smog problems, such as Los Angeles, most action in respect to air pollution has come as part of an ongoing federal air-pollution-control program which takes the familiar form of encouraging regulation of air pollutors and research. Noise control is one of the interests of professionals in the Department of Transportation.

A Closing Note

Early planners of the "city beautiful" school imagined that city design alone could solve social problems. We know now only that design may have some independent effect, especially perhaps as to the expression social disorganization will take. Yet physical features are more easily changed than human behavior, so they were among the first features that reformers worked with. In the following chapter we deal with urban services that more directly deal with problems of the human condition—some quite successfully, some less so.

SELECTED READINGS

Abrams, Charles: "The Uses of Land in Cities," Scientific American, 213:150–160, September, 1965. (Argues that taxing policy is the most effective method of land-use regulation.)

Adrian, Charles R.: "Metropology and the Planner," Planning 1962, American Society of Planning Officials, Chicago, 1962. (Discusses the psychological role of the regional planner as the conscience of the community and distinguishes this task from the self-image planners have of themselves as creators of a well-ordered community.)

"The Agony of the Commuter," Newsweek, Jan. 18, 1971, pp. 44–49.

Altshuler, Alan A.: The City Planning Process: A Political Analysis, Cornell University Press, Ithaca, N.Y., 1965.

Anderson, Martin: The Federal Bulldozer: A Critical Analysis of Urban Renewal, The M.I.T. Press, Cambridge, Mass., 1964. (A harsh criticism. No longer considered as excessive as it was when first published.)

Babcock, Richard: The Zoning Game: Municipal Practices and Policies, The University of Wisconsin Press, Madison, Wis., 1966. (Zoning laws and practices in the United States and other countries.)

Butler, G. D.: Introduction to Community Recreation, 4th ed., McGraw-Hill Book Company, New York, 1967.

Catanese, Anthony J.: Planners and Local Politics, Sage Publications, Inc., Beverly Hills, Calif., 1974. (Calls for the integration of planning, politics, and the private sector in an effort to produce greater achievements than planners have in the past.)

Chapin, F. Stuart, Jr.: Urban Land Use Planning, 2d ed., Harper & Row, Publishers, Incorporated, New York, 1965.

Crenson, Matthew: The Un-Politics of Air Pollution, Johns Hopkins Press, Baltimore, 1970.

Davies, J. Clarence, III: Neighborhood Groups and Urban Renewal, Columbia University Press, New York, 1966. (The neighborhoods to be renewed and those surrounding them are often centers of opposition to renewal plans.)

Doig, Jameson W.: Metropolitan Transportation Politics and the New York Region, Columbia University Press, 1966. (Advocates a regional policy.)

Drury, Margaret: Mobile Homes: The Unrecognized Revolution in American Housing, rev. ed., Praeger, New York, 1972.

Editors of Fortune: The Exploding Metropolis, Anchor Books, Doubleday & Company, Inc., Garden City, N.Y., 1958. (Essays on large urban problems.)

Greer, Scott: Urban Renewal and American Cities, The Bobbs-Merrill Company, Inc., Indianapolis, 1965. (A review and evaluation in sociopolitical terms.)

Gruen, Nina Jaffe, and Claude Gruen: Low and Moderate Income Housing in the Suburbs, Praeger, New York, 1971. (Analysis of attitudes of residents of the Dayton region who will be affected by implementation of the "Dayton Plan.")

Heckscher, August: The City and the Arts, Institute of Local Government, University of Pittsburgh, Pittsburgh, Pa., 1964. (Municipal government and support of the institutions of fine arts.)

Hoar, Charles, and Demetrius Iatridis: Housing the Poor in Suburbia, Ballinger Publishing Company., Cambridge, Mass., 1974. (Five case studies of the conflicts resulting from locating lower-class persons in middle-class suburbs.)

Jacobs, Jane: The Death and Life of Great American Cities, Random House, Inc., New York, 1961. (A vigorous criticism of the housing and life-style preferences of the middle class and of urban planners.)

Kaplan, Harold: Urban Renewal Politics, Columbia University Press, New York, 1963. (Urban-renewal policy making in Newark is dominated by the professionals.)

Kaplan, Marshall, and others: The Model Cities Program: A History and Analysis of the Planning Process in Three Cities, Atlanta, Georgia; Seattle, Washington; and Dayton, Ohio; U.S. Department of Housing and Urban Development, Washington, 1969.

Lamb, Charles M.: Land Use Politics and Law in the 1970s, Program of Policy Studies, George Washington University, Washington, 1975. (Trends in land-use law.)

Lupo, Alan, Frank Colcord, and Edmund P. Fowler: Rites of Way: The Politics of Transportation in Boston and the U.S. City, Little, Brown and Company, Boston, 1971. (Case study of Boston, followed by discussion based on studies of eight other large cities.)

Makielski, Stanislaw J., Jr.: The Politics of Zoning, Columbia University Press, New York, 1966. (A study of New York City.)

Miller, David R. (ed.): Urban Transportation Policy: New Perspectives, Lexington Books, Lexington, Mass., 1972.

Moynihan, Daniel P. (ed.): Toward a National Urban Policy, Basic Books, Inc., New York, 1970. (A series of essays by outstanding scholars on a variety of urban-service problems.)

Mumford, Lewis: The City in History, Harcourt, Brace & World, Inc., New York, 1961. (Reviews the place of the city in human society through 5,000 years. Highly opinionated, but brilliant.)

Ostrom, Vincent: Water and Politics: A Study of Water Policies and Administration in the Development of Los Angeles, The Haynes Foundation, Los Angeles, 1953.)

Owen, Wilfred: The Accessible City, The Brookings Institution, Washington, 1972. (Transportation problems.)

Pressman, Jeffrey L.: Federal Programs and City Politics, University of California Press, Berkeley, 1975.

Rabinowitz, Francine: City Politics and Planning, Atherton Press, New York, 1969. (Discussion of planners' role in cities with differing types of power diffusion.)

Ranney, David C.: Planning and Politics in the Metropolis, Charles Merrill Publishing Co., Columbus, Ohio, 1969.

Reps, John W.: The Making of Urban America: A History of City Planning in the United States, Princeton University Press, Princeton, N.J., 1964.

Rosenbaum, Walter: The Politics of Environmental Concern, Praeger, New York, 1973.

Rossi, Peter H., and Robert A. Dentler: The Politics of Urban Renewal, The Free Press of Glencoe, New York, 1961.

Smerk, George M. (ed.): Readings in Urban Transportation, Indiana University Press, Bloomington, 1968.

Stacey, William A.: Black Home Ownership, Praeger, New York, 1972. (Study of black suburban area of Jacksonville, Florida.)

Stefferud, Alfred (ed.): Water, U.S. Government Printing Office, 1955. (A U.S. Department of Agriculture yearbook, discussing the problem in its many ramifications.)

Thomas, Norman C.: Rule 9: Politics, Administration and Civil Rights, Random House, Inc., New York, 1966. (A case history of a suburban realty code designed to discriminate against minority ethnic and racial groups.)

Thursz, Daniel: Where Are They Now? Health and Welfare Council of the Capital Area, Washington, 1966. (A study of the impact of relocation upon residents of a section of Washington, including where they moved to and the effects of such moves.)

Toll, Seymour I.: Zoned American, Grossman Publishers, New York, 1969. (History and function of zoning in the growth of cities.)

Wheaton, W. L. C., and others: Urban Housing, The Free Press of Glencoe, New York, 1966. (Thorough study of housing. Contributors include social scientists.)

Whyte, William H.: The Last Landscape, Anchor Books, Doubleday & Company, Inc., Garden City, N.Y., 1968. (Optimistic view of the politics of open space.)

Wilson, James Q. (ed.): The Metropolitan Enigma, Anchor Books, Doubleday & Company, Inc., Garden City, N.Y., 1968. (Collection of essays on urban services.)

Woodbury, Coleman: The Future of Cities and Urban Redevelopment, The University of Chicago Press, Chicago, 1953. (A major study conducted at the time the subject was first becoming a matter of general public concern.)

Chapter 15

Human Services in Cities[1]

The preservation of public safety through police and fire services, the provision of education, and the protection of the health and welfare of community residents form the subject matter of this chapter. The differences between these and the urban services described in the previous chapter are that these more directly attempt the structuring of human activities into what society defines as desirable patterns of behavior.

URBAN POLICE SERVICES

The Crime Problem

For generations Americans have been aware that our crime rate was among the highest of the Western nations and that it was rising. What makes today's conditions different is the fact that minor crimes against persons and property are now so out of control as to make large areas of core cities unliveable for those with families, and to offer life only under a state of seige for others. The risks of going to jail are roughly 23 to 1 against it if you commit a robbery; they are about 5 to

[1] For the most part, health, education, and welfare functions today are the responsibility, not of cities, but of state, county, and special-district governments. See Charles R. Adrian, *State and Local Governments*, McGraw-Hill Book Company, New York, 4th ed., 1976; and recent texts in American national government.

1 against success if you start a small business.[2] Crime does pay. These further aspects of urban crime deserve note: (1) crime is increasingly the activity of amateurs, particularly of very young amateurs, (2) much of street crime and home robberies are drug related, (3) the crime blight is spreading out to the suburbs and into small cities, (4) about 60 percent or more of crimes are committed by blacks, (5) the highest crime rates, as has always been the case, are concentrated among the male youth of the very poor, and (6) many types of crimes of the sort that are on the increase (such as random terrorist attacks at airports or in public buildings) are so bizarre to most people that they have difficulty understanding them, much less helping to prevent them. In the present case, this incidence is exacerbated by racial discrimination, whereby young blacks can view crime as a way of striking back; though in fact the victims of their crimes are, more often than not, other blacks.

Some Other Police Problems

The police are plagued with other problems, but the most significant of these are those that hamper their efforts in controlling crime, such as: (1) The police still occasionally face the problems of crowd control in respect to riots and demonstrations, even though this type of activity has been sharply reduced since the collapse of the Vietnam war. Occasionally, but less frequently than in the past, they blunder in overreaction. (2) Almost every year an instance of police corruption is discovered in some large or middle-sized city. (3) The police are hampered in their work by their poor public image, especially among minority groups and among those under twenty-five. In addition, much of the public is apathetic and doubts that the police can do much about the crime problem. (They may well be right—for reasons discussed below.)

Some Proposed Programs

If core-city crime has done nothing else, it has awakened the police themselves to the fact that the old ways of dealing with crime are no longer good enough. Essentially we can discern two approaches in the variety of programs proposed, each based on different assumptions. One emphasizes increased efficiency of the police forces themselves through such efforts as professional training and coordination of activities. The other argues that crime will not decline to acceptable levels until its root causes are ameliorated. The causes are themselves a debatable and uncertain matter, but here is a partial listing of typical kinds of programs proposed:

1 Professionalized technical training of police.
2 Coordination of activities of local, state, and federal agencies.
3 Improvement of the administration of justice by the courts.
4 Crime-prevention activities: ranging from proposals for gun control to more foot patrols in neighborhoods, civilian police aides, decentralized police stations, crackdowns on drug activities, and special programs for juveniles.
5 Attack at root causes: poverty, lack of meaningful jobs, and racial dis-

[2] An example used by Anthony Downs in a speech at Michigan State University, 1972.

crimination, all of which make society's rules appear illegitimate to the poor, the blacks, and browns. The effort includes the movement of blacks and browns into positions of authority in urban governments and politics and the hiring of more black and brown police.

6 Research into the general causes of crime.

A major difficulty is that not much is known about the causes of crime. Some noncapitalist countries have high crime rates while countries with mixed economies, such as the United Kingdom, have low rates. Japan, a rich nation with an economic system similar to the United States, has one of the lowest crime rates in the world. Cultural, social, and economic factors appear to be important in the causes and rates of crime. It is not at all clear that police policies, rates of expenditure on anticrime programs, size of forces, punishment policies, or any other governmental efforts can have much effect upon the crime rate.

Even police-detection practices do not appear to have much effect upon crime rates or the arrest chances of suspects. A 1976 report of practices in 156 law-enforcement agencies concluded that:[3]

1 "The single most important determinant of whether or not a case will be solved is the information the victim supplies to the patrol officer."

2 If a suspect is not promptly identified by the victim or witnesses, "the perpetrator, by and large, will not be subsequently identified."

3 The work of detectives accounts for the solution of only 10 percent of the cases involving commercial burglary, robbery, and homicide.

4 Detectives spend much time carrying out role expectations imposed upon them by the public, which is no doubt strongly influenced by television, even though these activities are usually unnecessary. "Fingerprint dusting, mug shot showing, or questioning witnesses are often done without any hope of developing leads, but simply for public relations."

The report concluded that police departments would do well to have fewer detectives and more patrol officers on the street. It is not clear, however, that such a change or any others would make much difference.

Performance Measures

For years only two types of crime statistics have been available. Both are of some use, but both are basically unreliable. The Uniform Crime Reports of the FBI are suspect because they are prepared by chiefs of police and in some cases have been clearly inaccurate. Statistics on prison inmates are only of unsuccessful criminals, those who have been caught. One of the goals of the Law Enforcement Assistance program of the federal government is the collection of statistics. Also, under the program, the Attorney General is required to make reports on crime every two years. This may produce more accurate statistics on crime and criminals.

[3] A report of the Rand Corporation to the U.S. Law Enforcement Assistance Administration, February 14, 1976.

Local Organization

Police departments, by tradition, are organized along quasi-military lines. The head of the police department is commonly a professional police officer called the chief. In some cities, especially in the largest cities, the highest-ranking uniformed officer may be subordinate to a lay department head, called the commissioner, director, or in a few cities, the chief. The lay department head usually does not perform details of departmental administration, but serves as liaison officer between the force and the chief executive. At one time a council committee administered the police department, and in the last half of the nineteenth century, it was common for the department to be operated by a semiautonomous board. This is still the case in about seventy cities but is increasingly giving way to control of the department by the chief executive.

Under the chief, and depending largely upon the size of the city, are numerous supervisory officers arranged in a hierarchy. They are traditionally given military titles: assistant chiefs, then majors or inspectors (especially if the city is large enough to have precinct or district stations), captains, lieutenants, and sergeants. The patrol officers make up the broad base of the pyramid. Detectives may outrank patrol officers, or they may merely be patrol officers with a special job-position classification.

The force is organized according to the nature of the tasks performed (e.g., patrol and traffic divisions). Larger cities are divided into geographical districts, or precincts, especially for administering the patrol force. In some cities, some of the specialized divisions may also be decentralized so that they operate out of the district stations. Since police work, particularly that of the patrol division, is continuous, the force is also divided into platoons, or shifts.[4]

State and Federal Activities

Most states have provided two services to city police in the past: criminal records and laboratory services, and a state highway police or patrol that may also have programs in police training and may conduct investigations of major crimes in rural and small-city areas. (States have also always provided National Guard troops when local police have not been able to control a situation or are on strike. In 1975, Governor Edmund G. Brown, Jr., of California, proposed a specially trained unit of the National Guard to take over in the event of police strikes, such as that in San Francisco that year.) To these, since 1968, have been added administration of major federal law-enforcement-assistance programs. The Omnibus Crime Control and Safe Streets Act of 1968 was the first major federal program in the law-enforcement area and was set up as a block grant, with the states designated as the units to supervise the spending of funds by local units. Major additions to the federal program include: those made in 1970 (collection of statistics and purchase of telecommunications equipment), the Crime Control Act of 1973 (administration of justice, an Attorney General's report on crime, incentives

[4] On police organization, see O. W. Wilson, *Police Administration,* 3d ed., McGraw-Hill Book Company, New York, 1972.

to coordination among local units, and training programs by the National Institute of Law Enforcement and Criminal Justice), and in 1974, the Juvenile Justice and Delinquency Prevention Act (a national program including one in respect to runaway youth). Previous to 1968 the major federal activities were through the FBI and included cooperation with local police in seeking criminals wanted by them, laboratory aid, and training for local police. Also important to local police were a series of decisions by the Supreme Court during the 1960s on such matters as legitimate search and seizure and interrogation and charging of suspects. Police and others have sometimes argued that an overconcern by federal judges for the rights of criminals has been at the expense of the rights of other citizens.

What of the Future?

The next ten years or so should show a marked rise in the professional quality of urban-police services. Less promising are the efforts made thus far to discover and reduce root causes of poverty, crime, and antisocial behavior.

OTHER LAW-ENFORCEMENT AGENCIES

The Courts

The courts in smaller cities often exercise jurisdiction only over minor offenses, particularly traffic violations. Their powers thus are not much greater than the justice of the peace courts in rural areas. In such cities, the significant courts are those established by the state on a county or district basis. Generally, however, in larger cities, the municipal courts are given added jurisdiction and sometimes special names to indicate their greater powers. Municipal courts of this type are in some states equivalent to the state courts established at the county level. But in other states, municipal courts have somewhat different jurisdictions. Municipal judges are generally paid on a salary basis, and in the larger cities their salaries may be higher than those of the state supreme court justices. Local judges are often elected on a nonpartisan ballot and serve for relatively long terms.

In the past, local courts were clearly under the control of urban political organizations. Today such influence still exists, but the courts, like the police, have undergone greater and greater professionalization. In most states, municipal courts have been closely meshed into the total state court system, unlike justice of the peace courts, which tend still to have greater independence and lack of professionalization. Such a system is headed by the state supreme court and may perhaps have an additional appellate level of courts, with county courts and municipal courts in the larger cities carrying most of the judicial load as courts of original jurisdiction. The municipal courts in smaller cities and the justice of peace courts remain for minor violations.

The City Attorney

City attorneys are less important political officials than their counterparts at the county, state, or federal level. They are almost always appointed rather than elected, with their primary duty being that of giving legal advice to the city government and representing it in court. Less frequently are they involved in the prosecution of violators, though this aspect of their position is growing in importance. Nevertheless, the district or state's attorney, an official of the state who is generally elected by county voters, more frequently is the local prosecutor of importance because state law is generally involved in the important cases. Crusading district attorneys, like Thomas E. Dewey in the 1930s and 1940s, have worked closely with local grand juries exposing crime within cities, but such action by city attorneys is much rarer. Allied with the district attorney's office is the sheriff. In most urban areas, an informal agreement exists between city and county law-enforcement officials for the sheriff to be the chief law-enforcement officer outside the city limits and the city police to be the chief law-enforcement agency in each municipality. The sheriff's office frequently provides jail facilities for serious offenders, though in larger cities such facilities also exist.

The Jail

The city jail is usually administered by the police department. The local prison is likely to be primarily of the congregate type of design with a large bullpen to house most prisoners. There may be a few cells to segregate notoriously tough prisoners and the violently insane. Jails are seldom constructed to meet the multifunctional demands placed upon them. They house a great variety of persons: major offenders awaiting trial; habitual misdemeanants, many of them psychopaths; elderly degenerates; youthful minor offenders; traffic violators; drunks locked up for a single night; vagrants; material witnesses; and others. (In some states jail facilities for urban and rural areas alike are provided by the county under the sheriff.)

At least 1 million persons spend some time in jail each year. It is doubtful if many profit from the experience. The general public has never regarded jails as being of much importance and does not approve of the expenditure of large amounts of money "to make things comfortable for crooks and drunks." Police administrators of jails, in the great majority of cases, are concerned with custody, and little effort is made in most cities to identify the personal problems which helped cause incarceration. Even less effort goes toward rehabilitation or preventive activities.

Many professional students of police administration believe that the image of the police officer would be better if the police could be freed from responsibility for the custodial function of operating the jail. An independent custodial agency or one under the control of the prosecutor who is responsible for preparing criminal cases would serve to eliminate some of the suspicions as to what happens to an individual while in the hands of the police and awaiting trial. Much of the criticism of the police has concentrated upon the treatment of the accused immediately after they are taken into custody and upon the conditions existing in the jail while they are awaiting trial. Although many police executives would prefer to be free of responsibility for this portion of the criminal-justice process, apathy, lack of understanding of the process, and fear of increased costs make such a separation of responsibilities difficult to achieve.

URBAN FIRE SERVICES

Color, Drama—and Carelessness

American cities have the finest fire equipment in the world, but they also have the greatest annual fire losses. Such losses in the United States exceed 1,000 million dollars annually—most of it in cities. Americans are not economy-conscious. Europeans, endowed with fewer of nature's gifts, must be conservationists. Americans, for example, are seldom prosecuted for contributory negligence in cases of fires. Losses, it is felt, are somehow "paid by the insurance company." Insurance rates are not associated with fire rates. (In nearly all American states, fire-insurance rates are determined by the quality of fire-defense equipment in each community, with no consideration given to actual fire-loss experience. Performance is assumed rather than examined.)

The politics of fire prevention is colored by the low priority it is given by the general public. Fire fighters sometimes regard assignment to the prevention bureau as exile resulting from presumed incompetence or disciplinary considerations. The head of the bureau may be an experienced fire fighter who was injured in line of duty; that is, the office may be treated as a sinecure rather than as a grave responsibility for an especially trained person. Members of the bureau may expect to be pressured to approve various materials and building arrangements. Few departments have adequate test facilities and must depend on reports of federal agencies or the state fire marshal. They usually end up banning only the most obviously unacceptable materials or designs, for they may lack needed information on hazards and, in any case, are likely to find it difficult and unpleasant to order someone to clean up trash or make expensive repairs. In some cases, persons are assigned to the bureau on a rotating basis, which is likely to mean that about the time they begin to gain some special skills, they are reassigned to fire fighting. But this recruiting pattern is sometimes made necessary because the typical fire fighter does not want assignment permanently to prevention work.

Special Programs

The largest cities, and frequently entire metropolitan areas, combine in setting up academies to train local fire fighters. Training programs involve not only physical conditioning but also instruction in the use of equipment, chemicals, and explosives, in fire-fighting techniques, in ventilation, and in making fire-prevention inspections.

Europeans have long placed heavy emphasis upon fire-prevention procedures, but the idea has received serious attention in the United States only since the 1920s. In their prevention activities, fire departments depend heavily upon routine inspections performed by the neighborhood fire stations. They seek to correct common hazards (e.g., accumulated rubbish, dirty chimneys, defective heating equipment). Periodically, technical surveys by engineers are made in some cities to suggest major improvements in the use and construction of buildings.

Fire prevention also involves the granting of permits, licenses, and certificates of approval (e.g., for the design of fire escapes, the use of dry-cleaning materials, the licensing of motion-picture operators, and the installation of oil burners). It is the responsibility of the city council (and in some cases of the state legislature) to provide adequate fire-prevention codes. The department also investigates the causes of fires and seeks to give publicity to fire statistics.

Departmental Organization

Fire-department organization generally parallels that of the police department. At least fifty cities still have a lay fire commissioner in charge, although in others, departments are headed by professional chiefs chosen from the departments or, in a few instances, from fire departments in other cities. Fire or safety boards still appoint the chief in quite a few cities, and in nearly one hundred weak-mayor cities the council makes the appointment. Normally, however, the appointment is made by the chief executive. In all but small cities, district stations are established with a company under the command of a lieutenant or captain. In very large cities, several companies in a section of the city may be organized into a battalion or district. In suburbs and small cities the volunteer fire fighters usually learn a good deal about the government of the community (political gossip is one of the staples around the firehouse) and often become important figures in local election campaigns. They may be active because the mayor has chosen them with an eye to developing a low-voltage political device, or because they have stakes in the decisions of the council (allowances for clothing, a new pumper), or simply because they are a well-knit group that enjoys politics as a game and have time on their hands in which to play it.

The core cities of urban areas typically have modern, professional fire departments. The larger the city, the more specialized the equipment is likely to be. Suburbs and small cities, on the other hand, often depend upon amateur departments. Some small residential communities make it a practice to hire a few full-time members who staff the station and equipment, with volunteer amateurs on call to follow along at each fire alarm. Other municipalities, especially suburbs, are following the practice of training people as both police and fire fighters.

It is a peculiar phenomenon of American life, best left to the explanation of psychologists, perhaps, that citizens will be apathetic in responding to calls for volunteers for blood donations, civil defense, or even the staffing of a charity booth at a church bazaar, but will establish waiting lists to join a volunteer fire department. In fact, volunteer companies were such powerful interest groups in New York and Philadelphia that they were able to prevent the installations of professional systems in those cities until 1865 and 1870, respectively, even though the first paid department had been inaugurated in Boston as early as 1837. This urge to assist is useful to the city government but is also a nuisance at times.

In some cities, especially smaller ones, police and fire services are combined into a single unit under one head. Employees are trained as both police and fire fighters. Efforts to secure adoption of such integrated units have met with considerable opposition from trade unions, however, for they see it as a way to increase work without an equal increase in pay. In a few communities, private fire-fighting services are still provided on a fee basis—a practice that was common in the early nineteenth century.

Performance Measures

States generally require fire chiefs to make estimates of loss, and of course insurance companies also collect such figures. But as in the police area, there are no generally good sources for such figures, and as previously noted, performance of the department is not reflected in local insurance rates.

State and Federal Programs

The state fire marshal's office is the major aid to urban fire-fighting forces. About two-thirds of the states provide for statewide training courses, which are available to all cities and villages in the training of their forces. In addition, many state fire marshal's offices collect statistics, inspect the causes of major local fires or where arson is suspected, and make tests on the flammability of building materials.

Federal efforts in respect to fire fighting are few. In 1973 a Fire Prevention and Control bill passed the U.S. Senate. It passed both houses the next year. It has many of the features of the Law Enforcement Assistance program, with a national academy for training and grants for equipment and research. Fire departments have benefitted most from the federal revenue-sharing program, a source of funds for many urban fire-equipment purchases. Federal agencies do have regulations concerning dangerous and flammable toys and materials. In some cases, these regulations have been criticized for being overly cautious, in contrast to the usual criticism that local officials are too lenient. Local fire fighting has been adversely affected by court decisions which have raised doubts about conditions under which inspections may be made of private residences.

What of the Future?

Fire fighting is not yet seen as a high-priority urban service. The major need is for improved prevention programs. Fire fighting is one of the few areas that unitl very recently was without a federal-support program. Americans seem content to live with high fire losses in life and property. This appears to be true even though arson was on the increase in the 1960s and 1970s and there were many needless deaths in apartment houses, old hotels, and nursing homes.

OTHER PUBLIC SAFETY FUNCTIONS

Cities also have responsibility for overseeing the use of devices to determine weights and measures, for smoke abatement, prevention of water pollution, noise abatement, civil defense, traffic engineering, and the licensing of persons engaged in various activities which are viewed as having a special relationship to the public health or safety. In recent years, emphasis on ecological problems has resulted in more serious attention being paid to water and air pollution by industry. Licensing is always a potential area of corruption, for some permits, such as those to operate a taxi fleet or to sell liquor, may be worth much more than the amount paid for them to the city because they are in scarce supply. In some cities, upon approval, these licenses can be transferred from one person or firm to another and can be, in effect, sold for a large profit. Even when licenses are easily secured, they may still be of economic importance to the recipients, who cannot continue in their trade or profession if the license is suspended or revoked for any reason.

PUBLIC EDUCATION

The American educational system faces four major problems at the very least. One is that of finances and the financial inequalities which result from having a multiplicity of school districts. A fortunate location of industry for one district may permit it to raise the same taxes per capita as another neighboring district, but it need levy only one-half the property tax. State-aid formulas and federal grants to some degree attempt to level these differences, but they still exist in dramatic form. Especially hard hit are suburbs of modest homes with no commercial or industrial base and some core-city districts, where a declining tax base is coupled with major problems of social disorganization in the schools. (The pattern varies, however. The four largest cities in California all have average to above-average assessed valuation per pupil.)

In the 1970s, the use of the general property tax as the basis for financing the schools was challenged in the courts. It was argued that the variation in the amounts of assessed valuation per pupil from one district to another constituted a violation of the constitutional right of equal protection of the laws. Although the United States Supreme Court ruled that this was not the case relative to the United States Constitution, the California case held that the situation violated the provision for equal protection in the state constitution and ordered that a system of equal financing be worked out within a reasonable time period. The ruling overlooked the fact that (1) poor students do not necessarily live in poor districts (poor people often live near commercial and industrial areas and, in California, 70 percent of the property tax is paid by business and industry) and (2) the amount spent per pupil has nothing to do with students' educational performances.[5] Even so, these cases raised political problems that were certain to create difficulties for school financing and concepts of social equity in the last years of the 1970s.

A second problem is that of school bussing. In the widely publicized Detroit case, the Court ruled (1975) that bussing could not be ordered across district lines, effectively sealing off the core city. Bussing within districts with heavy

[5] See *San Antonio Ind. School Dist. v Rodriguez,* 93 S. Ct. 1278 (1973), *Serrano v. Priest,* 487 P. 2d 1241 (1971); a research note, "A Statistical Analysis of the School Finance Decisions: On Winning Battles and Losing Wars," *Yale Law Journal,* 81:1303, 1328–1329, 1972, which shows that poor people are not concentrated in low-tax-base districts in Connecticut; also the various studies that use the data of the Coleman Report: James Coleman, *Equality of Educational Opportunity,* Washington, 1966; especially Christopher Jencks and others, *Inequality: A Reassessment of the Effect of Family and Schooling in America,* Basic Books, Inc., New York, 1972; and Daniel P. Moynihan and Frederick Mosteller (eds.), *On Equality of Educational Opportunity,* Random House, Inc., New York, 1972.

black populations has resulted in "white flight" and arguments that such a policy is counterproductive. The entire subject has generated much emotional rhetoric on both sides, and all concerned seem to behave as if they knew what the effects—good or bad from their points of view—might be. In fact, the likely results (as distinguished from judicial intentions) are quite uncertain. In 1975 and 1976, violence occasionally erupted concerning bussing in several cities, notably Boston. A constitutional amendment was proposed to prevent bussing for the sake of achieving racial parity in schools. The best approach to equality of educational opportunity (much less of educational utilization) remains a matter of controversy.

A third problem is that of school curriculum. Traditionally, this has been the responsibility of professional educators, a responsibility that many critics argue they have not handled well. The averages on national college entrance test scores have been steadily declining for some years; but what is perhaps more disquieting, the absolute numbers of high scores has been declining as well, indicating that the decline is not wholly accounted for by the larger number of poor who have been taking the college entrance examinations.

A fourth problem is that of the control of schools. In some cities, people complain that the teachers' unions dominate most policy, with other opinions and goals ignored. In other cases, some groups, especially blacks, have sought "community" or subdistrict control of school curricula and personnel. Some have argued that such decentralization of control would have benefits in helping parents to identify with their children's schools and make school offerings more appropriate for each particular class or subculture. New York City and Detroit have experimented with decentralized schools, but the results are unclear.[6]

Some Programs

The answer of most school professionals to these problems has been a request for more funds and greater professionalization. The answer of their critics has tended to be requests for performance measures. The state of Oregon now requires graduates to demonstrate reading, writing, and mathematical proficiency on a state test, before being awarded a high school diploma. In respect to the variations in financial support, more states are attempting to move school financing from the local property tax to the state general fund. The problems of discrimination will be solved when jobs and the opening of housing opportunities for blacks and other racial minorities also become an accomplished fact. Whether these can be achieved through school-bussing programs is still part of the public debate and very much in doubt so far as available evidence is concerned.

James B. Conant, after his visits to classrooms in the slum areas of several large cities, reported that almost every kind of problem of social disorganization was faced daily by some of the pupils. Both boys and girls became involved in gang fights; many had seen brutality in their homes. Most commonly they came from homes in which the parents were divorced, where one or both parents were

[6] Mario Fantini and Marilyn Gittell, *Decentralization: Achieving Reform,* Praeger Publishers, New York, 1973.

alcoholics, or where the parents faced serious emotional problems. Girls of high school age, when surveyed, reported their greatest problem as avoiding molesters between the sidewalk and their family's apartment upstairs. Another discouraging finding relevant to education was that in some slum schools the students changed almost completely over the course of a year because of dropouts and moving in and out of slum neighborhoods. Thus Conant, like many other educators, concluded that the schools can be only minimally effective under such conditions. They cannot be expected to reform society but must depend on other agencies, both private and governmental, to correct the worst problems. Welfare programs might have an impact if coupled with opportunity to qualify for productive positions in the economy. The solution thus seems related to a circle of frustration in which persons cannot be properly trained for better positions because of their present conditions.

School Organization

The special status of education has been buttressed by what amounts almost to a credo of public education in the United States. That credo holds that public education must be treated as nonpolitical and controlled locally. It should be organized separately from all other services at the local level (though this separateness is not preserved at the state level, where it is a part of state government, or at the national level, where it is part of a cabinet department with health and welfare). In addition, its relations with the public should be "nonpartisan."

Each state has a state department of education headed by a chief state school officer. The heads of state departments of education have been elective, particularly in the South, Midwest, and West. Under pressure from professional educators, however, there is a growing trend to appointment either by the governor or by members of the state boards of education. Increasingly, such agencies are becoming dominated by the values of the professional educators who run them.

Most states operate their schools through numerous local school districts. In the past, these often had the same geographic boundaries as cities, villages, or townships, but such is not necessarily the case today. States, through financial aid and legislative pressure (requiring each school district to have a high school, for example), have encouraged consolidation of districts. The number of local districts has dropped from 127,422 in 1932 to 34,678 in 1962, and 26,983 by 1967: a reduction of 80 percent. By 1972, the number was 15,781, a further reduction of almost 40 percent. Thus the central city in a metropolitan area is likely to have a school district that includes the whole of that city. But it may also, particularly in smaller metropolitan areas, include parts of the suburban fringe area. In suburban areas, the school-district boundaries frequently do not follow city boundaries but may include in one district large parts of the unincorporated area and even several suburban cities. The pattern depends on local inclination, state law, and historical accident. Quite commonly, the independent local school district does not have the same boundaries as do the cities or other local governments where they exist.

Because most states operate their schools through small districts, many of which have limited resources, intermediate school units also often exist. These units, operating between the state and local district levels, include counties, parts of counties, and various other groupings of districts.

At both the state and intermediate levels, the principal responsibility has been not the operation of schools or control of school policy but the furnishing of consultative, advisory, and statistical services. There has been, however, a trend toward the exercise of regulatory and inspection functions by these levels of administration. The state department has also often been given a veto power over proposed school consolidations and, in some states, has control over the approval of textbooks, school bonding, or plans for school buildings and equipment purchases.

Legally, school districts are merely "creatures of the state" to be structured as state authorities desire. Politically, however, these local districts have significant power. Because of the strong tradition of local control of education in the United States, occasionally conflicts erupt between local school districts and the state board.

The arguments for local autonomy of course relate to the desire to keep education free of partisan politics. At present, education is perhaps at the pinnacle of isolation from other units of local government, though the picture has changed somewhat in respect to state agencies. With increased state and federal aid and regulations, there may be a tendency to strengthen the school districts' ties to other local units of government, particularly those at the county level.

Local School-District Organization

The organization within the local school district is generally decided upon by the citizens of that district from among the choices permitted by state law. In general, the internal organization is very similar to that of the council-manager system of government. In place of a council, a school board usually of five to seven members serves, holding three- or four-year terms. Board members in 85 percent of the nation's school districts are elected, almost always on a nonpartisan ballot. They then appoint a school superintendent who serves at their pleasure, that is, one who may be dismissed if he or she loses the confidence of the board majority. The superintendent is generally a professionally oriented administrator without previous local ties, who plans to follow a career in school administration and may, in the course of time, move on to other positions in another city or state. This person almost always has an advanced academic degree.

Variations from this scheme occur most usually in the nation's largest cities. Here school board members are more frequently appointed; in fact, in the nation's four largest school systems, this is the case. In addition, terms are often longer. The system is often similar to the Missouri plan of judicial appointment: A "citizens' committee" proposes a list of nominees from which the mayor appoints a board member. The choice is confirmed at an election. The reasons for variations from the usual practice are probably two. First, campaigns in large districts are a wearisome and costly business, particularly in nonpartisan elections. A former president of the St. Louis board once said: "I could name fifty outstanding men and women who have turned me down simply because they don't want to get involved in the campaigning. We've taken some second-rate people because of this."[7] Secondly, in the larger cities such campaigns often get involved in partisan politics, perhaps because the party is a major means of gaining votes in a large constituency for a race in which relatively few voters may be interested.

According to the professionals' ideal model, the local school board is responsible for policy making while professional administrators and teachers carry out its decisions. Thus, the professional aspect of the educational system is presumably insulated from political questions. In fact, just as we have found to be the case in respect to managers in the council-manager system, the role of the school superintendent in the ideal model is not always a description of reality. The line between a professional matter to be handled by educational experts and one involving policy is difficult to draw. Only within communities having a homogeneous value system is there likely to be an absence of political tensions in the carrying out of education functions. Where disagreements exist within the community over the proper educational policies to be followed, the school superintendent is almost inevitably drawn into the political battle to champion her or his professional views.

School Elections

Evidence from a number of sources suggests that the interest of average citizens in schools only comes to the fore on financial matters or on those questions that sporadically pique their interest because of their dramatic or scandalous nature. Attendance at school board meetings rarely includes more than the members themselves. Voter turnout at school board elections is generally low, usually even lower than in municipal elections. The opinions of local community leaders would ". . . put the school tax rate in first place, school building and expansion programs second, bond issues to support such programs third and the school budget fourth. Teachers' salaries ranked fifth. . . . The respondents indicated no particular interest in curriculum, textbooks, subversive activities, personalities, athletics, race relations, and independence of the schools."[8] Half of those replying did not know how long their school superintendent had served, well over one-half could not name the president of their school board, and two-thirds did not vote in the last school election. However, 71 percent had voted in the last bond-issue election, although 26 percent did not know how the election had turned out. Seventy-seven percent said they had never attended a school board meeting and less than three percent said they attended often. Well over half did not belong to the Parent-Teachers Association or to other similar groups. Another study made for the U.S. Office of Education by the Stanford University Institute for Communication Research found that roughly one-half the voters "show no evidence of any participation in school affairs and no interest in such partici-

[7] Peter Binzen, "How to Pick a School Board," *Saturday Review,* Apr. 17, 1965.

[8] Roscoe Martin and Frank J. Munger (eds.), *Decisions in Syracuse,* Indiana University Press, Bloomington, Ind., 1961, pp. 52–55.

pation." The study reported that only about a third took an active part in school affairs and their knowledge about the school program was "only slight."[9]

Similarly in Detroit, in at least one election, there was difficulty in recruiting a full slate of candidates, while a group in St. Louis was so sure of general lack of information by voters that they kept a forty-five-hour vigil so that their candidates would be first in line for filing. High position on the ballot, they calculated, was worth 4.5 percent of the vote since many voters only voted for the top names.[10]

Thus it appears that for most voters the information gathering and participation costs are too great to justify a great deal of involvement in educational matters. Those with children regularly show greater concern, but even in their case, involvement is low. Only when a sizable amount of funds is to be spent or when an issue is presented dramatically do voters become much interested in the operation of their school system.

A number of scholars noting that a professional administrative elite largely controls school policy, have argued for a decentralization of school districts, especially in large cities as a method of reducing citizen participation costs. Marilyn Gittell states:[11]

> In large city educational systems . . . professionalism combined with the cumulative development of a highly bureaucratic structure have reinforced the depersonalization process. The result is an insulated system in which decision-makers and decision-making are closed off from a wide group of potential participants. Generally a central headquarters staff maintains a tight hold on power, rationalizing its role in the shibboleths of professional competence . . . the political system is obligated to construct favorable arrangements for [citizen] involvement.

Federal Programs

The basic Elementary and Secondary Education Act dates from 1965 and was designed as a means for equalizing educational advantages. The act has been extended with changes in program and aid formulas. The 1974 version contained a proviso that school children could be bussed only to the closest or next closest school to their place of residence in any effort to achieve racial balance in the schools.

Change for the Future

The local school in America today is in the process of change. On the one hand, state governments following the advice of educators have encouraged consolidation, and this has resulted in larger and more professional school systems. As the nation becomes more technologically oriented, citizen leaders are also showing increasing concern about the quality of local educational programs and their content. It is likely, though far from certain, that continued emphasis will be

[9] Richard F. Carter, *Voters and Their Schools,* School of Education, Institute for Communication Research, Stanford University, Palo Alto, Calif., 1960, pp. 7 and 16.

[10] Peter Binzen, *op. cit.*

[11] Marilyn Gittell, "Saving City Schools," *National Civic Review,* 57:21–26, January, 1968.

given to upgrading the nation's schools with a lessening of local controls. States and even the federal government can be expected to impose more standards in the future. Among the greatest difficulties still unresolved are those of de facto segregation by race and the related problem of the quality of educational training in slum areas. If these problems are to be met, it is likely that the impetus for change must come both from outside the schools and from educators themselves.

PUBLIC HEALTH

The Nation's Health

Cities, with their high concentration of people in confined areas, are natural targets for communicable diseases. For this reason, local governments have for centuries had responsibilities for the protection of health. The idea that some diseases were in some manner contagious was discovered long ago. Resulting from this knowledge came the practice of having cities require the isolation of afflicted persons. The pesthouse was an early form of isolation. Quarantining of such persons in their houses also became a municipal responsibility. A flag or sign beside the doorway of the homes of those with contagious diseases was the responsibility of the public health officer.

During the Great Plague (bubonic plague) that struck London in 1665 and 1666, for example, the houses of the afflicted were marked with red crosses on the door, "searchers" were sent out to certify the cause of deaths, and municipal authorities sent a man out to kill the dogs of the city, for these creatures were mistakenly blamed for spreading the disease.[12] Cities, now aided by a considerable amount of progress in medical knowledge, still perform similar functions. In recent decades, their tasks have become even greater and their successes in lowering the death rate ever more impressive.

Another development in municipal health activities, and a logical extension of the older practice of isolation, came with the discovery of the techniques of vaccination and inoculation against communicable diseases. A conflict has developed over the question of whether these practices are "treatments" that should be cared for by private physicians or preventive medicine and, as such, a public health function. In the United States, the former view has generally prevailed, except for the vaccination of school children in some cases and the emergency treatment of populations in the event of epidemics.

A third factor in the development of public health departments was the popularity of the filth theory of disease in the middle years of the nineteenth century. This notion led to heavy emphasis upon sanitation, especially the construction of sewers, the collection of garbage, and the abatement of nuisances. During this period public health departments became common and were expanded in size beyond that of a local physician acting on a part-time basis. Although the collection and disposal of sewage and garbage is still a function of the health

[12] See Johannes Nohl, *The Black Death,* Ballantine Books, Inc., New York, 1960, chap. 5, "Administrative Precautions."

department in some cities, it has generally been transferred to the public works department. But the health department is still responsible for the health supervision of such activities, and it has been entrusted with an ever increasing number of other functions.

Public Health Administration

The American Public Health Association believes that specialization is so important in a proper health program that its Committee on Local Health Units has recommended the establishment of health units so organized as to contain not less than 50,000 people in each of them.[13] Smaller units not only cannot develop specialization but are likely to be unable to finance a successful program. This means, of course, that the county or a special-purpose district would have to be used as the health unit, except for fair-sized cities. The professional organization also suggests that there should be one public health nurse for each 5,000 people and one sanitarian for each 25,000 people. Few communities in the nation meet these and other standards of the association, however. Cities and villages are still the standard units established by state law, although county and city-county departments are increasingly taking over health functions in urban areas and standards are rising. For example, Michigan law provides that any city failing to maintain a full-time health officer comes automatically under the county health department, and that the city and county may, by mutual agreement, share the services of a single health officer to supervise both departments. Its state health department encourages the consolidation of county departments. In 1975, there were eighty-three counties but only thirty-five health departments serving local cities, counties, or substate regions. It is likely that health units will be rapidly consolidated in most states only through the incentive of conditional federal or state grants-in-aid.

The trend today is toward municipal health departments under a single head responsible to the chief executive. Most municipalities, however, still make use of the traditional board of health. (General municipal health departments first became popular in the heyday of the independent board and commission.) Quite a few cities still have boards but have stripped them of administrative powers, leaving them with but an advisory function. This is, in fact, the structure recommended by the American Public Health Association.

The board of health usually consists of physicians and lay persons. In some cities, at least one seat must be given to an engineer. The American Public Health Association and other medical groups favor a heavy representation of physicians on the board. This can perhaps be justified on the basis of the superior interest of these persons, but they are also wanted there to "protect" the private medical profession against those who would expand the scope of public health functions.

The health officer in small cities is a local physician, often serving on a part-time basis. In larger cities, a person with professional training in public health and the degree of Doctor of Public Health, as well as that of M.D., is often employed. The specialized professional degree affords training in sanitation, pub-

[13] American Public Health Association, *Local Health Units for the Nation,* The Commonwealth Fund, New York, 1946.

lic administration, and other fields, in addition to medical training. In the largest cities, the health officer's time is fully occupied with administration, and technical functions are left to subordinates.

Public Health Functions

A great many health activities are performed or aided by state health departments and by federal agencies, especially by the U.S. Public Health Service of the Department of Health, Education, and Welfare. But the principal direct health services are performed by local governments. Except in small communities, the health department is normally divided into several specialized divisions.

Communicable-disease control is one of the most effective of public health programs. Typhoid fever has largely been eliminated by inspection of water and milk, yellow fever and malaria by draining swamps, and typhus through ratproofing programs. Tuberculosis control was at one time a major activity but has been reduced by better conditions of work, housing, and diet.

Venereal diseases are usually treated by a special division of the department. These diseases, like tuberculosis, must be controlled through treatment. Protection against them can be achieved only through health education. The venereal-disease-control section has the major task of persuading people to apply for its help voluntarily and of overcoming the sufferer's wish to keep secret a socially disapproved ailment. Health departments have sought to encourage people to come forward for treatment by making their services available to all, regardless of ability to pay, and by locating treatment clinics as inconspicuously as possible.

Federal grants for venereal-disease control are made to local units. Modern medicines have been very effective in treatment. However, an unknown, but no doubt very large, number of cases requiring treatment are never brought to the attention of either private practitioners or public health clinics, and in the 1970s, the incidence of venereal diseases was sky-rocketing.

A public health program that is growing in importance is that of substance abuse. The overuse of alcohol and other drugs is now treated as a medical as well as a police problem. The Alcohol and Drug Education Act provides for research and the establishment of demonstration projects. A number of urban centers now have drug education centers, as well as special programs for alcoholics.

Maternal and Child Care The principal functions of this division are of an educational nature. It offers lectures, pamphlets, publicity releases, and other information services designed to reduce ignorance concerning childbearing among prospective mothers and fathers. The division also gives advice on child care and child rearing. Many cities operate prenatal and postnatal clinics and provide for home visits by public health nurses. The division works closely with hospitals offering free maternity service to the indigent, and it licenses and regulates midwifery in those states where this practice is still permitted.

Sanitary Inspections Many municipal functions related to sanitation are administered outside of the health department. Swamps are drained, water supplied, and sewage disposed of by the public works department or by independent departments, but health aspects are supervised by the health department.

The municipal department shares many inspection duties with state and federal agencies. Milk must be inspected to guard against watering and against the presence of tuberculosis and typhoid as well as several other types of germs that may be found in raw milk. Local slaughterhouses, if not inspected by representatives of the U.S. Department of Agriculture, are inspected by the local health department. Retail food establishments are inspected and food handlers examined for communicable diseases by the health department, or under its supervision.

In checking the premises of retail food establishments, sanitation-division personnel usually follow the practice of unexpected and irregular inspections. If illegal and unsanitary conditions are found, the usual practice is to issue a warning. In the case of extreme or repeated violations, licenses may be suspended or revoked.

Municipal Hospitals Municipal hospitals have become common throughout the nation as part of a public health program. There are over 250 city hospitals and over 60 city-county hospitals in the United States. Hospitals in cities under 100,000 are usually managed by semiautonomous boards, while in larger cities they tend to be controlled by the city health departments. In smaller cities, the budget is also usually autonomous, with the council having no power of review, but in larger cities municipal hospitals as a rule are treated as simply another city agency.

Generally speaking, the smaller the city, the more likely its hospital is to be completely self-supporting, or nearly so. In very few cities of over 50,000 is the municipal hospital even 50 percent self-supporting. The difference is made up from funds appropriated by the city or sometimes the county or state. Municipal hospitals in larger cities exist to a great extent to care for police and indigent cases. The smaller the city, generally speaking, the more likely is the hospital tc be a general-service institution. Larger cities are also more likely to operate special hospitals for the treatment of contagious diseases, tuberculosis, poliomyelitis, and mental disorders.

The oldest municipal hospital in the United States, the Philadelphia General, dates from 1732. The largest municipal institution, New York's famed Bellevue, is only four years younger. The city of New York also operates eighteen other hospitals and sanatoria. There are, however, municipal hospitals in cities of all sizes, including about one hundred cities of under 5,000 population.

Public Health Education This division seeks to increase longevity by teaching citizens the principles of personal hygiene and the need for proper medical care and consultation, and warning them about certain dangers to health. The division may conduct public lectures, issue news releases and public service announcements to press, radio, and television, and furnish lecturers to clubs, school assemblies, and other get-togethers. For example, the division may help the National Cancer Society warn the public of the "seven danger signals of cancer"; in the summer it may issue public service announcements to local radio stations reminding parents of the symptoms of heart disease; or it may issue news releases to the press warning of the dangers of food poisoning in an unrefrigerated cream puff.

The Staff Services

A staff function of general interest is the collection of vital statistics for the community: records of births, of deaths and their causes, and of communicable diseases. The public health laboratory furnishes analyses of blood, sputum, and other samples in helping physicians diagnose diseases. It also may analyze food suspected of being tainted. As a staff service, public health nurses are furnished to aid the divisions in charge of communicable diseases, tuberculosis, venereal diseases, maternal and child care, public health education, and outpatient care.

Federal Programs

In 1975, Congress overrode President Ford's veto of the Health Services and Nurses Training Act. Among the features of this act were expansion of community mental health centers, migrant health programs, and such new programs as those for treatment of hypertension, rape prevention and control, and treatment of hemophilia. It expanded nurses' training and extended the life of the National Health Service Corps.

Continuing Issues

Health controversies in urban centers are related to the following: (1) the establishment of hospitals for the chronically ill (a group of increasing size in our society, a by-product of lengthening life expectancy); (2) the development of home-care programs by local health units through which patients not in need of hospitalization or other institutional care may be cared for and followed up in their own homes after hospital release; (3) the public purchase of polio vaccine for children; (4) the development of publicly financed medical-service centers in small towns with too little population to support hospitals or even physicians; (5) expanded services to ghetto residents who cannot afford medical care. All these and some other items being urged as proper areas for public health activity are controversial.

PUBLIC WELFARE

Cities at one time provided the major public welfare services, but these functions are now largely financed by federal and state governments, with local administration through counties, where they exist. The city's main responsibilities are supplementary, for persons who fail to qualify under major categorical programs, although in most states even these functions are now under county jurisdiction. These may include some of the poor, including children whose parents cannot or will not support them, and old people who can neither work nor support themselves from their savings. Delinquents, disabled persons, and the mentally handicapped are also taken care of by welfare agencies. The administration of these "welfare cases" is a major task taken alone in some large cities. City public welfare agencies are sometimes entrusted, in addition, with responsibility for the licensing of private child-care agencies, the provision of foster care for children unable to live in their own homes, adoption services, work with children's courts, provision for medical and dental care for the needy, and the supervising of private charities.

Pre-employment Training

The federal program under the Comprehensive Employment and Training Act of 1973 recognized that different urban areas had different pre-employment training needs. A major aspect of the program was decentralizing a large share of decision making about programs while retaining approval rights at the state and national levels. The act also encouraged cooperative programs across regions and, in addition, established a job corps for young men and women from low-income families. In this program, what had been seen until recently as primarily a state or federal function was shared with officials at the local level, so that programs would more closely be tailored to local needs and conditions.

COMMISSIONS AGAINST DISCRIMINATION

". . . Because of Race, Color, or Creed."

In an attempt to bring social democracy abreast of political democracy, a movement after World War II sought to secure the establishment of laws providing for employment without regard to race, color, or creed, and for equal opportunities in housing.

A large number of cities of over 200,000 population—and many smaller places, if they have substantial self-conscious minorities—have adopted charter amendments or ordinances providing for fair employment and equal opportunities for all citizens. This is true of most of the largest cities of the nation outside the South.

The rules so established seek to prevent discrimination in employment because of the race, religion, color, or national origin of the employee. They apply to cases of private employment in business and industry, to labor-union membership, and to discriminatory practices toward employees in governmental agencies.

Discrimination in employment is not uncommon. Even city personnel agencies have permitted discrimination in the hiring of municipal employees, though their rules may formally forbid it. In some instances, personnel agencies have actually abetted such discrimination.

Most "human relations" groups have avoided coercion or punishment in their attempts to eliminate discrimination. In fact, most municipal commissions have only advisory and noncoercive powers, although some of them have power to bring court actions against offenders, which may result in both restraining orders and criminal punishments. Most human relations agencies, however, depend upon education, conferences, persuasion, social pressure, and the threat of unfavorable publicity to produce compliance.

There is some question as to whether the municipality has adequate jurisdiction to provide for equal opportunities. The problem is at least statewide in nature and now most states take action in this area.

Some cities which lack equal-opportunity ordinances have established interracial or intergroup negotiating committees to help improve relations between persons of different ethnic, racial, or religious group membership. They have no coercive powers, but they are sometimes objected to by improvement associations who fear that real equality would threaten property values.

Because of Sex

Women's groups have been especially active since 1970 in pushing grievances to the point of court cases in respect to public hiring, salary, and promotion practices. The initial evidence suggests that in many jurisdictions they have legitimate grievances. Another group active in some larger cities and in university communities is homosexuals who argue that they should not be discriminated against when seeking public employment.

COMPREHENSIVE COMMUNITY DEVELOPMENT

Beginning with the Kennedy administration, the federal government undertook a variety of community-development programs. The purpose was not to aid one form of human behavior or one aspect of physical design but to undertake a broad-scale attack. The initial focus of these programs, adopted mainly during the Johnson administration, was the poverty areas of the core city, but under the Nixon administration the programs were broadened to include all cities. These programs were different in two ways: they melded together both physical design and human-service projects, and they left a larger share of choice among possible programs at the local level.

The "War on Poverty"

The Kennedy administration fathered the Economic Opportunity Act of 1964, which was pushed through Congress by President Johnson. It undertook an "unconditional war on poverty." The Office of Economic Opportunity had a number of responsibilities but the part of its program that attracted most interest and attention was that of Community Action, with its ambiguous requirement of "maximum feasible participation" by community residents. The goal was that of mobilizing an urban community of low-income citizens to attack a host of problems that beset them, and attempt to pull the community up with federal funds and their own bootstraps. The administration of this program would be through a new local agency, with its own administrators separate from local government. It could choose from a variety of projects such as those of job training, the Head Start program for preschoolers, legal aid, homemaking, neighborhood centers, and health care. In time Community Action foundered in two respects: Some of its projects were poorly chosen and administered. Failure to follow strict accounting procedures sometimes led to financial irregularities. Secondly, some of its citizen leaders and administrative staff were accused by local officials of viewing community action as a means of mobilizing the poor to topple the local political power holders. The program was finally phased out by the Nixon administration and revenue sharing substituted for it. However some of the more successful projects such as Head Start were retained, as was a Community Action agency with reduced status and funds.

Model Cities

A second attempt was made by the Johnson administration to change the social and physical environment of core cities. The Model Cities program was set up by the Demonstration Cities and Metropolitan Development Act of 1966. It provided for liberal grants to specific city neighborhoods to establish what were to be demonstration projects, much as the county agricultural agent might provide in one field a demonstration of five strains of corn all grown under the same environmental conditions. The city would set up a special agency and would design its own program to upgrade the Model Cities area, which at first was the heart of core-city slums, but in time was expanded in some cities to include moderate-income areas. The program again was broad-scale community development involving both physical design and human services, such as efforts to improve health care, education, crime control, housing, economic development, and even transportation (busses for the elderly or children), in fact, any effort that might reasonably be interpreted as upgrading the quality of life for residents in an urban slum. It was intended that federal funds be concentrated in roughly half a dozen cities as the demonstration city model would suggest. However, the number of participating cities quickly rose to 150, and some of the same problems that beset Community Action and OEO dogged Model Cities. It met the same fate under the Nixon administration: cutback in funds and finally dismantlement with the advent of revenue sharing.

Community Development

The Housing and Community Development Act of 1974 followed something of the same format as the 1960s legislation, but with significant differences. First, funds were allocated to every city in the nation, rich or poor, black or white, suburb or core city. Second, while there was a requirement for hearings at which citizens might testify, the final proposals for projects were made by the city council and mayor, rather than by poverty-area residents or administrators employed by a Model Cities or Community Action agency. Third, the projects were to be administered through city-government departments. The form of the grant was a block grant which listed eight broad areas in which projects might be undertaken. The core requirement was that the purpose should be to upgrade housing and community facilities for residents. Thus some communities used the funds for parks or recreation centers, or facilities to aid the elderly or handicapped, or for teen-age centers, or for such projects as drug education centers or the recycling of paper, while many core cities had development programs that continued very much in the Model Cities tradition. Critics argued that funds were being allocated to suburbs for luxury services while core cities floundered in financial difficulty. At the same time it could be argued that the program did bring the concept of concerted community development to all of the nation's cities rather than only to the core poverty areas and that it was in many ways an invigorating shot in the arm for local government, encouraging attempts at improvement in the quality of urban life.

A Closing Note: Governing Urban America Tomorrow

City governments are likely to continue to play an important part in decisions about services to urban people. The tasks of municipalities in the future, as in the past, will be to perform those functions that are demanded by influential groups—within the limits of revenues that can be raised through the political process. In determining types and levels of services and how to pay for them, government will, as always, have to strike a balance.

The American culture is a product created by people interacting with one another. It is an independent variable which must be accepted as a basis for understanding present and future American government. Projections seem to show that the future, despite fads and momentary concerns and crises, holds "more of the same," with increasing pressures of the same sort that have existed for many years. Citizens in the future will be called upon to meet the problems of living together in vast numbers, problems that seemingly will become more complicated rather than simpler as times passes. If the political process as well as trends in government services are understood by students, these future challenges will become more understandable.[14] Above all, they should recognize that American government, at all levels, involves negotiation and compromise. The end result is one that satisfies few people completely, but one that is at least acceptable to most.

SELECTED READINGS

Berude, Maurice R., and Marilyn Gittell: Confrontation of Ocean Hill-Brownsville, Frederick A. Praeger, New York, 1969.

Brandstatter, A. F., and Allen A. Hyman: Fundamentals of Law Enforcement, Sage Publications, Beverly Hills, Calif., 1971.

Brandstatter, A. F., and Louis A. Radelet: Police and Community Relations: A Sourcebook, The Macmillan Company, New York, 1968.

Chevigny, Paul: Police Power, Police Abuse in New York City, Vintage Books, New York, 1969.

Cohen, Bernard, and Jan M. Chaiken: Police Background Characteristics and Performance, D. C. Heath and Company, Lexington, 1973. (An empirical study of New York City police.)

Commission on Community Health Services: Health Is a Community Affair, Harvard University Press, Cambridge, Mass., 1966. (Emphasizes intergovernmental aspects of these services and the interaction of public and private aspects.)

[14] On trends, see Charles R. Adrian and Charles Press, *American Politics Reappraised,* McGraw-Hill Book Company, New York, 1974.

The Danforth and Ford Foundations: The School and the Democratic Environment, Columbia University Press, New York, 1970.

Downs, Anthony: Who Are the Urban Poor? rev. ed., Committee for Economic Development, New York, 1970.

——: Urban Problems and Prospects, Markham, Chicago, 2d edition, 1976. (Deals with core-city problems.)

Eley, Lynn, and Thomas W. Casstevens (eds.): The Politics of Fair-Housing Legislation: State and Local Case Studies, Chandler, San Francisco, 1968.

Fischer, Linda A.: The Use of Services in the Urban Scene: The Individual and the Medical Care System, University of North Carolina Center for Urban and Regional Studies, Chapel Hill, 1971.

Gittell, Marilyn: Participants and Participation: A Study of School Policy in New York City, Frederick A. Praeger, New York, 1967.

——, and T. Edward Hollander: Six Urban School Systems: A Comparative Study of Institutional Response, Frederick A. Praeger, New York, 1968.

——, and Alan Hevesi (eds.): The Politics of Urban Education, Frederick A. Praeger, New York, 1969.

Goldsmith, Jack, and Sharon S. Goldsmith (eds.): The Police Community, Dimensions of an Occupational Subculture, Palisades Publishers, Pacific Palisades, Calif., 1974.

Hahn, Harlan (ed.): American Behavioral Scientist, complete issue titled "Police and Society," 13:May–August, 1970.

Harrington, Michael: The Other America, Macmillan, New York, 1963. (Classic study on poverty in America of the 1960s.)

Herman, Harold, and Mary E. McKay: Community Health Services, International City Management Association, Washington, 1968.

Iannaccone, Laurence: Politics, Power and Policy: The Governing of Local School Districts, Charles E. Merrill Publishing Company, Columbus, 1970.

Klonoski, James R., and Robert Mendelsonn (eds.): The Politics of Local Justice, Little Brown, Boston, 1970.

Lamb, Curt: Political Power in Poor Neighborhoods, John Wiley and Sons, New York, 1975. (Argues, based on many interviews in many poor areas, that militancy is an "effective tactic" for the poor.)

Long, Norton: The Unwalled City: Reconstituting the Urban Community, Basic Books, New York, 1972.

Masotti, Louis H.: Education and Politics in Suburbia, The New Trier Experience, The Press of Western Reserve University, Cleveland, 1967. (Politics in a rich suburban school district.)

Meranto, Philip: School Politics in the Metropolis, Charles E. Merrill Publishers, Columbus, Ohio, 1970.

Moynihan, Daniel P.: Maximum Feasible Misunderstanding, Community Action in the War on Poverty, Free Press, New York, 1972. (Criticism of citizen participation by one of the act's authors.)

—— (ed.): Toward a National Urban Policy, Basic Books, New York, 1970. (Collection of essays by experts on urban service problems.)

Municipal Fire Administration, 7th ed., International City Management Association, Chicago, 1967. (Describes professional values, standards, procedures, and goals.)

Municipal Police Administration, 5th ed., International City Management Association, Chicago, 1961. (Describes professional values, standards, procedures, and goals.)

Ostrom, Elinor: "On the Meaning and Measurement of Output and Efficiency in the

Provision of Urban Police Services," Journal of Criminal Justice, 1:93–112, 1973.
Perry, David C.: Police in the Metropolis, Charles E. Merrill Publishers, Columbus, Ohio, 1975.
Pollinger, Kenneth J., and Annette C. Pollinger: Community Action and the Poor, Praeger, New York, 1972. (Study of New York City's Community Action program in a Bronx neighborhood.)
Public Management, complete issue, "What Now for Fire Service?" November, 1970.
Rainwater, Lee, and William Yancey (eds.): The Moynihan Report and the Politics of Controversy, The M.I.T. Press, Cambridge, Mass., 1967. (Essays concerning and reprint of the report arguing that black social conditions are related to family structure.)
Reischauer, Robert D., and Robert W. Hartman: Reforming School Finances, The Brookings Institution, Washington, 1973.
Rossi, Peter H. (ed.): Ghetto Revolts, Aldine, Chicago, 1970. Urban Affairs Quarterly, "Special Issue on the Urban Negro," September, 1968.
Rubinstein, Jonathan: City Police, Farrar, Straus and Giroux, New York, 1973.
Saunders, Charles B., Jr.: Upgrading the American Police: Education and Training for Better Law Enforcement, The Brookings Institution, Washington, 1970.
Steiner, Gilbert Y.: Social Insecurity: The Politics of Welfare, Rand McNally & Company, Chicago, 1966. (A major study, using the analytical tools of political science.)
Usdan, Michael D., and others: Education and State Politics, Teachers College Press, Columbia University, New York, 1969. (School politics, especially of finance, in twelve states.)
Van der Slik, Jack R. (eds.): Black Conflict with White America, Charles E. Merrill, Columbus, Ohio, 1970.
Viteritti, Joseph P.: Police, Politics, and Pluralism in New York City, Sage Publications, Beverly Hills, Calif., 1973. (Police policy making in the nation's largest city.)
Wilson, James Q. (ed.): City Politics and Public Policy, John Wiley, New York, 1968. (See especially Part IV, the study of comparative traffic law enforcement by John A. Gardiner, and the study of two cities, one with professionalized police force and one not, and the handling by police of juvenile cases by James Q. Wilson.)
——: Varieties of Police Behavior: The Management of Law and Order in Eight Communities, Harvard University Press, Cambridge, Mass., 1968. (Analysis of police systems in Albany, Newburgh, Oakland, Syracuse, Amsterdam, Brighton, Highland Park, and Nassau County. Police styles are characterized as the watchman, legalistic, or service types.)
—— (ed.): The Metropolitan Enigma, Anchor Books, Doubleday & Company, Inc., Garden City, N.Y., 1968. (Essays on service problems of cities.)
Wilson, O. W.: Police Administration, 3d ed., McGraw-Hill Book Company, New York, 1972.
Zimmer, Basil G., and Amos H. Hawley: Metropolitan Area Schools, Sage Publications, Beverly Hills, Calif., 1968. (Survey of attitudes of residents toward schools in six metropolitan areas.)

Suggested Readings

In general, see Charles Bryfogle, *City in Print: Urban Studies Bibliography,* Dawson and Co., Tucson, Ariz., 1974, with subsequent supplements.

PERIODICALS

The following are important periodicals, but they do not necessarily exhaust the field. The periodicals of state municipal leagues provide much detail. For a list of these publications, see the *Municipal Year Book,* International City Management Association, Washington, published annually.

American City. Monthly. Much detail on administrative developments and less attention to politics and reform action than is found in the *National Civic Review.* Many pictures and a great deal of advertising of the most recent municipal equipment.

American Journal of Public Health. Monthly. American Public Health Association.

American Municipal News. Monthly. Current municipal developments and practices.

City. Bimonthly. National Urban Coalition.

Journal of Housing. Monthly. National Association of Housing Officials. Housing and redevelopment news.

Municipal Finance. Quarterly. Municipal Finance Officers' Association. Also publishes a biweekly *News Letter.*

National Civic Review. Monthly. Formerly the *National Municipal Review.* Perhaps the best source of news of a general nature. Emphasizes political action, especially of the reform type.

National Tax Journal. Quarterly. National Tax Association. Features information on municipal taxation.

Nation's Cities. Monthly. National League of Cities.

Newsletter. Monthly. American Society of Planning Officials.

New York Times. Daily. Reports important political and administrative developments throughout the country if of general interest.

Police Chief. Quarterly. International Association of Chiefs of Police.

Public Employee. Monthly. The American Federation of State, County, and Municipal Employees. The labor viewpoint, especially on personnel practices.

Public Management. Monthly. International City Management Association. A major source of news on administration.

Public Personnel Management. Bimonthly. International Personnel Management Association. Includes developments in municipal personnel administration.

Public Utilities Fortnightly. Management and technical problems of utilities operation.

Public Welfare. Quarterly. American Public Welfare Association.

Recreation. Monthly. National Recreation Association.

Urban Affairs Quarterly. Sponsored by the City University of New York.

Urban Reporter. Twice monthly. Urban Research Corporation.

Urban Research News. Biweekly. Sage Publications, Inc.

Suggested Readings

FOR SPECIFIC LOCALITIES

Albuquerque

Cline, Dorothy I., and T. Phillip Wolf: "Albuquerque: The End of a Reform Era," in Leonard E. Goodall (ed.), Urban Politics in the Southwest, Institute of Public Administration, Arizona State University, Tempe, Ariz., 1967.

Atlanta

Banfield, Edward C.: Big City Politics, Random House, Inc., New York, 1965, chap. 1, "Atlanta: Strange Bedfellows."

Hunter, Floyd: Community Power Structure, University of North Carolina Press, Chapel Hill, N.C., 1953.

Jennings, M. Kent: Community Influentials: The Elites of Atlanta, The Macmillan Company, New York, 1964.

Austin

MacCorkle, Stuart A.: Austin's Three Forms of Government, The Naylor Company, San Antonio, 1973. (A history of the city's politics.)

Olson, David M.: "Austin: The Capital City," in Leonard E. Goodall (ed.), Urban Politics in the Southwest, Institute of Public Administration, Arizona State University, Tempe, Ariz., 1967.

Baltimore

Lukas, J. A.: "Boss Pollack: He Can't Be There but He Is," Reporter, 27:35–36, July 19, 1962.

Martin, Harold H.: "The Case of the Bouncing Mayor," The Saturday Evening Post, Sept. 24, 1955, pp. 19ff. (Story of Mayor Thomas D'Alesandro.)

Baton Rouge

Havard, William C., and Floyd Corty: Rural-Urban Consolidation: The Merger of Governments in the Baton Rouge Area, Louisiana State University Press, Baton Rouge, La., 1964.

Birmingham

Levine, Charles H.: Racial Conflict and the American Mayor, D. C. Heath and Company, Lexington, 1974, chap. 6, "Birmingham: The Politics of Hegemony."

Boston

Banfield, Edward C.: Big City Politics, Random House, Inc., New York, 1965, chap. 2, "Boston: The New Hurrah."

Blackwood, George: "Boston Politics and Boston Politicians," in Murray B. Levin, The Alienated Voter: Politics in Boston, Holt, Rinehart and Winston, Inc., New York, 1960, chap. 1.

Curley, James M.: I'd Do It Again, Prentice-Hall, Inc., Englewood Cliffs, N.J., 1957. (By the city's long-time boss.)

Chicago

Banfield, Edward C.: Political Influence, The Free Press of Glencoe, New York, 1961. (The Chicago political style.)

Gosnell, H. F.: Machine Politics: Chicago Model, The University of Chicago Press, Chicago, 1937.

Gottfried, Alex: Boss Cermak of Chicago, University of Washington Press, Seattle, Wash., 1962. (A psychological study of Chicago's boss of the early 1930s.)

Liebling, A. J.: Chicago: The Second City, Alfred A. Knopf, Inc., New York, 1952. (An entertaining, though hostile, study.)

Merriam, Charles E.: Chicago: A More Intimate View of Urban Politics, The Macmillan Company, New York, 1929.

Meyerson, Martin, and Edward C. Banfield: Politics, Planning and the Public Interest, The Free Press of Glencoe, New York, 1955.

Rakove, Milton: Don't Make No Waves; Don't Back No Losers, Indiana University Press, Bloomington, Ind., 1976. (A much more lighthearted approach to Daley's machine than is Royko's book.)

Royko, Mike: Boss: Richard J. Daley of Chicago, E. P. Dutton and Son, New York, 1970. (By a journalist. Sharply critical of Daley.)

Waters, Harry, and Frank Maier: "Chicago's Daley: How to Run a City," Newsweek, Apr. 5, 1971. (A balanced account.)

Wendt, Lloyd, and Herman Kogan: Big Bill of Chicago, The Bobbs-Merrill Company, Inc., Indianapolis, 1953. (A biography of Mayor William H. Thompson.)

Cincinnati

Straetz, Ralph A.: PR Politics in Cincinnati, New York University Press, New York, 1958.

Cleveland

Levine, Charles H.: Racial Conflict and the American Mayor, D. C. Heath and Company, Lexington, 1974, chap. 4, "Cleveland: The Politics of Immobilism."

Dallas

Thometz, Carol Estes: The Decision-makers: The Power Structure of Dallas, Southern Methodist University Press, Dallas, Tex., 1963.

Denver

Bridge, Franklin M.: Metro-Denver: Mile-high Government, Bureau of Governmental Research, University of Colorado, Boulder, Colo., 1963.

Detroit

Banfield, Edward C.: Big City Politics, Random House, Inc., New York, 1965, chap. 3, "Detroit: Balancing Act."

Kornhauser, Arthur: Attitudes of Detroit People toward Detroit, Wayne State University Press, Detroit, Mich., 1952.

Mowitz, Robert, and Deil Wright: Profile of a Metropolis, Wayne State University Press, Detroit, Mich., 1962.

El Paso

Banfield, Edward C.: Big City Politics, Random House, Inc., New York, 1965, chap. 4, "El Paso: Two Cultures."

Fort Worth

Spain, August O.: "Fort Worth: Great Expectations—Cowtown Hares and Tortoises," in Leonard E. Goodall (ed.), Urban Politics in the Southwest, Institute of Public Administration, Arizona State University, Tempe, Ariz., 1967.

Gary

Levine, Charles H.: Racial Conflict and the American Mayor, D. C. Heath and Company, Lexington, 1974, chap. 5, "Gary, The Politics of Racial Partisanship."

Houston

McCleskey, Clifton: "Houston: Tripartite Politics," in Leonard E. Goodall (ed.), Urban Politics in the Southwest, Institute of Public Administration, Arizona State University, Tempe, Ariz., 1967.

Jersey City

Fleming, T. J.: "City in the Shadow," The Saturday Evening Post, 235:80–83, Jan. 6, 1962.

McKean, Dayton D.: The Boss: The Hague Machine in Action, Houghton Mifflin Company, Boston, 1940.

Kansas City

Dorsett, Lyle W.: The Pendergast Machine, Oxford University Press, New York, 1968.

Gabis, Stanley: "Leadership in a Large Manager City: The Case of Kansas City," The

Annals of the American Academy of Political and Social Science, 353:52–63, May, 1964. (Post-Pendergast politics.)

Los Angeles

Ainsworth, Edward M.: Maverick Mayor, Doubleday & Company, Inc., Garden City, N.Y., 1966. (The story of Mayor Samuel Yorty.)
Banfield, Edward C.: Big City Politics, Random House, Inc., New York, 1965, chap. 5, "Los Angeles: Pre (Civil) War."
Bollens, John C., and Grant B. Geyer: Yorty: Politics of a Constant Candidate, Palisades Publishers, Pacific Palisades, Calif., 1973. (Mayor, 1961–1973.)
Brodie, F. M.: "Parks and Politics in Los Angeles," Reporter, 32:39–42, Feb. 11, 1965.
Carney, Francis M.: "The Decentralized Politics of Los Angeles," The Annals of the American Academy of Political and Social Science, 353:107–122, May, 1964.
Crouch, Winston W., and Beatrice Dinerman: Southern California Metropolis: A Study in Development of Government for a Metropolitan Area, University of California Press, Berkeley, Calif., 1963.
Mayo, Charles G.: "The 1961 Mayoralty Election in Los Angeles: The Political Party in a Non-partisan Election," Western Political Quarterly, 17:325–337, June, 1964.

Miami

Banfield, Edward C.: Big City Politics, Random House, Inc., New York, 1965, chap. 6, "Miami (Dade County): Yes, but . . ."
Sofen, Edward: The Miami Metropolitan Experiment, Indiana University Press, Bloomington, Ind., 1963.

Milwaukee

Hoan, Daniel W.: City Government: The Record of the Milwaukee Experiment, Harcourt, Brace & World, Inc., New York, 1936.
Schmandt, Henry J., and William H. Standing: The Milwaukee Metropolitan Study Commission, Indiana University Press, Bloomington, Ind., 1965.

New Haven

Dahl, Robert A.: Who Governs? Yale University Press, New Haven, Conn., 1961.
Talbot, Allan R.: The Mayor's Game, Richard Lee of New Haven and the Politics of Change, Praeger Publishers, New York, 1970.

New York

Bellush, Jewell, and Stephen M. David (eds.): Race and Politics in New York City, Praeger Publishers, New York, 1971. (Articles on various basic governmental functions.)
Carter, Barbara: "New York City—Can It Be Governed?" Reporter, 30:42–45, Jan. 30, 1964.
Cook, Frederick J., and Gene Gleason: "The Shame of New York," The Nation, Oct. 31, 1959, entire issue.
Fitch, Lyle C., and Annmarie H. Walsh (eds.): Agenda for a City, Sage Publications, Inc., Beverly Hills, Calif., 1970. (A number of specialists write on issues confronting New York.)
Glazer, Nathan: "Is New York City Ungovernable?" Commentary, 32:185–193, September, 1961.
Hamburger, Philip: "That Great Big New York Up There," The New Yorker, Sept, 28, 1957, pp. 47–82. (A profile of Mayor William O'Dwyer.)

——: "The Mayor: Profile of Robert F. Wagner," The New Yorker, Jan. 26, 1957, pp. 39–67; Feb. 2, 1957, pp. 39–69.

Hapgood, David: Purge that Failed: Tammany versus Powell, McGraw-Hill Book Company, New York, 1962.

Hentoff, Nat: "The Mayor," The New Yorker, Oct. 7, 1967, and May 3, 1969. (Profiles of Mayor John Lindsay.)

Lowi, Theodore J.: At the Pleasure of the Mayor: Patronage and Power in New York City, 1898–1958, The Macmillan Company, New York, 1964.

Makielski, S. J.: Politics of Zoning: New York, 1916–1960, Columbia University Press, New York, 1965.

Sayre, Wallace S., and Herbert Kaufman: Governing New York City, Russell Sage Foundation, New York, 1960. (Available in paperback.)

Oklahoma City

Mauer, George J.: "Oklahoma City: In Transition to Maturity and Professionalization," in Leonard E. Goodall (ed.), Urban Politics in the Southwest, Institute of Public Administration, Arizona State University, Tempe, Ariz., 1967.

Philadelphia

Banfield, Edward C.: Big City Politics, Random House, Inc., New York, 1965, chap. 7, "Philadelphia: Nice While It Lasted."

Crumlish, Joseph D.: A City Finds Itself: The Philadelphia Home Rule Charter Movement, Wayne State University Press, Detroit, Mich., 1959.

Gilbert, Charles E.: Governing the Suburbs, Indiana University Press, Bloomington, Ind., 1967.

McKenna, William J.: "The Pattern of Philadelphia Politics, 1956–1963," Economics and Business Bulletin (Temple University), 16:19–24, December, 1963.

Reichley, James: The Art of Government: Reform and Organization Politics in Philadelphia, The Fund for the Republic, New York, 1959.

Pheonix

Goodall, Leonard E.: "Pheonix: Reforms at Work," in Leonard E. Goodall (ed.), Urban Politics in the Southwest, Institute of Public Administration, Arizona State University, Tempe, Ariz., 1967.

St. Louis

Banfield, Edward C.: Big City Politics, Random House, Inc., New York, 1965, chap. 8, "St. Louis: Better than She Should Be."

Schmandt, Henry J., Paul G. Steinbricker, and G. D. Wendel: Metropolitan Reform in St. Louis, Holt, Rinehart and Winston, Inc., New York, 1962.

San Antonio

Crane, Bill: "San Antonio: Pluralistic City and Monolithic Government," in Leonard E. Goodall (ed.), Urban Politics in the Southwest, Institute of Public Administration, Arizona State University, Tempe, Ariz., 1967.

San Diego

Wilcox, Robert F.: "San Diego: City in Motion," in Leonard E. Goodall (ed.), Urban Politics in the Southwest, Institute of Public Administration, Arizona State University, Tempe, Ariz., 1967.

San Francisco

Bean, Walton: Boss Ruef's San Francisco, University of California Press, Berkeley, Calif., 1952.

Wirt, Frederick M.: "Alioto and the Politics of Hyperpluralism," Trans-action, April, 1970, pp. 46–55. (San Francisco, "Government by Clerks.")

——: Power in the City: Decision Making in San Francisco, University of California Press, Berkeley, 1974. (Oddly, the first book-length study of the city's politics by a political scientist. An excellent work.)

Seattle

Banfield, Edward C.: Big City Politics, Random House, Inc., New York, 1965, chap. 9, "Seattle: Anybody in Charge?"

Toledo

Stinchcombe, Jean L.: Reform and Reaction, City Politics in Toledo, Wadsworth, Belmont, Calif., 1968.

Tucson

Joyner, Conrad: "Tucson: The Eighth Year of the Seven-Year Itch," in Leonard E. Goodall (ed.), Urban Politics in the Southwest, Institute of Public Administration, Arizona State University, Tempe, Ariz., 1967.

Tulsa

Hanson, Bertil: "Tulsa: The Oil Folks at Home," in Leonard E. Goodall (ed.), Urban Politics in the Southwest, Institute of Public Administration, Arizona State University, Tempe, Ariz., 1967.

Wichita

Carpenter, Dwight M.: "Wichita: Cowboys, Crises and Tuesday Night Fights," in Leonard E. Goodall (ed.), Urban Politics in the Southwest, Institute of Public Administration, Arizona State University, Tempe, Ariz., 1967.

Index